W9-AHG-702

VALUATION:
MEASURING AND MANAGING THE VALUE OF COMPANIES

WILEY PROFESSIONAL BANKING AND FINANCE SERIES

EDWARD I. ALTMAN, Editor

VALUATION:
MEASURING AND MANAGING THE VALUE OF COMPANIES

Tom Copeland
Tim Koller
Jack Murrin

McKinsey & Company, Inc.
Corporate Finance Practice

WILEY

JOHN WILEY & SONS

New York • Chichester • Brisbane • Toronto • Singapore

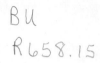

Library of Congress Cataloging in Publication Data:

Copeland, Thomas E., 1946–
    Valuation: measuring and managing the value of companies / Thomas
Copeland, Tim Koller, Jack Murrin.
    p. cm. — (Wiley professional banking and finance series.
ISSN 0733-8945)
    Includes bibliographical references.
    ISBN 0-471-51024-6
    1. Corporations—Valuation—Handbooks, manuals, etc. I. Koller,
Tim. II. Murrin, Jack. III. Title. IV. Series.
HG4028.V3C671989
658'5—dc20
                                                                        89-38192
                                                                            CIP

ISBN 0-471-51024-6

Printed in the United States of America

10 9 8 7 6 5 4 3

Dedication

This book is dedicated to our parents to thank them for their loving support through the years: George and Irene Copeland, David and Jeannette Koller, and John and Wilma Murrin.

Series Preface

When John Wiley and I launched the Wiley Professional Banking and Finance Series in 1982, we noted the dynamic nature of financial markets beginning in the mid to late 1970s. We expected this trend to continue through the 1980s, as, indeed, it has. Today, the same prospects for dramatic change and the need to monitor and chronicle these changes into the 1990s continue.

We are very pleased with the quality and quantity of output from our continued efforts to publish books written by experts in diverse fields related to our central theme of financial innovation. We expect to continue to publish definitive, authoritative works on specialized subjects for practitioners and theorists, as well as compendiums and handbooks on more general topics, ranging from financial markets and investment policy to consumer, commercial, and investment banking.

It is a continued pleasure for me to work with such a distinguished publisher, and I look forward to a productive association in the years leading up to 2000. Of one thing I am sure: the constant innovations in banking and finance will provide fertile ground for generating ideas and topics for important new works in this series.

EDWARD I. ALTMAN

Max L. Heine Professor of Finance
Stern School of Business
New York University

Preface

This is an unusual book. It is intended to be at once a guide to doing valuations of companies rigorously and well, a treatment of some special issues in valuation (for example, how to value financial institutions), and a perspective on how the corporate environment—and, therefore, the challenge for corporate managers—has changed. Value and valuation are more important than ever. This book is about how to reckon true value.

We hope it is a book you will use again and again. If we have done our job well, it will soon be full of underlinings, marginal notations, and highlighting. This is no coffee-table book. It is a tool, to be deployed in the pursuit of value.

In the last decade, two separate streams of thinking and activity—corporate finance and corporate strategy—have come together with a resounding crash. Corporate finance is no longer the exclusive preserve of financiers. Corporate strategy is no longer a separate realm ruled by CEOs. The link between strategy and finance has become very close and clear. Participants in the financial markets are increasingly involved in business operations through leveraged buyouts, hostile takeovers, and proxy contests. At the same time, chief executives have led their companies to become increasingly active players in the financial markets through self-generated restructurings, leveraged recapitalizations, leveraged buyouts, share repurchases, and the like. Financing and investment are now inextricably linked.

This new reality presents a challenge to business managers: the need to *manage value*. They need to focus as never before on the value their corporate and business-level strategies are creating. In the quest for value, they find that they must consider such radical alternatives as selling the "crown jewels" or completely restructuring operations. And they need more systematic and reliable ways to look for opportunities in the turbulence resulting from the confluence of strategy and finance. For instance, as a result of restructurings, companies face unprecedented opportunities to acquire assets and businesses that may be worth more to them than to their original owners.

WHY THIS BOOK?

Our firm, McKinsey & Company, Inc., works with hundreds of companies each year on strategies to make lasting improvements in their performance. Often this work has a significant financial component, such as counsel on potential restructurings, acquisition programs, merger transactions, divestitures, and international ventures. At McKinsey, then, finance is not simply a specialized practice area, but an integral part of our overall service to clients.

This book grew out of a special research project in our Corporate Finance Practice aimed at developing approaches to valuation and financial thinking that effectively link finance to strategy. We have drawn on leading-edge academic thinking as well as our own research to devise clear and sound ways to calibrate value in a variety of contexts that we encounter frequently in our work with clients. These include valuing single-business companies; assessing the value-creation and restructuring potential in multi-business companies; evaluating acquisitions; analyzing international and multinational business opportunities; and using option-pricing methods to value strategies based on the flexibility they give.

Our primary goal in this book is to *demystify* the field of valuation. We hope that value-based thinking and the application of sophisticated valuation approaches will soon become commonplace. We believe that clear thinking about valuation and skill in using valuation to guide business decisions are prerequisites for success in today's competitive environment. Value needs to be understood clearly by CEOs, business managers, and financial managers alike. Heretofore, valuation has been left to "experts" and used in special situations. Too often, it has been viewed as a specialized discipline unto itself, rather than as a key tool for running businesses better. But valuation is not a rarefied art or arcane science.

In this book we hope to lift the veil on valuation by explaining, step by step, how to do it well. We spell out valuation frameworks that we use in our consulting work, and we bring these frameworks to life with detailed case studies that highlight the practical judgments involved in developing and using valuations. Most important, we discuss how to use valuation to make decisions about courses of action for a company.

WHO SHOULD USE IT?

This book began as a guide for McKinsey consultants. By publishing it, we hope to reach, and help, a wider audience.

- *Business managers.* Now more than ever, leaders at the corporate and business-unit levels need to know how to assess the value of alternative strategies. They need to know how much value they can create through restructurings and other major transactions. Beyond this, they need to instill a managing-value mindset throughout their organizations.

- *Corporate finance practitioners.* Valuation approaches and the linkage between finance and strategy are important to chief financial officers, merger and acquisition specialists, corporate finance professionals within companies and on Wall Street, and corporate development managers and strategists. Value—how to assess it, create it, and communicate it—lies at the core of their roles and responsibilities.

- *Investors, portfolio managers, and security analysts.* These professionals should find this volume a useful guide to applying cash flow valuation approaches. This is the purest form
  of fundamental security analysis, since it links the value of
  the company directly to the economic returns it can generate
  from its businesses and assets.

Moreover, while our case examples and the formats of our
illustrations are geared toward U.S. situations, the fundamental
principles of valuation and the valuation approaches described
here are applicable in any country. With minor adjustment, they
can be used in Europe and the Far East. Market conditions and
the availability of information differ from country to country, but
the techniques themselves are a bedrock on which managers and
investors can build their assessments of value.

WHEN TO USE IT

First and foremost, this book is written for those who want to
improve their ability to create value for the stakeholders in their
business. It will be of most use when a need exists to do the
following:

- *Estimate the value of alternative corporate and business strategies*
  and the value of specific programs within those strategies.
  These strategies include such initiatives as new product
  introductions, capital expenditures, joint venture agreements, and new market entries.
- *Assess major transactions* such as mergers, acquisitions, divestitures, recapitalizations, and share repurchases.
- *Review and target the performance of business operations.* It is
  essential to know whether and to what extent a business as
  currently performing and configured is creating value.
  Equally important is the need to understand which operating measures have the greatest prospects for enhancing
  value.
- *Communicate with key stakeholders,* especially stockholders,
  about the value of the business. Our fundamental premise is

that the value of a company derives from its ability to generate cash flows and cash flow based returns on investment. In our view, many companies could do a much better job than they now do of communicating with the market and other players about the value of their plans and strategies. But first they need to become value managers themselves and understand what value they are creating and why.

STRUCTURE OF THE BOOK

This book is organized into three clusters of chapters. In the first cluster—Chapters 1, 2, and 3—we discuss the link between business strategies and value. In Chapter 1, we make the case that *managing value* is a central role and challenge for senior managers today. This is due to the increasingly complex competitive environment and especially to the emergence of an active market for corporate control. In Chapter 2, we develop a picture of what it means to *be* a value manager. We do this through a detailed case study based on the actual experiences of a CEO who needed to restructure his company and build a new managing-value philosophy throughout it. Chapter 3 rounds out the section on managing value. In it we review our fundamental premise that managing value effectively means focusing on *cash flows* and cash flow rates of return from business activities. We make the case that traditional accounting measures can be useful tools for understanding cash flow returns, but are no substitute for these more direct indicators of value.

The next group of chapters—Chapters 4-8—is a self-contained handbook for doing valuations of single-business companies. In it we describe, step by step, a general approach to discounted cash flow valuation and how to implement it. This includes how to identify and forecast free cash flows, estimate the appropriate opportunity cost of capital, identify sources of value, and interpret results. As a further aid to the practitioner, we walk through the valuation of an actual company (Preston Corporation) from the outside using publicly available information.

The final block of chapters—Chapters 9-13—is devoted to valuation in more complex situations. We have included a chapter on valuing multibusiness companies that shows how to estimate the value of each part of the portfolio, the corporate center, and so forth. There is a chapter on valuation of multinational companies, and another on assessment of acquisitions. We explore the application of option-pricing theory to corporate assets and liabilities (such as convertible debt). And we discuss the principles of valuation applicable to financial intermediaries such as banks, an exceedingly intricate area that is growing in importance with the wave of bank mergers, S & L failures, and international financial combinations.

TOM COPELAND
TIM KOLLER
JACK MURRIN

New York, New York
September 1989

Acknowledgments

No book is solely the effort of its authors. This book is certainly no exception, especially since it grew out of the collective work of McKinsey's corporate finance practice and the experiences of consultants throughout our Firm. Many people at McKinsey deserve special thanks for their help in taking this volume from concept to reality.

For their guidance and encouragement, we thank Fred Gluck and Ennius Bergsma.

For help in developing the original drafts of this book as an internal guide for our consultants, we owe a special debt to Dave Furer. Ahmed Taha deserves special mention for his contribution to the case materials on valuation. Shyanjaw Kuo provided extensive help on options pricing applications, based on knowledge developed in an ongoing McKinsey research project in collaboration with Alo Ghosh, Jon Weiner, and Juan Ocampo. The chapter on acquisitions benefitted from work undertaken by our Corporate Leadership Center whose key contributors were John Patience, Steve Coley, and Jack Welch. Finally, Madeleine James provided excellent analytical support to back up and illustrate many of the points in the book.

We are also grateful to the large number of finance-savvy

consultants and specialists around our Firm who provided input to our efforts after reviewing and using early drafts. Several people in particular must be mentioned: Peter Bisson, Will Draper, Russ Fradin, Bill Barnett, David Willensky, Mikel Dodd, Claudia Baler, Michelle Petigny, Bill Trent, and Bill Pursche.

For their help in preparing the manuscript and exhibits, we owe thanks to: Lenora Cannegieter, Carmen Hernandez, Rosanna Perfetto, and Robin Pastrana. John Donovan and the rest of the team in our excellent (and patient) visual aids and report production departments here in New York also did a terrific job.

Gene Zelazny provided his charting know-how while Vera Deutsch added her design touch to the exhibits and cover.

Last, but not least, from McKinsey, we thank Mark Goldberg and Bill Matassoni for their help in arranging to have this manuscript published and providing input to its overall shape. Mark especially deserves an award for his willingness to talk about the book 3 times per day over a period of 1½ years.

The Wiley editorial and production team has been great too: Karl Weber, Maryan Malone, Michael Bass, Lorraine Anderson, and Randy Miyake.

Finally, heartfelt thanks to Karen Copeland and Marjorie Murrin for enduring the late nights, weekends, and parts of "vacations" we consumed to write this book. Your support and encouragement are truly appreciated.

Tom Copeland
Tim Koller
Jack Murrin

Contents

Appendices

VALUATION:
MEASURING AND MANAGING THE VALUE OF COMPANIES

Part I

Company Value and the Manager's Mission

1

Managing Value: Key to Winning Strategies

Many companies in America are moving quickly and confidently in the wrong direction. They believe that they are becoming leaders in their industries; instead, they are becoming leading targets for raids and proxy fights.

Often, the reason has nothing to do with the quality of their products and services or with the abilities of their people. It has to do with an unduly cramped construction of strategy—a construction that does not focus on *managing value*.

Today's business environment is rife with challenges—ranging from more volatile interest rates to decreasing returns to vertical integration—that have a major impact on the value of many companies. At the same time, investors in capital markets have become less forgiving of substandard performance by managers. Shareholders have become more active in protecting and furthering the value of their investments, and a loose confederation of takeover entrepreneurs has been extremely successful in displacing some managements and forcing others to restructure to boost shareholder value.

The successful companies of the 1990s will be those that make managing value a central tenet of their corporate and business strategies. They will be able to take the greatest advantage of the opportunities and threats that confront them, while eluding the raiders' grasp.

VALUE: THE GAME IS CHANGING

Arguably, fifteen or twenty years ago, top managements could run their companies successfully with only a crude understanding of value. "Rule of thumb" accounting numbers were a sufficient basis for most business decisions. However, today's environment places a premium on a thorough understanding of value and on the ability to manage it, due to the following factors:

- Large firms have become subject to intense competition and often enjoy little or no advantage from size per se over small and medium-sized companies.
- The business environment is turbulent, forcing managers to reassess their business positions continually, and frequently make decisions that have a major effect on value, such as divesting product lines, entering into joint ventures, and changing distribution approaches.
- Business is "disintegrating" as the advantages of vertical integration, horizontal integration, and multibusiness ownership erode in situation after situation.

These factors, which are summarized in Exhibit 1.1, mean that business as usual is not good enough. Managers are faced with a stream of challenges in their businesses that have major implications for value.

The Playing Field Is More Level

Historically, a connection has existed between sheer size and a corporation's ability to create value. In many markets size alone provided larger firms with important competitive advantages over smaller players. But many of these traditional advantages are

Exhibit 1.1 **THE NEED TO MANAGE VALUE**

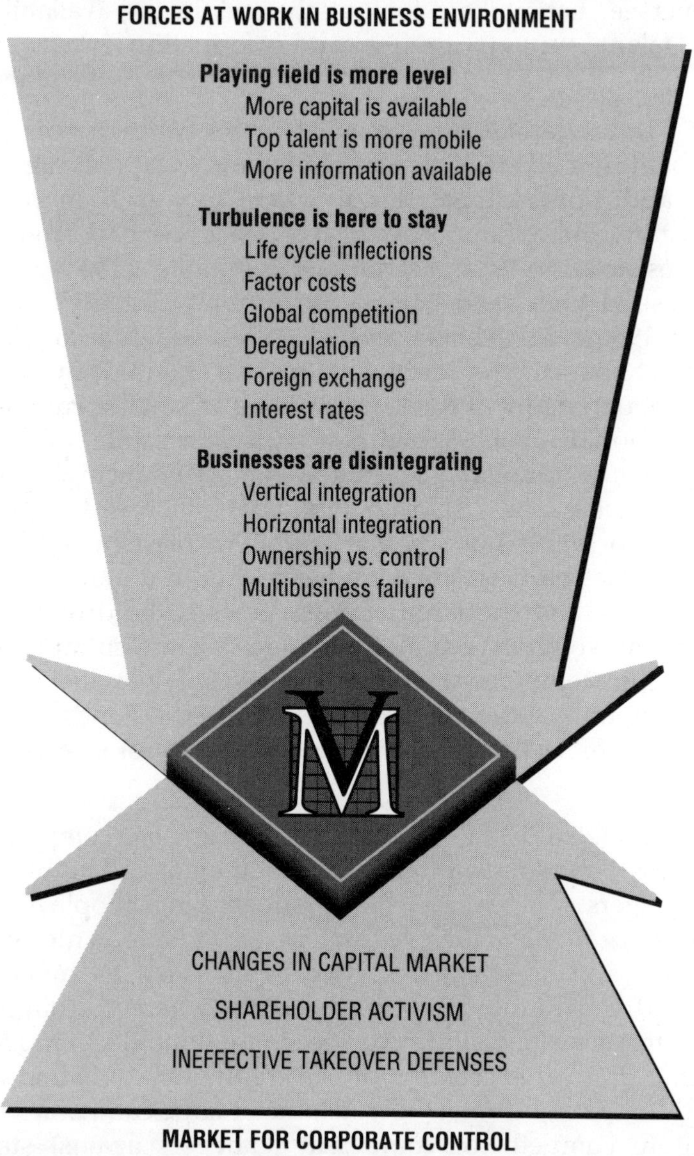

FORCES AT WORK IN BUSINESS ENVIRONMENT

Playing field is more level
More capital is available
Top talent is more mobile
More information available

Turbulence is here to stay
Life cycle inflections
Factor costs
Global competition
Deregulation
Foreign exchange
Interest rates

Businesses are disintegrating
Vertical integration
Horizontal integration
Ownership vs. control
Multibusiness failure

CHANGES IN CAPITAL MARKET

SHAREHOLDER ACTIVISM

INEFFECTIVE TAKEOVER DEFENSES

MARKET FOR CORPORATE CONTROL

much less important today and managers in larger companies need to reassess their ability to add value to the large enterprises they oversee. Let's take a look at changes in the availability of capital, talent, support services, and information.

Capital   Today capital is more widely available than ever before to companies of all sizes. In an era of venture capital, high-yield bonds, and global capital flows, where money is in constant search of investment opportunities, access to needed funds is no longer restricted to large, established companies. The volume of newly issued high-yield bonds, for example, leaped from $2.1 billion in 1980 to $27.8 billion in 1988. While widely recognized as a source of financing for leveraged buyouts and raids by takeover entrepreneurs, many of these funds went to smaller entities that formerly would not have had access to debt capital other than through banks. Similarly, leveraged-buyout financing, typically used for smaller deals, shot up from $0.8 billion in 1979 to over $50 billion in 1988—more than a fiftyfold increase in eight years. Today, market participants continue to talk of a glut of venture capital funds, and the large supply seems to be driving down returns. The volumes may not continue to grow so rapidly, but the blue-chip companies clearly no longer enjoy exclusive access to large amounts of capital on competitive terms. Funds are readily available for well-managed firms, regardless of size.

Talent   Top talent is more mobile too. Fortune 500 companies no longer have a monopoly on the most competent and highly qualified managers. To be sure, many outstanding people work in large organizations. However, talent has flooded into smaller companies and specialized service firms, such as investment banks and consulting firms, to the point where recruiters and social critics alike bewail the ever-declining numbers of top MBAs and other graduates seeking jobs in traditional industrial firms. Beyond competing for new recruits, many large companies find it difficult to compete for competent managers against start-up situations, smaller companies, and enterprises that have been taken private via a leveraged buyout. We can expect to see more rather than less of this trend.

Support services Support services are also more readily available. In many areas—for example, transportation and distribution—the development of highly focused service industries with national scope is making efficient support and market access available on an unbundled or contingent basis to most players, regardless of size. Moreover, third-party providers, be they in raw materials procurement, components manufacturing, assembly, distribution, or sales, are often more responsive and efficient than in-house suppliers. It no longer takes a large company to have access to top-quality capabilities. What large companies do in-house, the smaller company can contract for externally.

Information Information is more widely available. Large firms used to have a substantial edge over smaller competitors in gathering market and competitive information. No longer. The information services industry has grown rapidly, from $11 billion in 1980 to a projected $30 billion in 1990. Information is available to any subscriber, regardless of size. The number of on-line data-bases available in the market has increased more than eight times since 1980, due to the declining cost of computers and magnetic storage devices. Competitive advantage now lies not in the assembly of information, but rather in using it for decisions.

Turbulence Is a Fact of Life

In addition to the reduced advantages of size, the business environment has become extremely unstable. This instability demands that companies rethink their overall corporate and business-unit strategies almost continuously. This has implications for valuation approaches. In a relatively stable environment, rules of thumb such as accounting-based earnings can be used for decision making, normally without causing serious errors. But in today's ever-changing environment, characterized by frequent restructurings, takeovers, and other major investment-related decisions, cash flow based analysis is the only way to ensure that actions create value for shareholders. Rules of thumb will not do.

Because turbulence is the reality today, it is worth reflecting briefly on how many factors are changing and how they affect the value-creation decisions of managers.

Life-cycle inflections   Many companies are facing "life-cycle in-flections." Their core businesses have matured and profitable reinvestment opportunities in them are drying up. At the same time these businesses can be generating large cash flows. Indus-tries such as oil, cable TV, food, and tobacco are clear examples. As product life cycles continue to shorten, companies can expect to experience life-cycle inflections more frequently.

In this situation, companies must adjust reinvestment prac-tices quickly; otherwise, shareholder value will decline. Un-fortunately, it can be difficult for top management to tell a mature business unit that delivers 90 percent of the firm's profits that it will not get any of the cash to reinvest; after all, it was responsible for generating the cash in the first place. However, the result of not adjusting reinvestment practices can be devastating. From 1979 to 1982, even though on average every dollar put into U.S. oil drilling programs was predicted by many to be worth only seventy cents, oil companies invested heavily in exploration. The stock market reaction was extremely negative, with the market valuing many oil companies below the value of their proven reserves. It was cheaper for a time to "buy oil on Wall Street" than to explore for it, provided that the buyer stopped the value-destroying reinvestment of the cash flow produced by the re-serves. The lesson is that continued investment generates rising earnings, but does not necessarily create value, unless the cash flow returns on reinvestment are above the cost of capital.

Changes in factor costs   Major changes can also take place in factor costs. For example, the real estate holdings of department store chains often include downtown stores that have become ailing properties that barely break even. On the other hand, these stores sit on sites that are potentially very valuable in other uses. If such a firm's management has an eye for a deal, they will realize that the downtown real estate has little economic value as a retail store and should be sold, for example, to an office de-veloper.

Global competition   We are all familiar with global competition and its effect on whole industries such as autos and phar-maceuticals. In the decade ahead, we can expect to see this trend continue and result in more restructurings, acquisitions, and alliances around the globe. The scheduled removal of customs and other regulatory barriers within the European Community will have a tremendous impact on competition in Europe and cause a substantial reshuffling of corporate relationships. Those players who think through their strategies in terms of value creation will be the clear winners, and will prey on those who do not.

Deregulation   In the United States, the deregulation of the airline, banking, and trucking industries is creating a need for major adjustments and fleet-footedness. Deregulation is occurring in other countries, too. And privatization of government-owned firms, such as the United Kingdom's British Telecom, is changing the competitive landscape.

Volatile foreign exchange rates   Foreign exchange rates have become highly volatile. For example, the massive swings in the value of the dollar relative to other currencies have had a major impact on competitive positions in industries ranging from automobiles to forest products. It is small consolation to be the most efficient operator in an industry if the advantage is wiped out by a 50 percent increase in the cost of your input currency mix versus competitors'. Today as never before, major capital-investment decisions, even in "hard currency" countries, must take into account exposure to exchange-rate movements. Beyond this, managements must assess the value of an array of financial and operational hedging/exposure-management approaches, including swaps, options, local currency financing, and changes to the terms of sales and supply contracts.

Volatile interest rates   Interest rates have been volatile, too. Changes in interest rates affect demand for capital equipment, consumer durables, and housing construction. They therefore have implications for the future cash flows and value of most businesses. In today's environment of highly leveraged acquisitions, restructurings, and major recapitalizations, volatile interest rates can play havoc with the best-thought-out plans.

Fortunately, as with foreign-exchange exposure, a range of

tools is available to manage interest-rate exposure. These include fixed- and floating-rate borrowings, interest-rate caps, collars, and swaps. Those who are adept at managing value will be able to identify their exposures and tailor their capital structures to produce the lowest cost of capital consistent with prudent management of financial risk.

Indeed, active management of exposures is a requirement today. Being overexposed can have disastrous consequences if interest rates rise, including the ultimate defeat of bankruptcy. Being too conservative can be a problem, too, since management is thereby failing to capture the tax benefit of the interest associated with leverage. They may even be paying the tax penalty that arises from holding excess cash and marketable securities.

Some managements find this out the hard way, when raiders use their own cash flows and balance sheets to back financing for a takeover. Smart managements assess the level and riskiness of the free cash flows their businesses generate and structure their financing to maximize tax benefits while preserving flexibility to deal with new opportunities or adverse circumstances. In their search for value, they ignore accounting-based rules of thumb, such as debt-to-equity ratios. They are not overly concerned with maintaining high ratings from the debt-rating agencies. They concern themselves first and foremost with the proper financial structure for their particular circumstances based on the risks and opportunities their businesses face.

To sum up, the business environment is turbulent. Businesses are facing a stream of unprecedented challenges—challenges that will have a major impact on shareholder value. Gauging that impact properly, as an integral part of decision making, requires a deeper understanding of value than can be gleaned from relying on rules of thumb, such as growth in earnings per share.

Businesses Are Disintegrating

The efficiency and market responsiveness of focused competition are making the traditional integrated competitor vulnerable, and also shaking the foundations of multibusiness companies. The advantages formerly enjoyed by integrated and multibusiness companies are eroding in several ways.

Breakdown of vertical integration Consider the decreasing advantage to vertical integration. Many industries were dominated for decades by heavily integrated competitors. Examples include automobiles, steel, oil, financial services, electricity generation, even hotels. The premise was that participation in most, if not all, of an industry system was needed to compete effectively and would provide the greatest returns. However, over the last decade or two it has become clear that unbundled, "disintegrated" competitors can do just as well as and often better than their integrated competitors.

The key is to understand industry dynamics and concentrate resources in the stages that really matter. It is best to participate in stages where a company can develop competitive advantage and where returns will be greatest. The flip side of this is avoiding overly competitive stages, or those whose returns will be lower or below the cost of capital.

The classic example is the oil industry, which for fifty years or more consisted of fully integrated competitors—companies competing all the way from exploration to gasoline retailing. Today, little or no advantage accrues to being fully integrated in oil. An actively traded market in crude oil ensures access to a market for the player who competes only in exploration and production. Likewise, the competitor who chooses to compete only in refining or gasoline retailing has little problem getting access to wholesale markets.

This plays havoc with the economics of integrated producers. When integrated oil companies examine the value they create at each stage of the industry chain, they can find, for example, that substantial value created in one area, perhaps exploration, is masking value destruction in another, say, gasoline retailing. More efficient retailers, often linked to convenience stores, are earning high returns on thin margins due to lower capital requirements, while the outlets of the majors are earning below their cost of capital. Meanwhile, upstream in exploration, the majors' large exploration and production organizations could be destroying wealth because they focus on rules of thumb, such as maintaining the reserve-to-production ratio, rather than on value creation. Smaller companies, like it or not, don't often have the luxury of such thinking—they must focus on economic drilling programs or they won't be able to raise the capital required to operate.

The situation in oil is not unique. Markets everywhere are becoming more efficient. Companies now need to rethink not only how well they compete at each stage in their businesses, but whether they should be in those stages in the first place.

Separation of ownership and control   Closely related to the break-down of vertical integration is the fact that ownership and control need no longer be one and the same. Companies that historically have had their capital invested in many stages of an industry system are finding that they can retain control over the assets and activities in selected stages while avoiding the need to invest in them. The net result is higher returns and fewer funding constraints.

Prime movers behind this trend toward separation of owner-ship and control at the asset level have been the increasingly sophisticated capital markets intermediaries and investors. Trade-able instruments and private placements backed by a wide array of assets burst onto the scene in the 1980s. This has enabled companies to make dramatic changes in their strategies. For ex-ample, in banking, securitization of credit is allowing companies to focus on selected stages of the lending chain and outperform integrated providers. In one instance, efficient mortgage origina-tors have been freed from the shackles of limited deposit bases by selling mortgage securities into the secondary market. Now they can exploit fully their comparative advantage in underwriting, processing, and servicing mortgage loans. Likewise, securitized credit has provided an opportunity for automobile companies to step up their auto financing activities, cutting deeply into the auto loan business of commercial banks.

As another example, consider hotels. The business system in this industry has been "decoupled." Major hotel companies like Marriott are able to focus their investment on the stages where they create most value: site selection, construction, and op-erations. They can turn ownership over to others who, due to tax advantages and risk preferences, are better owners than public corporations. A similar trend is taking hold in soft drink bottling, as illustrated by the recent creation of Coca-Cola Enterprises. This vehicle allows Coca-Cola to influence the strategy and operations of major bottlers, without needing to own them.

Today, companies do not necessarily need to own each stage in the industry chain to control it to advantage.

Breakdown of horizontal integration   Horizontal integration, too, is proving less valuable than was once thought. In a nutshell, the idea behind horizontal integration is that by combining normally separate, but related, businesses a company can create a cost or quality advantage over competitors. Examples include food manufacturers who sell multiple brands to supermarkets; banks and other financial companies, some of which think of themselves as financial supermarkets; advertising agency conglomerates such as Saatchi and Saatchi that believe clients will buy market research, strategic consulting, human resources services, and the like from a single source; and department stores that attempt to sell a wide range of goods to a given set of customers.

Horizontal integration—sometimes called cross-selling—*can* work as a strategy. However, it is difficult to bring off and more often than not fails. When can it work? When true economies of scale exist in the production, sale, and/or distribution of a *group* of products; when the costs of coordinating delivery of multiple products do not outweigh those scale economies; when it is relatively expensive for buyers to search for alternative sources of supply; and/or when a common brand name can deliver tangible superiority in the form of the customer–vendor relationship.

Unfortunately, these conditions do not hold in as many circumstances as companies think. Often some scale economies do exist, but they do not extend across many products or services. Furthermore, technology coupled with more active intermediate markets is making it possible to capture these scale economies without being a broad-line competitor. More problematic is the high cost of coordinating a wide range of products and services. The obvious direct costs are manageable. The indirect costs, broadly defined, are the problem. Fixed and variable costs do not behave as predicted when products are added to a range. The complexity of the logistics involved makes costs rise faster in practice than they would appear to on paper. Beyond this, the responsiveness of the organization suffers. That old adage "Jack of all trades, master of none" comes into play. Specialized competitors are able to cherry-pick the best products and customers with tailored and differentiated products and more focused and responsive delivery systems.

To make matters more difficult for the broad-line, horizontally integrated firm, customers are more able than ever before to shop around and buy on an unbundled basis. They are more sophisticated. Information about competitive product offerings is more readily available. Moreover, buyers are under intense pressure themselves to ensure they get value for money.

Demise of multibusiness companies Nowhere is disintegration occurring more spectacularly than in the demise of many multibusiness companies. Corporate raiders and leveraged-buyout firms have made large sums by simply dismembering some of them. Why is such value there for the taking? Several reasons can be given.

First, operating synergies among businesses are often more apparent than real. Earlier we argued that the benefits of vertical integration and horizontal integration have eroded in many industries. In practical terms, this means that not so many synergies—situations in which two businesses together are worth more than the sum of the parts—exist as might have been the case in the past. When synergies do exist, they are certainly worth capturing, but they should not be presumed to exist.

Many multibusiness firms have separable businesses in their portfolios that might be worth more on their own, and in some cases in combination with the business of a different owner. The result is pressure for restructuring.

Second, stock market investors are not as naive as some multibusiness managers assume. The emergence of conglomerates in the late 1960s and early 1970s was in part due to the belief that investors have a single-minded enthusiasm for companies who have rising earnings per share. Since by making acquisitions, companies could make earnings per share grow (especially if they practiced the art of creative accounting), we saw a spate of acquisitions by a group of voracious companies. A phrase was even coined to describe their strategies: the conglomerate growth model. However, as we will discuss in a later chapter, the stock market is driven by cash flow returns, not accounting numbers—and especially not artificially sweetened accounting numbers. The conglomerates' stock market performance reflects the fact that despite rising earnings per share, the underlying economic returns of the conglomerators were weak. This should not be surprising, since it has been documented widely that the majority of acquisition programs fail to create value for their perpetrators. They do reward selling shareholders nicely, but not the shareholders of the buyers.

Another stock market related argument sometimes invoked in favor of multibusiness companies is that investors prefer companies with diversified earnings bases. This belief is usually put into practice when companies begin to search for a "third leg" or "fourth leg" for their business portfolios. Unfortunately, little evidence exists that investors do in fact value moves made mainly for purposes of diversification.

Why should they? Investors can easily pick their own mix of companies to own if diversification of risks is what they are after; they need not pay someone else a significant sum to do it on their behalf. When management will probably pay a 40-percent to 50-percent or more premium to buy into another line of business, simple diversification is obviously a poor motive for creating—or maintaining—a multibusiness company. Investors are no better off. If you have a better idea about how to manage or change the new business, that is another matter and could be valuable. However, diversification purely for the sake of diversification is not.

Third, the scale economies in multibusiness ownership are negligible. Beyond the often-overrated advantages from operating synergies among businesses, very few scale economies result for most companies from owning multiple businesses. Some cost savings may be realized from centralizing support services such as finance, accounting, data processing, and human resources. However, three problems often occur with these savings:

- They are more likely to exist on paper than in reality as more staff are needed than supposed to serve the disparate needs of the businesses.

- Some of the scale economies could be achieved by the businesses on their own. For example, they could use third-party providers who can operate data processing systems less expensively than many corporations' centralized facilities.

- To realize the benefits of centralizing corporate services, companies often have to pay a price in terms of responsiveness. The result is less-effective management of the business unit being "served" by the corporate staff. The ultimate irony is that after a while it is not unusual to see business-unit managers begin to rebuild their original staffs to provide the service they need. This happens all the time in the systems area. The end result is a big central staff *plus* a business-unit staff. So much for the savings.

Finally, major *diseconomies* of scale result from owning multiple businesses for all but the best corporate centers. A few companies such as General Electric, Emerson Electric, Pepsico, and Hanson Trust (a U.K. company), have demonstrated skill in owning multiple businesses. They have been able to leverage their high-caliber-but-lean corporate staffs and superior management systems to foster outstanding performance in their businesses. For these companies, arguably, no one else could own their businesses and generate greater returns than they can. Consequently, these top companies are seldom the subject of rumors about raiders.

Unfortunately, most companies do *not* have advantages in owning multiple businesses per se. Often, multibusiness companies have severe disadvantages when it comes to creating value. Problems of inflexibility and complacency are manifest in most (not all) large enterprises. Managements in larger companies are often farther from their markets, slower to respond to competitors, and—in the worst of situations—can be rewarded more for avoiding mistakes and playing by the rules than for taking prudent risks and creating value. Furthermore, even with the best of intentions and the systems to back them up, companies find that managing a large, diverse enterprise is complex.

With complexity come costs, in several layers. Most obvious is the direct spending at the corporate center. This can have a large impact on shareholder value—often more than 20 percent. Next comes the cost of divisional staffs and the time of managers down the line to respond to the demands of the corporate center. Net result: multiply the direct corporate center costs several times to get the true figure.

What you discover rather quickly is that—even leaving aside inflexibility, mixed incentives, and the like—maintaining a large corporate structure is very costly. This is not to suggest that corporate centers do not add value to the businesses they oversee; rather, given the costs, they must add substantial value to be economically viable. Unfortunately, in too many instances they do not.

In the final analysis, the net effect of size, integration, and diversification is often negative; the *tax* it imposes can be a *net destroyer of value*. This makes intuitive sense. How else could we explain the sizable fortunes that have been amassed by the breakup artists or leveraged-buyout firms? Mounting evidence shows that financial structuring plays only a small part in this. And the track record for many deals is long enough to indicate that their successes are not derived just from cutting reinvestment to unsustainable levels.

THE MARKET FOR CORPORATE CONTROL

In the early 1960s, academics coined the phrase "market for corporate control" to describe the market for buying and selling companies, as opposed to the market for products and services. In the 1980s, this market for control over companies, their assets, and the opportunity to generate value from them has been very active, to say the least. Dramatic takeovers have become commonplace and debate about them fills the popular and business press. The pace of merger and acquisition activity seems unrelenting. In 1988, according to *Fortune* magazine, the top fifty deals totaled $111.8 billion, a new record. This booming market occurred despite the stock market crash in late 1987, which might have scared off potential acquirers, especially heavily leveraged ones.

While at any given time different explanations can be offered for merger and acquisition activity, ranging from rising stock prices to a "cheap" dollar, more fundamental forces are usually at work. Currently they suggest that a relatively high level of activity in the market for corporate control will persist. Three of the most important forces are

- fundamental changes in capital markets that facilitate takeovers,
- less willingness among shareholders to tolerate weak performance, and
- the failure of legal protections for managements to completely prevent hostile takeovers.

The implication of all this for managements is that *managing value*, while becoming increasingly difficult, *is no longer optional*. Let's take a brief look at these three key forces in the development of the market for corporate control.

Changes in Capital Markets

The capital markets have changed dramatically, to the point where enormous volumes of funds are available to back acquisitions and restructurings. Institutional money has flooded into leveraged-buyout funds in search of high returns. The high-yield bond market is large and active. Banks are eager to finance acquisitions and buyouts since they earn high fees and spreads on this business at a time when many of their other, more traditional activities are marginally profitable at best. Foreign banks are eager to crack U.S. markets. Lacking at this stage deep expertise and contacts in the United States, they can use their enormous capital resources to finance acquisitions in the hope of building credibility, skills, and banking relationships. On top of all this, the large merger and acquisition departments of Wall Street investment banking and law firms have grown accustomed to earning large fees from contests for control. They ensure that few stones are left unturned in the search for more deals to do and fees to earn.

The point is this: a lot of money and talent is looking for companies to acquire and restructure. Today's computing technology and analytical techniques make it easier than ever before to identify potential targets. Moreover, size is no longer much protection against takeover attempts because the funding pool is so deep. The feverish bidding by multiple suitors for RJR Nabisco shows that the capital markets can take even a $25-billion deal in stride. In fact, size is an attraction! It means bigger fees for advisors and larger dollar returns for acquirers.

Shareholder Activism

At the same time that funding for takeovers has become more available, shareholders are becoming impatient with managements who do not focus on value creation—and they are doing something about it. Even though a legal fiction has always existed that shareholders are owners of corporations, the reality was quite different, until recently. If a shareholder did not like the performance of a company, he or she was wasting time attending its annual shareholders' meeting. Stock owners basically voted with their feet, selling their shares rather than getting involved in proxy battles at the annual meeting. In fact, shareholders were such a docile lot that those who did make proposals to be voted on at the annual meeting were treated like errant children or labeled gadflies.

That is changing dramatically. Not only has the proportion of stock owned by large investors grown rapidly, but investors are also increasingly ready to intervene directly when management is underperforming. Fund managers, who are evaluated annually on the basis of the amount by which their investment returns exceed the performance of the market, face enormous pressures. Consequently, they are more willing to have their voices heard if they disagree with management's actions and performance.

As an illustration, look at the lengths to which Texaco had to go to mollify shareholders in its battles with Carl Icahn, an especially well-known and successful corporate raider. Or consider the acrimony between shareholders and managements concerning "poison pills," antitakeover devices that, if activated, would require the would-be acquirer to purchase a large block of the target's or its own shares, thereby making a takeover prohibitively expensive. In annual shareholders' meetings, institutional investors who control blocks of shares, such as the California Public Employees Retirement System, are starting to wage proxy battles with management on the abolition of poison pills. In 1987, several motions for the abolition of poison pills attracted more than 40 percent of the available votes. In 1988, one carried for the first time, in a May 24 vote of the shareholders of Santa Fe Industries. Investors are starting to take a much more interventionist stand, and the results to date can only encourage them to do so.

Ineffective Takeover Defenses

Obviously, the wave of takeovers and restructurings has not gone unnoticed by corporate managements and other groups. In an effort to fend off unwanted suitors, managements and their advisors have developed a wide range of defensive mechanisms. These include supermajority provisions, staggered boards, and poison pills. In addition, "antiraider" statutes aimed at protecting companies against hostile takeovers have been adopted in a number of states, such as Indiana. Not surprisingly, these steps have generated intense controversy and even greater demand for legal talent with expertise in mergers and acquisitions. They have succeeded in preventing the more questionable—and one could argue abusive—tactics, especially the two-tier, front-end-loaded takeover.

What these steps have *not* succeeded in doing is stopping the determined bidder. Most investment bankers and lawyers seem to agree that no permanent defense can be made against a well-financed, all-cash bid that exceeds the next-best offer on the table. Poison pills have a spotty track record when put to the test in the courts. Restrictive state statutes are being challenged vigorously and successfully by well-heeled bidders. High bids that attract a substantial majority of outstanding shares in tender offers are often not subject to the restrictive provisions in state statutes, anyway. Additionally, proxy contests can be used as an alternative avenue of attack to overcome blockages put in place by sitting directors, ultimately by removing the directors or calling special shareholders' meetings to amend the bylaws directly. And the federal government has taken a more laissez-faire attitude toward antitrust enforcement, so that once-potent deterrent has been weakened. Legal maneuvers and obstacles certainly make takeovers more expensive and time-consuming, but they do not stop them.

This is reinforced by the evolving legal role of the board in takeover situations. Once a company is "for sale," boards of directors are obligated to seek the highest price for shareholders. Moreover, their determination of what constitutes the best price attainable must now follow a relatively strict and objective process. Much less room exists for directors to exercise business judgment on these matters. In fact, directors risk potentially severe financial penalties if they fail to follow a process aimed at achieving the best offer for shareholders.

This was brought home sharply by the case of *Smith v. Van Gorkom*, which was decided by the Delaware Supreme Court in 1985. In that decision, the court held the directors of Trans Union Corporation *personally* liable for the difference between the amount they agreed to sell the company for ($55 per share) and the amount that the court decided was a fair price (about $56.50 per share) based on the evidence at the trial. The decision was based on the conclusion that the directors of Trans Union had not informed themselves adequately about the value of the company before agreeing to an acquisition proposal negotiated hastily by the CEO.

The directors were held to a higher level of care in evaluating the transaction than previously had been required. Prior to *Smith v. Van Gorkom*, the "business judgment doctrine" operated essentially to protect directors against second-guessing by outsiders such as shareholders. So long as they were "reasonably" informed, they were on solid ground. And besides, the test for being informed was comparatively weak. Now, however, directors must evaluate takeover proposals rigorously, and this usually involves receiving expert opinions about value from external advisors as well as the active consideration of a range of alternatives. These alternatives can, of course, include proposals aimed at keeping the company independent—for example, leveraged buyouts, leveraged recapitalizations, or management-initiated restructuring plans; but they must be shown to deliver higher value than competing offers. So now the standard of care is very strict once the board has decided to sell the company.

In addition, a company that is under siege finds it increasingly difficult to avoid being considered as "for sale." The business judgment doctrine still does operate, though less stringently, when a board that has not put the company up for sale receives an unsolicited offer. In this circumstance, some takeover defense lawyers have argued that boards can "just say no" to suitors without significant risk. However, common sense suggests that this approach is doomed to failure. If the directors fail to approve a credible bid for substantially above the share price, they will at the least invite shareholder protest and proxy battles, and their business judgment will be suspect. Beyond this, if they begin to consider a competing management proposal to deliver value, they may be found to have in effect decided to sell the company. In this case, they are subject to the precedent established in *Smith v. Van Gorkom*, which stipulates that the highest bidder should win. The bottom line is this: once a company is in play, the best offer for shareholders will win, regardless of whether this is to management's or the board's liking.

THE NEED TO MANAGE VALUE

As we argued at the outset, in a large number of situations significant value can be captured or released via restructuring, due to diseconomies of size, disintegration, and shocks to established business positions. Coupled with this, the emergence of a very active market for corporate control ensures that managements who do not take advantage of these opportunities will be under intense pressure. They will attract takeover attempts and proxy fights. More fundamentally, though, they will be failing to discharge their responsibility as managers to generate sustained high returns for their shareholders—a responsibility that has been made evident by the market for corporate control, but that has really been there all along.

To succeed in this environment, managements must avoid two fundamental misconceptions about the nature and ends of strategy for their enterprises—misconceptions that can lead them to work very hard on too few things. The first misconception is that *business strategy* is just a matter of figuring out how best to compete in markets for products and services. The second is that *corporate strategy* is just a matter of deciding which business to be in.

Strategy must go beyond these objectives to incorporate more explicitly the need to create value. This is true for both business strategy, which applies to single businesses, and corporate strategy, the game plan for multibusiness companies.

Managing Value and Business Strategy

The narrow—and traditional—definition of *business strategy* leads firms to focus on gaining market share and increasing earnings—moving toward a stronger position relative to other companies selling the same products and services. But measures taken to that end can ultimately decrease cash flow returns and the value created for shareholders.

The point here is not that businesses should not be trying to compete effectively in product and service markets; of course they should. But that effort has to be measured not only in terms of its impact on competition in a product or service market, but also in terms of its effect in the market for corporate control. A company that emphasizes the former at the expense of the latter can find itself in trouble very quickly.

What is the connection of business units to the market for corporate control? For corporations that are in only one business, business strategy and corporate strategy are the same. For multibusiness companies, if one business is building market share but destroying value, the entire corporation can be a takeover target.

The challenge for business-unit managers can be summed up in two words: *managing value.* To meet that challenge, every business-unit manager should know the answers to such questions as: What is the cash flow based value of our business? How does this compare with its potential market value? How much value will our current plans and strategies create versus business as usual? What are the key drivers of value in our business—for example, what is the effect on value of increased market share or growth, higher operating margins, better asset utilization, alternative capital structures? The trick is to focus not on traditional accounting measures, but on cash flows. In the game of managing value, cash is king. And managers who proceed from this premise are often surprised to find that reality confounds intuition. In some seemingly profitable businesses, growth actually destroys value. In others, growth increases value even if it drives down the average return on capital. Without an ongoing focus on managing value, a strategy that wins in a product or service market may lose in the market for corporate control.

Managing Value and Corporate Strategy

What is true for one business applies even more certainly to a company with multiple business units. Many of the popular frameworks for *corporate strategy* suggest that the key to success is picking the right mix of businesses—that if a company has a balanced or diversified portfolio of well-managed businesses, all will be well. That is an appealing vision, but it is too narrow; it overlooks entirely the need for corporations to manage value.

From a financial perspective, a multibusiness company is essentially a complex intermediary akin to a bank, as illustrated by the example in Exhibit 1.2. It takes funds from its owners and the capital markets and seeks to invest them in ways that will generate a return above the cost of capital—the return the owners could earn elsewhere in investments of similar risk. If corporate strategy were simply the sum of business-unit strategies, wouldn't it be cheaper just to cut out the intermediary and send the businesses in the portfolio out on their own? And since shareholders are served by legions of professional securities analysts and money managers, couldn't they pick companies to invest in directly? Why do they need high-priced corporate managements to do this for them?

The essence of corporate strategy is to figure out how the corporation, as intermediary, can add value to the businesses it oversees. In some firms, corporate centers may be able to add value by managing especially well—making sure that business-unit managers focus on cash flows, attracting and leveraging an exceptional corps of executives, helping business-unit managers develop effective strategies of their own. In other companies, added value may come from synergies among businesses—savings achieved, or efficiency gains realized, by combining functions across businesses or by serving, and leveraging, common

Exhibit 1.2 **THE CORPORATION AS INTERMEDIARY: MOBIL CORPORATION CUMULATIVE CASH FLOW, 1978–82,** $ Millions

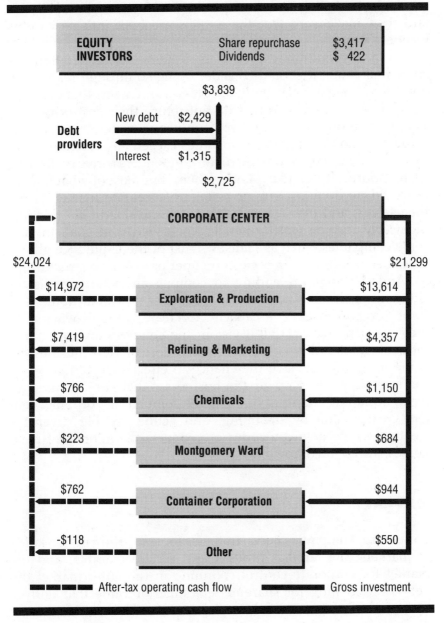

customer bases. In still others, what may be especially significant is the ability of the corporation to build superior skills—for example, in marketing consumer products or fostering innovation—and then make sure that these skills are built into its various business units.

As a corporation explores its options for generating incremental value, it should consider doing so through restructuring. Many companies include businesses and assets that could be worth more to others or that do not return their cost of capital. These situations represent opportunities to generate additional value, in amounts that can sometimes exceed 50 percent of what the firms are worth before restructuring. Raiders thrive on finding such opportunities and exploiting them. But most of what raiders do could be done as well or better by corporate managements themselves; and managements that become skillful at "raiding" themselves can be worth, literally, their weight in gold. In fact, some companies, such as Hanson Trust of the United Kingdom, base their corporate strategies on superior skill in restructuring.

And, without pretending to compile an exhaustive list of alternatives, we should mention one other special attribute that some companies have: a capacity to create value in ways only they can conceive of. Call it vision, the ability to imagine transformations of industries and the creation of new businesses. Some firms do not have the chance to effect such fundamental changes; they are competing in businesses that are not susceptible to sweeping changes. But in some companies, corporate centers create value by dreaming, and acting on, big dreams—creating whole new categories of products, definitions of businesses, ways to compete.

SUMMARY

To sum up, companies need strategies for competing in two kinds of markets: the familiar product and service markets, and the market for corporate control. Winning in the latter market depends on creating for shareholders superior value that derives from cash flow returns. *Managers at both the business-unit and corporate levels need to broaden their conceptions of stategy; they need to manage value.*

2

The Value Manager

High performance comes from creating as much value as possible from the businesses and assets a company owns—in other words, from managing value in a superior fashion. Companies that manage value well do not really need takeover defenses to protect them from raids. Raiding a corporation that manages value effectively would be pointless. There would be no obvious destruction of value to reverse, redundant staff to cut, nor businesses that could be sold to others for relatively high prices. Since the company's stock price would reflect its inherent value, no bargain purchase of the shares would be in the offing. All that would result from taking over a company that manages value aggressively would be a loss for the suitor, barring good luck. The target company's shareholders would receive the usual control premium for their shares, while the raider would be saddled with expensive financing and no quick and easy exit. It would, in short, be a speculator's nightmare come true.

Top managements in companies that manage value well are able to spend more of their time focusing on running and creating value from their businesses. They are relatively free from the distractions many of their colleagues face, some of whom seem to be in an unending struggle in the market for corporate control.

BECOMING A VALUE MANAGER

Fortunately, becoming a value manager is not a mysterious process that is open to only a few. It does require a different perspective from that taken by many managers today. It requires a focus on long-run cash flow returns, not quarter-to-quarter changes in earnings per share, as we will discuss in the next chapter. It also requires a willingness to adopt a dispassionate, value-oriented view of corporate activities that recognizes businesses for what they are—investments in productive capacity that either earn a return above their opportunity cost of capital or do not. The value manager's perspective, as detailed in Exhibit 2.1, is characterized by an ability to adopt a raider's view of the business and by a willingness to act on opportunities to create incremental value. Finally, and most important, it includes the need to develop and institutionalize a managing value philosophy throughout the organization. Focusing on shareholder value is not a one-time task to be done only when raiders are on the prowl, but rather an ongoing concern.

In essence, the process of becoming value-oriented has two distinct aspects. The first involves a restructuring that unleashes value trapped within the company. The immediate results from such actions can range from moderate to spectacular: for example, share prices that double or triple in a matter of months. At the same time, the price to be paid for such results can be high. It can involve divestitures, payoffs, and the need to adjust to the discipline of relatively high debt levels. Today, managements have little choice but to take these actions; otherwise, others will displace them and do it anyway.

Managements can avoid the need for cataclysmic change in the future by embracing the second aspect of the managing value process: developing a value-oriented approach to leading and managing their companies after the restructuring. This involves establishing priorities based on value creation; gearing planning, performance measurement, and incentive compensation systems toward shareholder value; and communicating with investors in terms of value creation. By taking these steps to ensure that managing value becomes a routine part of decision making and operations, management can keep the gap narrow between

Exhibit 2.1 **THE MANAGING VALUE PERSPECTIVE**

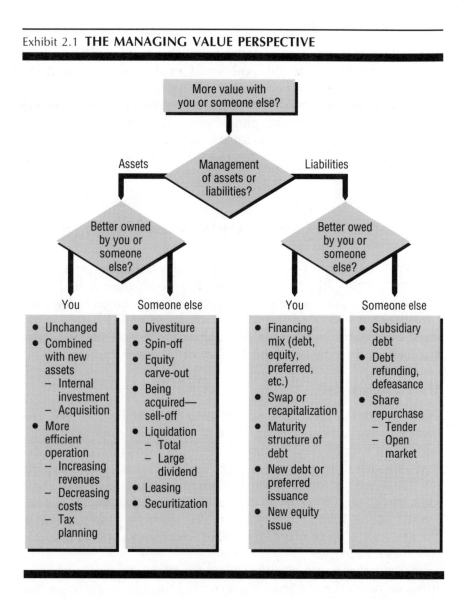

potential and actual value-creation performance. Consequently, the need for major restructuring that goes with large performance gaps will be less likely to arise. Those who manage value well can guide their companies in a series of smaller steps to the higher levels of performance that even the most comprehensive of restructurings effected by raiders cannot match.

In the balance of this chapter, we illustrate the integrated application of value management principles by presenting a case example distilled from the real-world experiences of client executives we have worked with. Our purpose is to show the process of transforming a company in terms of value to shareholders and management philosophy. The case serves as an overview of and framework for the application of the more detailed valuation approaches developed in the main body of this book.

THE CASE OF EG CORPORATION, PART 1: SITUATION

In early 1987, Ralph Demsky took the helm of EG Corporation as chairman and CEO. For the prior ten years, Ralph had been president of Consumerco, EG Corporation's largest division. Consumerco had been the original business of EG before it entered other lines of business through acquisition. Unfortunately, EG had recently become the subject of takeover rumors.

The EG Businesses

EG Corporation had sales of just over $3.5 billion in 1986. The company was in three main lines of business—consumer products, food service, and furniture—with its Consumerco, Foodco, and Woodco divisions.

Consumerco manufactured consumer products and sold them via a direct sales force to grocery and drug stores throughout the United States. It had a dominant market share (over 40 percent) in the majority of its product lines, all of which had a strong branded consumer franchise.

Woodco was a mid-sized player in the highly fragmented furniture business. Woodco had been created through acquisition and consisted of eight separate smaller companies acquired over a period of ten years. All served the mid- to lower-priced end of the market with complementary product lines. The Woodco companies sold their products under their original brand names. As of early 1987, the companies were still operated as autonomous units, but EG had begun to implement plans to combine the companies into one unit, consolidating currently separate administration, sales, and production functions to the extent feasible. They also planned to establish an "umbrella brand" to tie together the wide range of Woodco product offerings and establish a base for adding new lines.

Thus far, the Woodco businesses had turned in uneven financial results. Management capability in the eight businesses varied widely. Moreover, Woodco's business performance was to varying degrees dependent on keeping up with the latest in furniture styling and fashion. Some of the companies were very skilled in this area, but the disastrous consequences of missing the trends had been brought home over the years by their uneven performance. Despite this, Woodco's management was convinced that EG could build a large and successful business over the next few years. They believed consolidation would reduce Woodco's operating costs significantly and strengthen the company's management control over the businesses. They thought the new common sales and marketing thrust would lead to increased volumes and higher margins. The Woodco management's convictions were lent some credence by the existence of several other players in the industry that earned consistently high returns, achieved in part by rationalizing less-efficient companies that they had acquired.

Foodco, EG's third main division, was in the food service business. Foodco operated a small chain of fast food restaurants, as well as providing food service under contract to major corporations and other institutions around the country. It had been essentially built up from internal growth plus a few small acquisitions over the last five years. The former CEO had viewed Foodco as a major growth vehicle for EG and had backed aggressive expansion plans and the associated capital spending. As of early 1987, EG's Foodco unit was earning a profit but was still in the early stages of its development plan. It was a smaller player in the restaurant business and had only a few institutional food service accounts. In both businesses it faced formidable competition, but management believed that its operating approach and EG Corporation's Consumerco name recognition, which was being used as the branding proposition for Foodco, would establish Foodco as a major factor in the industry.

Beyond Consumerco, Foodco, and Woodco, EG Corporation

owned a few other smaller businesses: a property development company (Propco), a small consumer finance company (Finco), and several small newspapers (Newsco). No one currently employed by EG could recall why EG had acquired these businesses. They had been added to the portfolio in the 1960s. All were earning a profit, though they were small by comparison with EG's three main divisions. (See Exhibit 2.2.)

EG's Financial Performance

Overall, EG Corporation's financial performance had been mediocre for the last five years. Earnings growth had not kept pace with inflation, and return on equity had been hovering around 10 percent. Part of the problem was that EG had been hit with unfavorable "extraordinary items" that had depressed bottom line results. Beyond this, though, the company had failed to deliver on overall commitments for growth and operating earnings in its businesses for the last few years.

Exhibit 2.2 **THE EG CORP. BUSINESSES, 1986,** $ MILLIONS

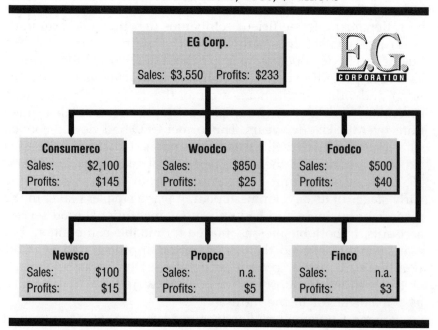

From an investor's standpoint, the company's stock price had lagged the market generally for the last several years. Analysts bemoaned the company's lackluster performance, especially in view of its strong brand position in Consumerco. They were disenchanted with the slow progress in building profits in other parts of the company. Some security analysts had gone so far as to speculate that EG would make a good breakup play for a raider. They noted too that the company's shares were widely held and that no friendly blocks of shares existed for management to count on to thwart a bid. Reflecting this view, and fueled by the frenzied pace of acquisition activity in many industries, EG's share price had risen by over 25 percent over the last several months. EG Corporation's board and senior management were anxious to avoid becoming involved in a takeover contest, but they were frustrated by their inability to convince the market that EG should be more highly valued.

Ralph Demsky's Ingoing Perspective

Ralph Demsky was very familiar with EG's worrisome corporate situation and had been a vocal advocate of a sharper focus on shareholder value at EG for several years. Ralph had been following the restructuring and leveraged-buyout phenomena and was convinced that great opportunities existed for EG to boost its value. Upon retirement of the previous chairman and CEO, the board had tapped Ralph to lead EG because of his controversial ideas and his strong operating track record leading Consumerco.

Ralph knew he needed to act fast. His plan was first to uncover and act on any immediate restructuring opportunities within EG. Then for the longer term he would put in place management systems and approaches to ensure EG did not pass up such opportunities in the future.

THE CASE OF EG CORPORATION, PART 2: RALPH AS RAIDER

During the first week of his tenure as CEO, Ralph initiated a project to assess restructuring opportunities within EG. He knew that raiders and others were running the numbers on EG, and he felt it was only a matter of time before someone took a major "investment position" in EG. He had to take action soon to build value for EG's shareholders. Moreover, stock analysts who commented on Ralph's appointment as CEO in their reports suggested that EG looked set for more "business as usual," since Ralph was a longtime EG insider. They said the only real play in EG shares would be as a takeover candidate. Ralph was determined to prove them wrong on this score. To do so, he would "raid" EG on its shareholders' behalf rather than let an interloper plunder EG. But first, Ralph needed to know where the opportunities lay; hence the project.

To carry it out, he structured a task force with him as chairman, the chief financial officer, and the heads of the businesses. Staff support for the valuation work was provided by analysts from the finance staff, while each business-unit head was responsible for getting the work on his or her business done. The team met twice a week to review progress, develop conclusions, and—importantly—keep up the tempo of the work. Ralph expected the project to provide actionable recommendations within six to eight weeks.

Ralph had thought long and hard about doing the review with a smaller team, perhaps consisting of him, the CFO, and several financial analysts, to maintain secrecy and speed up the process. However, he had rejected this alternative for several reasons. First, he wanted to draw on the best judgment of his senior managers about the prospects for their businesses. Second, because they would play a key role in carrying out the business improvements that were sure to be identified, he wanted to involve them from the outset. Finally, he wanted them to learn the process by doing it, since he planned to undertake a similar thorough review annually from now on.

As an analytical framework, Ralph envisioned investigating the value of EG's existing businesses along five dimensions, which he thought of as forming a restructuring pentagon (see Exhibit 2.3). The pentagon analysis would start with a thorough understanding of EG's current market value. Then the team would assess the current and potential internal values of EG's businesses based on expected cash flows, and would compare

Exhibit 2.3 **PENTAGON FRAMEWORK FOR ASSESSING RESTRUCTURING OPPORTUNITIES**

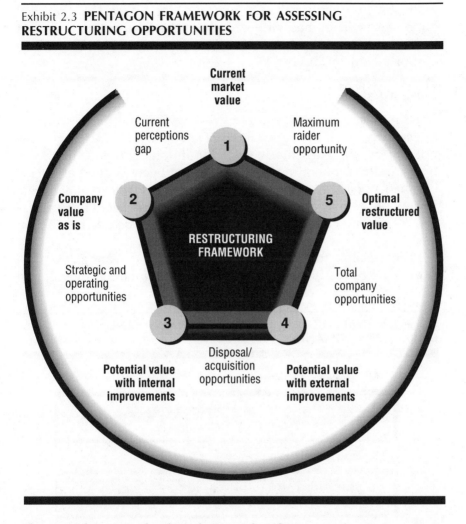

these with external sale values to develop restructuring options. All of these values would be tied back to EG's value in the stock market to estimate the potential gain to EG's shareholders. The comparison would also help to identify gaps in perceptions between investors and EG management about prospects for the businesses.

When their analysis was complete, Ralph and his team would have a thorough, fact-based perspective on the condition of EG's portfolio and their options for building value. They would also know just how serious the risk of a takeover—at least by a rational raider—was. They had all heard about the takeover rumors, but no one at EG knew whether and how a raider could really make any profit out of buying EG.

Current Valuation

The first thing Ralph did was to review EG's performance from the standpoint of its stockholders. He already knew that EG had not performed particularly well for its shareholders in recent times and that operating returns had not been as good as everyone had hoped. But Ralph wanted to be more systematic in his review of the market's perspective, so his team set about analyzing EG's market situation using the framework detailed in Exhibit 2.4.

What Ralph found was disturbing—and revealing. EG's return to investors had indeed been below the market overall and

---

Exhibit 2.4 **ANALYTIC FRAMEWORK FOR DIAGNOSING MARKET PERFORMANCE**

1. **Review market performance**

   - Determine returns to shareholders compared with other investments

2. **Analyze comparative corporate performance**

   - Develop initial picture of company performance that underlies market performance

3. **Understand corporate cash flow**

   - Identify where the corporation has been generating and investing cash and the return this investment is generating

4. **Synthesize market views**

   - Identify assumptions that form basis for current market value

below the returns for a roughly assembled set of "comparable" companies (see Exhibit 2.5). What also stood out from the analysis were a couple of events that had knocked down the value of EG relative to the market. In the period 1980 to 1985, EG had made several acquisitions to establish and build the Woodco furniture businesses. Ralph noticed a decline in EG's share price relative to comparables and the market around the date of each acquisition. In fact, when the team calculated the impact of these declines on EG's total value, they realized that the decline in EG's total value was about equal to the dollar amount of the premiums over market price EG had paid to acquire the companies. Evidently, the stock market did not believe EG would add any value to the acquired businesses. It had viewed the acquisition premiums EG

Exhibit 2.5 **EG CORP., COMPARATIVE SHAREHOLDER PERFORMANCE**

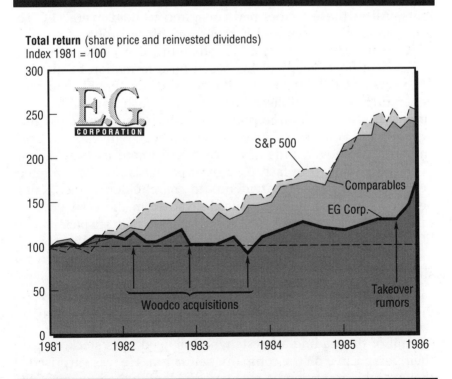

Total return (share price and reinvested dividends)
Index 1981 = 100

had paid as a damaging transfer of value from EG investors to the selling shareholders in the acquired companies.

Ralph thought that this made sense. Since EG had not in fact done anything to these companies since they were purchased, there was no reason for them to be worth any more than their preacquisition value. It didn't seem to matter that the deals had been carefully structured and financed in part with debt to avoid diluting EG's earnings per share. The market had seen through those gimmicks.

Looking next at the financial results of each of EG's businesses, the team noted that Consumerco had generated high, stable returns on capital (40+ percent) for the last five years. However, the business's earnings base was only growing at the pace of inflation. Meanwhile, EG's Woodco business had suffered steadily declining returns. The Foodco business's earnings, on the other hand, were growing, but returns on investment were low due to high capital investment requirements in the restaurants. All of these factors had conspired to hold overall EG returns on capital down and hamper growth in profits.

One investment analysis Ralph found especially intriguing was a cash flow "map" of EG based on information for the last five years (see Exhibit 2.6). What it showed was that EG had been generating substantial discretionary or free cash flow in the Consumerco business, a large portion of which had been sunk into Woodco and Foodco. Relatively little had been reinvested in Consumerco. Moreover, little of the cash had found its way back to EG's shareholders. In fact, on a five-year basis, EG had in effect been borrowing to pay dividends to shareholders. Since Ralph believed that shareholder value derived from the cash flow returns EG could generate, he became increasingly suspicious that EG had taken the cash Consumerco had generated and reinvested it in businesses that might not generate an adequate return for shareholders.

To round out his perspective on EG's valuation by the stock market, Ralph spent a day reading all the reports security analysts had written recently about the company. He then went to visit several of the leading analysts who followed EG's stock, to gain their perspective on the company's situation. He was surprised at the favorable reception he received. Evidently, the previous CEO

Exhibit 2.6 **EG CORP., CUMULATIVE CASH FLOWS,
5 YEARS ENDED DECEMBER 31, 1986,** $ MILLIONS

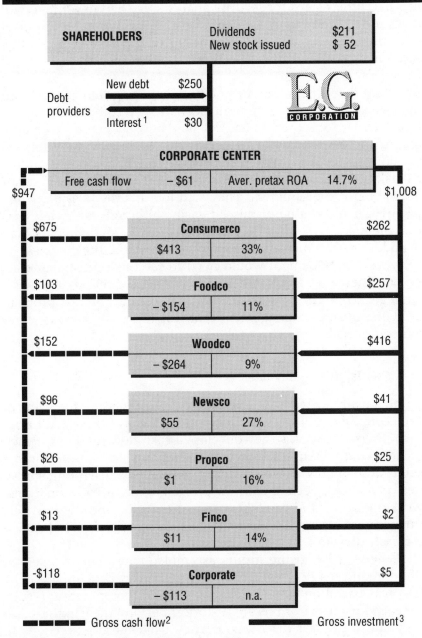

1. Equals after-tax operating profits plus depreciation.
2. Equals capital expenditures, acquisitions, increases in working capital, and other assets.
3. Net of tax benefit.

had had little regard for security analysts. He had never met with them individually to understand their views. When he did meet with them, it was always to tell them why the stock should be more highly valued, never to listen to what they thought about EG.

What Ralph heard about EG was disturbing, but agreed with his views. The analysts thought EG had been complacent for the last five years or more and had pursued new businesses with little regard for the returns to be generated. Moreover, they felt EG would remain an uninteresting investment candidate unless Demsky took actions to demonstrate more commitment to creating value for shareholders. They said too that the possibility of a takeover could not be dismissed easily, although their view was that the management of EG could do better for shareholders than a raider could since management understood the businesses. However, management would need to see this potential and act on it. They thought some real synergies were possible with strategic acquirers for some EG businesses, but the real problem at EG had been a management that was not really serious about generating value for shareholders.

EG's "As Is" Internal Value

Ralph's team turned their attention next to assessing the value of each component of EG's portfolio on the basis of projected future cash flows. To do this they developed cash flow models for each business and then set to work assembling key inputs for the projections, many of which were available from each unit's business plan. They needed to know projected sales growth, margins, working capital and capital expenditure needs, and the like. The finance staff meanwhile developed estimates of the cost of capital for each division.

When they had the inputs assembled, they ran two sets of discounted cash flow valuations as preliminary benchmarks. The first was based on simple extrapolations of the operating results for each business from recent historical performance; in this case, they chose the last three years. They used these projections to estimate the gross value of each EG business, as well as the cost of corporate headquarters activities and the value of nonoperating investments. Exhibit 2.7 shows the "value buildup" the team used to compare the total value to EG's market value. They noticed several points immediately. First, the total value based on history was substantially below the value of EG in the marketplace. Second, the Foodco food service/restaurant business would be worth far less than the capital EG had invested in it in over the last few years, unless performance improved dramatically. Third, the vast majority of EG's value was represented by the cash flow generated by Consumerco. Finally, the corporate headquarters costs, when viewed on a value basis, were a very large drag on overall EG value—almost 25 percent.

After reviewing the disturbing results of the historical extrapolations, Ralph asked the team to look at the value of EG assuming the performance estimates in the business plans were achieved. The results, shown in Exhibit 2.7, were also less than comforting. The total value of EG would be above its market value if the plans came true, but only by about 10 percent. On the face of it this was good news, but Ralph knew that the plans were

Exhibit 2.7 **EG CORP., VALUE BUILDUP COMPARISON, JANUARY 1987,** $ MILLIONS

E.G. CORPORATION	Historical extrapo- lation	Business plans	% difference
Consumerco	$1,750	$2,115	+21%
Foodco	300	275	−8
Woodco	200	600	+200
Newsco	175	200	+14
Propco	125	150	+20
Finco	25	35	+40
Corporate overhead	−425	−425	0
Total	$2,150	$2,950	+37%
Debt	−300	−300	
Equity value	**$1,850**	**$2,650**	+43%
Stock market value	2,400	2,400	
Value gap	**−$550**	**+$250**	
% of stock market value	−23%	+10%	

very aggressive, at least by normal EG standards. He especially did not like the idea that they would need to do all the hard work implied by the plans just to stand still from their shareholders' perspective. Apparently the market took for granted that EG would either improve its performance on its own, or someone would take it over soon and make the needed improvement. Ralph was beginning to think that EG would need to come up with some big ideas in order to create the impact on the value of his shareholders' investment that he was seeking during his tenure as CEO.

Ralph was interested also to note the change in value of the individual businesses projected by the plans. For example, Consumerco's plan performance would increase its value by about 20 percent over its value based on recent performance, which would have a large impact on EG, given Consumerco's large size. Foodco's value, on the other hand, would actually decline despite the fact that their plan involved substantial growth in the number of outlets and overall sales and earnings. To Ralph this could mean only one thing—as he had suspected, the returns on investment in the business were too low. Foodco management was more focused on growth than returns. In contrast, the Woodco consolidation looked set to improve the value of the furniture businesses dramatically, while the newspaper, finance, and property businesses would improve somewhat too.

At this stage, Ralph drew a few preliminary conclusions. First, Consumerco would have to do even better, given its large impact on the company. Second, Foodco would need to revamp its strategy to make sure it built value, not simply bulk. Third, Woodco's consolidation was far more important than he had thought and would need to succeed to maintain EG's value. Finally, EG would need to run pretty hard just to maintain shareholder value, and any missteps could precipitate a collapse in the share price and trigger a bid from another company.

EG's Potential Internal Value

After looking at EG's value "as is," Ralph's team tried to assess how much each business might be worth under more aggressive plans and strategies. Their first step was to identify the key value drivers for each business. They estimated the impact on the value

Exhibit 2.8 **EG CORP., VALUE DRIVERS: IMPACT OF CHANGES IN KEY OPERATING MEASURES,** PERCENT

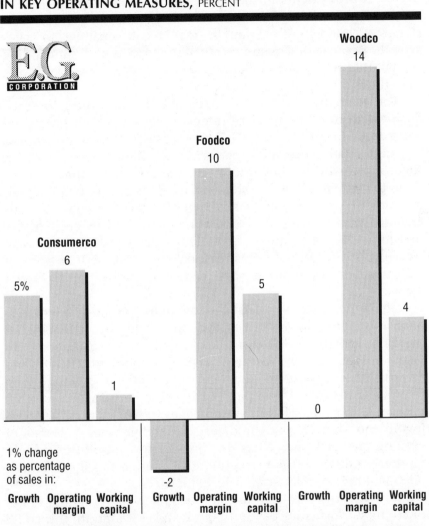

of each business of increasing sales growth by 1 percent, boosting margins by a point, and reducing capital intensity, while holding other factors in constant proportions. The results, shown in Exhibit 2.8, indicated that the key factors varied by business. Foodco, as Ralph suspected, was most sensitive to reductions in capital intensity and increased margins. Woodco was most sensitive to improvements in margins, which would hopefully come about as a result of the consolidation of the companies. Consumerco, interestingly enough, was most sensitive to sales growth. Because of Consumerco's high margins and outstanding capital utilization, each dollar of sales generated large profits and cash flows.

The team next set about assessing the prospects for each business to improve its performance. One approach they used was simply to compare each EG business with similar companies to gauge relative operating performance. They also broke down each of EG's businesses into a "business system" that allowed them to compare—step by step—relative costs, productivity, and investment for EG versus the competition, based on observations and analyses provided by operating managers in each of the divisions. These analyses, coupled with the financial comparisons, showed that it was reasonable to assume that some of EG's businesses could indeed be made to perform at much higher levels.

Consumerco, despite its already high margins, seemed to have room to increase prices over time and earn even higher margins. Moreover, the team discovered that Consumerco had been holding down research and development (R&D) and advertising spending to generate cash for EG's diversification efforts and to buffer the impact of EG's poor performance in other parts of its portfolio. Ralph's team believed that increased spending in the short term would lead to higher sales volumes of existing products, as well as the introduction of additional high-margin products to the marketplace. The impact of these actions on Consumerco is illustrated in Exhibit 2.9.

Woodco, the furniture division, also had the potential to improve its performance beyond plan by a large margin, if it could transform itself and perform at the levels of other top companies in its industry. However, this would likely require a change in Woodco's strategy after the consolidation, to focus less on growth and more on developing higher margins. To do this, Woodco would need to build management information and control systems that would allow Woodco management to keep a tight rein on its potentially volatile businesses. Woodco would also need to

Exhibit 2.9 **EG CORP., IMPACT OF POTENTIAL CONSUMERCO BUSINESS INITIATIVES,** $ MILLIONS

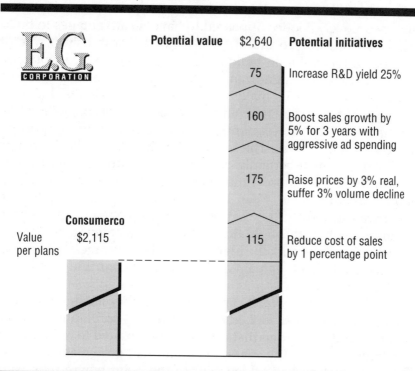

Potential value	$2,640	**Potential initiatives**
	75	Increase R&D yield 25%
	160	Boost sales growth by 5% for 3 years with aggressive ad spending
	175	Raise prices by 3% real, suffer 3% volume decline
Consumerco		
Value per plans $2,115	115	Reduce cost of sales by 1 percentage point

consider sticking more to the basic, mass-market segment of the business where strong operating skills would provide an advantage. This would probably involve abandoning plans to move the business more "up market," since while prices were higher and the potential rewards great, design skills were of utmost importance in this segment. Woodco would be better off sticking to its potentially strong core in the mass-market basic-furniture segments and seeking to maximize its advantage and returns there. Competitors' performance bore this out. Companies with highest returns had either a strong operational focus in higher-volume segments or downplayed manufacturing and won with innovative design. Companies who strayed into the middle ground—and there were many of them—turned in only marginal results.

On the other hand, Foodco, EG's restaurant business, looked

like it would continue to be a poor performer. The industry was extremely competitive. A few large players were earning respectable returns, but even they were struggling to maintain momentum. Moreover, Foodco appeared to have no advantages to build on. The Consumerco brand, which Foodco was using, was of little or no real value in building the business. Foodco would be unable to develop significant scale economies, at least for the foreseeable future. To make matters worse, Foodco had a voracious appetite for capital to build facilities, but was not generating a return on new investment sufficient to cover the opportunity cost of that capital. The team reckoned that the best strategy for Foodco almost certainly would involve cutting back to only its profitable locations and being much more circumspect about growth targets. Even then, it would be necessary to find some way to reduce the cost of capital employed in the Foodco business, either through franchising/management-contract approaches or substantially higher financial leverage. Otherwise, Foodco would likely remain an insignificant contributor to building EG's value.

Similar reviews were carried out for the smaller EG businesses. The team also looked critically at EG's corporate overhead situation and concluded that opportunities existed to reduce costs substantially. Over the years, EG's staff had grown at corporate. The divisions too had added staff to the point where they were functioning largely as freestanding operations. Ralph thought that a raider would almost certainly assume that 75 percent to 80 percent of the corporate costs could be eliminated. He himself thought 50 percent a reasonable target.

Ralph also urged his CFO to look hard at EG's financial structure and come up with an aggressive plan to take advantage of the tax advantages of debt financing. EG had heretofore had a policy of maintaining an AA rating from Standard & Poor's and liked to think of itself as a strong "investment grade" company. However, Ralph knew that many companies had taken on much higher debt levels and performed very well. In fact, the performance of many had been spectacular, as managers thought harder about how to generate additional cash flow and looked more critically at investment requirements and so-called fixed expenses.

EG had sizable and stable free cash flows that could support much higher debt. The Consumerco business, which generated the bulk of the cash, was recession-resistant. Ralph also knew that he did not need much reserve financial capacity in the financial markets of the 1980s and 1990s. To him, being considered investment grade or not was irrelevant; EG would be able to get access to funding if it needed it for a major expansion or acquisition, if it made economic sense. Otherwise, it was probably a poor investment in the first place.

By the CFO's calculations, EG could indeed carry a lot more debt than it did currently, depending on the interest coverage Ralph wished to maintain. Moreover, as the financial performance of the EG businesses improved, EG would be able to carry an even higher debt load comfortably. Ralph figured that at a minimum, EG could raise $500 million in new debt in the next six months and use the proceeds to repurchase shares or pay a special dividend. This debt would provide a more tax-efficient capital structure for EG, which would be worth about $200 million in present value to EG's shareholders, assuming a combined federal and state marginal tax rate of about 40 percent.

Putting it all together, Ralph concluded that the potential internal value of EG's businesses was at least $3.8 billion, which would be 50 to 60 percent above its current market value (see Exhibit 2.10). This was before considering any incremental value that might be garnered through the sale of particular EG businesses to owners who might do more with them, as might be the case with the relatively unattractive Foodco business.

Ralph and his team were beginning to feel better about their chances for turning EG into a high-performance company. They were anxious to get on to the next step, which was to look at the value of EG as a breakup candidate to see whether estimates of EG's potential value would be sufficient to ward off a breakup-oriented raider. They thought too that they would also uncover more ideas for improvement that they could undertake on behalf of their shareholders.

EG's External Value

Ralph's team decided to investigate the external value of EG's businesses under four different scenarios: sale to a "strategic buyer" (another company that could realize operating and stra-

Exhibit 2.10 **EG CORP., POTENTIAL VALUE VS. PLAN VALUE, JANUARY 1987,** $ MILLIONS

E.G. CORPORATION	Historical extrapolation	Business plans	Potential value	% difference
Consumerco	$1,750	$2,115	$2,640	+25%
Foodco	300	275	300	+9
Woodco	200	600	800	+33
Newsco	175	200 ⎫		
Propco	125	150 ⎬	410	+6
Finco	25	35 ⎭		
Corporate overhead	−425	−425	−225	−47%
Debt tax benefit	n.a.	n.a.	200	n.a.
Total	$2,150	$2,950	$4,125	+40%
Debt	−300	−300	−300	
Equity value	**$1,850**	**$2,650**	**$3,825**	**+44%**
Stock market value	2,400	2,400	2,400	
Value gap	**−$550**	**+$250**	**+$1,425**	
% of stock market value	−23%	+10%	+59%	

tegic "synergies"); a flotation or spin-off; leveraged buyout by management or a third party; and liquidation.

The team started with the easiest values to estimate: what the EG businesses would trade for in the market if spun off as independent companies. To estimate these values, they identified a set of publicly traded companies comparable to each EG business. They used current stock market valuation data (for example, price-to-earnings or P/E, market-to-book, market-to-sales ratios) to estimate the value of the EG businesses as freestanding entities. They found that a simple breakup into separate, publicly traded companies would not, at current market prices, provide any gain overall for EG shareholders. Some benefit would result from reduced corporate overhead burden, but the freely traded sum of the parts was less than the current share price of EG.

Likewise, estimates of the value of the businesses as leveraged-buyout candidates did not suggest that EG as a whole would be worth more in parts, especially after taking into account the taxes EG would have to pay on the sale of the units. The

Consumerco business with its strong, stable cash flow was a natural buyout candidate, but the other businesses were not.

The final financially oriented valuation Ralph's team considered was a complete or partial liquidation or decapitalization of the businesses. The only EG business of the three larger ones for which this might have made sense was the Foodco business, because of the real estate it encompassed. The restaurant property might be sold off piecemeal and the Foodco restaurant division shut down. To Ralph's team, a number of the units did appear to be worth more for their alternative real estate value than in their current incarnation as restaurants. However, this did not hold true for Foodco as a whole; the company was worth more as a going concern than in liquidation. The review of Foodco's properties *did* suggest to management, though, that they incorporate into their plans for Foodco the possibility of closing and selling some of those units, including some that were profitable.

One business the team found might be worth more liquidated than operated was EG's small consumer finance company. The business had become so competitive that the spreads between its borrowing costs and the rates it earned on the new loans it booked did not cover its operating costs of generating and processing new business. The team discovered that the existing loan portfolio might be sold for more than the entire business was worth, even under management's plans going forward. In effect, each year's new business was dissipating some of the value inherent in the existing portfolio of loans. The team was sure also that it would be relatively easy to sell the portfolio and exit the business altogether. A number of financial companies might buy the loans. Moreover, no links between the finance company and any of the other EG businesses would need to be untangled. Of course, EG would also consider the possibility of selling the entire business and searching for ways to make the company more viable, but it seemed likely that it would end up going out of business.

Reflecting on the values generated by a financially driven dismemberment of EG, Ralph saw clearly that the gains to be gotten from pure financial maneuvering would be limited. At EG's current market price, a raider would be foolish to try to acquire EG and sell its pieces in their current condition as freestanding units. The company was certainly not undervalued as currently operated. EG's management, or a potential acquirer, would need to make substantial improvements to the businesses to be able to increase the value of EG significantly. The best combination of financial plays for each business did not generate an increment over EG's current market value.

Finally, Ralph reviewed the team's findings on the value of EG's parts to strategic buyers—potential owners who would be able to make the improvements required to increase the value of the businesses. From these analyses, it was evident that Consumerco, EG's largest business, might be worth much more in the hands of another owner than it was now to EG and might still be worth more to them even after Ralph achieved the potential value he had identified earlier. A strategic buyer might see several sources of value in Consumerco. First was the ability to make the improvements to the growth and returns in the business Ralph's team had identified earlier. It was clear to Ralph that these opportunities were evident to any potential acquirer who looked at Consumerco, even using publicly available data. Important too was the potential for cost savings between the consumer businesses of certain potential buyers and Consumerco. For instance, sales forces could be combined and much of Consumerco's direct sales force eliminated. Potential savings could also be realized in the management of Consumerco itself, since it might be merged into an existing management structure at another consumer products company.

In addition to cost savings, an acquirer might believe it could improve Consumerco's business by injecting more vigorous marketing know-how into the business and improving its new product development activities. Ralph believed that these areas, while difficult to quantify, needed improvement at Consumerco, which was not known for the strength of its marketing team. It had grown accustomed to the high returns its dominant and essentially unchallenged brand recognition provided to its range of products. All these factors together suggested that Consumerco might be worth over $3.2 billion to a strategic buyer, which was much more than it was currently worth as run by EG (around $2 billion). It was also more than the $2.6 billion potential value of Consumerco to EG that Ralph's team had estimated previously as the best EG could do with the business. Since Consumerco was a large portion of EG's value, the whole company was at risk of a takeover by a buyer interested in getting its hands on Consumerco.

Potential strategic buyers existed for the other EG businesses too, and Ralph's team did their best to estimate the value of the EG businesses to each company. They thought Foodco would be attractive to another more established restaurant company who might follow one of two courses of action. On the one hand, they could accelerate Foodco's development and leverage their own management skills to improve the profitability of the Foodco units. Alternatively, they could convert the Foodco sites over to their own restaurant concept. Foodco did have quite a few reasonably good locations. In fact, it looked as though EG would be better off to sell Foodco if the potential prices were likely to be realized, since even after paying tax on the proceeds the Foodco business was unlikely to be worth as much under EG's plans.

The Woodco business, which was in the process of being consolidated, might be attractive to one of several other companies in the industry who had earned a reputation for buying and improving smaller furniture companies. However, it made little sense to sell Woodco when it was in the midst of the consolidation. Any potential buyer would not be willing to take the risk of having the business fall apart completely in the transition to new ownership. For all practical purposes, the Woodco business would not be salable for twelve to eighteen months at anything other than a distressed sale price. By the end of eighteen months, though, EG would be in a good position to evaluate a sale. The business would be streamlined and Ralph would have a better idea about the ability of Woodco's management to improve performance to approach that of the industry leaders. If Woodco could perform that well on its own, EG would be better off to retain it and perhaps use it as a base for making additional furniture company acquisitions. If Woodco did not look able to reach higher performance levels, it could be sold at that time to another player in the industry and for a much better price than today.

Exhibit 2.11 shows the conclusions the team drew about estimated values for the EG businesses under the different sce-

narios. In total, they concluded that, even allowing for difficulty
in selling Woodco at this time, EG could be worth substantially
more than its current stock price if sold piece by piece to the best
potential owners of each business.

EG's Restructuring Plan

Ralph's team had analyzed EG's value from multiple perspectives, both internal and external. Having done so, they were
in a good position to develop an overall restructuring plan for the
company. The plan would have to boost EG's value to its
shareholders substantially. They knew that a raider or strategic
buyer pursuing Consumerco would find the economics of acquiring EG tempting. The returns to a raider interested in breaking up
EG would be at least 80 to 100 percent if the deal were leveraged
in the typical fashion (see Exhibit 2.12). Likewise, a strategic
buyer could end up owning Consumerco at an attractive net price
if it bought EG and were patient in selling off the other parts of
the company. It was obvious to Ralph's group that EG's whole
management team would be out of a job if they didn't act to boost
EG's value, and boost it fast.

Fortunately, Ralph believed EG could match or better a potential acquirer's actions through his own restructuring plan. This
would also be likely to yield greater returns to EG's shareholders
than selling out to a raider, even at a hefty 40 to 50 percent
premium over market. As shown in Exhibit 2.13, the team identified, business area by business area, the actions an acquirer of
EG, or the party to whom it would ultimately sell the business,

Exhibit 2.11 **EG CORP., COMPARISON OF EXTERNAL VALUE
ESTIMATES BY BUSINESS, JANUARY 1987,** $ MILLIONS

	Consumerco	Foodco	Woodco	Propco	Finco	Newsco
LBO	$2,500	290	n.a.	n.a.	n.a.	180
Spin-off	2,000	280	55	n.a.	25	140
Liquidation	n.a.	260	25	130	50	n.a.
Strategic buyer	3,250	350	155	175	35	190
Highest value	**3,250**	**350**	**155**	**175**	**50**	**190**

Exhibit 2.12 **EG CORP., ECONOMICS OF POSSIBLE RAIDER'S "BUST-UP" TAKEOVER,** $ MILLIONS

POTENTIAL BREAKUP PROCEEDS	(Millions)	
Gross sales prices	$ 4,170	
Taxes on sales	-155	
Payoff of E.G. debt	-300	
Net proceeds	$ 3,715	
Transaction costs	-75	
After-tax interest on acquisition debt	-253	
Payoff of acquisition debt	-2,808	
Proceeds to equity	$ 579	
LIKELY INVESTMENT		
Market value of equity	$ 2,400	
Takeover premium at, say, 30%	720	1-year return = 86%
Total purchase price	$ 3,120	
Debt financing (90%)	2,808	
Equity invested by raider	$ 312	

might take. Matched against these were the actions Ralph and his management team could take. It was clear that EG could do as well as or better than the outsiders in most areas.

Ralph's plan would produce a large gain for EG shareholders if he were successful in executing it. Exhibit 2.14 and 2.15 show the projected sources of increase in the value of EG's stock and the increment over EG's recent share value in the market. In a nutshell, Ralph's restructuring plan would entail these moves:

- Stopping further expansion in Foodco and putting the company up for sale
- Putting the finance company portfolio up for sale, and taking steps to wind down the rest of its business activities
- Accelerating the consolidation of the Woodco companies and reorienting plans for its direction after the consolidation

Exhibit 2.13 **EG CORP., COMPARISON OF RESTRUCTURING ACTIONS**

Area	Raider action	EG action
Consumerco	Sell to acquirer in consumer business	Cut cost of sales Reorganize sales force Increase advertising, R&D Build marketing skills
Foodco	Sell to larger food service company	Sell
Woodco	Sell to management	Keep and consolidate; sell if in two years management cannot reach next level of performance
Propco	Sell	Sell
Finco	Sell	Liquidate
Newsco	Sell	Sell
Corporate	Eliminate	Cut by 50%; decentralize remainder
Financing	High leverage during breakup	Set leverage to maintain BB rating to capture tax benefits

to focus on boosting returns in basic furniture markets rather than expanding into more upscale segments

- Making improvements in the Consumerco business aimed at doubling its already high value: increasing prices, investing more in advertising and new products, rationalizing the large direct sales force to boost productivity, hiring several top-flight marketing executives from leading consumer companies, cutting back on staff functions that had been allowed to grow unchecked

- Selling the newspaper and property development companies—valuable properties, but needless distractions for EG

- Launching a review of corporate overheads, starting from the premise that EG could operate with only a handful of

Exhibit 2.14 **EG CORP., VALUE CREATED THROUGH RESTRUCTURING, JANUARY 1987,** $ MILLIONS

	Historical extrapolation	Restructuring action	% difference	
Consumerco	$1,750	$2,900	**+66%**	**Improvements**
Foodco	300	350	**+17**	**Sale**
Woodco	200	800	**+300**	**Consol./sale**
Newsco	175	190	**+9**	**Sale**
Propco	125	160	**+28**	**Sale**
Finco	25	45	**+80**	**Liquidation**
Corporate overhead	−425	−225	**−47**	**Cuts**
Debt tax benefit	n.a.	200	**n.a.**	
Total	$2,150	$4,420	**+106%**	
Debt	−300	−300		
Equity value	**$1,850**	**$4,120**	**+122%**	
Stock market value	2,400	2,400		
Value gap	**−$550**	**−$1,720**		
% of stock market value	−23%	+72%		

people by moving to a holding-company type structure, with staff functions pushed down into the divisions
- Recapitalizing the company by borrowing $500 million and targeting a BB rating for EG going forward, rather than its historically conservative AA rating
- Developing a strategy for communicating with the investment markets about the restructuring plan and its potential impact on the value of EG

Ralph and his team were confident that their plan would work well. Since they could take immediate steps, they also expected to get a quick and favorable response to the program.

THE CASE OF EG CORPORATION, PART 3: RALPH AS VALUE MANAGER

EG's restructuring plan did in fact result in an increase in the price of its shares. When the plan was announced, EG's price jumped

Exhibit 2.15 **EG CORP., VALUE BUILDUP, JANUARY 1987,** $ MILLIONS

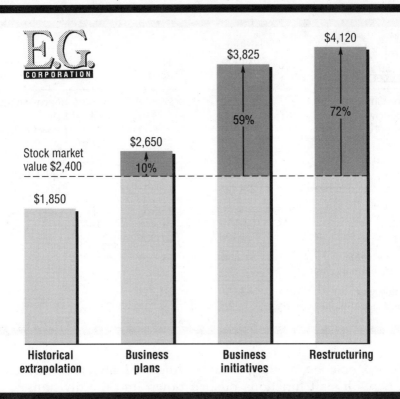

immediately. Then, when investors saw that EG was in fact taking the actions it had promised, the stock price rose further. Over the first six months of 1987, EG's shares increased over 40 percentage points above the stock market average increase. The analysts who followed EG dropped their talk of takeovers and applauded the "transformation" of the company.

Needless to say, Ralph and his team were feeling pleased with the results. Ralph regretted having had to reduce the corporate staff and sell some of EG's businesses, but took some comfort from the knowledge that he did it in a more orderly and humane way than an outsider would have. Despite his successes, though, Ralph knew he had a lot more work ahead to see his restructuring plan through to completion. Furthermore, he knew he needed to begin the job of building an orientation toward managing value into the company's ongoing activities. Otherwise, he feared that people throughout the company would soon become complacent about EG's performance, and the accumulation of untapped value potential would begin anew. He wanted to build on the fragile momentum he had established.

Ralph planned to take five steps to build EG's ability to manage value:

1. Focus planning and business performance reviews around value creation.
2. Evaluate strategic investment decisions explicitly in terms of their impact on value.
3. Restructure EG's compensation system to foster an emphasis on creating shareholder value.
4. Begin communicating with investors and analysts more clearly about the value of EG's plans.
5. Reshape the role of EG's CFO.

Ralph's plans and thinking in each of these areas are set out in the following paragraphs.

Put Value into Planning

Ralph was convinced that one of the main reasons EG Corporation had gotten into the position it had was a lack of focus on value creation in developing corporate-level and business-unit plans. Likewise, evaluations of the performance of the businesses had had only a vague focus on value. Ralph firmly believed that it was the responsibility of all senior managers to focus on value creation. Going forward, Ralph would ensure that company plans included a thorough analysis of the value of each of the businesses under alternative scenarios. He would also make sure that EG used the restructuring pentagon approach on an annual basis to identify any restructuring opportunities within EG's portfolio.

This new focus on value would also require some changes in the way EG thought about its corporate strategy. For the next year or so, EG clearly would need to focus on carrying out its restructuring. In effect, EG's corporate strategy for the next year would be to restructure itself. However, beyond that, Ralph would need to develop a plan for sustaining EG's advantage in the market for corporate control. To do this, he would need to get clear about the company's real skills and assets and in which businesses they would be most valuable. Most important, he would ensure that the value of these skills could be identified in terms of higher margins, growth rates, and the like before building action plans around them. Too often in the past, Ralph was convinced, EG had done a perfunctory analysis of its capabilities and entered businesses without a clear idea of how and why EG would be a better owner and able to create value for its shareholders. As a first step, later in the year Ralph would establish a task force to begin inventorying and analyzing EG's skills and assets compared with competition, as well as ideas for new businesses EG might enter.

At the business level, EG's new focus on value would require some changes too. The restructuring review had pointed out a number of specific strategic and operating actions that the various business managers would need to take. Beyond this, management in the business units would need to think differently about their operations. They would need to focus on what was driving the value of their businesses—whether it was volume growth, margins, or capital utilization. Everyone had been used to focusing on growth in earnings, but what would matter going forward would be growth in value and economic returns on investment. Sometimes this would mean foregoing growth in the business that would have been accepted in years gone by. At other times, managers would have to get more comfortable with the idea of reporting lower earnings when investment in research and development or advertising with a longer-term payoff made economic sense. Ralph knew that these changes would be difficult for his management group, because they had not been encouraged to think this way in the past. To help bring about change, he decided to share with them the results of the overall corporate restructuring analysis and to develop a series of training seminars for senior division management about shareholder value.

Finally, Ralph knew that it was simply not good enough to *demand* that his managers' plans and strategies have creation of value as an objective. He would have to reinforce this in his dealings with them on a formal and informal basis. He planned to position himself to play the role of an active "investor" in his company's businesses. He was not there to tell the division managers how to run their businesses. Instead, he was there to ensure that they were running them in a way that would build their values as investments. In monthly and quarterly business reviews, he would ensure that the focus of discussion when it came to financial results was performance against key objectives for the value drivers. If he lapsed into his company's old habits of worrying about quarter-to-quarter earnings growth, then his managers would not take him seriously and would revert to business as usual. His performance standards would certainly be tough. He would let his managers know that while a plan is important, if he as an outside investor saw an opportunity to "raid" their businesses to create more value, he would do so and they would find their lives very uncomfortable indeed.

Assess Value of Strategic Investments

Injecting a value-creation focus into EG's planning and performance review processes would make a big difference. However, Ralph knew he needed to make changes in the way the company looked at major spending proposals in the areas of capital expenditures and acquisitions.

To evaluate capital expenditures, EG had been using discounted cash flow analysis for at least five years, as had most other companies. This was fine and good, but Ralph saw two problems. First, capital expenditures were not linked tightly enough to the strategic and operating plans for the businesses. Because of this, capital expenditure proposals were very difficult to evaluate; they were out of context. Second, EG had been using a corporationwide hurdle rate to assess capital investment proposals. From his restructuring review of EG, Ralph knew that each of the EG businesses involved a different degree of risk, so the hurdle rates for assessing capital investments should be different too. To make matters worse, the hurdle rate was much too high, having been set in an attempt to "smoke out" unrealistic operating projections. The result was an ineffective capital expenditure process. Ralph figured that many investments that earned above their cost of capital were being passed up because they did not meet EG's extremely high hurdle rate. On the other hand, major capital investments were not evaluated as closely as they should be since the whole process had degenerated into a numbers game about assumptions. In the future, Ralph intended to tie the capital expenditure cycle in closely with the strategic and operating plans to ensure that evaluation of capital spending was done in a realistic, fact-based way. He would also ensure that the finance staff developed appropriate hurdle rates that would differ by division to reflect the relevant opportunity cost of capital.

Ralph knew that one of EG's biggest problems in the past had been the evaluation of acquisitions. He knew they had paid way too much for the Woodco acquisitions in the early 1980s. In his restructuring review, he had seen the impact of paying too much for them on the company's share price. Fortunately, as CEO he would have direct control over the decision to pursue acquisitions. He would insist that when proposing an acquisition, the relevant operating manager and CFO do a thorough valuation analysis based on cash flow returns for the transaction. He would not make the mistake his predecessor had of believing that just because he could make the accounting earnings and dilution figures look good in the first year or two of an acquisition, it made sense from a value standpoint.

To Ralph it was really quite simple. Either the cash flow value to EG's shareholders of an acquisition would be above the price EG would have to pay, or Ralph would not make the acquisition. And he believed that value could be assessed in a relatively systematic way—much more systematically than had been done in the past.

First, EG management would evaluate the target's business on an "as is" basis, just as they had done for EG. Next, they would use the restructuring pentagon approach to identify improvements that could be made to the value of the company on a stand-alone basis. The management of the target company might or might not be capable of making these improvements on their own. Likewise, Ralph would ensure that EG management knew whether they were capable of making the changes. Third, EG management would evaluate the potential for synergies with other EG businesses on a systematic basis. These synergies would be evaluated in concrete terms for their impact on value. Finally, EG management would think about the strategic options the acquisition would create. These would be difficult to value and to evaluate, but could nevertheless be important. For example, an acquisition might give EG an option on a new technology in one of its businesses, or access to a new market, both of which could have substantial value in the future under the right conditions.

Armed with this information, Ralph would be much better able to evaluate the value of any particular acquisition and be much clearer than EG management had ever been in the past. He would know how much EG could afford to pay. Equally important, he would know more specifically what to do with the business after it had been acquired. Before entering negotiations, Ralph would also have his team assess the value of the target to other potential acquirers; in this way he could be sure that he would not enter into a fruitless bidding contest or end up buying the company at a price higher than he needed to. He certainly did not want to fall into the trap of paying all of the potential value of the candidate to the selling shareholders. After all, why should EG do all the work and the sellers receive all the rewards?

Acquisition proposals would also be subjected to a new test. EG management would no longer presume that the best way to pursue a new business idea was by acquisition. Ralph would ensure that they considered entering the business on their own or via joint venture as an alternative to the "big bang" acquisitions that always seem like a quick and easy solution at the time, but afterward cause no end of problems for the company's performance.

Tie Compensation to Value

Ralph believed that one of the most powerful levers he could use in building a value-creation focus throughout EG was the compensation system. At present, the package contained relatively little performance-based incentive for top managers. They did receive a bonus, but it was a relatively modest proportion of total compensation. They also received stock options, but few viewed these as significant in terms of their ability to build capital for doing a good job. It was also clear to Ralph that the top-management incentives did not focus on value creation. Bonus payouts were geared toward achievement of earnings-per-share targets, which as he knew did not always correlate well with creating value. In addition, the compensation of business-unit managers was tied more closely to the performance of EG as a whole than it was to the fortunes of their particular business unit.

Ralph wanted a much sharper edge to his compensation system for senior managers. He hoped to develop a structure that would promote performance like that seen in leveraged-buyout situations, where the same management group under new ownership was able to generate substantially higher returns for the owners of the business. He wanted to build into his approach the same carrot-and-stick incentives present in a buyout. In an LBO, managements have a powerful incentive to build the value of their businesses because of the equity stake they receive. They must focus on identifying and acting quickly on short-term improvements in order to meet high debt payments, but must also focus on the long term since their ultimate payoff usually comes from taking the company public several years down the road. They are encouraged to both build the future value of the business and wring out short-term improvement opportunities. Added to the incentive picture is the fact that if the managers do not perform well, not only will they not receive the buildup of wealth they have envisioned, but they will also be out of a job since their lenders and investors will not tolerate substandard performance for very long.

To develop a workable plan, Ralph asked his head of corporate human resources to develop an alternative structure that would meet certain objectives. First, it should have a large incentive portion to it that had the prospect of generating large returns for managers who were capable of creating outstanding value for shareholders. Second, the compensation needed to be linked to the value created in specific businesses, not corporation-wide. Third, it would need to discourage short-term game playing and ensure that executives had an interest in the long-term health of their businesses. Consequently, Ralph thought the awards and payout should vest over a three-to-five-year period. Finally, he wanted it to be truly equitylike. Many of the stock options that EG had outstanding now, for instance, had been issued at prices substantially higher than the current market value. While the company stock was near or above the issuance price, the options had an incentive effect. But when stock fell way out of the money, the options were viewed as largely worthless regardless of what the EG managers did to create value.

Ralph figured that several schemes were potentially capable of meeting his objectives, and asked his human resources executives to consider plans involving phantom stock for each of the divisions; a deferred compensation program structured around a return-on-investment versus investment-base grid that would reflect changes in the value of the business; as well as a more operationally focused plan using the attainment of goals on particular value drivers over time as a basis for compensation awards. Ralph was confident that through these plans he would be able to devise one that would suit EG's situation. If for some reason he could not, he was ready and willing to consider the option of selling up to 20 percent of the major businesses in a public offering so as to provide a basis for giving management an equity stake in each business that had a traded market value.

Develop Investor Communications Strategy

Ralph planned to continue working hard to build the company's credibility with Wall Street analysts and investors. As a key part of this, it would be essential for EG to track analyst views on its performance and prospects on a regular basis. Ralph wanted to do this for two reasons. First, he would be able to ensure that the market had sufficient information to evaluate the company at all times. Second, Ralph knew that the market was smart. He could learn a lot about the direction of his industry and competitors from the way investors evaluated his shares and those of other companies. He did not believe that he could, nor would he try to, fool the market about EG. He was convinced, though, that it was sound strategy to treat investors and the investing community with the same care that the company showed its customers and employees. Had previous management taken the time to really understand what the market was saying about EG, the company might have been less likely to get into the difficult position it had fallen into.

In addition to tracking the analysts' opinions and meeting with them regularly, Ralph thought EG should be more active and clearer in communicating with the investors. Henceforth, his communications with the market at security analyst meetings and in press releases would focus on what EG was doing to build value for shareholders. He even thought it might be a good idea to have a section in the annual report entitled something like "Perspective on the Value of Your Company" that would discuss clearly and in some depth the company's strategies for creating value.

He thought that EG could even go so far as to publish its estimates of the value of the company, as long as the assumptions were spelled out clearly. Ralph knew that this communications strategy would be a break with the practices of many companies and with EG's recent past. However, Ralph did not really think investors got much benefit from the mechanical—and usually vague—explanations of changes in year-to-year performance typically found in the annual reports of many companies. Likewise, the glossy photographs and glowing language in the front sections of many annual reports did little to give investors a clear sense of where a company was going and what the status of their investment was.

Reshape CFO's Role

Critical to the success of Ralph's efforts to build a value-creation focus into EG was the need to upgrade the role of the CFO. It was clear to Ralph that the link between business strategy and financial strategy was becoming tighter; on top of this, corporate strategies, since they are designed to create an advantage in the market for corporate control and financial markets, are by definition intertwined with financial considerations. Furthermore, it was going to take a lot of work to make managing value a key element of EG's strategy and management approaches. Ralph would need a strong executive who would be able to help him push this through.

Historically, EG financial officers had been focused entirely on financial matters such as running the treasury operation, producing financial reports, and negotiating the occasional deal. Ralph needed much more, and since his current CFO was due to retire at the end of the year, he felt this was a perfect opportunity to redefine the role.

Ralph's concept was to create a new position that would blend corporate strategy and finance responsibilities. The officer would act as a bridge between the strategic/operating focus of the division heads and the financial requirements of the corporation and its investors. Ralph drafted a job description for this position, which in EG's case would carry the title of executive vice-president for corporate strategy and finance. This description is set out in Exhibit 2.16. Key responsibilities of the new role would be to act as a kind of "super CFO" and take the lead in developing a value-creating corporate strategy for EG, as well as to work with Ralph and the division heads to build a value-management capability throughout the organization.

The EVP would also be responsible for managing the normal financial affairs and financial reporting of the corporation, but his or her success would be measured mainly in terms of how well EG made the transition to a corporation that managed value in a superior way. For example, if the EVP were successful, in a year or so EG would have a first-draft corporate strategy in place, a clearly articulated financial strategy that supported it, and division heads and key managers who were thinking and acting in terms of value creation when submitting plans and proposals. Security analysts would also have a much clearer understanding of EG's strategy and the reason why it would not make sense to view the company as a breakup candidate. Longer term, the EVP's success would be measured as part of a team who would provide shareholders with superior returns, assist in launching several new value-creating expansion opportunities, and establish EG with a reputation in the financial community as a leading-edge, value-managing company.

Ralph Demsky expected his five-part plan for building a sharper focus on value into EG could take as long as two years to become a well-accepted part of EG's management approach.

Exhibit 2.16 **JOB DESCRIPTION: EXECUTIVE VICE PRESIDENT FOR CORPORATE STRATEGY AND FINANCE, EG CORPORATION**

Job Concept

The EVP will act as key advisor to the CEO and division heads on major strategic and operational issues, and will manage EG's financial and planning functions. Responsibilities will include:

- Corporate strategy
- Financial strategy
- Budgeting and management control, and
- Financial management.

Corporate strategy   The EVP will take the lead role in coordinating the development of a value-maximizing overall corporate strategy for EG:

- Ensuring that plans are in place to create maximum value for EG from its current businesses
  - —Assessing the value creation potential of plans on an ongoing basis
  - —Ensuring that plans focus on key issues by (1) challenging key assumptions and the rationale for changes in performance, and (2) providing external reference points for value-creation opportunities (for example, value of the businesses to alternative owners)
  - —Acting as a sounding board for the CEO and division heads on critical proposals
  - —Establishing financial measurement standards and developing systems to monitor performance against goals
- Supporting the development of corporate expansion strategies to create additional shareholder value
  - —Developing perspectives on market opportunities in businesses closely related to current businesses
  - —Assessing EG's skills and assets in place for pursuing opportunities and suggesting programs to build skills to fill gaps
  - —Conducting business and financial evaluations of specific proposals
- Planning and executing major transactions required to implement EG's strategies

Exhibit 2.16 Continued

Financial strategy The EVP will have responsibility for developing, recommending, and executing an overall financial strategy for EG that supports its business strategies and captures maximum value for its shareholders:

- Developing value-creating capital structure and dividend policy recommendations
- Designing and managing a strategy for communicating the key elements of EG's plans and performance to investors and the financial community
- Negotiating and executing all major financial transactions, including borrowings, share issuances, and share repurchases

Budgeting and management control   The EVP will design and implement processes to ensure that EG managers have the right information to set goals, make decisions, and monitor performance:

- Coordinating preparation of short-term operating budgets
- Developing key performance measures for each business unit
- Ensuring that business units have adequate management controls in place
- Evaluating business-unit performance in conjunction with the CEO and division heads

Financial management   The EVP will ensure the effective and efficient management of EG's financial operations:

- Ensuring that all external reporting and compliance obligations are fulfilled
- Establishing controls to safeguard EG's assets
- Ensuring the integrity and efficiency of cash, receivables, and payables management
- Filing and paying all tax obligations
- Pursuing opportunities to reduce EG's tax burden
- Maintaining strong day-to-day relationships with EG's banks

Exhibit 2.16 Continued

* Managing EG's pension fund
* Managing EG's risk management programs

Success Criteria

If the EVP is successful: .

One year from now:
* A well-defined corporate strategy will have been created, and early phases of execution will have been completed
* A clearly articulated financial strategy will have been developed and implementation will have begun
* Division heads and key managers will think in terms of shareholder value creation when developing their plans and evaluating proposals
* The financial management functions will be operating smoothly
* Security analysts will understand EG's strategy and evaluate it as a strong operating company rather than a breakup candidate

Three years from now:
* EG will have provided shareholders with superior returns
* EG will have begun pursuing several value-creating expansion initiatives (most likely through internal investments)
* Security analysts will view EG as a leading-edge "value manager" of its businesses

Major Resources

The EVP's staff will include the treasury, controller's, planning, and tax departments. In addition, the financial staffs of the operating units will have dotted-line reporting relationships to the EVP. The EVP will have broad discretion in organizing the staff.

Key Organizational Relationships

The EVP's integrating role will require close working relationships with all the other key executives at EG:

* *CEO:* The EVP will provide recommendations and analyses to the CEO on all major issues. The EVP will carry out the financial policy decisions made by the CEO.

Exhibit 2.16 Continued

- *Operating-Unit Heads:* The EVP will work with the operating-unit heads to ensure the smooth functioning of the planning, reporting, and control systems, and to resolve conflicts between corporate and business-unit priorities. The EVP will also counsel the operating-unit heads on finance-related issues and provide analytical support for special projects.

The EVP and staff will manage the relationships with key outside groups, including:

- Investors, financial analysts, rating agencies, and the financial press;
- Financial institutions (banks and investment banks);
- External auditors; and
- Regulators and tax authorities.

Critical Skills/Requirements for the Job

The EVP should bring a broad business perspective and should possess the following characteristics:

- Seasoned business judgment and superior analytical abilities, particularly in strategic business and financial analysis
- Ability to take an independent stance and challenge the ideas of the CEO and operating managers while maintaining their respect and confidence
- Presence to deal with the financial community
- Ability to lead/orchestrate negotiations in major transactions
- Strong administrative and people management skills

In addition, the EVP should have familiarity with the following:

- Financial markets
- Financial and managerial accounting
- Treasury operations
- Taxation

It would require the recruitment of the new EVP and substantial time and attention from Ralph himself. Focusing planning and performance measurement on value creation, evaluating all major decisions in terms of impact on value, redesigning the compensation system for senior management, and communicating more clearly and consistently with the stock market would help to ensure that EG maintained an advantage in the market for corporate control and produced outstanding value for shareholders. Moreover, by following this much more integrated approach, it would be easier for EG to set corporate priorities in the future, since major decisions would be brought back to the common benchmark of their impact on the value of the company.

SUMMARY

The ability to manage value is an essential part of developing sound corporate and business strategies—strategies that create value for shareholders and maintain an advantage in the market for corporate control. As the case of EG Corporation shows, managing value is not a mysterious process. Valuation techniques and approaches can be complex in their details, but are relatively straightforward in their objectives and applications. Our objective in the balance of this book is to demystify the approaches needed to implement value management in most companies.

As in the EG case, managing value consists of taking three broad steps: first, *taking stock* of the value-creation situation within the company and identifying restructuring opportunities; second, *acting* on those opportunities, which usually involves major transactions such as divestitures and acquisitions as well as reorganization of the company; and third, *instilling* a value-creation philosophy into the management approaches of the company. This three-step process is outlined in Exhibit 2.17.

It should be clear that a managing-value focus does not create value through financial manipulations. Rather, it creates value through developing sound strategic and operating plans for a company's businesses. The link between sound strategy and value creation is a tight one. As many CEOs have learned, financial manipulations on their own seldom work.

Exhibit 2.17 **THE MANAGING-VALUE PROCESS**

1. Take stock

> Identify restructuring opportunities
> - Conduct restructuring analysis (pentagon approach)
> - Assess business strategies and plans
> - Develop restructuring and expansion scenarios

2. Act

> Execute restructuring program
> - Execute internal initiatives
>   Accelerate growth
>   Increase margins
>   Cut costs
>   Decapitalize
> - Execute external initiatives
>   Sell/spin off businesses
>   Recapitalize
>   Acquire new businesses

3. Instill

> Build managing-value approach
> - Put value into planning
> - Rethink capital investment process
> - Tie compensation to value created
> - Develop investor communications strategy
> - Reshape CFO role

Many companies thankfully are not in as desperate a condition as we outlined for EG Corporation. Most companies, however, *would* benefit from a thorough review of restructuring opportunities. Despite this, we know of relatively few companies that have made the attempt to institutionalize a managing-value approach to their business. Perhaps it is because many companies who have gone through massive restructuring believe that it will only happen once. However, we believe, as we discussed in the first chapter of this book, that restructuring and an active market for corporate control are now facts of corporate life. Consequently, managers need to ensure that they identify and act on value-creation opportunities regularly—not just once when the raider is knocking at the door, but on an ongoing basis. This is best done through fundamental changes in the way their businesses are structured and operated. By acting now, value managers can avoid the need to react under duress later.

3

Cash Is King

On October 1, 1974, the *Wall Street Journal* published an editorial lamenting the widespread focus on earnings per share as an indicator of value:

> A lot of executives apparently believe that if they can figure out a way to boost reported earnings, their stock prices will go up even if the higher earnings do not represent any underlying economic change. In other words, the executives think they are smart and the market is dumb. . . .
>
> The market is smart. Apparently the dumb one is the corporate executive caught up in the earnings-per-share mystique.

Unfortunately, our experience shows that many corporate managers still worship earnings per share, and thus are still betting that the market is dumb. They do have good reasons for this belief. Earnings per share is a simple calculation that answers many business questions quite well. But the virtue of simplicity can also be a vice. Earnings per share ignores the effects of many natural or contrived peculiarities of accounting. It can therefore lead, or allow, managers to make choices that destroy value in the long term, often without the short-term share price improvement they hoped for.

The key problem with maximizing accounting earnings can be demonstrated with an example of another common valuation approach. Cable television companies are sometimes valued by placing a monetary value on each subscriber, say $2,000 each. Using the number of subscribers as a comparable for share value suggests that the latter can be increased simply by signing up more subscribers. But if that is accomplished by slashing subscriber fees, for instance, value actually might be destroyed rather than increased.

The essential problem with the cable television dollars-per-subscriber approach is that it does not value what directly matters to investors. Investors cannot buy a house or car with subscribers. Nor can they use subscribers to make additional investments. Only the cash flow generated by the business can be used for consumption or additional investment. The price-per-subscriber approach is useful only when the number of subscribers is a good proxy for cash flow. That occurs only when all cable systems generate the same cash flow per subscriber.

Similarly, accounting earnings is useful for valuation only when earnings is a good proxy for the expected long-term cash flow of the company. Not all companies generate the same cash flow for each dollar of earnings, however, so earnings approaches are generally only useful for first-cut value approximations. They fail as a comprehensive management tool.

As the *Wall Street Journal* editorial goes on to say, "To us the lesson is clear: If the manager keeps his eye on the long-run health of the enterprise, the stock price will take care of itself." That message gives rise to a question: What valuation tool is most consistent with the goal of long-term value creation? We believe that the manager who is interested in maximizing share value should use discounted cash flow (DCF) analysis, not earnings per share, to make decisions. The DCF approach captures all the elements that affect the value of the company in a comprehensive yet straightforward manner. Furthermore, the DCF approach is strongly supported by research into how the stock markets actually value companies.

DCF CAPTURES ALL ELEMENTS OF VALUE

Either explicitly or implicitly, all management decisions are based on some valuation model. The manager tries to take those actions that will increase the value of the company's shares. It is therefore to the manager's advantage to base his or her decisions on the model that most accurately reflects share value. We will show that the DCF approach—an economic model—provides a more sophisticated and reliable picture of a company's value than the accounting approach, although the latter is simpler and can be made to serve well in many instances.

First, let's define the two competing valuation approaches that we will be comparing throughout this chapter.

- In the *accounting approach,* all that matters is the accounting earnings of the business. Value is simply earnings times some multiple (the price-to-earnings or P/E ratio). In its extreme form, the accounting approach says that only this year's or next year's earnings matter. A more complex form discounts the future stream of earnings at some rate.
- In the *DCF approach,* the value of a business is the future expected cash flow discounted at a rate that reflects the riskiness of the cash flow.

A simple example will illustrate the difference between the two models. Exhibit 3.1 shows the projected income statements of two companies. Based on this accounting information, would you pay more for Longlife Company or Shortlife Company? Both the level and expected growth rates of earnings are identical, so most people would be inclined to pay the same price for both companies.

Exhibit 3.2 shows the projected cash flow statements for the two companies. Longlife Company uses manufacturing equipment that must be replaced every three years, while Shortlife Company uses equipment that must be replaced every year but costs one-third what Longlife's equipment costs. In addition, Shortlife does a better job of collecting its receivables.

Now which one would you pay more for? Most people would pay more for Shortlife, because most people prefer to have cash now rather than later. Note that the total cash flow over the entire six-year period is the same for both companies, though Shortlife shareholders get their cash earlier.

Exhibit 3.1 **PROJECTED INCOME OF LONGLIFE AND SHORTLIFE COMPANIES**

Longlife Company	Year 1	2	3	4	5	6
Sales	1,000	1,050	1,100	1,200	1,300	1,450
Cash expenses	(700)	(745)	(790)	(880)	(970)	(1,105)
Depreciation	(200)	(200)	(200)	(200)	(200)	(200)
Net income	100	105	110	120	130	145

Shortlife Company	Year 1	2	3	4	5	6
Sales	1,000	1,050	1,100	1,200	1,300	1,450
Cash expenses	(700)	(745)	(790)	(880)	(970)	(1,105)
Depreciation	(200)	(200)	(200)	(200)	(200)	(200)
Net income	100	105	110	120	130	145

This example illustrates the accounting approach's main weakness: it does not consider the investment required to generate earnings or its timing. Longlife Company has less value than Shortlife because it invests more capital (or the same amount of capital earlier) to generate the same level of sales and earnings. The accounting approach ignores the difference by concentrating on the P/E ratio as a function of expected eanings growth.

The DCF model, however, comprehends the difference in value by factoring in the capital expenditures and other cash flows required to generate the earnings. DCF analysis can do this because it is based on the idea that an investment adds value if it generates a return on investment above the return that can be earned on investments of similar risk. This approach is widely used by companies to evaluate capital spending proposals. The DCF model applies this approach to entire businesses, which are effectively just collections of individual projects.

So why has the accounting approach persisted all these years?

Exhibit 3.2 **PROJECTED CASH FLOW OF LONGLIFE AND SHORTLIFE COMPANIES**

Longlife Company	Year 1	2	3	4	5	6	Cumu-lative
Net income	100	105	110	120	130	145	710
Depreciation	200	200	200	200	200	200	1,200
Capital ex-penditures	(600)	0	0	(600)	0	0	(1,200)
Incr in receivables	(250)	(13)	(13)	35	45	(23)	(219)
Cash to/(from) shareholders	(550)	292	297	(245)	375	322	491

Shortlife Company	Year 1	2	3	4	5	6	Cumu-lative
Net income	100	105	110	120	130	145	710
Depreciation	200	200	200	200	200	200	1,200
Capital ex-penditures	(200)	(200)	(200)	(200)	(200)	(200)	(1,200)
Incr in receivables	(150)	(8)	(8)	(15)	(15)	(23)	(219)
Cash to/(from) shareholders	(50)	97	102	105	115	122	491

Like most things that stand the test of time, it works very well in certain situations. When earnings reflect cash flow, the accounting approach provides a reasonably good proxy for discounted cash flow. It is when earnings and cash flow diverge that the accounting approach comes up short.

For example, suppose Longlife Company has just figured out a way to increase its earnings each year by 10 percent by increasing invested capital commensurately. Both the accounting approach and DCF analysis would suggest that the value of Longlife should increase by 10 percent as well, because both earnings and cash flow increase by 10 percent each year. So the accounting approach would appear to be incrementally correct in this situation.

Now suppose that Longlife's controller has figured out a way to increase the first year's earnings by 10 percent by recording some revenues in year 1 that would otherwise appear in year 2. The increase in year 1's earnings is exactly offset by the decrease in year 2's. The most extreme accounting approach would say that the value of Longlife has increased by 10 percent. As we will see in the next section, it is possible to create a more sophisticated accounting model. This model would see higher year 1 earnings but a lower growth rate and reduce the P/E ratio accordingly so the increase in value would be lower. (But how do you figure out the right P/E ratio?) In any event, the DCF model would not be fooled. Cash flow has not changed, so Longlife's value would be unchanged in the DCF model.

A REFINED ACCOUNTING MODEL

Before maligning the accounting approach too much, we should show how to develop a more sophisticated accounting model that mimics the DCF model pretty well under some circumstances. This entails finding a way to incorporate the *quality* of earnings into the P/E ratio so that we can differentiate between companies with identical earnings but different cash flows or risks.

Let us construct another simple example, using Value Inc. and Volume Inc., as shown in Exhibit 3.3. Both companies have identical earnings once again, but Value Inc. has a larger cash flow. Let us value the companies using DCF analysis.

If we assume that both companies have identical risk, we can discount their cash flows at the same discount rate, say 10 percent. Both companies also continue their respective earnings and cash flow growth rates forever. Using some algebra that helps us deal with growing perpetuities, we can compute the value of Value Inc. to be $1,500 and Volume Inc. to be $1,000. This also means that Value Inc. has a P/E ratio of 15 and Volume Inc. of 10.

The key to Value Inc.'s larger cash flow and higher value is that it does not invest as much capital to generate additional earnings. For example, Value Inc. invests only $25 in the first year

Exhibit 3.3 **CASH FLOWS OF VALUE INC. AND VOLUME INC.**

Value Inc.	Year 1	2	3	4	5	. . .
Net income	100	105	110	116	122	. . .
Net investment	(25)	(26)	(28)	(29)	(30)	. . .
Cash to/(from) shareholders	75	79	83	87	91	. . .
Volume Inc.	Year 1	2	3	4	5	. . .
Net income	100	105	110	116	122	. . .
Net investment	(50)	(53)	(55)	(58)	(61)	. . .
Cash to/(from) shareholders	50	53	55	58	61	. . .

to generate $5 additional earnings the next year, while Volume Inc. invests $50 to generate the same incremental earnings. Value Inc. earns a return of 20 percent on its new capital, while Volume Inc. earns a return of only 10 percent on its new capital.

In this simplified world, we can develop a simple formula that allows us to predict the P/E ratios of the two companies. That formula is as follows:

$$\text{P/E ratio} = \frac{1 - g/r}{k - g}$$

where

g = the long-run growth rate in earnings and cash flow
r = the rate of return earned on new investment
k = the discount rate

This formula correctly calculates the P/E ratios for Value Inc. and Volume Inc.

For Value Inc.:

$$P/E = \frac{1 - 5\%/20\%}{10\% - 5\%} = 15$$

For Volume Inc.:

$$P/E = \frac{1 - 5\%/10\%}{10\% - 5\%} = 10$$

This formula improves the performance of the accounting valuation approach by adding investment and risk to the equation. But more important, it helps to highlight the shortcomings of the naive accounting model. For example, what is the impact on Value Inc.'s value if it can increase its growth rate from 5 percent to 8 percent, while the return on incremental capital declines from 20 percent to 10 percent? The basic accounting model suggests that Value Inc.'s value will increase as a result of the higher earnings growth. Our formula, however, tells us that the new P/E ratio should be 10 and the resulting value should be $1,000, a substantial decline in value. So higher growth in this situation will yield a decline in value, but only the refined accounting model leads us to the right conclusion.

While our refined accounting approach works pretty well in a simplified world, it begins to break down once we add real-world complications.

- Varying accounting treatments for inventories, depreciation, and other items make it difficult to measure the incremental return on investment consistently across companies.
- Inflation distorts the relationship of accounting earnings to cash flow.
- Cyclicality is not dealt with by the accounting model, which attempts to capture an entire cycle in a single P/E ratio.
- The pattern of investments and their returns is not so simple that investments are made in one year and earn constant returns in all succeeding years.

- The base level of earnings must be normalized to eliminate any nonrecurring items.

We could develop an extremely complex version of the accounting model to handle these and other considerations, but in most cases the DCF model is simpler to work with since it already explicitly incorporates key valuation parameters like investment and risk.

IS THE STOCK MARKET NAIVE?

We have shown that the DCF model is conceptually superior to the accounting model. To be useful, however, it must also reflect how the stock market actually behaves. We are often confronted by managers who suggest that even though they agree with the DCF model, the market just does not behave that way: the market naively responds only to short-term earnings fluctuations.

It is true that the market does respond to quarterly earnings reports. The market would be foolish not to, because these earnings reports often convey important information. For example, increases in quarterly earnings can signal higher levels of cash flow in the future. So earnings reports also matter to the DCF model, but they are not the only thing that matters.

As the *Wall Street Journal* editorial from which we quoted earlier asserts, the market is not fooled by cosmetic earnings increases; only earnings increases that are associated with improved long-term cash flow will increase share prices. Substantial evidence supports the view that the market takes a sophisticated approach to assessing accounting earnings. This evidence can be grouped into three classes:

1. Studies showing that accounting earnings are not very well correlated with share prices
2. Studies demonstrating that earnings window dressing does not improve share prices
3. Studies showing that the market evaluates management decisions based on their expected long-term cash flow impact, not their short-term earnings impact

Accounting Earnings Are Not Well Correlated with Share Prices

According to the accounting model, a strong correlation should exist between earnings-per-share (EPS) growth and shareholder returns. Exhibit 3.4, using P/E ratios as a proxy for how investors value earnings growth, shows that the actual correlation between P/E ratios and earnings growth for the S&P 400 is weak. In fact, many of the companies on the chart have strong earnings growth but low P/E ratios.

Exhibit 3.4 **LOW CORRELATION BETWEEN EPS GROWTH AND P/E RATIO FOR S&P 400**

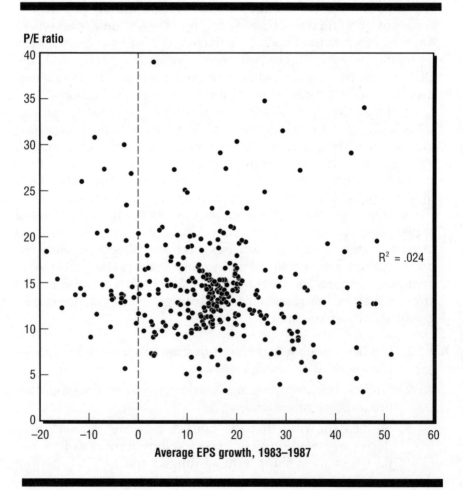

A comparison of Albertson's and Giant Food, two major supermarket chains, highlights the weak correlation between earnings growth and shareholder returns. As you can see in Exhibit 3.5, the earnings-per-share growth of the two companies was about equal during the period 1979–87, but Giant's shareholders were three times as well off as Albertson's at the end of that period. One dollar invested in Albertson's in 1977 was worth $8 at the end of 1987 (including dividends), while the same amount invested in Giant was worth $25. This can be clearly explained by the companies' return on equity over the nine years. Albertson's return on equity declined steadily while Giant's improved substantially. These changes were due to fundamental business improvements by Giant relative to Albertson's.

- Giant's operating margin improved; Albertson's declined. As a result, Albertson's sales had to grow faster to generate the same earnings growth.
- Giant's inventory turnover improved; Albertson's deteriorated.
- Giant increased its financial leverage; Albertson's reduced its debt levels.

So it is clear that earnings growth is a poor indicator of value creation. We can find better indicators, but no single indicator can capture all the elements captured by DCF analysis. For example, many researchers would argue that some measure of return on invested capital is the single best indicator of value creation. This is consistent with the DCF model, because the DCF model says that value is created when invested capital earns returns above its cost. Unfortunately, no evidence exists to show a strong correlation between accounting returns on capital and the value of a company.

The correlation is weak because it is impossible to capture the essence of a complex cash flow pattern in one number. Consider two companies starting at the same point and with identical expected returns on capital over their cost of capital. One company plans to invest twice as much as the other, however. As a result, the company with higher investment and faster growth

Exhibit 3.5 **SHAREHOLDER VALUE AND EPS GROWTH, GIANT FOOD VS. ALBERTSON'S**

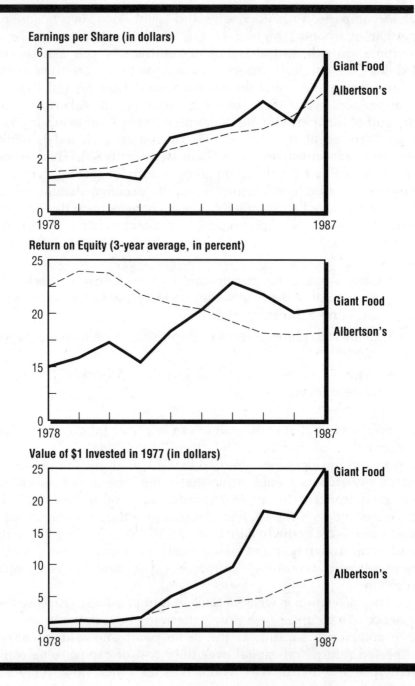

should have a higher market/book value despite identical returns on capital.

Only the DCF model captures both returns and growth. We recently applied the DCF model to about thirty companies, using forecasts from the Value Line Investment Survey, and found very strong correlations with the companies' market values (Exhibit 3.6). While these results are not scientific, they are consistent with our experience that DCF is very good at explaining companies' market values.

Exhibit 3.6 **HIGH CORRELATION BETWEEN MARKET VALUE AND DCF VALUE FOR 30 COMPANIES**

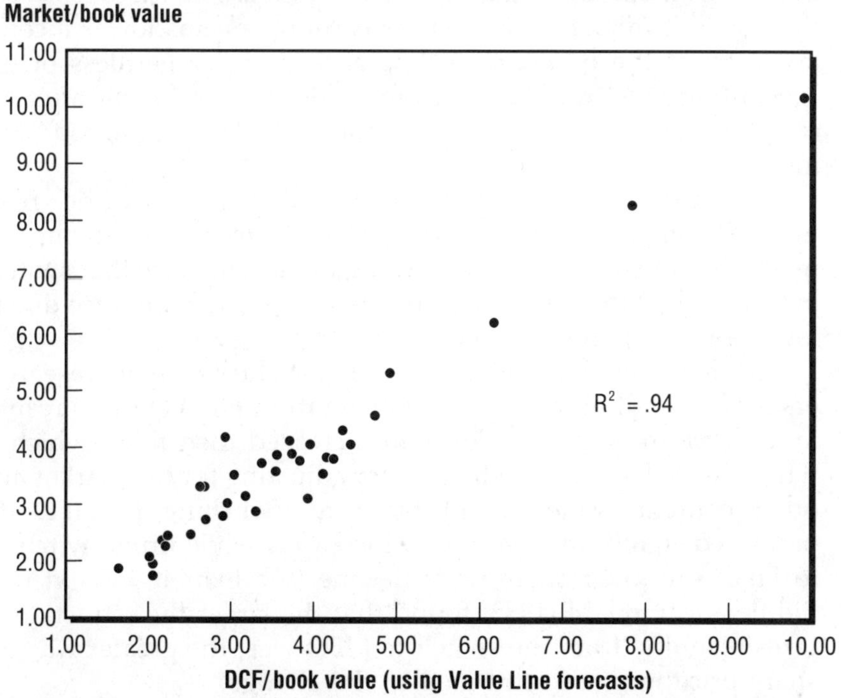

Market/book value

$R^2 = .94$

DCF/book value (using Value Line forecasts)

Source: McKinsey analysis.

Earnings Window Dressing Does Not Help Share Prices

The accounting model also suggests that the market might be fooled by accounting techniques that improve earnings. Academic studies have shown that the market is not deceived by accounting techniques. The most persuasive of these studies have focused either on inventory accounting or on techniques used to account for mergers and acquisitions.

Inventory accounting is one area where the U.S. tax authorities require that the method used for financial reporting also be used for calculating taxable income. As a result, the choice of accounting method affects both earnings and cash flow, but in opposite directions. In periods of rising prices (for as long as any of the authors can remember), the last-in-first-out (LIFO) inventory method results in lower earnings than the first-in-first-out (FIFO) method, because the cost of goods sold is based on the more recent, higher costs. Lower earnings means lower income taxes. Since the pretax cash flow is the same regardless of the accounting method, LIFO accounting leads to a higher after-tax cash flow than FIFO accounting, despite the lower reported earnings.

A number of researchers have looked at the stock price reaction of companies that have switched from one accounting method to the other. The accounting model suggests that switching from FIFO to LIFO should result in a lower share price due to lower earnings, and vice versa.

While the evidence is not entirely conclusive, some researchers have found, in fact, that switching from FIFO to LIFO results in a *higher* share price due to an increased cash flow, which is what the DCF model predicts. After adjusting for the market and other contemporaneous effects, firms switching to LIFO experienced significant share price increases, while firms switching to FIFO saw their share price decline (see Exhibit 3.7). In fact, Biddle and Lindahl (1982) found that the larger the reduction in taxes resulting from the switch to LIFO was, the greater was the share price increase attributed to the change.

Other studies that prove window dressing to be of little value involve mergers and acquisitions. A business combination that is accounted for as a purchase requires that the difference between

Exhibit 3.7 **EFFECT OF INVENTORY ACCOUNTING CHANGE ON SHARE VALUE**

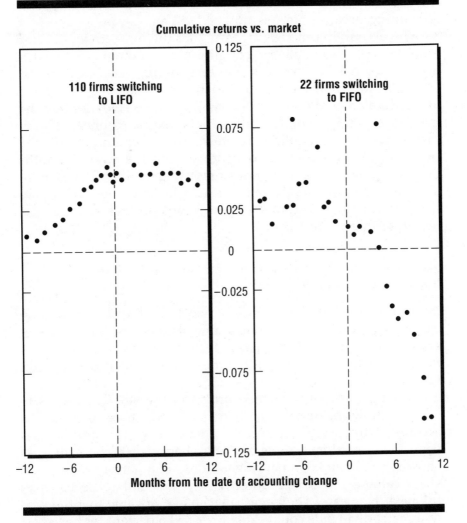

Cumulative returns vs. market

110 firms switching to LIFO

22 firms switching to FIFO

Months from the date of accounting change

Source: S. Sunder (1973), p. 18.

the price paid for the target and the book value of its assets (with some adjustment) be recorded as an asset called goodwill and amortized over a period of generally forty years. Under a pooling-of-interests accounting, on the other hand, the acquisition is reported at book value with no goodwill or amortization. Since goodwill amortization is not deductible for tax purposes, the company's cash flow is the same regardless of the accounting method. Reported earnings, however, are higher under pooling accounting because there is no goodwill amortization.

The accounting model suggests that the market would react more favorably to pooling accounting than to purchase accounting because of the former's higher earnings. The DCF model suggests no difference because cash flow would be the same. Hong, Kaplan, and Mandelker (1978) found no evidence that the market responds favorably to the higher earnings under a pooling-of-interests accounting. Interestingly, companies using the purchase method performed better during the twelve months preceding the merger than companies using pooling. This is probably due to some self-selection bias. The poor performers are likely to attempt to improve their earnings through selective use of accounting techniques.

Sacrificing Long-term Cash Flows for Short-term Earnings Improvement Does Not Work

A lot of confusion about how the market evaluates accounting earnings has to do with the time frame of investors. Many managers believe that the stock market focuses too narrowly on near-term earnings. They believe that the market does not give credit for long-term investments.

A simple test of the time horizon of the stock market is to examine how much of a company's current share price can be accounted for by its expected dividends over the next several years. For a random sample of twenty Fortune 500 companies, as shown in Exhibit 3.8, an average of only 11.8 percent of the total share value could be accounted for by dividends expected over the next five years. The largest percentage of value that the next five years' dividends could explain was 20.6 percent for Lone Star Industries. So from this test, the market appears to take a long view. More rigorous analyses described in the following paragraphs also support this view.

We showed earlier that pure accounting manipulation does not fool the market. But managers can do other things to improve earnings at the expense of long-term cash flow. For example, they can reduce spending on research and development or capital

Exhibit 3.8 **PRESENT VALUE OF EXPECTED DIVIDENDS VS. SHARE PRICE FOR 20 FORTUNE 500 COMPANIES, OCTOBER 1988**

Company	Share price	Present value of dividends expected over next 5 yrs.	Dividends as percentage of stock price
Aluminum Company of America	$55	$5.71	10.4%
Becton, Dickinson & Company	57	3.91	6.9
Bristol-Myers Company	45	8.10	18.0
Champion Spark Plug Company	13	1.03	7.9
Chesapeake Corp.	21	2.21	10.5
Coleman Company, Inc.	37	5.17	14.0
Esselte Business Systems, Inc.	33	3.79	11.5
Exxon Corporation	45	8.95	19.9
Fieldcrest Cannon, Inc.	22	2.56	11.6
Grumman Corp.	22	4.16	18.9
Jefferson Smurfit Corp.	27	1.92	7.1
Johnson Controls, Inc.	35	4.35	12.4
Lone Star Industries, Inc.	32	6.58	20.6
McDonnell Douglas Corporation	72	11.25	15.6
Medtronic, Inc.	80	5.30	6.6
Newmont Mining Corporation	36	2.61	7.2
Nucor Corp.	42	1.82	4.3
Reynolds Metals Company	54	4.08	7.6
Rohm and Haas Company	34	4.25	12.5
Westvaco Corp.	30	3.59	12.0
Average			11.8%

Source: Value Line; McKinsey analysis.

goods. Reducing R&D spending will increase earnings (and cash flow) in the short run, potentially at the expense of the development of profitable new products for the long run. Similarly, cutting back on value-adding capital spending will increase short-term profits because new capital projects often earn low profits in their earlier years.

A group of Securities and Exchange Commission economists examined the stock price reaction to announcements by sixty-two companies that they were embarking on R&D projects (Office of the Chief Economist, 1985). As Exhibit 3.9 shows, the

Exhibit 3.9 **STOCK MARKET REACTION TO RESEARCH AND DEVELOPMENT ANNOUNCEMENTS, AVERAGE OF 62 COMPANIES**

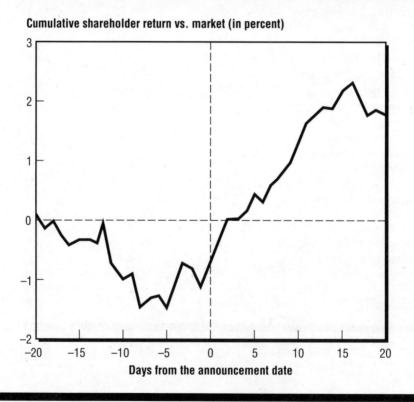

Cumulative shareholder return vs. market (in percent)

Days from the announcement date

Source: Office of the Chief Economist, Securities and Exchange Commission (1985).

market had a significant positive reaction to these announcements.

To illustrate this, we looked at the R&D spending of six major pharmaceutical companies. R&D spending is generally treated as an expense in the year incurred regardless of future benefits. Exhibit 3.10 shows that contrary to what the accounting model would suggest, the companies with the highest levels of spending on R&D tended to have the highest P/E ratios. While these results are not at all scientific, they do cast serious doubt on the view that the stock market penalizes companies that invest a lot in research and development.

Exhibit 3.10 **R&D SPENDING VS. P/E RATIOS FOR SIX MAJOR PHARMACEUTICAL COMPANIES, OCTOBER 1988**

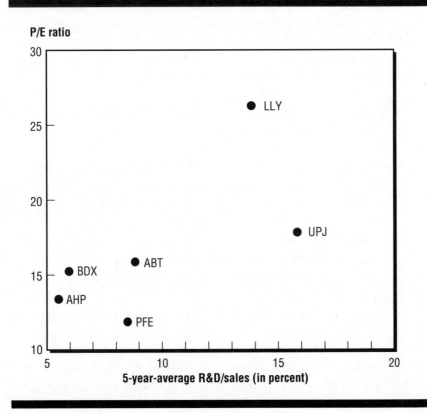

Source: Compustat.

The evidence on capital spending supports the DCF model as well. McConnell and Muscarella (1985) examined the stock market's reaction to announcements of increased capital expenditure levels. For a sample of 349 such announcements (that contained no other company-specific information) by industrial firms from 1975 to 1981, the stock market reacted positively to spending increases and negatively to spending decreases, with one exception. The results were the opposite for oil and gas exploration and development. Apparently, the market did not believe that oil and gas exploration was a profitable investment at the time. Given the subsequent decline in oil prices and the high cost of exploration in the United States relative to other parts of the world, the market was probably right. In any case, it is clear that the market does not arbitrarily penalize companies for making long-term investments.

In fact, as Woolridge (1988) found, the stock-market gains from the announcement of long-term strategic investments can be substantial. Consider these examples of the reaction of share prices on the day of and the day following such announcements (even after adjusting for market movements):

- McDonald's announced in February 1988 that it would open restaurants in Sears stores. The value of its shares went up 2.6 percent or $225 million.
- Disney's share value increased 3.6 percent or $280 million in March 1987 when it announced its plan to build Euro-Disneyland. The project will cost $2 billion and will take years to pay off.
- In February 1988, Westinghouse announced a joint venture with Daimler-Benz to make rail transit systems. Its shares rose 3 percent or $215 million on the announcement.

Conversely, the market also reacts favorably when companies write off bad investments, despite the negative short-term earnings impact. While the complex nature of write-offs prohibits comprehensive statistical analysis, Mercer (1987) looked at forty major write-offs from 1984 to 1986 and found that 60 percent of them resulted in share price increases. Furthermore, 75 percent of write-downs resulting from abandonment of entire businesses were associated with share price increases. The following summarizes the write-off experience of several companies.

- Sohio's $163 million write-off in 1984 of its Mukluk oil well in the Beaufort Sea led to a 6.5 percent increase in its share price around the announcement day. Poor drilling results had been announced previously and already were discounted in the share price. The write-off could be interpreted as good news if it meant that Sohio would no longer be committing cash to a losing effort.
- Beatrice took a $280 million write-off in 1983 as part of a long-term program to improve its future profitability, including write-downs of its Tropicana division, reserves for divestitures of fifty businesses, and a charge for the early retirement of some employees. Beatrice's share price increased 13 percent on the announcement. The announcement conveyed good news: management's realization of its past mistakes and its intention to avoid future mistakes.
- In contrast to the favorable reactions, Natomas suffered a 9 percent price decline following its $87 million write-off in 1982. In this case, however, the write-off resulted from a revised engineering survey indicating that oil reserves had been overestimated by six million barrels. The stock price decline is really attributable to the value lost in the future cash flow in the oil reserves rather than the accounting event itself.

Another piece of evidence supporting the view that the market values cash not earnings draws from changes in leverage and its impact on share prices and earnings per share. Copeland and Lee (1988) studied 161 exchange offers and stock swaps from 1962 to 1984. The accounting model suggests that the earnings-per-share impact of the transaction determines the share price reaction. The study showed that the earnings-per-share (EPS) impact did not matter. What mattered was whether the transaction was leverage-increasing or leverage-decreasing. The average percent-

age changes in share value upon the announcement of the transactions relative to the changes in the market average were as
follows:

	EPS-increasing transactions	EPS-decreasing transactions
Leverage-increasing transactions	3.77%	8.41
Leverage-decreasing transactions	−1.18	−0.41

On average, leverage-decreasing transactions resulted in
negative share price reactions, regardless of the earnings-per-
share impact. Furthermore, Copeland and Lee concluded that the
most likely explanation for the direction of the share price
changes is that investors interpret these leverage-changing transactions as management's signals of future cash flow. For example,
insiders could use leverage-increasing transactions to increase
their ownership position and to exploit their superior knowledge
regarding the future cash flows of their companies. Therefore,
leverage-increasing transactions could signal strong cash flows in
the future.

SUMMARY

Managers who use the DCF approach to valuation, focusing on
long-term cash flow, ultimately will be rewarded by higher share
prices. The evidence from the market is conclusive. Naive attention to accounting earnings will lead to value-destroying decisions. These could, in turn, result in a takeover attack by suitors
who believe they can run the company better.

Part II

Cash Flow Valuation:
A Practitioner's Guide

4

Framework for
Valuation

To use discounted cash flow (DCF) analysis for decisions like
acquisitions, divestitures, or for developing corporate strategies,
you need a framework that answers practical questions like:

- How is cash flow defined?
- What is an appropriate discount rate?
- For how long a time period should you forecast cash flow?

This chapter begins to answer these and other practical valuation questions, and presents a framework for valuing businesses
and strategies. It is followed by chapters that describe a step-by-
step approach to using the framework.

THE RECOMMENDED DCF FRAMEWORK

While a number of alternative DCF frameworks are conceivable,
we recommend an approach we will refer to as the "components
model." This approach asserts that the value of a company's
equity is equal to the sum of the present value of the various cash

flow streams that ultimately add up to the cash flow to the equity holders (dividends, share repurchases, and share issues). Exhibit 4.1 illustrates this approach for a single-business company. Rather than value the equity directly as the present value of the dividends and other cash flow to shareholders, the equity is

Exhibit 4.1 **SIMPLE COMPONENT VALUATION OF A SINGLE-BUSINESS COMPANY**

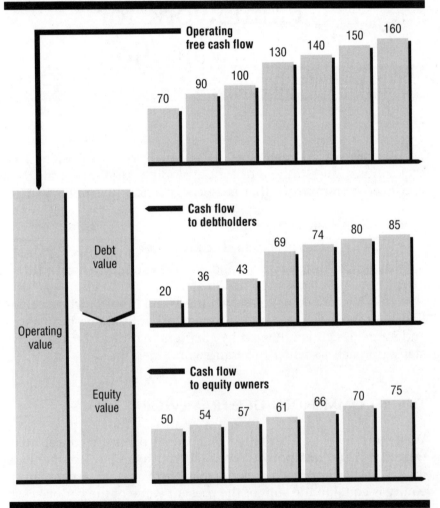

valued as the present value of the operating free cash flow less the present value of the cash paid to and received from the company's debtholders. As long as the discount rates are selected properly to reflect the riskiness of each cash flow stream, the components approach will result in exactly the same equity value as the direct discounting of cash flow to the shareholders.

This approach is especially useful when extended to a multi-business company, as shown in Exhibit 4.2. The equity value of the company equals the sum of the values of the individual operating units plus cash-generating corporate assets, less the cost of operating the corporate center and the value of the com-

Exhibit 4.2 **COMPONENT VALUATION OF A MULTIBUSINESS COMPANY**

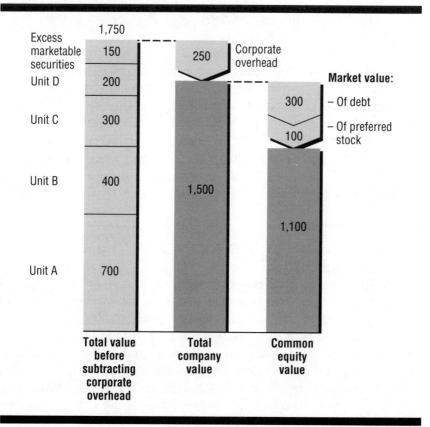

pany's debt. The exhibit helps to highlight the reasons for recommending this approach.

- Valuing the components of the business, instead of just the equity, helps in identifying and understanding the separate investment and financing sources of value for the equity holders.
- This approach helps to pinpoint key leverage areas in the search for value-creating ideas.
- It can be applied consistently at different levels of aggregation and is consistent with the capital budgeting process most companies are already familiar with.
- It is sophisticated enough to deal with the complexity of most situations, while at the same time it is easy to implement with simple personal computer tools.

Let us now apply the model to a simple single-business company. (Later we will discuss more complex situations.) The value of the company's equity equals the present value of its operations less the value of its debt (our example company has no other nonequity obligations like preferred stock). The value of operations and debt is equal to their respective cash flows discounted at a rate that reflects the riskiness of these cash flows. Exhibit 4.3 is a simple valuation summary for the Hershey Foods Corporation.

Value of Operations

The value of operations equals the discounted value of expected future free cash flow. Free cash flow is equal to the after-tax operating earnings of the company plus noncash charges less investments in working capital, property, plant and equipment, and other assets. It does not incorporate any financing-related cash flows such as interest expense or dividends. Exhibit 4.4 shows a summarized free cash flow calculation for the Hershey Foods Corporation. Free cash flow is the correct cash flow for this valuation model because it reflects the cash flow generated by a company that is available to all providers of the company's capi-

Exhibit 4.3 **HERSHEY FOODS CORPORATION, VALUATION SUMMARY,** $ MILLIONS

	Year	Free cash flow (FCF)	Discount factor @ 11.5%	Present value of FCF
	1987	85	0.8969	77
	1988	110	0.8044	88
	1989	121	0.7214	87
	1990	133	0.6470	86
	1991	146	0.5803	85
	1992	161	0.5204	84
	1993	177	0.4667	83
	1994	195	0.4186	81
	1995	214	0.3754	80
	1996	235	0.3367	79
Continuing value		4,583	0.3367	1,543
Value of operations				2,374
Less: Value of debt				(254)
Equity value				2,120
Equity value per share				23.50

tal, both debt and equity. In fact, free cash flow is also equal to the sum of the cash flows paid to or received from all the capital providers (interest, dividends, new borrowings, debt repayments, and so on).

For consistency with the cash flow definition, the discount rate applied to the free cash flow should reflect the opportunity cost to all the capital providers weighted by their relative contribution to the total capital of the company. This is called the weighted average cost of capital (WACC). The opportunity cost to any investor equals the rate of return the investor could expect to earn on other investments of equivalent risk. The cost to the company equals the investors' costs less any tax benefits received by the company (for example, the tax shield provided by interest expense). Exhibit 4.5 shows a sample WACC calculation for Hershey Foods.

Exhibit 4.4 **HERSHEY FOODS CORPORATION, FREE CASH FLOW CALCULATION,** $ MILLIONS

Free Cash Flow	1985	1986	Fore-cast 1987	Fore-cast 1988	Fore-cast 1989
Revenues	1,996	2,170	2,387	2,625	2,888
Operating expenses	(1,745)	(1,893)	(2,083)	(2,291)	(2,520)
Earnings before interest and taxes (EBIT)	251	277	304	334	368
Cash taxes on EBIT	(95)	(108)	(116)	(111)	(122)
Net oper profits less adj taxes	156	169	188	224	246
Depreciation	50	56	63	70	77
Gross cash flow	205	225	251	293	322
Change in working capital	15	39	18	20	22
Capital expenditures	109	147	145	160	176
Incr in net other assets	3	95	2	3	3
Gross investment	126	281	166	183	202
Operating free cash flow	79	(56)	85	110	121
Financing flow					
Net interest expense after tax	8	7	16	27	28
Decrease/(increase) in net debt	27	(198)	14	17	21
Common dividends	44	48	56	65	73
Share repurchases	0	87	0	0	0
Financing flow	79	(56)	85	110	121

An additional problem in valuing a business is its indefinite life. One approach is to forecast the free cash flow for one hundred years and not worry about what comes after, because its discounted value will be tiny. Alternatively, you can make the problem tractable by separating the value of the business into two time periods, during and after an explicit forecast period. In this case,

$$\text{Value} = \frac{\text{Present value of cash flow}}{\textit{during} \text{ explicit forecast period}} + \frac{\text{Present value of cash flow}}{\textit{after} \text{ explicit forecast period}}$$

Exhibit 4.5 **HERSHEY FOODS CORPORATION, WACC CALCULATION**

Source of Capital	Proportion of total capital	Opportunity cost	Tax benefit	After-tax cost	Contribution to weighted average
Debt	25.0%	9.9%	39.0%	6.0%	1.5%
Equity	75.0%	13.3%	–	13.3%	10.0%
Weighted average cost of capital (WACC)					11.5%

The value after the explicit forecast period is referred to as the continuing value. Simple formulas can be used to estimate the continuing value without the need to forecast the company's cash flow in detail for an indefinite period. For example, one approach estimates the continuing value using the following formula:

$$\text{Continuing value} = \frac{\text{Net operating profit less adjusted taxes}}{\text{Weighted average cost of capital}}$$

Value of Debt

The value of the company's debt equals the present value of the cash flow to the debtholders discounted at a rate that reflects the riskiness of that flow. The discount rate should equal the current market rate on similar-risk debt with comparable terms. In most cases, only the company's debt outstanding on the valuation date must be valued. Future borrowings can be assumed to have zero net present value because the cash inflows from these borrowings will exactly equal the present value of the future repayments discounted at the opportunity cost of the debt.

Value of Equity

The value of the company's equity is simply the value of its operations less the value of its debt.

OTHER DISCOUNTED CASH FLOW FRAMEWORKS

Other discounted cash flow frameworks yield the same results as the component approach we recommend. However, each has drawbacks, and their usefulness for practical applications is limited.

Direct Discounting of Equity Cash Flow

Valuing a company's equity by directly discounting the cash flow to the equity holders (dividends and share repurchases) is intuitively the most straightforward valuation technique. Unfortunately, it is not as useful or easy to implement as the components approach. Discounting equity cash flow provides less information about the sources of value creation and is not as useful for identifying value-creation opportunities. Furthermore, it requires careful adjustments to ensure that changes in projected financing do not incorrectly affect the company's value.

For example, a common error that we see in discounted equity valuations is an inconsistency between the company's dividend policy and the discount rate used. First, a base valuation is performed that results in a value of, say, $15 per share. Next, the dividend payout ratio is increased but the operating performance remains constant (for example, there is no change in revenues or margins). Presto! The equity value has just increased because of the higher dividend payments despite the constant operating performance. The error here is that the discount rate was not changed. Increasing the dividend payout ratio requires more use of debt. More debt means riskier equity and a higher discount rate for the equity.

Using Real Instead of Nominal Cash Flow and Discount Rate

Another valuation approach is to forecast cash flow in real terms (for example, in constant 1988 dollars) and discount this cash flow at a real discount rate (for example, the nominal rate less expected inflation). However, most managers think in terms of nominal rather than real measures, so nominal measures are often easier to communicate. Interest rates are generally quoted nominally rather than in real terms (excluding expected inflation). Moreover, we have found that since historical financial statements are stated in nominal terms, forecasting future statements in real terms is difficult and confusing.

Discounting Pretax Cash Flow Instead of After-tax Cash Flow

The approach we recommend uses after-tax cash flow and an after-tax discount rate. It is conceptually valid to use pretax cash flow and a pretax discount rate, as the following example illustrates.

$$\text{Value} = \frac{\text{After-tax cash flow}}{\text{After-tax discount rate}}$$

$$\text{After-tax cash flow} = \text{Pretax cash flow} \times (1 - \text{tax rate})$$
$$\text{After-tax discount rate} = \text{Pretax discount rate} \times (1 - \text{tax rate})$$

Substituting into the initial equation gives

$$\text{Value} = \frac{\text{Pretax cash flow} \times (1 - \text{tax rate})}{\text{Pretax discount rate} \times (1 - \text{tax rate})}$$

$$\text{Value} = \frac{\text{Pretax cash flow}}{\text{Pretax discount rate}}$$

However, real-world after-tax cash flow is not simply pretax cash flow adjusted by the tax rate, because taxes are based on accrual accounting (for example, the tax benefit of purchasing a machine is received in a different period from when the machine is paid for). As a result, no practical way exists to calculate a pretax discount rate. You cannot simply gross up the discount rate to a pretax rate and discount pretax cash flow. It is virtually impossible to perform a valid real-world discounted cash flow analysis using the pretax approach.

Formula-based DCF Approaches Instead of Explicit Discounted Cash Flow

Formula-based DCF approaches make simplifying assumptions about a business and its cash flow stream (for example, constant revenue growth and margins) so that the entire discounted cash flow can be captured in a concise formula. Unfortunately, these formulas are most often too simple for real problem solving, though they may serve as valuable communication tools.

The Miller-Modigliani (MM) formula, while simple, is particularly useful for demonstrating the sources of a company's value. The MM formula shown in Exhibit 4.6 values a company as the sum of the value of the cash flow of its assets currently in place plus the value of its growth opportunities. The formula is based on sound economic analysis, so it can be used to illustrate the key factors that will affect the value of the company.

Option-Pricing Models

Option-pricing models are variations on standard discounted cash flow models that adjust for the fact that management de-

---

Exhibit 4.6 **THE MILLER-MODIGLIANI DCF FORMULA**

Value of entity = Value of assets in place + Value of growth

$$\text{Value of assets in place} = \frac{E(NOPLAT)}{WACC}$$

and is determined by

- level of expected cash flows after taxes, E(NOPLAT), where NOPLAT stands for net operating profit less adjusted taxes
- weighted average cost of capital (WACC) after tax

$$\text{Value of growth} = K[E(NOPLAT)]N \left[\frac{r\text{-}WACC}{WACC(1 + WACC)} \right]$$

and is determined by

- rate of return on invested capital (r) in excess of WACC
- investment rate (K)—that is, the percentage of cash flows invested in new projects
- interval of competitive advantage (N)

---

cisions can be modified in the future as more information becomes available. Option models hold particular promise for valuing strategic and operating flexibility such as opening and closing
plants, abandoning operations, or natural resource exploration
and development. Chapter 12 discusses how option pricing might
be used as the technology is further developed.

SUMMARY

This chapter has introduced the DCF valuation framework. The
value of the company's equity equals the value of its operations
less the value of its debt. The value of operations is the discounted value of its expected free cash flow, using an opportunity
cost of capital.

The following chapters describe a step-by-step approach to
valuing a company, as summarized in Exhibit 4.7. They explain
both the technical details, such as how to calculate free cash flow
from complex accounting statements, and how to interpret the
valuation through careful financial analysis.

Exhibit 4.7 **STEPS IN A VALUATION**

1. Forecasting free cash flow (Chapter 5)

- Identify components of free cash flow
- Develop integrated historical perspective
- Determine forecast assumptions and scenarios
- Calculate and evaluate the forecast

2. Estimating the cost of capital (Chapter 6)

- Develop target market value weights
- Estimate cost of nonequity finance
- Estimate cost of equity

3. Estimating continuing value (Chapter 7)

- Determine the relationship between continuing value and DCF
- Decide forecast horizon
- Estimate the parameters
- Discount to the present

4. Calculating and interpreting results (Chapter 8)

- Develop and test results
- Interpret results within decision context

5

Forecasting Free Cash Flow

Free cash flow is a company's true operating cash flow. It is the total after-tax cash flow generated by the company that is available to all providers of the company's capital, both creditors and shareholders. It can be thought of as the after-tax cash flow that would be available to the company's shareholders if the company had no debt. Free cash flow is generally not affected by the company's financial structure,* even though the financial structure may affect the company's weighted average cost of capital and therefore its value.

It is essential to define free cash flow properly to ensure consistency between the cash flow and the discount rate used to value the company. A company's free cash flow is calculated by subtracting the amount the company invests in new capital from the gross cash flow available from operations (operating earnings plus noncash charges). On the following pages, Exhibit 5.1 demonstrates the typical free cash flow calculation derived from a hypothetical company's income statement (Exhibit 5.2) and balance sheet (Exhibit 5.3).

---

*Financing decisions of a company with unused tax loss carry-forwards or an alternative minimum tax liability may affect its free cash flow. Also, business disruptions may be associated with debt levels that are too high.

109

Exhibit 5.1 **XYZ COMPANY, FREE CASH FLOW CALCULATION**

Free Cash Flow	1986	1987
Earnings before interest and taxes (EBIT)	$1,450	$1,500
− Taxes on EBIT	(701)	(600)
+ Change in deferred taxes	20	100
= Net operating profit less adjusted taxes (NOPLAT)	769	$1,000
+ Depreciation	387	400
= Gross cash flow	$1,156	$1,400
Increase in working capital	123	150
+ Capital expenditures	587	600
+ Investment in goodwill	0	0
+ Increase in net other assets	30	50
= Gross investment	$ 740	$ 800
Gross cash flow	$1,156	$1,400
− Gross investment	(740)	(800)
= **Free cash flow from operations**	$ 416	$ 600
+ Nonoperating cash flow	0	0
= **Total cash flow before financing**	$ 416	$ 600

Financial Flow	1986	1987
Change in excess marketable securities	12	(20)
− After-tax interest income*	(8)	(10)
+ Decrease in debt	(70)	30
+ After-tax interest expense*	221	250
+ Dividends	161	200
+ Share repurchase	100	150
= **Total financial flow**	$ 416	$ 600

*Marginal tax rates of 49 percent in 1986 and 42 percent in 1987 were used to calculate after-tax interest income and expense.

Exhibit 5.2 **XYZ COMPANY, INCOME STATEMENT**

	1986	1987
Revenues	$14,500	$15,000
− Cost of goods sold	(9,667)	(10,000)
− Selling, general, and administrative expense	(2,996)	(3,100)
− Depreciation	(387)	(400)
− Goodwill amortization*	(20)	(20)
= **Operating income**	**$ 1,430**	**$ 1,480**
+ Interest income	15	17
− Interest expense	(434)	(431)
= Income before income taxes	$ 1,011	$ 1,066
− Provision for income taxes	(495)	(426)
= **Net income**	**$ 516**	**$ 640**
Retained earnings at beginning of year	$ 3,505	$ 3,860
+ Net income	516	640
− Dividends	(161)	(200)
= **Retained earnings at end of year**	**$ 3,860**	**$ 4,300**

*Not a deductible expense for tax purposes; therefore, in 1987, EBIT = operating income + goodwill = $1,500.

A company's free cash flow must equal its financial cash flow. That is, the total cash generated by the company's operations (plus nonoperating cash flow, if any) must equal the net payments to all the company's creditors and shareholders. Conversely, if free cash flow is negative, it must equal the net funds provided by the company's shareholders and creditors (for example, via new issues of debt or equity).

This equality between operating and financial flows helps ensure that the free cash calculation is correct. The complexity of

Exhibit 5.3 **XYZ COMPANY, BALANCE SHEET**

	1985	1986	1987
Cash	$ 87	$ 90	$ 100
+ Excess marketable securities	308	320	300
+ Accounts receivable	2,800	2,900	3,000
+ Inventories	3,200	3,310	3,400
= Short-term assets	$ 6,395	$ 6,620	$ 6,800
+ Gross property, plant, and equipment	7,000	7,500	8,000
− Accumulated depreciation	(2,400)	(2,700)	(3,000)
= Net property, plant, and equipment	$ 4,600	$ 4,800	$ 5,000
+ Goodwill	540	520	500
+ Other assets	920	950	1,000
= **Total assets**	**$12,455**	**$12,890**	**$13,300**
Short-term debt	$ 1,060	$ 1,030	$ 1,000
+ Accounts payable	1,980	2,050	2,000
+ Accrued liabilities	880	900	1,000
= Short-term liabilities	$ 3,920	$ 3,980	$ 4,000
+ Long-term debt	3,400	3,500	3,500
+ Accumulated deferred income taxes	380	400	500
+ Common shares	1,250	1,150	1,000
+ Retained earnings	3,505	3,860	4,300
= Total shareholders' equity	$ 4,755	$ 5,010	$ 5,300
= **Total liabilities and shareholders' equity**	**$12,455**	**$12,890**	**$13,300**

some financial statements often leads to mistakes in free cash flow calculations. Errors can be minimized by always calculating the company's financial flow and ensuring that it equals the sum of free cash flow and nonoperating cash flow.

Developing a forecast of free cash flow involves four basic steps:

1. Defining the relevant components of free cash flow. Which elements of the company's cash flow are included in free cash flow and which are not?

2. Developing an integrated historical perspective of the company's performance, particularly in terms of its key value drivers.

3. Developing the forecast assumptions for all the elements of free cash flow and relevant scenarios.

4. Calculating and evaluating the resulting free cash flow forecast in terms of the key value drivers.

STEP 1: IDENTIFY THE RELEVANT COMPONENTS OF FREE CASH FLOW

Exhibit 5.1 shows the major components of free cash flow and financial flow. The following paragraphs define each of these major components.

Earnings Before Interest and Taxes (EBIT)

EBIT is the pretax income that a company would have earned if it had no debt. It includes all types of "operating" income (the distinction between operating and nonoperating cash flows is described later). It is often equal to the line "operating income" on the company's income statement. Depreciation should be subtracted in calculating EBIT but goodwill amortization should not.

Taxes on EBIT

Taxes on EBIT represent the income taxes that are attributable to EBIT. They are the taxes the company would pay if it had no debt or excess marketable securities. They equal the total income tax provision (current and deferred) adjusted for the income taxes attributed to interest expense, interest income, and nonoperating items. Using figures for our XYZ Company, 1987 taxes on EBIT are calculated as follows:

	Total income tax provision from income statement	$426
+	Tax shield on interest expense	181
−	Tax on interest income	(7)
−	Tax on nonoperating income	0
=	Taxes on EBIT	$600

The taxes related to interest expense, interest income, and nonoperating items are calculated by multiplying the marginal tax rate by the item. (The marginal tax rate is generally the statutory marginal rate, including state and local taxes. However, companies with tax loss carry-forwards or those subject to the alternative minimum tax may have different marginal rates.)

Change in Deferred Taxes

For valuation purposes, taxes should be stated on a cash basis. The provision for income taxes in the income statement generally does not equal the actual taxes paid in cash by the company due to differences between GAAP accounting and accounting for taxes. The adjustment to a cash basis can be calculated from the change in accumulated deferred income taxes on the company's balance sheet.

Net Operating Profit Less Adjusted Taxes (NOPLAT)

NOPLAT represents the after-tax operating profits of the company after adjusting the taxes to a cash basis. It is important because it is used in the calculation of the rate of return on invested capital.

Depreciation

Depreciation includes all the noncash charges deducted from EBIT except goodwill amortization (which is not added back to NOPLAT because it was not deducted in calculating NOPLAT). It also includes the amortization of intangible assets with definite lives such as patents and franchises.

Gross Cash Flow

Gross cash flow represents the total cash flow thrown off by the company. It is the amount available to reinvest in the business for maintenance and growth without relying on additional capital.

Change in Working Capital

The change in working capital is the amount the company invested in working capital during the period. Only operating working capital should be included. Nonoperating assets, excess marketable securities, and interest-bearing liabilities (short-term debt and the current portion of long-term debt) are excluded.

Capital Expenditures

Capital expenditures include expenditures on new and replacement property, plant, and equipment. Capital expenditures can be calculated as the increase in *net* property, plant, and equipment on the balance sheet plus depreciation expense for the period. (Technically, this calculation results in capital expenditures less the net book value of retired assets.)

Investment in Goodwill

The investment in goodwill equals the amount of expenditure to acquire another company in excess of the book value of its net assets. Theoretically, goodwill has an indefinite life and should always be stated on a gross basis—that is, before accumulated amortization. In any year, the investment in goodwill is best calculated as the net change in the goodwill account on the balance sheet plus the amortization of goodwill in that period. This ensures that goodwill amortization does not affect free cash flow in either gross cash flow or gross investment.

Increase in Net Other Assets

The increase in net other assets equals the expenditure on all other operating assets including capitalized intangibles (patents, trademarks), deferred expenses, and net of increases in noncurrent, non-interest-bearing liabilities. These can be calculated directly from the change in the balance sheet accounts plus any amortization included in depreciation.

Gross Investment

Gross investment is the sum of a company's expenditures for new capital, including working capital, capital expenditures, goodwill, and other assets.

Nonoperating Cash Flow

Nonoperating cash flow represents the after-tax cash flow from items not related to operations.

Free cash flow explicitly does not include nonoperating cash flow. Caution must be exercised, however, in considering an item to be nonoperating. Any nonoperating cash flow must be reflected in the value of the company explicitly. We do this by defining the total value of the company as the discounted present value of the company's free cash flow plus the value of its after-tax nonoperating cash flow.

$$\begin{array}{l}\text{Present value of} \\ \text{company's free} \\ \text{cash flow}\end{array} + \begin{array}{l}\text{Present value of} \\ \text{after-tax nonoper-} \\ \text{ating cash flow}\end{array} = \begin{array}{l}\text{Total value of} \\ \text{company}\end{array}$$

Cash flow items that are sometimes considered nonoperating include cash flow from discontinued operations, extraordinary items, and the cash flow from investments in unrelated subsidiaries. Remember, though, that the present value of any nonoperating cash flow must be reflected in the total value of the company.

It is generally not advisable to consider a recurring cash flow as nonoperating. The company's risk and therefore its cost of capital reflects all its assets and its cash flow. Arbitrarily excluding items from free cash flow may violate the principle of consistency between free cash flow and cost of capital.

Change in Excess Marketable Securities

Changes in excess marketable securities and the related interest income are considered financial cash flows for two reasons:

1. Excess marketable securities generally represent temporary imbalances in the company's cash flow. For example, the company may build up cash while deciding what to do with it. These excess marketable securities are not generally directly related to the company's operating decisions.
2. Considering these changes as financial cash flow makes valuation easier. Marketable securities are generally much

less risky than the operations of the firm. As marketable securities grow or decline in relation to the size of the company, the company's overall level of risk and its cost of capital should rise or fall. Modeling the change in the cost of capital is complex. It is much easier to consider the value of a company as the sum of the value of its operating free cash flow plus the present value of the cash flow related to its excess marketable securities, where the risk of each component is relatively stable over time.

Excess marketable securities are the short-term cash investments that the company holds over and above its *target* cash balances to support operations. The target balances can be estimated by observing the variability in the company's cash and marketable security balances over time and by comparing against similar companies.

Recognize also that the investment in marketable securities (government securities and commercial paper) is a zero-net-present-value investment. The return on this investment just compensates for its risk. Therefore, the present value of the cash flow related to these marketable securities must equal the market value of the excess marketable securities on the company's books at the time of the valuation.

After-tax Interest Income

The after-tax interest income on excess marketable securities equals the pretax income times 1 minus the appropriate marginal income tax rate. The marginal tax rate should be consistent with the rate used for the adjustment of taxes on EBIT.

Change in Debt

The change in debt represents the net borrowing or repayment on all the company's debt, including short-term debt.

After-tax Interest Expense

The after-tax interest expense equals the pretax interest expense times 1 minus the company's marginal income tax rate. The marginal tax rate should be consistent with the rate used for the adjustment of taxes on EBIT.

Dividends

Dividends include all cash dividends on common and preferred shares.

Share Issues/Repurchases

Share issues/repurchases include both preferred and common shares and the effects of conversions of debt to equity. This figure can be calculated by taking the change in total equity plus dividends less net income.

The foregoing items are fairly standard for most companies. A number of special items may also be relevant, including operating leases, pensions, minority interest, investments in unconsolidated subsidiaries, and foreign currency translation gains/losses.

Operating Leases

Operating leases are any lease obligations that the company has not capitalized. Operating leases represent a type of financing and should be treated as such. Therefore, we adjust the company's financial statements to treat operating leases as if they were capitalized. First, reclassify the implied interest expense portion of the lease payments from an operating expense (usually in cost of goods sold, or selling, general, and administrative expense) to an interest expense. This increases EBIT by the amount of implied interest. Do not forget to adjust the EBIT taxes as well.

Also, reflect changes in the implied principal amount of the leases in gross investment and the change in debt. This mimics the effects that would have occurred had the leases been capitalized. Chapter 6 suggests an approach for estimating the principal amount of the leases. The implied interest expense is the principal amount times an appropriate interest rate.

Pensions

The company's pension costs are included in the cost of goods sold, or selling, general, and administrative expense. Normally, nothing special need be done in the free cash flow or the valuation related to pensions. If the company has a significantly overfunded or underfunded plan, however, care must be taken to ensure that the related cash flow is treated consistently in the valuation. Overfunded or underfunded pension plans can be handled in one of two ways:

1. Adjust the forecasted pension expense so that the overfunded or underfunded pension is eliminated over time. Do not treat the current amount of overfunding or underfunding as a separate item in the valuation, because that would be double counting.
2. Do not reflect the overfunding or underfunding in the pension expense forecast. The current amount of the after-tax overfunding or underfunding must be included as a separate item added to or subtracted from the valuation.

Minority Interest

A minority interest occurs when a third party owns some percentage of one of the company's consolidated subsidiaries.

The related cash flow should be included as part of the company's financial flow since a minority interest is simply another form of financing. The relevant cash flow amount equals the income statement amount less the change in the minority interest on the balance sheet. This should equal the dividends paid to the minority shareholder less any capital contributions received by the company from the minority shareholders.

Investments in Unconsolidated Subsidiaries

The cash flow associated with unconsolidated subsidiaries can be handled in one of two ways:

1. Include the cash flow in free cash flow.
2. Exclude the cash flow from free cash flow but include the present value of the cash flow as a separate item in the valuation.

The first approach is simpler and should be used unless the amount of the cash flow is material in size, *and* the operations of the subsidiary are not related to the core operations of the company. The first approach is recommended because the company's cost of capital probably reflects its holdings in these subsidiaries. Excluding the subsidiaries could violate the consistency between free cash flow and cost of capital.

The related cash flow can be calculated by subtracting the balance sheet increases in the investment-in-subsidiaries account from the income related to the subsidiaries (this works whether they are accounted for on the equity or cost method). The cash flow should also be adjusted for related income taxes.

Foreign Currency Translation Gains/Losses

The change in the cumulative foreign currency translation gains or losses account is driven by the changes in translation rates applied to both assets and debt. As a practical matter, you generally cannot separate the asset and debt gains or losses without internal information. Therefore, treat these gains/losses as nonoperating cash flow in the free cash flow. If you have the information needed to separate the asset from the debt effects, treat the gains/losses on assets as adjustments to free cash flow and the gains/losses on debt as financial cash flow. (See Financial Accounting Standards Board Statement No. 52 for a complete discussion of foreign currency accounting.)

STEP 2: DEVELOP AN INTEGRATED HISTORICAL PERSPECTIVE

A sound understanding of the company's past performance provides an essential perspective for developing a good forecast of future performance. This perspective should be based on an analysis of the company's free cash flow and key value drivers, both over time and compared with other companies.

The key value drivers are summarized in Exhibit 5.4. Most important among them are the rate of return on invested capital relative to the weighted average cost of capital and the amount the company invests in new capital at this rate to generate growth.

Exhibit 5.4 **THE KEY VALUE DRIVERS**

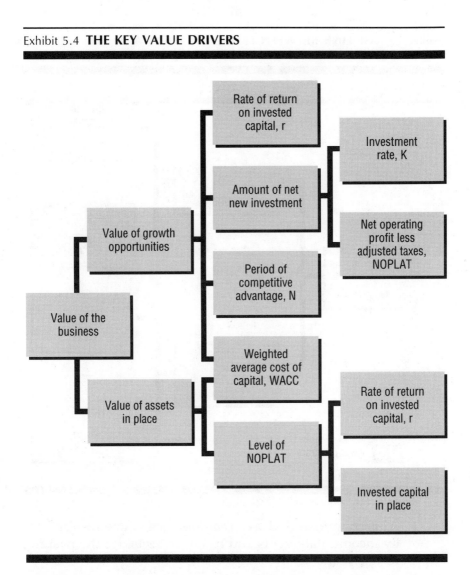

A direct link obviously exists between those value drivers and free cash flow, as demonstrated in Exhibit 5.5. By understanding the value drivers—especially the return on invested capital and the investment rate—we can develop insights into the likely behavior of free cash flow and value creation in the future.

Performing an integrated historical analysis involves the following tasks:

Exhibit 5.5 **THE LINK BETWEEN FREE CASH FLOW AND THE KEY VALUE DRIVERS (XYZ Company, 1987)**

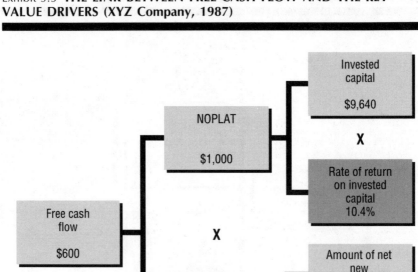

Value drivers

1. Analyzing historical free cash flow statements, supported by income statements and balance sheets, for the past five to ten years
2. Analyzing the rate of return on invested capital over the historical period
3. Analyzing the historical investment rate and its implications
4. Drawing conclusions about the sustainability of the company's rate of return in excess of its weighted average cost of capital

Analyzing Historical Financial Statements

Analysis of the historical free cash flow statements, income statements, and balance sheets should focus on three areas:

1. *Gross cash flow.* What are the components of the company's gross cash flow?
2. *Gross investment.* Is gross investment more or less than gross cash flow? Where has the company been investing capital? What are the relative proportions of working capital, fixed assets, and other assets?
3. *Financing.* How has the company been financing its investment? How has it been distributing its excess cash flow? What are the levels of debt and marketable securities?

Each area should be analyzed in terms of the following:

- What are the trends in each item over time, both absolutely and relative to other items?
- How do the items fluctuate? Have any radical fluctuations occurred, and what accounts for them?
- How does the company compare with its competitors?

Analyzing the Rate of Return on Invested Capital

The rate of return on invested capital is the single most important value driver. A company creates value for its shareholders only when it earns rates of return on invested capital that exceed its cost of capital. The rate of return on invested capital is defined as follows:

$$\text{Return on invested capital} = \frac{\text{Net operating profit less adjusted taxes}}{\text{Invested capital}}$$

Net operating profit less adjusted taxes (NOPLAT) was defined earlier. Invested capital is the sum of operating working capital, net property, plant, and equipment, and net other assets (net of noncurrent, non-interest-bearing liabilities), and is generally measured at the beginning of the period. Invested capital can also be calculated from the liability side of the balance sheet. Exhibit 5.6 demonstrates the calculation of invested capital for the XYZ Company.

Exhibit 5.6 **XYZ COMPANY, INVESTED CAPITAL CALCULATION***

	1986	1987
Current assets (excludes excess marketable securities)	$6,300	$ 6,500
− Non-interest-bearing current liabilities	(2,950)	(3,000)
= Net working capital	$3,350	$ 3,500
+ Net property, plant, and equipment	4,800	5,000
+ Goodwill*	540	540
+ Net other operating assets	950	1,000
= **Invested capital**	**$9,640**	**$10,040**
Debt	$4,530	$ 4,500
+ Common equity*	5,030	5,340
+ Deferred income taxes	400	500
	$9,960	$10,340
− Excess marketable securities	(320)	(300)
− Nonoperating assets	0	0
= **Invested capital**	**$9,640**	**$10,040**

*Before cumulative goodwill amortization of $20 in 1986 and $40 in 1987. (It also may be instructive to exclude goodwill from the capital base when calculating the rate of return. The rate of return on invested capital excluding goodwill may be a better indicator of the underlying economics of the company and the industry. It may also be a better predictor of possible future returns. Consider an example. Company A is considering buying Company B. Company B currently earns 12 percent on invested capital against its cost of capital of 12 percent. Company A expects that it can increase Company B's return to 15 percent because of proprietary processes that it can apply to Company B's operations. However, Company A must pay a premium to acquire Company B. Company A buys Company B at a price that results in Company A's earning 13 percent on its capital invested in Company B, including goodwill in invested capital. Excluding goodwill, Company A's return on Company B is 15 percent, as expected. The 15 percent return may be a better indicator of Company A's ability to create value in the future by investing and growing Company B's operations internally, instead of through additional acquisitions.)

This definition of the rate of return on invested capital is a better analytical tool for understanding the company's performance than return on equity or return on assets, because it focuses attention on the true operating performance of the company. We should note, however, that the rate of return as defined here suffers from the same problems as other accounting-based measures of performance. It is plagued by both arcane accounting rules and the problem that assets and some expenses are recorded at historical costs and, therefore, distorted by inflation. Still, this measure is superior to similar measures like return on equity or return on total assets. Return on equity can easily confuse operating performance with financing decisions. Return on total assets is computed many ways, so its problems depend on the approach. As an example, consider that non-interest-bearing liabilities are not deducted from the denominator, total assets. Yet the implicit financing cost of these liabilities is included in the expenses of the company and, therefore, deducted from the numerator. So the return on total assets includes at least one internal inconsistency.

The rate of return on invested capital should be analyzed from two perspectives:

1. The return on total invested capital as an indicator of the overall performance of the company.
2. The return on incremental invested capital as an indicator of whether new capital is creating value. This understanding is essential because the return on incremental invested capital is a key value driver underlying the forecast. Note that this can only be calculated by assuming that all of the change in NOPLAT in any period is attributable to new investment, not to changes in the rate of return on existing capital.

A useful way to organize an analysis of the rate of return is to develop a return-on-invested-capital tree as demonstrated in Exhibit 5.7. (The numerical examples use data taken from Exhibits 5.2, 5.3, and 5.6.) The component measures of the return on invested capital are industry- and company-specific. For example, wholesalers typically have slim margins and high turnover, while telephone companies have high margins and low capital turnover. These ratios may also reflect the company's operating strategy relative to its competitors. A company may decide to use more laborsaving devices than its competitors; thus, its higher margins might compensate for lower capital turnover.

Analyzing the Investment Rate

The second most important value driver is the net investment rate. The net investment rate measures investment in new opportunities relative to the cash flow generated by the company. Note that the investment rate can be greater than 100 percent if the company uses external sources of capital (for example, new debt or equity) to finance current investment.

$$\text{Net investment rate} = \frac{\text{Net new investment}}{\text{NOPLAT}}$$

$$= \frac{\text{Gross investment} - \text{Depreciation}}{\text{NOPLAT}}$$

Analyzing the investment rate should be directed to understanding the following:

1. What has the investment rate been?
   - How has it changed year by year? Are there any significant items or changes that should be explained?
   - What is the cumulative average rate over the recent past? (The cumulative average is calculated by dividing the sum of the net new investment over a number of years by the sum of NOPLAT over the same period. It is not a simple average of each year's investment rates.)

Exhibit 5.7 **XYZ COMPANY, RATE OF RETURN ON INVESTED CAPITAL, 1987**

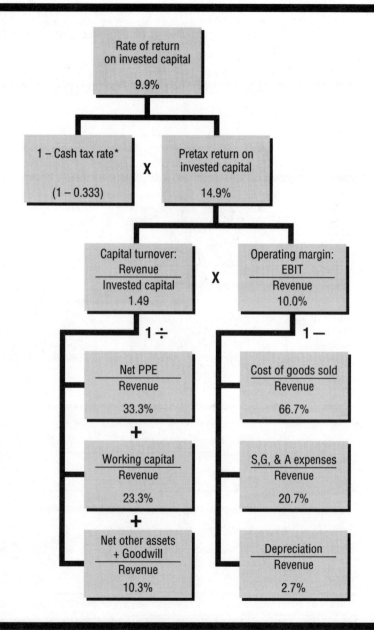

$$^*\text{Cash tax rate} = \frac{\text{EBIT taxes} - \text{Change in deferred taxes}}{\text{EBIT}}$$

$$= \frac{600 - 100}{1500}$$

$$= 33.3\%$$

2. What has been driving the investment rate? Use a tree similar to the one in Exhibit 5.8 to analyze the investment rate.

   • Analyze the components of the investment rate in terms of overall asset intensity and incremental asset intensity.

Exhibit 5.8 **XYZ COMPANY, DETERMINING THE INVESTMENT RATE, 1987**

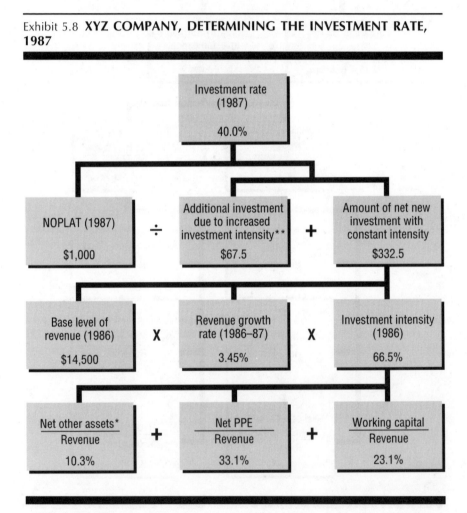

*Before goodwill amortization.
**From 1986 to 1987 the company's investment intensity increased from 66.48 percent to 66.93 percent. Multiplying the increase in intensity, 0.45 percent, by 1987's revenues of $15,000 yields additional investment of $67.5.

- Analyze the company's growth in revenues by undertaking a typical industry competitive analysis. Particularly understand the factors underlying demand for the company's products, and how much investment is required to meet demand. Has investment relative to sales changed over time?

3. What are the implications of the investment rate for

- growth in NOPLAT, since growth is the product of the rate of return on invested capital and the investment rate?

- the financial decisions of the company? Is the company raising new capital to fund investment or is it generating excess cash that it must disburse?

Drawing Conclusions About the Sustainability of Rates of Return

The final key value driver is the length of time over which the expected rate of return on invested capital will exceed the company's weighted average cost of capital. (This is also generally assumed to be the length of the forecast horizon.) In Exhibit 5.4 we called this the period of competitive advantage. The objective here is to gather clues about the sustainability of returns. Conclusions about the sustainability of returns will be based mostly on forward-looking information, but a historical analysis is a useful starting point. This involves the following:

1. Examining the level and trends in the rate of return on invested capital for the entire industry and individual competitors.

2. Using industry structure and competitive analysis to understand what has been driving changes in rates of return and to formulate hypotheses for the future. In particular,

- if the industry is currently performing well, how long will this last?

- if the industry is not healthy, will rationalization take place, and when?

Consider, for example, whether the industry is young and highly competitive without any entry barriers or mature with natural entry barriers such as government regulation or economies of scale.

STEP 3: DEVELOP FORECAST ASSUMPTIONS AND SCENARIOS

A key element of the forecast process is to develop the forecast assumptions. Good forecasts are based on a thorough analysis of the company's economics, industry competitive dynamics, and the underlying demand for the company's products. No universal rules exist for forecasting, but you need to think about the following:

1. Determining the overall structure of the forecast
2. Developing relevant scenarios
3. Developing a point of view about a forecast for each variable
4. Deciding on the length of the forecast

Determining the Overall Structure of the Forecast

The structure of the forecast is the order in which the variables are forecasted and the way in which they relate to each other. The best forecast structure begins with an integrated income statement and balance sheet forecast. The free cash flow can then be derived from them.

It is possible to forecast free cash flow directly rather than going through the income statement and balance sheet; however, we do not recommend it. If you forecast free cash flow first, you must construct the balance sheet anyway to properly evaluate the relationships between the cash flow/income statement items and the balance sheet accounts.

If you do not construct the balance sheet, it is easy to lose sight of how all the pieces fit together. A recent experience provides an example. A team doing a valuation tried to simplify the forecasting process by ignoring the balance sheet. The company's history showed that it usually generated about two dollars in sales for each dollar of net fixed assets. By the end of the team's forecast, the company was generating five dollars in sales for each dollar of net fixed assets. The team had not intended this result and did not even know it was happening because it had not constructed a balance sheet and supporting ratios.

The balance sheet also helps to identify the financing implications of the forecast. It shows how much capital must be raised or how much excess cash will be available.

The most common approach to forecasting the income statement and balance sheet is a demand-driven forecast. A demand-driven forecast starts with sales. Most other variables (expenses, working capital) are driven off the sales forecast. Use the return-on-invested-capital tree to organize the forecast and as a consistency check.

Developing Relevant Scenarios

Generally, no single forecast can truly represent the expected performance of a company. Instead, it is better to forecast the company's performance for a variety of scenarios. A scenario is a picture of the company under a unified set of circumstances and a plausible set of forecast assumptions. Considering alternative scenarios does not mean mechanically changing the sales growth rate by 10 percent. Instead, it means developing hypothetical situations like the following:

- *The company introduces a major new product line and sales take off.* This scenario should factor in how the competition would respond in terms of competing products and pricing. It should also deal with how the company would handle the strain of the higher sales level in areas like manufacturing and distribution.

- *A substitute product enters the market.* How would the company respond? Would it just lose sales or would it retaliate? What organizational changes would be made to compete in the new environment?

Each scenario should be valued independently of the others. A weighted average of the scenario values based on expected probabilities could be used to assess the overall value of the company.

Analytical frameworks such as the Structure-Conduct-Performance model or Porter's competitive analysis framework are helpful for developing scenarios because they systematically lay out the factors that should be considered. A brief list of factors to consider in developing scenarios includes the following:

- The potential for new products or technological break-throughs that would affect demand for the company's products

- The ability of the company to differentiate its products from those of its competitors

- Potential changes in government policy or regulation, such as environmental laws or international trade barriers

- The financial strength and strategies of the company's key competitors

- Changes in consumer tastes or lifestyles, or other factors that may affect demand for the industry's products

- The strategies of the company's suppliers and the availability of key raw materials

Consult a text on strategy analysis for a complete analysis of factors that should be considered in developing scenarios.

Finally, sensitivity analyses (measuring the impact on value of changes in key variables) should be conducted for each scenario. The purpose of sensitivity analysis is to understand how changes in variables affect the value of the company. For example, does a 1 percent increase in the sales growth rate increase the value of the company more or less than a 1 percent increase in the operating margin? This type of analysis identifies the critical assumptions in the forecast and potential areas of focus for value-creating efforts.

Developing a Point of View About a Forecast for Each Variable

Forecasts of valuation variables should draw upon a careful analysis of industry structure and a company's internal capabilities.

Analyzing the historical level of valuation variables is a useful starting point. Once these levels have been calculated, several questions should be addressed to gain insight into the future level of each valuation variable.

- What characteristics of the industry have had the greatest impact on value drivers in the past?
- What company-specific capabilities have had the greatest impact on historical value drivers?
- Are industry characteristics and company capabilities expected to maintain historical patterns in the future? If not, what is expected to change?
- What must change in the industry or the company to cause a significant shift in the historical level of the company's value drivers?

Alternative scenarios can be generated by assuming different industry structures and company capabilities. For example, the industry may be characterized by rapid growth and few substitutes. One scenario may assume that these conditions will continue for a certain time period, with industry growth eventually slowing due to the introduction of good substitutes. This would normally translate into declining revenue growth in the valuation forecast period.

As this demonstrates, forecasts should be driven primarily by strategic rather than financial analysis. While a full discussion of strategic analysis is beyond the scope of this book, we will comment on two important financial issues: inflation and risk.

Inflation We recommended that free cash flow forecasts and discount rates be estimated in nominal rather than real currency units. *For consistency, both the free cash flow forecast and the discount rate must contain the appropriate expected inflation rate.* In general, we will need to estimate a rate of change in prices for each cash flow component. Selling prices might increase at 5.5 percent, for example, while costs are expected to increase at 4.0 percent, with the exception of the depreciation tax shield, which is unaffected by inflation.

Do not forget that expected inflation rates in costs as well as revenues must be estimated in a fashion consistent with the general inflation rate in the discount rate. A common error is that the marketing department of a company estimates the inflation rate for sales; the production department, for costs; and the economics staff, for the general discount rate; but they fail to check their independent estimates for consistency. All estimates must be consistent with the same assumptions about general inflation.

To provide a specific example, suppose the market rate of interest can be broken down into general expected inflation of 4.5 percent and a real interest rate of 2.5 percent. Revenue forecasts have two components: rates of change in expected unit output and rates of change in unit prices. The nominal rate of growth in revenues must reflect both components. Furthermore, the expected rate of change in unit prices must be tied to the general expected inflation forecast—for example, 1 percent above general inflation. Assuming that the rate of change in expected unit output is 3 percent, the expected growth rate in revenues would be roughly 8.5 percent—that is, 4.5 percent general inflation plus 1 percent real price increase plus 3 percent real growth in unit sales.

The nominal discount rate for free cash flow will be a risk-adjusted weighted average cost of capital that contains general expected inflation and real rates of growth economywide. The same nominal discount rate applies to all cash flows.

We can derive the expected general inflation rate that is consistent with the discount rate from the term structure of interest rates. The term structure is based on yields to maturity of U.S. government bonds. Nominal interest rates reflect lenders' expectations of future inflation. Lenders expect to be compensated for expected losses due to inflation as well as default and market risk. Exhibit 5.9 shows the term structure of interest rates at three points in time. Inflationary expectations are clearly reflected in each. In 1981, short-term interest rates were high, reflecting the market's belief at that time that future inflation would be lower than near-term inflation. In 1984, inflationary expectations were lower than in 1981, and the market believed long-term inflation would be higher than short-term inflation. In 1988, inflationary expectations were even lower.

Exhibit 5.9 **TERM STRUCTURE OF INTEREST RATES AT THREE POINTS IN TIME**

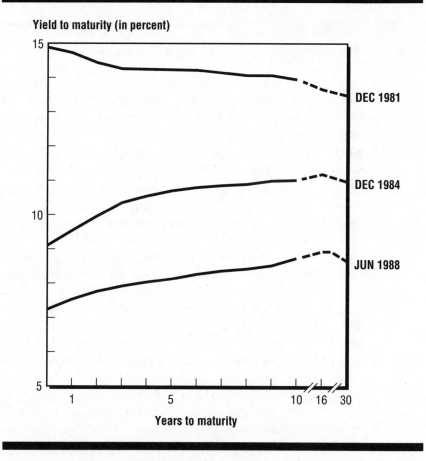

The term structure of interest rates provides a market-based estimate of expected inflation over time. This should be the best estimate for valuation purposes, for these reasons:

- Most economists', or econometric, forecasts of inflation rarely extend beyond one or two years, far too short a period for valuation.
- Market-based estimates provide a broader consensus view (with investors' money at stake) than individual forecasts.

- Empirical analysis suggests that market-based estimates are the least biased (see Fama and Gibbons 1984, or Hardouvelis 1988).

The expected inflation rate over a given period can be derived from the term structure of interest rates as follows:

1. Determine the nominal risk-free rate of interest for the time period over which you want to estimate inflation (use the same interval that will be used to calculate the weighted average cost of capital).

2. Estimate the real rate of interest. This is a controversial issue and different sources provide different estimates. Ibbotson Associates estimate the real rate as the difference between the annualized rate of return on U.S. Treasury bills and the Consumer Price Index (for all urban consumers, not seasonally adjusted). For the interval 1926 to 1988, their real rate is 0.44 percent per year. During the interval 1966 to 1980, the annual inflation rate was 6.9 percent and the realized T-bill rate was 6.3 percent, resulting in a negative real return of 0.6 percent. During the most recent period, 1981 to 1988, inflation was 3.6 percent and T-bill rates were 7.8 percent, yielding the highest real rate in half a century, 4.2 percent. The Department of Commerce estimates the real rate of growth in GNP at 3.3 percent per year during the 1967 to 1984 interval. In any single year, it has been as high as 6.8 percent and as low as minus 2.1 percent. Our recommendation is that you use a 2- to 3-percent real rate for forecasts over the next ten years. This range produces what seem to be reasonable estimates of expected inflation when 0.4 percent does not. Also, the 2- to 3-percent range is close to the Ibbotson Associates' twenty-six-year average (1960 to 1986)—that is, 2.97 percent—and to longer-term Commerce Department estimates.

3. Calculate the expected inflation rate from the nominal and real rates using the formula derived in Exhibit 5.10:

$$\text{Expected inflation} = \frac{(1 + \text{Nominal rate})}{(1 + \text{Real rate})} - 1$$

Exhibit 5.10 **NOTES ON CALCULATING EXPECTED INFLATION**

Estimating the expected inflation rate is more complicated than simply subtracting the real rate from the yield to maturity. For example, what is the expected rate two years out? On June 30, 1988, the yield to maturity for a two-year T-bond was 7.97 percent. It is a geometric average of two one-year nominal rates. If we designate "Nom" as the nominal rate, "r" as the real rate, and "infl" as the expected inflation rate, the algebraic relationship is as follows:

$$(1 + Nom_2)^2 = (1 + r_1)(1 + infl_1)(1 + r_2)(1 + infl_2)$$

We also know that for the first year, the yield to maturity is as follows:

$$(1 + Nom_1) = (1 + r_1)(1 + infl_1)$$

Taking the ratio of these two equations, using the two-year rate from June 1988, 7.97 percent, and assuming a real rate of 2.5 percent gives us the expected rate of inflation in the second year.

$$\frac{(1.0797)^2}{(1.0762)} = \frac{(1.025)(1 + infl_1)(1.025)(1 + infl_2)}{(1.025)(1 + infl_1)}$$

$$(1 + infl_2) = \frac{(1.0797)^2}{(1.0762)(1.025)} = 1.0568$$

Note that the market's estimate of inflation in the second year, 5.68 percent, is different from 5.47 percent, which is the answer you would get if you simply subtracted the (constant) real rate, 2.5 percent, from the yield to maturity in the second year.

The same procedure can be used to estimate the market's estimate of expected inflation for each year in the future, or as an average across N years. For example, suppose we wanted to know the average expected inflation across a ten-year period. We can solve the following equation:

$$(1 + inflation)^{10} = \frac{(1 + Nom)^{10}}{(1 + r)^{10}}$$

Exhibit 5.10 Continued

Taking the 10th root of each element gives

$$(1 + \text{inflation}) = \frac{(1 + \text{Nom})}{(1 + r)}$$

$$1 + \text{inflation} = \frac{1.0880}{1.025} = 1.0615$$

Expected inflation over the ten years starting June 1988 was 6.15 percent.

Risk How does the riskiness of the company's expected cash flow get incorporated into its value? Two types of risk must be considered. Default risk is reflected in the estimation of expected cash flow, and portfolio (undiversifiable) risk is reflected in the discount rate. As described in the next chapter, the discount rate that will be used to discount expected free cash flow is a risk-adjusted discount rate. This rate reflects the premium that investors expect to earn for undertaking the undiversifiable risk of investing in the company. The expected free cash flow forecast weights each possible cash flow scenario, including bankruptcy, by the probability that it might occur. The forecast should represent your best guess of the company's performance under the set of circumstances for that scenario.

Deciding on the Length of the Forecast

For practical purposes, most forecasts should be divided into two periods: an explicit forecast period (say ten years) and the remaining life of the company (year 11 on). A detailed forecast is done for the first period. Cash flow from the second, more distant, period is valued based on a continuing-value formula.

The explicit forecast period should be long enough so that the company reaches a steady state by the end of the period. The steady state can be described as follows:

- The company earns a constant rate of return on all new capital invested during the continuing-value period.
- The company earns a constant rate of return on its base level of invested capital.
- The company invests a constant proportion of its earnings back into the business each year.

The most common approach is to make the forecast period as long as you expect the company to have sustainable rates of return on new investment above the company's cost of capital. Microeconomic analysis suggests that over time, competition will drive the returns in most industries to the level of the cost of capital. Once the company's returns have converged on its cost of capital, it is relatively simple to estimate the company's continuing value. Therefore, forecasting until convergence simplifies the continuing-value problem. If this is your approach, the forecast period should be for as long as returns above the weighted average cost of capital are sustainable.

When in doubt, make a longer rather than shorter forecast. We would rarely use a forecast period of less than seven years. The forecast period should never be determined by the company's own internal planning period. Just because the company forecasts out only three years is not justification to use three years for the valuation. A rough forecast beyond three years is certainly better than no forecast.

If a company is in a cyclical industry, it is important that your forecast capture a complete cycle. Failure to do so may result in wildly unrealistic continuing-value assumptions, because the up or down phase of the cycle may be projected to last forever. It is best to put long-run forecasts (averaging out cyclical effects) into your continuing-value assumptions.

STEP 4: CALCULATE AND EVALUATE THE FREE CASH FLOW FORECAST

The final step in the forecasting process is to construct and evaluate the free cash flow forecast. The forecast should be evaluated the same way the company's historical performance was analyzed. Understand how the forecast translates into the key value drivers: rate of return on invested capital, the investment rate, and the time period of sustainable rates of return over the cost of capital. These questions should be addressed:

- Is the company's performance on the key value drivers consistent with the company's economics and the industry competitive dynamics?
- Is revenue growth consistent with industry growth? If the company's revenue is growing faster than the industry's, which competitors are losing share? Will they retaliate? Does the company have the resources to manage that rate of growth?
- Is the return on capital consistent with the industry's competitive structure? If entry barriers are coming down, shouldn't expected returns decline? If customers are becoming more powerful, will margins decline? Conversely, if the company's position in the industry is becoming much stronger, should you expect increasing returns? How will returns and growth look relative to the competition?
- How will technology changes affect returns? Will they affect risk?
- Can the company manage all the investment it is undertaking?
- Finally, understand the financing implications of the forecast. Will the company have to raise large amounts of capital? If so, can it obtain the financing? Should it be debt or equity? If the company is generating excess cash, what options does it have for investing the cash or returning it to shareholders?

PRESTON CORPORATION

FORECAST OF FREE CASH FLOW

The balance of this chapter illustrates the development of a free cash flow forecast using the Preston Corporation as a case example. Preston Corporation is a regional trucking company that transports freight by motor carrier. It carries truckload shipments, higher-fee less-than-truckload shipments, and special commodities. Less-than-truckload shipments account for 73.5 percent of its revenues.

Preston competes with hundreds of other carriers throughout its areas of service, as well as with railroads, airlines, and shipper-operated trucks in some regions. Preston has 8,262 employees and is subject to regulation by the Interstate Commerce Commission, the Department of Transportation, and the Federal Maritime Commission.

The Motor Carrier Act of 1980 has led to substantial deregulation of and intense competition in the industry; however, a significant shakeout and recently firming rates indicate that some relief for Preston and the rest of the industry may be forthcoming.

Preston Corporation is publicly owned and its common stock is traded in the over-the-counter market.

PRESTON CASE, STEP 1: IDENTIFY THE RELEVANT COMPONENTS OF FREE CASH FLOW

Exhibits 5.11 through 5.16 define the relevant components of Preston's historical free cash flow and illustrate its calculation. They include an income statement, a balance sheet, a free cash flow statement, supporting calculations, and a number of relevant ratios. Preston's marginal tax rate (for calculating the taxes related to interest expense and income) was assumed to be 49 percent through 1986: a 46-percent federal rate plus 3 percent for state and local taxes, allowing for their deductibility from federal taxes. A 45-percent marginal tax rate was assumed in 1987, composed of a 40-percent federal rate and 5 percent for state and local taxes, again net of the federal benefit.

PRESTON CASE, STEP 2: DEVELOP AN INTEGRATED HISTORICAL PERSPECTIVE

Overall, Preston's performance has been poor. The trucking industry has been suffering as a result of its deregulation in 1980. This deregulation allowed a large number of smaller, low-cost carriers, attracted by high industry profitability, to enter the industry. Substantial rate discounts resulted as companies competed for market share. This intense competition caused many carriers to leave the industry, and further price declines resulted as the remaining carriers sought to capture the market share held by

Exhibit 5.11 **PRESTON CORPORATION, HISTORICAL INCOME STATEMENT,** $ MILLIONS

Income Statement	1981	1982	1983	1984	1985	1986	1987
Revenues	$197.6	$222.3	$272.3	$299.5	$350.0	$418.9	$505.4
Operating expenses	(175.4)	(206.9)	(249.6)	(274.7)	(327.5)	(383.6)	(467.4)
Depreciation expense	(12.8)	(9.3)	(11.2)	(13.0)	(15.0)	(17.7)	(26.4)
Operating income	9.4	6.1	11.5	11.8	7.5	17.6	11.6
Amortization of goodwill	0.0	0.0	0.0	0.0	0.0	(0.1)	(0.6)
Nonoperating income	1.8	1.8	1.7	3.2	0.3	0.3	(0.5)
Interest income	0.0	0.0	0.0	0.0	0.9	0.7	0.6
Interest expense	(0.1)	(0.4)	(0.8)	(1.0)	(3.4)	(4.1)	(10.1)
Earnings before taxes	11.1	7.5	12.4	14.0	5.3	14.4	1.0
Income taxes	(5.3)	(2.4)	(5.8)	(5.2)	(1.0)	(7.1)	(0.7)
Income before extraordinary items	5.8	5.1	6.6	8.8	4.3	7.3	0.3
Effect of accounting change	0.5	0.0	0.0	0.0	0.0	0.0	5.8
Net income	$6.3	$5.1	$6.6	$8.8	$4.3	$7.3	$6.1

Statement of Retained Earnings	1981	1982	1983	1984	1985	1986	1987
Beginning retained earnings	$60.6	$64.8	$67.8	$70.0	$76.0	$78.2	$82.6
Net income	6.3	5.1	6.6	8.8	4.3	7.3	6.1
Common dividends	(2.1)	(2.1)	(2.8)	(2.8)	(2.8)	(2.9)	(2.9)
Adjustments	0.0	0.0	(1.6)	0.0	0.7	0.0	0.0
Ending retained earnings	$64.8	$67.8	$70.0	$76.0	$78.2	$82.6	$85.8

Exhibit 5.12 **PRESTON CORPORATION, HISTORICAL BALANCE SHEET,**
$ MILLIONS

	1981	1982	1983	1984	1985	1986	1987
Operating cash	$4.0	$4.4	$5.4	$6.0	$6.0	$8.4	$10.1
Excess marketable							
securities	10.9	3.0	20.5	10.3	0.0	5.8	3.2
Trade receivables	17.9	24.4	33.0	33.3	43.9	49.8	57.7
Other receivables	1.5	2.0	2.7	2.7	6.2	4.9	5.7
Inventories	1.9	2.1	2.8	2.5	9.0	10.9	11.9
Prepaid expenses	4.3	5.1	5.3	6.0	2.4	4.4	5.0
Current assets	40.5	41.0	69.7	60.8	67.5	84.2	93.6
Gross property,							
plant, & equip	100.0	117.7	128.2	155.6	204.7	272.5	297.6
Accumulated de-							
preciation	(37.7)	(42.3)	(48.7)	(56.5)	(71.9)	(86.9)	(103.4)
Net property,							
plant, equip	62.3	75.4	79.5	99.1	132.8	185.6	194.2
Goodwill	0.0	0.0	0.0	0.0	3.2	24.7	24.4
Other assets	0.5	1.2	1.2	3.1	3.4	6.2	8.3
Total assets	$103.3	$117.6	$150.4	$163.0	$206.9	$300.7	$320.5
Short-term debt	$0.3	$0.8	$0.9	$1.5	$11.5	$12.5	$20.7
Accounts payable	7.3	11.0	11.9	10.5	14.2	16.2	18.9
Other current							
liabilities	13.9	13.5	18.2	18.5	21.4	27.8	28.8
Total current							
liabilities	21.5	25.3	31.0	30.5	47.1	56.5	68.4
Long-term debt	3.7	8.6	13.2	17.4	38.4	112.9	122.4
Deferred income							
taxes	8.7	11.0	12.6	15.5	19.6	25.1	20.3
Common stock	4.6	4.9	23.6	23.6	23.6	23.6	23.6
Retained earnings	64.8	67.8	70.0	76.0	78.2	82.6	85.8
Total common							
equity	69.4	72.7	93.6	99.6	101.8	106.2	109.4
Total liabilities							
and equity	$103.3	$117.6	$150.4	$163.0	$206.9	$300.7	$320.5

Exhibit 5.13 **PRESTON CORPORATION, HISTORICAL FREE CASH FLOW,** $ MILLIONS

Free Cash Flow	1982	1983	1984	1985	1986	1987
Revenues	$222.3	$272.3	$299.5	$350.0	$418.9	$505.4
Operating expenses	(206.9)	(249.6)	(274.7)	(327.5)	(383.6)	(467.4)
Depreciation expense	(9.3)	(11.2)	(13.0)	(15.0)	(17.7)	(26.4)
Adjustment for operating leases	0.8	0.9	1.0	1.1	1.2	0.9
Adjusted EBIT	6.9	12.4	12.8	8.6	18.8	12.5
Taxes on EBIT	(2.1)	(5.8)	(4.6)	(2.6)	(9.2)	(5.6)
Change in deferred taxes	2.3	1.6	2.9	4.1	5.5	1.0
NOPLAT	7.1	8.2	11.1	10.1	15.1	7.9
Depreciation	9.3	11.2	13.0	15.0	17.7	26.4
Gross cash flow	16.4	19.4	24.1	25.1	32.8	34.3
Change in working capital	5.1	5.6	2.4	10.4	2.5	8.3
Capital expenditures	22.4	15.3	32.6	32.2	26.5	35.0
Capitalized operating leases	0.7	0.7	0.8	0.9	1.0	(2.3)
PPE from acquisitions	0.0	0.0	0.0	16.5	44.0	0.0
Investment in goodwill	0.0	0.0	0.0	3.2	21.6	0.3
Increase in other assets	0.7	0.0	1.9	0.3	2.8	2.1
Gross investment	28.9	21.6	37.7	63.5	98.4	43.4
Operating free cash flow	($12.5)	($2.2)	($13.6)	($38.4)	($65.6)	($9.1)
Nonoperating cash flow	0.9	0.9	1.6	0.2	0.2	(0.3)
Total cash flow before financing	($11.5)	($1.4)	($12.0)	($38.3)	($65.4)	($9.4)

Financial Cash Flow	1982	1983	1984	1985	1986	1987
Incr/(Decr) excess mkt securities	($7.9)	$17.5	($10.2)	($10.3)	$5.8	($2.6)
After-tax interest income	0.0	0.0	0.0	(0.5)	(0.4)	(0.3)
Decr/(Incr) in debt	(5.4)	(4.7)	(4.8)	(31.0)	(75.5)	(17.7)
After-tax interest expense	0.2	0.4	0.5	1.7	2.1	5.6
Decr/(Incr) cap oper leases	(0.7)	(0.7)	(0.8)	(0.9)	(1.0)	2.3
Implied interest on oper leases	0.4	0.5	0.5	0.6	0.6	0.5
Common dividends	2.1	2.8	2.8	2.8	2.9	2.9
Decr/(Incr) in common	(0.3)	(17.1)	0.0	(0.7)	0.0	0.0
Financial cash flow	($11.5)	($1.4)	($12.0)	($38.3)	($65.4)	($9.4)

Exhibit 5.14 **PRESTON CORPORATION, HISTORICAL FINANCIAL DATA,**
$ MILLIONS

Taxes on EBIT	1982	1983	1984	1985	1986	1987
Total tax provision	$2.4	$5.8	$5.2	$1.0	$7.1	$0.7
Tax shield on interest expense	0.2	0.4	0.5	1.7	2.0	4.5
Tax on oper lease adjustment	0.4	0.4	0.5	0.5	0.6	0.4
Less: taxes on interest income	0.0	0.0	0.0	(0.4)	(0.3)	(0.3)
Less: taxes on nonop income	(0.9)	(0.8)	(1.6)	(0.1)	(0.1)	0.2
Taxes on EBIT	$2.1	$5.8	$4.6	$2.6	$9.2	$5.6

EBIT Tax Rate	1982	1983	1984	1985	1986	1987
Taxes on EBIT	$2.1	$5.8	$4.6	$2.6	$9.2	$5.6
Divided by EBIT	6.9	12.4	12.8	8.6	18.8	12.5
= EBIT Tax Rate	30.57%	46.77%	36.02%	30.41%	48.97%	44.84%

Change in Working Capital	1982	1983	1984	1985	1986	1987
Increase in oper cash	$0.4	$1.0	$0.6	$0.0	$2.4	$1.7
Increase in accts receivable	7.0	9.3	0.3	14.1	4.6	8.7
Increase in inventories	0.2	0.7	(0.3)	6.5	1.9	1.0
Increase in other current assets	0.8	0.2	0.7	(3.6)	2.0	0.6
(Increase) in accts payable	(3.7)	(0.9)	1.4	(3.7)	(2.0)	(2.7)
(Increase) in other current liabs	0.4	(4.7)	(0.3)	(2.9)	(6.4)	(1.0)
Net change in working capital	$5.1	$5.6	$2.4	$10.4	$2.5	$8.3

Investment in Goodwill	1982	1983	1984	1985	1986	1987
Incr/(Decr) in balance sheet goodwill	$0.0	$0.0	$0.0	$3.2	$21.5	($0.3)
Amort of goodwill	0.0	0.0	0.0	0.0	0.1	0.6
Investment in goodwill	$0.0	$0.0	$0.0	$3.2	$21.6	$0.3

Nonoperating Cash Flow	1982	1983	1984	1985	1986	1987
After-tax nonoperating income	$0.9	$0.9	$1.6	$0.2	$0.2	($0.3)
Other	0.0	0.0	0.0	0.0	0.0	0.0
Nonoperating cash flow	$0.9	$0.9	$1.6	$0.2	$0.2	($0.3)

Exhibit 5.15 **PRESTON CORPORATION, HISTORICAL INVESTED CAPITAL,** $ MILLIONS

	1981	1982	1983	1984	1985	1986	1987
Current assets	$29.6	$38.0	$49.2	$50.5	$67.5	$78.4	$90.4
Non-interest current liabs	(21.2)	(24.5)	(30.1)	(29.0)	(35.6)	(44.0)	(47.7)
Working capital	8.4	13.5	19.1	21.5	31.9	34.4	42.7
Net property, plant, & equip	62.3	75.4	79.5	99.1	132.8	185.6	194.2
Capitalized operating leases	6.6	7.3	8.0	8.8	9.7	10.7	8.4
Goodwill	0.0	0.0	0.0	0.0	3.2	24.7	24.4
Other assets	0.5	1.2	1.2	3.1	3.4	6.2	8.3
Total invested capital	$77.8	$97.4	$107.8	$132.5	$181.0	$261.6	$278.0
Total debt	$4.0	$9.4	$14.1	$18.9	$49.9	$125.4	$143.1
Capitalized operating leases	6.6	7.3	8.0	8.8	9.7	10.7	8.4
Deferred income taxes	8.7	11.0	12.6	15.5	19.6	25.1	20.3
Common equity	69.4	72.7	93.6	99.6	101.8	106.2	109.4
	88.7	100.4	128.3	142.8	181.0	267.4	281.2
Less: excess mkt securities	(10.9)	(3.0)	(20.5)	(10.3)	0.0	(5.8)	(3.2)
Less: nonop assets	0.0	0.0	0.0	0.0	0.0	0.0	0.0
Total invested capital	$77.8	$97.4	$107.8	$132.5	$181.0	$261.6	$278.0
Invested cap ex goodwill	$77.8	$97.4	$107.8	$132.5	$177.8	$236.9	$253.6

Exhibit 5.16 PRESTON CORPORATION, HISTORICAL RATIOS FOR FORECAST ASSUMPTIONS, $ MILLIONS

	1981	1982	1983	1984	1985	1986	1987
Operations							
Revenue growth		12.5%	22.5%	10.0%	16.9%	19.7%	20.6%
Operating exp/revenues	88.8%	93.1%	91.7%	91.7%	93.6%	91.6%	92.5%
Gross margin	11.2%	6.9%	8.3%	8.3%	6.4%	8.4%	7.5%
Depreciation/revenues	6.5%	4.2%	4.1%	4.3%	4.3%	4.2%	5.2%
Operating margin	4.8%	2.7%	4.2%	3.9%	2.1%	4.2%	2.3%
Working Capital/Revenues							
Operating cash	2.0%	2.0%	2.0%	2.0%	1.7%	2.0%	2.0%
Trade receivables	9.1%	11.0%	12.1%	11.1%	12.5%	11.9%	11.4%
Other receivables	0.8%	0.9%	1.0%	0.9%	1.8%	1.2%	1.1%
Inventories	1.0%	0.9%	1.0%	0.8%	2.6%	2.6%	2.4%
Prepaid expenses	2.2%	2.3%	1.9%	2.0%	0.7%	1.1%	1.0%
Accounts payable	3.7%	4.9%	4.4%	3.5%	4.1%	3.9%	3.7%
Other current liabs	7.0%	6.1%	6.7%	6.2%	6.1%	6.6%	5.7%
Net working capital	4.3%	6.1%	7.0%	7.2%	9.1%	8.2%	8.4%
Prop, Plant, & Equipment (PPE)							
Gross PPE/revenues	50.6%	52.9%	47.1%	52.0%	58.5%	65.1%	58.9%
Net PPE/revenues	31.5%	33.9%	29.2%	33.1%	37.9%	44.3%	38.4%
Capital expenditures		$22.4	$15.3	$32.6	$32.2	$26.5	$35.0
Depreciation		$9.3	$11.2	$13.0	$15.0	$17.7	$26.4
Depr/gross PPE		9.3%	9.5%	10.1%	9.6%	8.6%	9.7%
Retirements/gross PPE		4.7%	4.1%	4.1%	(0.3%)	1.3%	3.6%
Taxes							
EBIT tax rate	49.0%	30.6%	46.8%	36.0%	30.4%	49.0%	44.8%
Marginal tax rate		49.0%	49.0%	49.0%	49.0%	49.0%	45.0%
Incr def tax/gross PPE		2.0%	1.2%	1.9%	2.0%	2.0%	0.3%
Incr def tax/tax prov		95.8%	27.6%	55.8%	410.0%	77.5%	142.9%
Other							
Goodwill/revenues	0.0%	0.0%	0.0%	0.0%	0.9%	5.9%	4.8%
Amortization of goodwill	$0.0	$0.0	$0.0	$0.0	$0.0	$0.1	$0.6
Other assets/revenues		0.5%	0.4%	1.0%	1.0%	1.5%	1.6%
Cap oper leases/revenues	0.3%	3.3%	2.9%	2.9%	2.8%	2.5%	1.7%

the exiting carriers. Moreover, because they were not hampered by the restrictive work practices tolerated during the days of regulation, nonunion carriers were better positioned to take advantage of deregulation than were unionized carriers.

However, the industry outlook appears to be brightening. Recent rate increases have not been heavily discounted and it appears that the industry has resolved to end the rate wars that have plagued its profitability. This price firming, in addition to recent increases in demand, has led to higher revenues and operating margins for Preston and for the rest of the industry. This trend may continue, but the decision of a major carrier or of several smaller carriers to attempt to gain market share by reducing rates could touch off further rate wars.

A large degree of consolidation has also occurred in the industry, and more consolidation is likely, although its pace may be slowed as the firming of rates retards potential bankruptcies. More takeovers seem possible in the future, and Preston has been regarded as a possible takeover target. (*Value Line* notes in its July 1, 1988, edition that "much of this [share price] rise is attributable to Preston's earnings improvement, but we suspect that with the stock trading below book value and the recent outbreak of takeover bids in the industry, buyout speculation is partly responsible.")

Developing Historical Financial Statements

To develop a complete historical perspective on Preston's performance, we must examine the behavior of its key value drivers and other noteworthy issues in its financial statements. This information gives us a basis for our forecasts and alerts us to factors that may influence our valuation. We can make several observations about Preston's historical financial statements.

Acquisitions   Preston made several acquisitions in 1985 and 1986; therefore, the pre-1985 data are not entirely comparable with subsequent years' data. In our forecasts the later data should be given more weight than the earlier data.

Deferred taxes   Beginning January 1, 1987, Preston reported its deferred income tax liability using the liability method, whereby the deferred tax liability is calculated using the tax rates that are expected to exist when the items that give rise to the deferred taxes reverse. Preston had previously used the deferred method, whereby deferred tax expense is calculated using the tax rates that exist when the deferral occurs. The result of this change was to increase Preston's 1987 net income by $211,000 ($.04 per share), and its cumulative effect on prior years was to increase the 1987 net income by

$5,752,000 ($1.00 per share). This is a one-time effect that should not affect the forecast.

Consolidation   One issue of consolidation that is often material to the valuation of a company is the extent to which the parent corporation guarantees the debt of its subsidiaries. Preston Corporation has guaranteed the secured notes of its wholly owned subsidiaries, Reeves Transportation Company and Bowie Hall Trucking, Inc., as well as the unsecured note of its subsidiary Smalley Transportation Company. Because these subsidiaries are fully consolidated, we have already accounted for the effect of all loan guarantees on the parent. Were the subsidiaries not wholly owned, the loan guarantee would be an off-balance-sheet liability of the parent and would affect its cost of capital.

Inventory accounting   Because Preston is a service business, its inventory is much less than that of a company that sells a tangible product. However, at least two components of its balance sheet—fuel and operating supplies, and tires on equipment in service—fall into this category. Preston Corporation uses LIFO inventory accounting. This means that the market value of inventory is understated during and following inflationary periods. Often LIFO inventory reserves (the difference between inventories at current cost and their stated LIFO value) are referred to as off-balance-sheet assets. However, for each extra dollar of future increase in LIFO reserves, an extra dollar of expense accrues against future profits; consequently, the two items cancel out. The only valuation effect of LIFO is that it often permits earlier realization of a tax shield, an effect that is already captured on the income statement.

Depreciation   Preston uses straight-line depreciation in its annual report, and it uses accelerated depreciation for tax purposes. Therefore, we must use the straight-line depreciation numbers when computing cash flow. The difference between tax depreciation and book depreciation is reflected in the deferred taxes account and consequently in the free cash flow—that is, Preston pays in cash fewer taxes than its books indicate it should pay.

Pension plans   As of December 31, 1986, the date of the last available information, Preston had an unfunded pension liability of approximately $20 million. Because we have not included the eventual funding of this liability in our cash flow forecasts, we will need to subtract the after-tax present value of these payments ($12.2 million) from the entity value estimates that we develop later in the valuation process.

Labor contracts   As of December 1987, approximately 42 percent of Preston's employees were employed by its largest subsidiary, Preston Trucking, and were members of the International Brotherhood of Teamsters, Chauffeurs, Warehousemen, and Helpers of America. They were covered by a three-year contract with the industry that expired on April 1, 1988, and a new three-year contract commenced on that date. These were the only employees of Preston Corporation covered by a collective bargaining agreement during that time period.

Labor contracts affect Preston's costs and, thus, its free cash flow. Because Preston owns substantial nonunion subsidiaries, it may have a cost advantage because it is not burdened by inflexible working rules to the same extent as its unionized competitors. However, we probably cannot assume that Preston will be able to pay lower wages to its nonunionized workers. Often, equivalent wages are necessary to ensure continued nonunionization.

Stock options   As of December 31, 1987, Preston reported having 231,676 options outstanding with an average exercise price of $20.55 and stock appreciation rights equal to the income tax incurred by the exercise of the executive stock options outstanding. In addition, in February 1988, it issued 331,500 nonqualified stock options with similar stock appreciation rights. These options have an exercise price of $11.25, but they cannot be exercised unless the fair market value of Preston's stock is at least $21.25 per share. The total value of the outstanding executive options ($4.5 million) must be subtracted from the entity value to obtain a valuation of Preston's equity.

Preferred stock   Although no preferred stock is outstanding, Preston is authorized to issue 2,500,000 no-par-value preferred shares. This provision in its charter allows the board of directors to issue additional shares without shareholder approval and thus may be intended to make a hostile takeover difficult.

Lawsuits and government actions   Preston states that no material legal or government actions are pending against it. If such actions were pending, the present value of their expected cost to Preston would have to be subtracted from our valuation.

Analyzing the Rate of Return on Invested Capital

Exhibit 5.17 displays the key value drivers for Preston's historical performance. The after-tax rate of return on invested capital has averaged 6.9

Exhibit 5.17 **PRESTON CORPORATION, HISTORICAL KEY VALUE DRIVERS**

	1981	1982	1983	1984	1985	1986	1987
Return on Invested Capital							
Revenues/avg capital		2.5	2.7	2.5	2.2	1.9	1.9
× EBIT/revenues		3.1%	4.6%	4.3%	2.5%	4.5%	2.5%
= Pretax ROIC		7.9%	12.1%	10.6%	5.5%	8.5%	4.6%
Operating tax rate		(2.7%)	33.9%	13.4%	(17.3%)	19.7%	36.9%
After-tax ROIC		8.1%	8.0%	9.2%	6.4%	6.8%	2.9%
At ROIC ex goodwill		8.1%	8.0%	9.2%	6.5%	7.3%	3.2%
Increm pretax ROIC			36.6%	2.2%	(11.5%)	15.8%	(12.9%)
Increm after-tax ROIC			7.3%	16.4%	(2.7%)	7.8%	(14.8%)
Return on avg equity		7.2%	7.9%	9.1%	4.3%	7.0%	0.3%
Return on sales		2.3%	2.4%	2.9%	1.2%	1.7%	0.1%
Investment Rates							
Net investment rate		275.4%	127.2%	222.9%	481.1%	533.8%	207.1%
(five-yr rolling avg)						356.4%	344.8%
Growth Rates							
Sales		12.5%	22.5%	10.0%	16.9%	19.7%	20.6%
NOPLAT			15.4%	35.2%	(9.1%)	49.8%	(47.5%)
EPS		(12.5%)	9.4%	33.3%	(51.1%)	65.1%	(95.9%)
Per Share Measures							
EPS (before extra items)	$1.23	$1.08	$1.18	$1.57	$0.77	$1.27	$0.05
Dividends per share	$0.45	$0.44	$0.50	$0.50	$0.50	$0.50	$0.50
Book value per share	$14.73	$15.36	$16.94	$17.27	$17.68	$18.44	$19.00
Avg shares outstanding (millions)	4.7	4.7	5.6	5.6	5.6	5.8	5.8
Financing							
Coverage (EBIT/interest)	94.0	15.3	14.4	11.8	2.2	4.3	1.1
Long-term debt/total cap	4.8%	8.8%	12.2%	13.1%	21.2%	43.2%	44.0%
Total debt/total cap	5.1%	9.7%	13.1%	14.3%	27.6%	47.9%	51.5%
Dividend payout ratio	36.2%	41.2%	42.4%	31.8%	65.1%	39.7%	966.7%
Working Capital							
Day's sales outstanding	33.1	40.1	44.2	40.6	45.8	43.4	41.7
Adj working cap/sales	4.3%	6.1%	7.0%	7.2%	9.1%	8.2%	8.4%
Current ratio	1.9	1.6	2.2	2.0	1.4	1.5	1.4

percent over the past six years. Excluding goodwill, the return has averaged 7 percent. These returns have remained relatively stable over time; however, they have declined somewhat in recent years, and the 1987 returns were less than half of the average returns of the prior years.

Over the same time period, the components of the return on invested capital (ROIC) also have declined. The operating margin dropped dramatically in 1985 and 1987, and capital turnover has steadily declined throughout the last six years.

Exhibit 5.18 compares the components of Preston's return on invested capital in 1987 to those of several other national network and interregional less-than-truckload carriers. Preston underperforms these comparables in almost every aspect.

Its higher operating expenses/revenue ratio results in an operating margin that is 36 percent below the comparable companies' average. Preston's overall operating margin (EBIT/revenue) has fluctuated between relatively low levels of 2.4 percent and 4.6 percent since 1982. As a result, the growth in NOPLAT has varied dramatically during the same period (from −47.4 percent to 49.2 percent). In addition, Preston has a higher amount of working capital; net property, plant, and equipment; and other assets per dollar of revenue than the comparable companies. As a result, it has a capital turnover ratio of 1.9 versus a 2.5 comparable average. These factors result in Preston Corporation's after-tax return on invested capital being nearly four percentage points lower than the average of the comparable companies (2.9 versus 6.9 percent).

The main culprit in Preston's declining operating margin is the intense rate competition that has plagued the industry since its deregulation in 1980. As we discussed earlier, this deregulation allowed an influx of new carriers into the industry and spurred rate wars as all carriers competed for market share. While the rates declined, however, the operating expenses, such as labor, fuel, and insurance, facing Preston and the rest of the industry continued to rise. As a result of these trends, operating margins have fallen dramatically. When projecting future operating margins, therefore, we will pay close attention to expectations of future trends in rates and in certain expenses (such as those established by the new labor contract with the Teamsters).

We also want to analyze Preston's historical performance relative to comparable companies in the industry. Unless we include comparable companies in our analysis, we will be unable to determine which aspects of Preston's performance occurred because of conditions that affected the entire industry and which aspects appear to be unique to Preston. With this information we are better able to project how expected industry trends will affect Preston. That is, in light of our expectations of improving rates, can we

Exhibit 5.18 **COMPARISON OF RATES OF RETURN ON INVESTED CAPITAL, 1987**

Company	$1 - \dfrac{\text{Operating expenses}}{\text{Revenue}} +$	$\dfrac{\text{Depreciation}}{\text{Revenue}} =$	Operating margin
Roadway Services	91.0%	6.0%	3.0%
Carolina Freight	91.8	4.8	3.4
Consolidated Freightways	91.2	4.4	4.4
Arkansas Best	90.5	5.6	3.9
Yellow Freight	89.9	5.6	4.5
Viking Freight	90.8	4.8	4.4
Average	90.9%	5.2%	3.9%
Preston	92.3%	5.2%	2.5*%

Company	$1 \div \dfrac{\text{Working capital}}{\text{Revenue}} +$	$\dfrac{\text{Net PPE}}{\text{Revenue}} +$	$\dfrac{\text{Long-term assets and goodwill}}{\text{Revenue}} =$	Capital turnover
Roadway Services	12.4%	28.6%	0.8%	2.4
Carolina Freight	5.2	33.2	1.0	2.5
Consolidated Freightways	7.2	26.0	8.6	2.4
Arkansas Best	5.6	32.0	2.1	2.5
Yellow Freight	5.2	36.9	1.1	2.6
Viking Freight	5.8	37.6	0.7	2.3
Average	6.0%	32.4%	2.4%	2.5
Preston	8.5%	37.5%	6.2%	1.9

Company	Operating margin $\times$	Capital turnover $\times$	Cash $1 - \text{tax rate} =$	After-tax return on invested capital
Roadway Services	3.0%	2.4	72.1%	5.2%
Carolina Freight	3.4	2.5	86.1	7.4
Consolidated Freightways	4.4	2.4	61.5	6.5
Arkansas Best	3.9	2.5	67.0	6.6
Yellow Freight	4.5	2.6	77.0	9.0
Viking Freight	4.4	2.3	64.5	6.5
Average	3.9%	2.5	71.4%	6.9%
Preston	2.5*%	1.9	63.1	2.9%

*Includes adjustment for operating leases.

expect Preston's performance to lag or lead those of its competitors? In addition, by comparing the components of Preston's operating margins to those of its competitors, we gain insights into the areas in which Preston is lagging its competitors. These areas could be those that management should focus on improving.

This same analysis is necessary for capital turnover, the other component of return on invested capital. We noted earlier that Preston lags the rest of the industry in every element of capital turnover. Preston's high level of long-term assets and goodwill to revenue likely can be explained by the fact that Preston has recently made a number of acquisitions. However, the existence of its high working-capital-to-revenue ratio and net property, plant, and equipment-to-revenue ratio suggests that Preston may not be managing its working capital and fixed assets as efficiently as its competitors do.

Analyzing the Investment Rate

The investment rate is also an important value driver. Investment by Preston in working capital; property, plant, and equipment; or other long-term assets and goodwill uses cash that would otherwise become free cash flow, available to debtholders and equityholders. However, if this investment earns returns greater than Preston's cost of capital, then the value of Preston will increase as a result of this investment (because the present value of the free cash flow it will generate is greater than the free cash flow that it uses).

Preston's historical investment rates, measured as a percentage of NO-PLAT, are shown in Exhibit 5.17. The net investment rate has fluctuated wildly, from 127.2 percent in 1983 to 533.8 percent in 1986. These fluctuations are largely due to acquisitions and other timing effects (for example, random total working capital fluctuations from year to year can lead to reasonably large swings in the calculated level of annual investment in working capital). The average net investment rate for the past five years is 344.8 percent, and the investment rate for 1987 was 207.1 percent.

Exhibit 5.19 shows the 1987 investment rate of Preston and comparable companies. Although Preston's investment rate is nearly twice the comparable companies' median rate, 89.7 percent, this may be accounted for by Preston's relatively low NOPLAT as a percentage of revenue in 1987. Preston appears to be maintaining a significant investment rate in the face of a low return on its assets. This indicates to us that rather than creating value for its shareholders, Preston's investment is actually destroying value.

Drawing Conclusions About the Sustainability of Rates of Return

We expect that Preston's rate of return will gradually increase over the forecast period, for these reasons:

Exhibit 5.19 **COMPARISON OF INVESTMENT RATES, 1987**

Company	Investment in working capital / NOPLAT	+	Investment in net PPE / NOPLAT	+	Investments in other long-term assets and goodwill / NOPLAT	=	Investment rate
Roadway Services	−58.8%		104.8%		−0.9%		45.2%
Carolina Freight	−15.0		79.7		−2.1		62.7
Consolidated Freight-ways	9.2		78.8		0.8		88.8
Arkansas Best	−57.8		156.4		−7.8		90.8
Yellow Freight	18.6		89.6		−5.5		102.7
Viking Freight	−40.5		379.9		4.0		343.4
Average	−24.1%		148.2%		−1.9%		122.3%
Preston	105.1%		80.5*%		21.5%		207.1*%

*Adjusted for capitalized operating leases.

- While Preston's current rate of return is very low relative to that of comparable companies, management is taking steps to improve the performance. These include emphasizing more profitable geographic regions and concentrating on improving productivity and on cost control.
- Preston's current operating margin (as of July 1988) is showing a substantial increase from its historical low in 1987 due to several recent rate increases enacted by the industry.
- The period of rationalization in the trucking industry appears to be coming to a close. Fierce rate competition and a shakeout in the industry have alleviated much of the excess capacity that existed.

Therefore, we expect the industry to reattain normal rates of return.

PRESTON CASE, STEP 3: DEVELOP FORECAST ASSUMPTIONS AND SCENARIOS

Our forecast assumptions for Preston are outlined in Exhibit 5.20.

Exhibit 5.20 **PRESTON CORPORATION, FORECAST ASSUMPTIONS**, $ MILLIONS

	1988	1989	1990	1991	1992	1993	1994	1995	1996	1997	Perpetuity
Operations											
Revenue growth	20.8%	14.8%	12.6%	10.8%	9.3%	9.5%	9.4%	9.6%	9.7%	9.9%	9.4%
Operating exp/revenues	90.8%	90.4%	90.0%	89.6%	89.1%	89.1%	89.1%	89.1%	89.1%	89.1%	89.1%
Gross margin	9.2%	9.6%	10.0%	10.4%	10.9%	10.9%	10.9%	10.9%	10.9%	10.9%	10.9%
Depreciation/revenues	4.7%	4.5%	4.5%	4.5%	4.6%	-4.8%	5.0%	5.1%	5.3%	5.4%	5.5%
Operating margin	4.5%	5.1%	5.5%	5.9%	6.2%	6.1%	5.9%	5.7%	5.6%	5.4%	5.3%
Working Capital/Revenues											
Operating cash	2.0%	2.0%	2.0%	2.0%	2.0%	2.0%	2.0%	2.0%	2.0%	2.0%	2.0%
Trade receivables	11.9%	11.9%	11.9%	11.9%	11.9%	11.9%	11.9%	11.9%	11.9%	11.9%	11.9%
Other receivables	1.4%	1.4%	1.4%	1.4%	1.4%	1.4%	1.4%	1.4%	1.4%	1.4%	1.4%
Inventories	2.5%	2.5%	2.5%	2.5%	2.5%	2.5%	2.5%	2.5%	2.5%	2.5%	2.5%
Prepaid expenses	0.9%	0.9%	0.9%	0.9%	0.9%	0.9%	0.9%	0.9%	0.9%	0.9%	0.9%
Accounts payable	3.9%	3.9%	3.9%	3.9%	3.9%	3.9%	3.9%	3.9%	3.9%	3.9%	3.9%
Other current liabs	6.1%	6.1%	6.1%	6.1%	6.1%	6.1%	6.1%	6.1%	6.1%	6.1%	6.1%
Net working capital	8.7%	8.7%	8.7%	8.7%	8.7%	8.7%	8.7%	8.7%	8.7%	8.7%	8.7%
Prop, Plant, & Equipment (PPE)											
Gross PPE/Revenues	53.5%	52.1%	51.6%	52.3%	54.0%	56.1%	58.2%	59.9%	61.4%	62.5%	63.5%
Net PPE/revenues	33.6%	31.9%	30.8%	30.7%	31.3%	32.4%	33.4%	34.1%	34.5%	34.6%	34.6%
Capital expenditures	$40.0	$50.0	$55.0	$65.0	$75.0	$90.0	$100.0	$110.0	$120.0	$130.0	$140.0
Depreciation	$28.8	$31.7	$35.4	$39.4	$44.3	$50.0	$56.9	$64.5	$72.9	$81.9	$91.5
Depr/gross PPE	9.7%	9.7%	9.7%	9.7%	9.7%	9.7%	9.7%	9.7%	9.7%	9.7%	9.7%
Retirements/gross PPE	3.6%	3.6%	3.6%	3.6%	3.6%	3.6%	3.6%	3.6%	3.6%	3.6%	3.6%
Taxes											
EBIT tax rate	39.0%	39.0%	39.0%	39.0%	39.0%	39.0%	39.0%	39.0%	39.0%	39.0%	39.0%
Marginal tax rate	39.0%	39.0%	39.0%	39.0%	39.0%	39.0%	39.0%	39.0%	39.0%	39.0%	39.0%
Incr def tax/gross PPE	0.8%	0.8%	0.8%	0.8%	0.8%	0.8%	0.8%	0.8%	0.8%	0.8%	0.8%
Incr def tax/tax Prov	57.2%	41.4%	34.4%	30.6%	29.1%	31.4%	35.0%	38.6%	42.0%	44.9%	48.0%
Other											
Goodwill/revenues	3.9%	3.3%	2.9%	2.5%	2.2%	2.0%	1.8%	1.6%	1.4%	1.2%	1.1%
Amortization of goodwill	$0.6	$0.6	$0.6	$0.6	$0.6	$0.6	$0.6	$0.6	$0.6	$0.6	$0.6
Other assets/revenue	1.6%	1.6%	1.6%	1.6%	1.6%	1.6%	1.6%	1.6%	1.6%	1.6%	1.6%
Cap oper leases/revenues	1.5%	1.4%	1.4%	1.4%	1.4%	1.4%	1.4%	1.4%	1.4%	1.4%	1.4%

Determining the Overall Structure of the Forecast

The Preston forecast is a typical demand-driven forecast. An integrated income statement and balance sheet forecast are developed first, followed by the free cash flow statement.

Developing Relevant Scenarios

We are presenting the most probable scenario for Preston in this chapter. Chapter 8 presents and discusses two alternative scenarios.

Developing a Point of View About a Forecast for Each Variable

We have developed assumptions for the Preston forecast that are reasonable, given the historical performance of the company and expected trends in the industry.

Our approach to forecasting each item is certainly not the only appropriate technique. It would be impossible to enumerate all the possibilities. Therefore, we have chosen to simply present one method to indicate the types of issues that should be addressed.

Revenues   Revenue growth is determined by the growth in the quantity of carrier services provided (tonnage) and by the growth in prices (rates). Tonnage is largely determined by the level of industrial production and by the ability of the company to capture increased market share as the industry continues to undergo consolidation. Through the first half of 1988, Preston's tonnage was 18.7 percent higher than it was during the same period of 1987. After taking into account a seasonal drop in tonnage during the fourth quarter, we project total tonnage growth to be 16.2 percent in 1988.

The industry is currently facing a large upswing in demand, and as a result, many companies are operating at levels near their permanent capacity. For these reasons, we forecast a large increase in Preston's tonnage, slowing over the next several years to a permanent real growth level of 3 percent, which is our forecast of the long-term rate of real industrial production growth.

As discussed earlier, rates in the industry are firming. The industry enacted a 3.3 percent rate increase in October 1987 and additional 3.5 percent rate increases in April and late June 1988. This growth is in contrast to the recent rate stagnation faced by the industry due to increased competition since deregulation, and it is allowing the industry to move closer to achieving normal returns on its invested capital. However, rate increases are implemented slowly because approximately half of the industry's demand is locked in at defined rates in contracts. Thus, full rate increases cannot be achieved until these contracts expire.

We are therefore forecasting the recent and future rate increases to be gradually phased in, and thus we expect an increase of 4 percent during 1988 and a slow growth in rates over the next several years. We forecast the rate growth to eventually level off to the rate of expected inflation (see Exhibit 5.10 for the calculation of expected inflation from the term structure of interest rates). Our revenue growth forecast is as follows (the total revenue growth is the product rather than the sum of the component growth rates):

	Tonnage growth	Rate growth	Revenue growth
1988	16.2%	4.0%	20.8%
1989	9.5	4.8	14.8
1990	7.0	5.2	12.6
1991	4.8	5.7	10.8
1992	3.0	6.1	9.3
1993	3.0	6.3	9.5
1994	3.0	6.2	9.4
1995	3.0	6.4	9.6
1996	3.0	6.5	9.7
1997	3.0	6.7	9.9

Operating expenses   As shown in Exhibit 5.16, Preston's operating expenses as a percentage of revenues have fluctuated between 91.6 percent and 93.6 percent during the last five years. Over the past several years a few trends are apparent in specific components of this category. Claims and insurance costs as a percentage of revenues have risen by almost 40 percent since 1985. Much of this increase has been due to the occurrence of an unusually high number of severe accidents; therefore, we believe this trend will slacken. Over the same period, salaries, wages, and fringes as a percentage of revenues, and purchased transportation as a percentage of revenues, have experienced small yet steady increases and declines, respectively.

We forecast operating expenses to decline as a percentage of revenues during the next several years. A primary reason for this forecast is our expectation of continued rising rates. We believe that the recent rate increases enacted by Preston will more than offset the effects of the new three-year labor contract that took effect April 1, 1988, between the Teamsters and the trucking industry (and which calls for a 7-percent wage-cost increase in the first year, and a 2.5-percent to 3-percent increase in each of the following years). In addition, because of its relatively slow growth,

Preston's labor costs as a percentage of revenues will be less affected than those of faster-growing firms by the new contract. This is because newly and recently hired employees will receive the largest pay increases, and these employees are most prevalent at quickly growing firms. Overall, rates should rise more quickly than costs in the near future, and thus Preston's gross margin should also rise.

Depreciation expense   Depreciation as a percentage of gross property, plant, and equipment has remained in the 9 to 10 percent range over the past six years. This should not change, so we have forecasted depreciation to equal 9.7 percent of the prior period's gross property, plant, and equipment, the same as its 1987 level.

Working capital   For valuation purposes, we should define working capital to include only the "operating" types of working capital. In the case of Preston, it is defined as the sum of the operating cash, trade receivables, other receivables, inventories, and prepaid expenses less accounts payable and other current liabilities. It excludes excess marketable securities and short-term debt.

Working capital should be considered an investment—a use of potential free cash flow. It is an investment because a level of working capital is necessary to generate revenue and entails having cash tied up in inventories and accounts receivable rather than being available to debt and equity holders as free cash flow. Therefore, other things being equal, increases in working capital requirements reduce the value of a company.

We could not discern any trends in Preston's working capital as a percentage of revenues. Over the last three years, net working capital has remained in the range of 8.2 percent to 9.1 percent of revenues. None of the individual components has shown significant change, either. We will forecast Preston's working capital to remain about where it has been in relation to sales.

Consider the following when forecasting working capital:

- How does the company's inventory accounting method (LIFO versus FIFO) affect its reported inventories?
- Does the company's changing mix of businesses affect its need for working capital?
- Is the company planning any action to reduce its working capital (for example, just-in-time inventory system)?
- If a trend in working capital is discernible, will the improvement/ deterioration continue or will it stabilize?

We have chosen to focus on working capital as a percentage of revenues. We also could have looked at working capital growth rates or how
working capital changes in relation to changes in revenue levels.

Year-end working capital can be fairly volatile simply because it is
measured only on the last day of the year. Average measures are probably
more stable yet not generally available. Therefore, do not give too much
weight to minor, random, year-to-year fluctuations. Focus instead on major
trends.

Fixed assets and depreciation   Preston owns a variety of fixed assets,
including trailers, tractors, trucks, freight terminals, retail outlets for the sale
of salvaged freight, and tire-recapping facilities. Fixed assets are probably
the trickiest part of the forecast. Most of the company's revenues, costs, and
working capital are affected somewhat equally by inflation. Since fixed
assets are not replaced each year, however, it is difficult to forecast the cost
of replacing old assets that wear out.

For Preston, we have made some fairly simple assumptions. We assume
that it takes a stable amount of fixed assets to generate each dollar of sales.
We expect that the relatively low levels of inflation experienced over the
past several years will persist in the near future and will not materially alter
this assumption. Therefore, we predict that over the forecast period, the
ratio of revenue to property, plant, and equipment will remain near its
historical average. Note that these assumptions would not work well with
fast-growing companies or in an unstable inflationary environment.

Accumulated depreciation is the prior period's accumulated depreciation plus the current period's depreciation expense minus the book value of
assets retired in the current period.

We will assume that fixed assets are used until they are fully depreciated
and that they have no material scrap value. Therefore, the amount of assets
retired from gross property, plant, and equipment will equal the amount of
the reduction in accumulated depreciation. We have set the level of retire-
ments at 3.6 percent of gross property, plant, and equipment. This level is
equal to that experienced in 1987, which we believe to be a reasonable
rate.

Income taxes   We estimated Preston's historical marginal income tax rate
to be about 49 percent. This was a 46-percent federal rate plus an effective
3-percent state and local rate. The 1986 Tax Reform Act reduces Preston's
marginal federal rate to 40 percent in 1987 and to 34 percent beginning in
1988. Adding a provision for state and local taxes (net of the federal tax
benefit derived from them), we estimate Preston's marginal income tax rate
will be 45 percent in 1987 and 39 percent beginning in 1988. (The implied

state and local tax rate increases from 3 to 5 percent because Preston's investment tax credit shelter disappears and because the federal tax benefit resulting from the state and local tax shelter is diminished.)

Preston's EBIT tax rate has historically been below its marginal rate, as shown in Exhibit 5.14. This was primarily due to investment tax credits that have been eliminated by the 1986 Tax Reform Act. Therefore, we have forecasted Preston's EBIT tax rate to equal its marginal income tax rate.

The total income tax provision on the income statement is the sum of two elements: Preston's EBIT multiplied by the EBIT tax rate, and the marginal tax rate multiplied by Preston's net interest income and nonoperating income less its interest expense.

The increase in accumulated deferred income taxes as a percentage of the income tax provision has fluctuated widely. Deferred taxes can have a significant effect on the timing of free cash flow because they represent the delay of a cash outflow—taxes. They arise because a company uses a depreciation schedule to calculate its taxes that is different from the schedule it uses to produce its financial statements. We are forecasting the increase in accumulated deferred taxes to be 0.8 percent of Preston's gross plant, property, and equipment. This percentage is Preston's recent historical average.

Financing The amortization schedule for Preston's existing debt is provided in the annual report. New debt or marketable securities are created automatically in our forecast to balance the sources and uses of cash.

The interest rate on existing debt is forecast to equal the effective rate in 1987, 11 percent. The rate on new debt and operating leases is equal to Preston's current marginal borrowing rate of 11 percent. This rate is derived in the cost of capital chapter that follows.

We also expect Preston to have a $.50 per share dividend payout in 1988, and for the remainder of the forecast period we expect dividends to average approximately 43 percent of net income.

Other Goodwill amortization should remain constant at $0.6 million per year since we are not forecasting any acquisitions. The amount of goodwill on the balance sheet will decline each year by the amount of the amortization.

We possess very little information about the nonoperating income items, which are composed of gains (or losses) on the disposal of property and equipment and of the "other income" category on Preston's income statement. Thus we forecast zero growth in them. It is impossible to generalize about the treatment of nonoperating items; just be careful and remember to take them into consideration in your valuation.

"Other" assets on the balance sheet are forecast to remain at the same percentage of revenues as they were in 1987. Unfortunately, we possess no information regarding what this category contains. Therefore, we are assuming that a certain level of these assets is necessary to generate each dollar of revenue.

Deciding on the Length of the Forecast

As we discussed earlier, since its deregulation in 1980 the industry has suffered through a period of intense competition. However, the resulting shakeout in the industry and the recent rate increases indicate that this syndrome is ending. We are forecasting a continued gradual improvement and eventually a stabilization of the operating performance of Preston Corporation and of the industry. Although we expect this stabilization to occur within five years, we have chosen to provide for the reader a forecast horizon of ten years. As long as our explicit free cash flow forecasts for this additional five-year period are based on the same underlying assumptions as our continuing-value calculation, the length of our forecast horizon will not affect the valuation.

PRESTON CASE, STEP 4: CALCULATE AND EVALUATE THE FREE CASH FLOW FORECAST

Exhibits 5.21 to 5.26 on the following pages show the resulting forecast of Preston's income statement, balance sheet, free cash flow, and supporting information. But don't relax yet; this is only the beginning. We now have to evaluate this forecast.

We started the forecast by suggesting that we expect Preston's future performance to be better than its past performance. Exhibit 5.26 summarizes the key value drivers derived from the Preston forecast.

The incremental after-tax rate of return on net new invested capital averages 9.5 percent.* This is much higher than the historical average return of 2.7 percent. How can we account for this jump? The major change is the increase in operating margin that we are forecasting. As a result of improve-

---

*The first two years of incremental returns are high because they incorporate small changes in margins on the base level of capital. This points out one of the problems of interpreting incremental returns. These calculations assume that all NOPLAT increases are related to new capital and that none of the NOPLAT increase is associated with existing capital. Nevertheless, the incremental returns are the same whether they are attributed to existing or to new capital.

ment in margin, EBIT rises significantly, and thus the incremental rate of return also increases dramatically.

Will Preston benefit from the new tax law? Our forecast says that it will, yet we are concerned that existing competitive forces may cause Preston to return some of its tax windfall to consumers in the form of lower prices. Unfortunately, no one can be sure how corporate taxes work their way through the economy and who ultimately bears the corporate tax burden.

The forecasted net investment rate settles down to 97.3 percent in later years, well below the historical investment rate of 346 percent. However, this investment rate is entirely consistent with the projected revenue and NOPLAT growth rates of about 9.6 percent. Also, consider that since the decline in taxes is expected to increase Preston's rate of return, Preston's investment rate can be lower while Preston maintains the same rate of growth.

Exhibit 5.21 **PRESTON CORPORATION, FORECASTED INCOME STATEMENT,** $ MILLIONS

Income Statement	1988	1989	1990	1991	1992	1993	1994	1995	1996	1997	1998
Revenues	$610.8	$700.9	$789.5	$874.9	$955.9	$1,046.8	$1,145.3	$1,254.8	$1,376.6	$1,512.5	$1,654.5
Operating expenses	(554.5)	(633.7)	(710.5)	(783.7)	(852.1)	(933.2)	(1,021.0)	(1,118.6)	(1,227.2)	(1,348.3)	(1,474.9)
Depreciation expense	(28.8)	(31.7)	(35.4)	(39.4)	(44.3)	(50.0)	(56.9)	(64.5)	(72.9)	(81.9)	(91.5)
Operating income	27.4	35.5	43.6	51.8	59.4	63.6	67.4	71.6	76.5	82.3	88.0
Amortization of goodwill	(0.6)	(0.6)	(0.6)	(0.6)	(0.6)	(0.6)	(0.6)	(0.6)	(0.6)	(0.6)	(0.6)
Nonoperating income	(0.5)	(0.5)	(0.5)	(0.5)	(0.5)	(0.5)	(0.5)	(0.5)	(0.5)	(0.5)	(0.5)
Interest income	0.3	0.0	0.0	0.0	0.0	0.0	0.0	0.0	0.0	0.0	0.0
Interest expense	(15.4)	(16.9)	(18.8)	(20.6)	(22.6)	(24.7)	(27.8)	(31.2)	(34.8)	(38.7)	(42.7)
Earnings before taxes	11.1	17.5	23.7	30.1	35.7	37.8	38.5	39.4	40.7	42.5	44.3
Income taxes	(4.6)	(7.1)	(9.5)	(12.0)	(14.2)	(15.0)	(15.2)	(15.6)	(16.1)	(16.8)	(17.5)
Income before extra items	6.5	10.4	14.2	18.1	21.5	22.8	23.2	23.8	24.6	25.7	26.8
Effect of accounting change	0.0	0.0	0.0	0.0	0.0	0.0	0.0	0.0	0.0	0.0	0.0
Net income	$6.5	$10.4	$14.2	$18.1	$21.5	$22.8	$23.2	$23.8	$24.6	$25.7	$26.8

Statement of Retained Earnings	1988	1989	1990	1991	1992	1993	1994	1995	1996	1997	1998
Beginning retained earnings	$85.8	$89.5	$96.1	$105.1	$116.8	$131.9	$148.3	$165.1	$182.4	$199.2	$216.5
Net income	6.5	10.4	14.2	18.1	21.5	22.8	23.2	23.8	24.6	25.7	26.8
Common dividends	(2.9)	(3.8)	(5.2)	(6.4)	(6.4)	(6.4)	(6.4)	(6.6)	(7.8)	(8.4)	(9.0)
Adjustments	0.0	0.0	0.0	0.0	0.0	0.0	0.0	0.0	0.0	0.0	0.0
Ending retained earnings	$89.5	$96.1	$105.1	$116.8	$131.9	$148.3	$165.1	$182.4	$199.2	$216.5	$234.3

Exhibit 5.22 **PRESTON CORPORATION, FORECASTED BALANCE SHEET**, $ MILLIONS

	1988	1989	1990	1991	1992	1993	1994	1995	1996	1997	1998
Operating cash	$12.2	$14.0	$15.8	$17.5	$19.1	$20.9	$22.9	$25.1	$27.5	$30.2	$33.1
Excess marketable securities	0.0	0.0	0.0	0.0	0.0	0.0	0.0	0.0	0.0	0.0	0.0
Trade receivables	73.0	83.8	94.3	104.5	114.2	125.1	136.9	149.9	164.5	180.7	197.7
Other receivables	8.3	9.5	10.7	11.9	13.0	14.2	15.5	17.0	18.7	20.5	22.4
Inventories	15.3	17.6	19.8	22.0	24.0	26.3	28.7	31.5	34.5	38.0	41.5
Prepaid expenses	5.5	6.4	7.2	7.9	8.7	9.5	10.4	11.4	12.5	13.7	15.0
Current assets	114.4	131.2	147.8	163.8	179.0	196.0	214.4	234.9	257.7	283.2	309.8
Gross property, plant, & equip	326.9	365.1	407.0	457.3	515.9	587.3	666.1	752.2	845.1	944.7	1,050.7
Accumulated depreciation	(121.5)	(141.4)	(163.6)	(188.4)	(216.3)	(247.7)	(283.4)	(324.0)	(369.8)	(421.2)	(478.7)
Net property, plant, & equip	205.4	223.7	243.3	268.9	299.6	339.6	382.7	428.2	475.3	523.4	571.9
Goodwill	23.8	23.2	22.6	22.0	21.4	20.8	20.2	19.6	19.0	18.4	17.8
Other assets	9.8	10.9	12.2	13.06	14.8	16.2	17.8	19.4	21.3	23.4	25.6
Total assets	$353.3	$389.0	$426.0	$468.3	$514.8	$572.6	$635.1	$702.2	$773.4	$848.5	$925.1
Short-term debt	$18.2	$19.8	$83.4	$23.1	$24.7	$41.8	$28.9	$31.4	$34.2	$37.4	$40.4
Accounts payable	23.7	27.3	30.7	34.0	37.2	40.7	44.5	48.8	53.5	58.8	64.3
Other current liabilities	37.6	43.1	48.5	53.8	58.8	64.4	70.4	77.2	84.7	93.0	101.7
Total current liabilities	79.5	90.1	162.7	110.9	120.7	146.9	143.8	157.3	172.4	189.2	206.5
Long-term debt	118.1	115.5	51.4	49.7	48.7	32.1	31.2	30.5	30.0	29.5	29.5
New long-term debt	19.7	37.9	54.2	134.5	153.0	180.2	224.4	255.4	288.6	322.6	355.6
Deferred income taxes	22.9	25.8	29.1	32.8	36.9	41.6	46.9	52.9	59.7	67.2	75.6
Common stock	23.6	23.6	23.6	23.6	23.6	23.6	23.6	23.6	23.6	23.6	23.6
Retained earnings	89.5	96.1	105.1	116.8	131.9	148.3	165.1	182.4	199.2	216.5	234.3
Total common equity	113.1	119.7	128.7	140.4	155.5	171.9	188.7	206.0	222.8	240.1	257.9
Total liabilities and equity	$353.3	$389.0	$426.0	$468.3	$514.8	$572.6	$635.1	$702.2	$773.4	$848.5	$925.1

Exhibit 5.23 **PRESTON CORPORATION, FORECASTED FREE CASH FLOW**, $ MILLIONS

Free Cash Flow	1988	1989	1990	1991	1992	1993	1994	1995	1996	1997	1998
Revenues	$610.8	$700.9	$789.5	$874.9	$955.9	$1,046.8	$1,145.3	$1,254.8	$1,376.6	$1,512.5	$1,654.5
Operating expenses	(554.5)	(633.7)	(710.5)	(783.7)	(852.1)	(933.2)	(1,021.0)	(1,118.6)	(1,227.2)	(1,348.3)	(1,474.9)
Depreciation expense	(28.8)	(31.7)	(35.4)	(39.4)	(44.3)	(50.0)	(56.9)	(64.5)	(72.9)	(81.9)	(91.5)
Adjustment for operating leases	1.0	1.1	1.3	1.4	1.5	1.7	1.8	2.0	2.2	2.4	2.7
Adjusted EBIT	28.4	36.6	44.9	53.1	61.0	65.3	69.2	73.7	78.8	84.7	90.7
Taxes on EBIT	(11.1)	(14.3)	(17.5)	(20.7)	(23.8)	(25.5)	(27.0)	(28.7)	(30.7)	(33.0)	(35.4)
Change in deferred taxes	2.6	2.9	3.3	3.7	4.1	4.7	5.3	6.0	6.8	7.6	8.4
NOPLAT	19.9	25.3	30.6	36.1	41.3	44.5	47.6	51.0	54.8	59.2	63.8
Depreciation	28.8	31.7	35.4	39.4	44.3	50.0	56.9	64.5	72.9	81.9	91.5
Gross cash flow	48.8	56.9	66.0	75.5	85.6	94.5	104.5	115.5	127.7	141.1	155.3
Change in working capital	10.3	7.8	7.7	7.4	7.0	7.9	8.6	9.5	10.6	11.8	12.3
Capital expenditures	40.0	50.0	55.0	65.0	75.0	90.0	100.0	110.0	120.0	130.0	140.0
Capitalized operating leases	0.8	0.9	1.0	1.1	1.2	1.3	1.5	1.6	1.8	2.0	2.2
PPE from acquisitions	0.0	0.0	0.0	0.0	0.0	0.0	0.0	0.0	0.0	0.0	0.0
Investment in goodwill	0.0	0.0	0.0	0.0	0.0	0.0	0.0	0.0	0.0	0.0	0.0
Increase in other assets	1.5	1.1	1.4	1.3	1.3	1.4	1.5	1.7	1.9	2.1	2.2
Gross investment	52.7	59.8	65.1	74.9	84.5	100.7	111.6	122.8	134.3	145.9	156.7
Operating free cash flow	($3.9)	($2.9)	$0.9	$0.7	$1.1	($6.1)	($7.1)	($7.4)	($6.6)	($4.8)	($1.4)
Nonoperating cash flow	(0.3)	(0.3)	(0.3)	(0.3)	(0.3)	(0.3)	(0.3)	(0.3)	(0.3)	(0.3)	(0.3)
Total cash flow before financing	($4.2)	($3.2)	$0.6	$0.3	$0.8	($6.5)	($7.4)	($7.7)	($6.9)	($5.1)	($1.7)

Financial Cash Flow	1988	1989	1990	1991	1992	1993	1994	1995	1996	1997	1998
Incr/(Decr) in excess mkt securities	($3.2)	$0.0	$0.0	$0.0	$0.0	$0.0	$0.0	$0.0	$0.0	$0.0	$0.0
After-tax interest income	(0.2)	0.0	0.0	0.0	0.0	0.0	0.0	0.0	0.0	0.0	0.0
Decr/(Incr) in debt	(12.9)	(17.1)	(15.8)	(18.4)	(19.1)	(27.7)	(30.4)	(32.8)	(35.5)	(36.6)	(36.2)
After-tax interest expense	9.4	10.3	11.5	12.6	13.8	15.1	17.0	19.0	21.2	23.6	26.0
Decr/(Incr) in cap oper leases	(0.8)	(0.9)	(1.0)	(1.1)	(1.2)	(1.3)	(1.5)	(1.6)	(1.8)	(2.0)	(2.2)
Implied interest on oper leases	0.6	0.7	0.8	0.8	0.9	1.0	1.1	1.2	1.4	1.5	1.6
Common dividends	2.9	3.8	5.2	6.4	6.4	6.4	6.4	6.6	7.8	8.4	9.0
Decr/(Incr) in common	0.0	0.0	0.0	0.0	0.0	0.0	0.0	0.0	0.0	0.0	0.0
Financial cash flow	($4.2)	($3.2)	$0.6	$0.3	$0.8	($6.5)	($7.4)	($7.7)	($6.9)	($5.1)	($1.7)

Exhibit 5.24 PRESTON CORPORATION, FORECASTED FINANCIAL DATA, $ MILLIONS

	1988	1989	1990	1991	1992	1993	1994	1995	1996	1997	1998
Taxes on EBIT											
Total tax provision	$4.6	$7.1	$9.5	$12.0	$14.2	$15.0	$15.2	$15.6	$16.1	$16.8	$17.5
Tax shield on interest expense	6.0	6.6	7.3	8.0	8.8	9.6	10.8	12.2	13.6	15.1	16.6
Tax on oper lease adjustment	0.4	0.4	0.5	0.5	0.6	0.6	0.7	0.8	0.9	1.0	1.0
Less: taxes on interest income	(0.1)	(0.0)	0.0	(0.0)	(0.0)	(0.0)	(0.0)	0.0	(0.0)	(0.0)	0.0
Less: taxes on nonop income	0.2	0.2	0.2	0.2	0.2	0.2	0.2	0.2	0.2	0.2	0.2
Taxes on EBIT	$11.1	$14.3	$17.5	$20.7	$23.8	$25.5	$27.0	$28.7	$30.7	$33.0	$35.4
EBIT Tax Rate											
Taxes on EBIT	$11.1	$14.3	$17.5	$20.7	$23.8	$25.5	$27.0	$28.7	$30.7	$33.0	$35.4
Divided by EBIT	28.4	36.6	44.9	53.1	61.0	65.3	69.2	73.7	78.8	84.7	90.7
= EBIT tax rate	39.0%	39.0%	39.0%	39.0%	39.0%	39.0%	39.0%	39.0%	39.0%	39.0%	39.0%
Change in Working Capital											
Increase in oper cash	$2.1	$1.8	$1.8	$1.7	$1.6	$1.8	$2.0	$2.2	$2.4	$2.7	$2.8
Increase in accts receivable	17.9	12.0	11.8	11.4	10.8	12.1	13.1	14.6	16.2	18.1	18.9
Increase in inventories	3.4	2.3	2.2	2.1	2.0	2.3	2.5	2.7	3.1	3.4	3.6
Increase in other current assets	0.5	0.8	0.8	0.8	0.7	0.8	0.9	1.0	1.1	1.2	1.3
(Increase) in accts payable	(4.8)	(3.5)	(3.4)	(3.3)	(3.1)	(3.5)	(3.8)	(4.3)	(4.7)	(5.3)	(5.5)
(Increase) in other current liabs	(8.8)	(5.5)	(5.4)	(5.3)	(5.0)	(5.6)	(6.1)	(6.7)	(7.5)	(8.4)	(8.7)
Net change in working capital	$10.3	$7.8	$7.7	$7.4	$7.0	$7.9	$8.6	$9.5	$10.6	$11.8	$12.3
Investment in Goodwill											
Incr in balance sheet goodwill	($0.6)	($0.6)	($0.6)	($0.6)	($0.6)	($0.6)	($0.6)	($0.6)	($0.6)	($0.6)	($0.6)
Amort of goodwill	0.6	0.6	0.6	0.6	0.6	0.6	0.6	0.6	0.6	0.6	0.6
Investment in goodwill	$0.0	$0.0	$0.0	$0.0	$0.0	$0.0	$0.0	$0.0	$0.0	$0.0	$0.0
Nonoperating Cash Flow											
After-tax nonoperating income	($0.3)	($0.3)	($0.3)	($0.3)	($0.3)	($0.3)	($0.3)	($0.3)	($0.3)	($0.3)	($0.3)
Other	0.0	0.0	0.0	0.0	0.0	0.0	0.0	0.0	0.0	0.0	0.0
Nonoperating cash flow	($0.3)	($0.3)	($0.3)	($0.3)	($0.3)	($0.3)	($0.3)	($0.3)	($0.3)	($0.3)	($0.3)

Exhibit 5.25 **PRESTON CORPORATION, FORECASTED INVESTED CAPITAL**, $ MILLIONS

	1988	1989	1990	1991	1992	1993	1994	1995	1996	1997	1998
Current assets	$114.4	$131.2	$147.8	$163.8	$179.0	$196.0	$214.4	$234.9	$257.7	$283.2	$309.8
Non-interest current liabilities	(61.3)	(70.4)	(79.2)	(87.8)	(95.9)	(105.1)	(115.0)	(126.0)	(138.2)	(151.8)	(166.1)
Working capital	53.0	60.9	68.6	76.0	83.0	90.9	99.5	109.0	119.6	131.4	143.7
Net property, plant, & equip	205.4	223.7	243.3	268.9	299.6	339.6	382.7	428.2	475.3	523.4	571.9
Capitalized operating leases	9.2	10.1	11.1	12.3	13.5	14.8	16.3	18.0	19.8	21.7	23.9
Goodwill	23.8	23.2	22.6	22.0	21.4	20.8	20.2	19.6	19.0	18.4	17.8
Other assets	9.8	10.9	12.2	13.6	14.8	16.2	17.8	19.4	21.3	23.4	25.6
Total invested capital	$301.2	$328.8	$357.9	$392.7	$432.3	$482.4	$536.5	$594.2	$655.0	$718.4	$783.0
Total debt	$156.0	$173.1	$188.9	$207.3	$226.5	$254.1	$284.5	$317.3	$352.8	$389.3	$425.5
Capitalized operating leases	9.2	10.1	11.1	12.3	13.5	14.8	16.3	18.0	19.8	21.7	23.9
Deferred income taxes	22.9	25.8	29.1	32.8	36.9	41.6	46.9	52.9	59.7	67.2	75.6
Common equity	113.1	119.7	128.7	140.4	155.5	171.9	188.7	206.0	222.8	240.1	257.9
	301.2	328.8	357.9	392.7	432.3	482.4	536.5	594.2	655.0	718.4	783.0
Less: excess marketable secs	0.0	0.0	0.0	0.0	0.0	0.0	0.0	0.0	0.0	0.0	0.0
Less: nonoperating assets	0.0	0.0	0.0	0.0	0.0	0.0	0.0	0.0	0.0	0.0	0.0
Total invested capital	$301.2	$328.8	$357.9	$392.7	$432.3	$482.4	$536.5	$594.2	$655.0	$718.4	$783.0
Invested cap ex goodwill	$277.4	$305.6	$335.3	$370.7	$410.9	$461.6	$516.3	$574.6	$636.0	$700.0	$765.2

Exhibit 5.26 PRESTON CORPORATION, FORECASTED KEY VALUE DRIVERS

	1968	1989	1990	1991	1992	1993	1994	1995	1996	1997
Return on Invested Cap										
× Revenues/avg capital	2.0	2.2	2.3	2.3	2.3	2.3	2.2	2.2	2.2	2.2
EBIT/revenues	4.7%	5.2%	5.7%	6.1%	6.4%	6.2%	6.0%	5.9%	5.7%	5.6%
= Pretax ROIC	9.4%	11.6%	13.1%	14.2%	14.8%	14.3%	13.6%	13.0%	12.6%	12.3%
Operating tax rate	29.8%	31.0%	31.7%	32.1%	32.2%	31.8%	31.3%	30.8%	30.4%	30.1%
After-tax ROIC	6.6%	8.0%	8.9%	9.6%	10.0%	9.7%	9.3%	9.0%	8.8%	8.6%
AT ROIC ex goodwill	7.5%	8.7%	9.6%	10.2%	10.6%	10.2%	9.7%	9.3%	9.1%	8.9%
Increm pretax ROIC	80.1%	32.3%	29.1%	25.9%	21.0%	9.7%	7.6%	7.9%	8.6%	9.6%
Increm after-tax ROIC	60.7%	20.9%	19.0%	17.0%	14.1%	7.2%	5.8%	6.1%	6.5%	7.1%
Return on avg equity	5.8%	9.0%	11.5%	13.5%	14.5%	13.9%	12.9%	12.1%	11.5%	11.1%
Return on sales	1.1%	1.5%	1.8%	2.1%	2.3%	2.2%	2.0%	1.9%	1.8%	1.7%
Investment Rates										
Net investment rate	116.5%	109.2%	95.0%	96.5%	95.9%	112.5%	113.7%	113.2%	110.9%	107.0%
(five-yr rolling avg)	301.6%	250.7%	178.9%	109.4%	100.7%	101.9%	103.8%	107.2%	109.7%	111.3%
Growth Rates										
Sales	20.8%	14.8%	12.6%	10.8%	9.3%	9.5%	9.4%	9.6%	9.7%	9.9%
NOPLAT	151.9%	26.7%	21.3%	17.8%	14.5%	7.8%	6.8%	7.1%	7.6%	8.1%
EPS	2082.9%	59.2%	36.4%	27.4%	19.0%	6.0%	1.8%	2.4%	3.3%	4.6%
Per Share Measures										
EPS (before extra items)	$1.14	$1.81	$2.47	$3.15	$3.74	$3.97	$4.04	$4.13	$4.27	$4.46
Dividends per share	$0.50	$0.67	$0.90	$1.11	$1.11	$1.11	$1.11	$1.14	$1.35	$1.46
Book value per share	$19.63	$20.78	$22.35	$24.38	$27.07	$29.84	$32.77	$35.77	$38.68	$41.69
Avg shares outstanding (millions)	5.8	5.8	5.8	5.8	5.8	5.8	5.8	5.8	5.8	5.8
Financing										
Coverage (EBIT/interest)	1.8	2.1	2.3	2.5	2.6	2.6	2.4	2.3	2.2	2.1
Long-term debt/total cap	45.7%	46.6%	29.5%	46.9%	46.6%	44.0%	47.7%	48.1%	48.6%	49.0%
Total debt/total cap	51.8%	52.7%	52.8%	52.8%	52.3%	52.7%	53.0%	53.4%	53.9%	54.2%
Working Capital										
Day's sales outstanding	43.6	43.6	43.6	43.6	43.6	43.6	43.6	43.6	43.6	43.6
Adj working cap/sales	8.7%	8.7%	8.7%	8.7%	8.7%	8.7%	8.7%	8.7%	8.7%	8.7%
Current ratio	1.4	1.5	0.9	1.5	1.5	1.3	1.5	1.5	1.5	1.5

6

Estimating the
Cost of Capital

Both creditors and shareholders expect to be compensated for the opportunity cost of investing their funds in one particular business instead of others with equivalent risk. The weighted average cost of capital (WACC) is the discount rate, or time value of money, used to convert expected future cash flow into present value for all investors.

The most important general principle to recognize when developing a WACC is that it *must* be consistent with the overall valuation approach and with the definition of the cash flow to be discounted. To be consistent with the free cash flow approach we are using, the estimate of the cost of capital must

- comprise a weighted average of the costs of all sources of capital—debt, equity, and so on—since the free cash flow represents cash available to all providers of capital;
- be computed after corporate taxes, since the free cash flow is stated after taxes;
- use nominal rates of return built up from real rates and expected inflation, because the expected free cash flow is expressed in nominal terms (recall that in Chapter 5 we

suggested an approach to developing an estimate of expected inflation using the term structure of interest rates);

- adjust for the systematic risk borne by each provider of capital, since each expects a return that compensates for the risk taken;

- employ market value weights for each financing element, because market values reflect the true economic claim of each type of financing outstanding, whereas book values usually do not; and

- be subject to change across the cash flow forecast period, because of expected changes in inflation, systematic risk, or capital structure.

FORMULA FOR ESTIMATING THE WACC

The general formula we recommend for estimating the after-tax WACC is as follows:

$$WACC = k_b (1 - T_c) (B/V) + k_p (P/V) + k_s (S/V)$$

where

k_b = the pretax market expected yield to maturity on noncallable, nonconvertible debt

T_c = the marginal tax rate for the entity being valued*

B = the market value of interest-bearing debt

V = the market value of the entity being valued ($V = B + P + S$)

k_p = the after-tax cost of capital for noncallable, nonconvertible preferred stock (which equals the pretax cost of

---

*The marginal tax rate is the rate applied to a marginal dollar of interest expense. Usually it is the statutory rate. However, if the company has substantial tax loss carry-forwards or carry-backs, or faces possible bankruptcy so that its tax shields may never be used, the marginal tax rate can be lower than the statutory rate—even zero.

preferred stock when no deduction is made from corporate taxes for preferred dividends)

P = the market value of the preferred stock

k_s = the market-determined opportunity cost of equity capital

S = the market value of equity

We have included only three types of capital (nonconvertible, noncallable debt; nonconvertible, noncallable preferred stock; and equity) in this formula. The actual weighting scheme may be more complex, because a separate market value weight is required for each source of capital that involves cash payments, now or in the future. Other possible items include leases (operating and capital), subsidized debt (for example, industrial revenue bonds), convertible or callable debt, convertible or callable preferred stock, minority interests, and/or warrants and executive stock options. A wide variety of unusual securities—for example, income bonds, bonds with payments tied to commodity indexes, and bonds that are extendable, puttable, or retractable—may also be included.

Non-interest-bearing liabilities, such as accounts payable, are excluded from the calculation of WACC to avoid inconsistencies and simplify the valuation. Non-interest-bearing liabilities have a cost of capital, just like other forms of debt, but this cost is implicit in the price paid for the goods generating the liability and therefore shows up in the company's operating costs and free cash flow. Separating the implied financing costs of these liabilities from operating costs and free cash flow would be complex and time-consuming without improving the valuation.

The balance of this chapter describes the three related steps involved in developing the discount rate, or WACC:

1. Establishing target market value weights for the capital structure
2. Estimating the opportunity cost of nonequity financing
3. Estimating the opportunity cost of equity financing

As a practical matter, the three are performed simultaneously.

STEP 1: DEVELOP TARGET MARKET VALUE WEIGHTS

The first step in developing an estimate of the WACC is to determine a capital structure for the company you are valuing. This provides the market value weights for the WACC formula.

To accomplish this step, it is helpful to think in terms of a "target" capital structure, for two reasons. First, at any point a company's capital structure may not reflect the capital structure that is expected to prevail over the life of the business. For example, capital structure might be affected by recent changes in the market value of the securities outstanding and the "lumpiness" of financing activities, particularly those involving securities offerings. Moreover, management may have plans to change the capital mix as an active policy decision. All of these factors mean that future financing levels could be different from current or past levels.

The second reason for using a target capital structure is that it solves the problem of circularity involved in estimating the WACC. This circularity arises because we need to know market value weights to determine the WACC, but we cannot know the market value weights without knowing what the market value is in the first place—especially the market value of equity. And to determine the value of equity, which is the objective of the valuation process itself, we must discount the expected free cash flow at the WACC. In essence, we cannot know the WACC without knowing the market value of equity, and we cannot know the market value of equity without knowing the WACC.

One way out of the circularity problem is to simply iterate between the weights used in the WACC and the resulting value of equity. The second approach is to work with the idea of a target capital structure, which will not be affected by changes in the value of the company and which also avoids potentially incorrect conclusions about the impact of capital structure on value.

To develop a target capital structure for a company, we suggest using a combination of three approaches:

1. Estimate, to the extent possible, the current market value–based capital structure of the company.
2. Review the capital structure of comparable companies.

3. Review management's explicit or implicit approach to financing the business and its implications for the target capital structure.

Estimating Current Capital Structure

Where possible, you should estimate market values of the elements of the current capital structure and review how they have changed over time. The best approach for estimating the market value based capital structure is to identify the values of the capital structure elements directly from their prices in the marketplace. Thus, if a company's common stock is publicly traded, and its only other source of financing is corporate bonds that are also traded, the best way to develop a market value based capital structure estimate is to simply multiply the number of each type of outstanding security by its respective price in the marketplace. Most of the difficulty arises because sources of funds often are not traded in a marketplace where we can observe their prices directly.

You need to be prepared to deal with four broad categories of financing: debt-type financing; equity-linked/hybrid financing; minority interests; and common equity financing. In the paragraphs that follow, we provide guidance on how to estimate market values when market prices for the specific financing sources of the company are not available. Remember, should you be fortunate enough to have access to an actual market price, using it is always preferable to using a book value or other approximation.

Debt-type financing Financing forms in this category normally obligate the company to make a series of payments to the holders of the outstanding instruments, according to a payment schedule stipulated in the financing documents. Interest, coupon, or dividend payments may be fixed or variable. In this category fall short-term and long-term debt, leases, and some preferred stock. Their value depends on three factors: the agreed-upon payment schedule, the likelihood the borrower will make the payments as promised, and the market interest rates for securities with a similar pattern of expected payments.

Generally, their market value can be approximated without difficulty. The process is as follows:

1. Identify the contractually promised payments; for example, is the financing instrument a variable-rate note with interest determined each six months at a fixed spread over the prime rate, or a twenty-year zero-coupon bond?

2. Determine the credit quality of the instrument to be valued. Credit ratings are often available for even illiquid issues, or can be estimated from ratings on other company borrowings (adjusting for the security of the specific instrument in bankruptcy) or from bond rating models that attempt to mimic the behavior of the rating agencies. (The Alcar Group, Inc., markets a software package and database service called APT! that estimates bond ratings using standard financial ratios. Alcar's address is 5215 Old Orchard Road, Skokie, IL 60077.)

3. Estimate the yield to maturity for which the instrument would trade were it publicly traded, by reference to market yields on securities with equivalent coupons, maturities, and ratings.

4. Calculate the present value of the stream of financing payments, using the yield to maturity on an equivalent issue as your discount rate. The resulting present value should approximate the market value. (This is equivalent to discounting expected payments at the expected market equilibrium rate of return.)

This approach will work well in most cases, but a few special situations might call for a different approach.

• *Interest rate option features* such as "caps," "floors," and call provisions have an effect on future payments, depending on the level of interest rates. They therefore affect the value of the security that contains them. Two approaches can be taken to adjusting for these features. The first is to find a comparable security with a similar feature and use it as a proxy. The second is to use an option-pricing approach to estimate the value of the option feature separately (see Chapter 12).

- *Swaps.* Many companies enter into interest-rate and currency swap agreements that change the duration and/or currency profile of their financing. Swaps are off-balance-sheet transactions that are disclosed in the footnotes to the financial statements. They are also sometimes used by corporations to speculate on interest rates, and a company could have a debt swap outstanding even though it is financed entirely with common equity.

  For valuation purposes, swaps should be treated in the same way as any other financing instrument, with the promised cash flow in the agreement valued at the prevailing market rate. Practically speaking, this can be a complicated exercise and nearly impossible to do without specific information about the swap instruments themselves.

  Where possible, if you can associate a swap with a specific outstanding instrument, you should estimate the value of the "synthetic" security that the combination of the security plus swap creates. For example, a company may have issued floating-rate debt and entered into an interest-rate swap that converts it to a five-year fixed-rate instrument. In this case, you would estimate the value of the five-year instrument using the standard procedure noted earlier.

- *Foreign currency obligations.* If a company has financing outstanding in a currency other than its home currency, the value of this financing will need to be stated in terms of the company's home currency. This involves a two-step process. First, value the debt in foreign currency terms according to the standard procedure. Second, translate the resulting foreign currency market value into the home currency by using the *spot* foreign exchange rate. For example, if a U.S. company has issued ten-year Swiss franc bonds, it would first determine the market value of the bonds in Swiss francs, using Swiss interest rates for equivalent issues (if necessary), and then translate the result into current U.S. dollars.

- *Leases.* Leases substitute for other forms of debt and should therefore be treated like debt. Standard accounting principles divide leases into two classes: capital leases and operating leases. Capital leases, as defined by the Financial Accounting Standards Board (1976), are essentially those that transfer most of the ownership risk of the asset to the lessee. All other leases are considered operating leases.

  Capital leases are accounted for as if the lessee had purchased the asset and borrowed the funds. The present value of the lease payments is added to the company's assets with other fixed assets and to the liability side of the balance sheet alongside other debt. Operating leases do not appear on the balance sheet, and the lease payments are included with other operating costs. While the accounting treatment of capital and operating leases differs, the economics of the two types of leases are often similar. Some companies carefully structure leases to keep them off the balance sheet, but the accounting treatment should not drive your valuation analysis.

  Since capital leases are already shown as debt on the balance sheet, their market value can be estimated just like other debt. Operating leases should also be treated like other forms of debt. The market value of an operating lease is the present value of the required future lease payments (excluding the portion of the lease payment for maintenance) discounted at a rate that reflects the riskiness to the lessee of the particular lease. (Required future lease payments on both capital and operating leases are disclosed in the financial statement footnotes if they are significant.)

  As a practical matter, if operating leases are not significant, you should not bother to treat them as debt. Leave them out of the capital structure and keep the lease payments as an operating cost.

- *Callable debt.* The call feature gives the debt issuer the right to call in outstanding debt for a fixed premium above the face value. When interest rates fall, the call feature becomes valuable. Consequently, purchasers of fixed-rate debt that is callable (but not convertible) demand higher coupon rates to compensate them for the risk that their capital gain will be limited if interest rates fall. Callable debt is equivalent to straight debt less a put option; consequently, the coupon rate and yield to maturity may not be good estimates of the opportunity cost of capital. Instead, the option-pricing model should be used to estimate the opportunity cost of callable debt.

Equity-linked/hybrid financing   Companies commonly have, in addition to fixed-income obligations, financing that has all or part of its return linked to the value of all or part of the business. These financing forms include warrants and convertible securities (convertible debt and convertible preferred stock). When these securities are traded, their market value should be determined from their current market prices. When they are not traded, estimating their market value is more difficult than is the case with the fixed-income obligations.

- *Warrants.* Usually warrants represent the right to buy a set number of shares of the company's equity at a predetermined price. They can also be warrants to purchase other types of securities, such as preferred stock or additional debt. Warrants are essentially long-term options having an exercise period of five to ten years, with a "strike price" equal to the price the holder would pay, on exercise, to acquire the underlying security. Since they are options, warrants should be valued using option-pricing approaches. If the company you are valuing has a large number of warrants outstanding, their cost should be included in the company's WACC. (See Copeland and Weston 1988, 472–80.)

- *Convertible securities.* Convertible securities represent a combination of straight, nonconvertible financing and a specified number of warrants that comprise the conversion feature. Their value and their true opportunity cost cannot be determined properly without recognizing the value of the conversion feature (warrant). The stated interest rate on these issues is lower than on straight-debt equivalents because the conversion feature has value. Investors are willing to pay for this value by forgoing the higher yield available on nonconvertible securities. As with warrants, the extent of the yield they will forgo depends on how far in or out of the money the conversion feature is. The deeper in the money it is, the lower the traded yield, and vice versa. Since each convertible bond is a portfolio of straight debt and warrants, the true opportunity cost is higher than for straight debt but lower than for equity.

To deal with the existence of convertible securities in a company's capital structure, follow an approach similar to the one used for warrants.

In summary, hybrid securities are more difficult to value than straight nonequity financing. If they are very important in a particular situation, use the guidelines just set out and employ an option-pricing approach.

Minority interests   As discussed in Chapter 5, minority interests represent claims by outside shareholders on a portion of a company's business. Minority interests usually arise after an acquisition when the acquiring company does not purchase all of the target company's shares outstanding. They can also arise if the company sells a minority stake in one of its subsidiaries to a third party.

The treatment of minority interests depends on the information available. If the minority shares are publicly traded, then their approximate value can be determined directly from the market prices for the shares. If, as is more often the case, the shares are not traded, then theoretically we should value the *subsidiary* separately using the discounted free cash flow valuation approach and compute the value of the minority stake according to the percentage of the subsidiary's shares the minority shareholders own.

If information about the subsidiary's free cash flow cannot be developed, then the value of the minority stake could be approximated by applying price-to-earnings or market-to-book ratios for similar companies to the minority's share of income or net assets. Both of these items are disclosed in the financial statements—

sometimes separately for each subsidiary in which a minority interest exists.

Common equity   In addition to estimating the market values of the pure nonequity and equity-linked financing, we also need to determine the value of equity before we can determine the total market value capitalization of the company and hence the target market value weights for the WACC formula.

If a traded market for the company's common shares exists, follow the familiar approach of using current market price multiplied by the number of shares outstanding. The current market price is the best available estimate of the market value of the equity, and is superior to book values or averages of past market prices. It reflects investors' views about expected returns from holding the shares relative to alternative investments at the time of the valuation.

If a traded market does not exist for the shares, the situation is more difficult. This is one of the reasons why we might need to use comparables and discussions with management to estimate an implied target for the percentage of equity in the company's capital structure. These are discussed in the next section. Before proceeding to these approaches, though, we should note that we can develop an implied equity value by testing alternative values for the equity and the implications they would have for the market value weights in the WACC computation. These alternative weights can be used to develop first estimates of the cost of capital, and can be refined through a couple of iterations. Essentially, when the value of equity used in the WACC formula is approximately equal to the discounted cash flow value of equity produced by applying the discount rate to the free cash flows and the continuing value, then we have produced an implied economic capital structure for the business. (To follow this approach you will have had to estimate the market values of all the other financing components and an opportunity cost for each— discussed in the next section—as well as have in hand the free cash flow forecast and inputs to the continuing-value estimate. When described as part of a sequential process, this iterative approach sounds more complicated than it really is in practice, especially since the use of a PC-based valuation model makes the process of iterating relatively quick and easy.)

Reviewing the Structures of Comparable Companies

In addition to estimating the market value based capital structure of the company currently and over time, we should also review the capital structures of comparable companies. Two reasons exist for doing this.

First, comparing the capital structure of the company we are valuing with those of similar companies will help us understand whether our current estimate of capital structure is unusual. For the company's capital structure to be different is perfectly acceptable, but we should understand the reasons why it is or is not. For instance, is the company by philosophy more aggressive or innovative in the use of nonequity financing, or is the current capital structure only a temporary deviation from a more conservative target? Often, companies finance acquisitions with debt that they plan to pay down rapidly or refinance with a stock offering in the next year. Alternatively, is there anything different about the company's cash flow or asset intensity that, despite its being in a seemingly comparable situation, means that its target capital structure can or should be fundamentally different from those of comparable companies? Answers to questions such as these can help us decide on the company's future target capital structure relative to its current one.

The second reason for reviewing comparable companies is a more practical one: in some cases we cannot directly estimate the current financing mix for the company. For privately held or thinly traded companies, or for divisions of a publicly traded company, a market-based estimate of the current value of equity may not be available. In these situations, we can use comparables to help us assess the reasonableness of the estimate of the target proportion of equity developed through the iterative process described in the previous section.

Also, in the case of divisions of multibusiness companies, we may not even be able to determine the nonequity financing portion of the division's capital structure. One approach to this problem is to use the corporatewide capital structure. But this should be supplemented with a review of the approximate market value capital structures of similar companies. Chapter 9 provides more detailed guidance on handling the practical and conceptual problems of valuation for multibusiness companies, including how to develop relevant capital structures for each business.

Reviewing Management's Financing Philosophy

Where possible, we should discuss the company's capital structure policy with management to determine their explicit or implicit target market capital structure for the company and its businesses. In some cases, they will have in hand a very clear perspective on the capital structure they intend to employ on a division-by-division basis.

Even if management's approach is not well developed or is largely judgmental, we can still learn a lot from discussions with them about sensible targets for use in our valuation work. At some level, they will have targets for the types of financing they plan to employ. The targets may be expressed in terms of book values, but these can be converted into market values. Furthermore, management can provide insights into the factors that underlie their choice of financing and about comparable companies.

If we do not have direct access to management, we can glean similar information from the annual review sections of annual reports/10-Ks and from reports by security analysts.

In the next two sections we describe the approach to estimating the relevant opportunity costs for each type of financing commonly encountered, organized around fixed-income financing and common equity financing. In each case, we are seeking to estimate nominal, required rates of return since our free cash flow estimates are expressed in nominal terms.

STEP 2: ESTIMATE THE COST OF NONEQUITY FINANCING

In this section we discuss approaches to estimating market opportunity costs for financing forms that do not have explicit equity features. These include the following:

- Straight investment-grade debt (fixed and variable rate)
- Below-investment-grade debt (for example, "junk" bonds)
- Subsidized debt (for example, industrial revenue bonds)
- Foreign-currency-denominated debt
- Leases (capital leases, operating leases)
- Straight preferred stock

Straight Investment-Grade Debt

If the company has straight debt that is not convertible into other securities—like common stock—and that is not callable, then we can use discounted cash flow analysis to estimate the market rate of return and the market value of the debt. For investment-grade debt, the risk of bankruptcy is low. Therefore, yield to maturity is usually a reasonable estimate of the opportunity cost.

The coupon rate—that is, the historical (or imbedded) cost of debt—is irrelevant for determining the current cost of capital. Always use the most current market rate on debt of equivalent risk. A reasonable proxy for the risk of debt is Moody's or Standard & Poor's bond rating. If the bond rating is not available, you will need to calculate traditional financial ratios—times-interest-earned, debt-to-equity, working capital, and so on—in order to compare the entity you are valuing with known firms, as a means of estimating the bond rating. (The APT! software package and database service by Alcar estimates bond ratings by using standard financial ratios.)

Many companies have variable-rate debt, either acquired through swaps, as an original security issue, or in the form of revolving bank loans. If the variable-rate loan has no cap or floor, then use the long-term rate, because the short-term rate will be rolled over and the geometric average of the expected short-term rates is equal to the long-term rate. If the variable-rate debt has a cap or floor, or if the interest payment is determined as a moving average of past rates, then an option is involved and the problem becomes much more complicated. For example, if market rates have risen and a variable rate loan is "capped out," then it becomes a "subsidized" form of financing that adds value to the company.

Below-Investment-Grade Debt

When dealing with debt that is less than investment grade, you must be aware of the difference between the expected yield to maturity and the promised yield to maturity. The promised yield to maturity assumes that all payments (coupons and principal) will be made as promised by the issuer. Consider the following simple example: a three-year bond promises to pay a 10 percent coupon at the end of each year, plus a face value of $1,000 at the end of the third year. The current market value of the bond is $951.96. What is the yield to maturity? If we use y to designate the promised yield to maturity, it can be computed by solving the following formula:

$$B_o = \sum_{t=1}^{3} \frac{Coupon_t}{(1 + y)^t} + \frac{Face}{(1 + y)^3}$$

where

B_o = the current market value of noncallable, non-convertible debt

Coupon = the promised coupon paid at the end of time period t

Face = the face value of the bond, promised at maturity

y = the promised yield to maturity

The solution is y = 12 percent. However, this promised yield to maturity assumes that the debt is default-free. Suppose that we expect a 5 percent chance that the bond will default and pay only $400.

If we were to rewrite the formula, putting the bond's expected payments rather than its promised payments in the numerator, we could calculate the market's *expected* rate of return as opposed to the promised rate of return implicit in the yield to maturity. As recomputed, the market expected rate of return on the risky debt would be 11.09 percent. Thus, the rate of return that the market expects to earn is 91 basis points lower than the promised yield to maturity. The promised yields on junk bonds are very different (frequently much higher) from the expected yields that the market anticipates on these risky securities. Thus, yields are not always what they seem.

Our problem, then, is that we need to compute the expected yield to maturity, not the quoted, promised yield. We can do this if we have the current market price of the low-grade bond and estimates of its expected default rate and value in default, or if we can estimate its systematic risk (beta). Unfortunately, the necessary data are usually unavailable.

As a reasonable fallback position, *use the yield to maturity on BBB-rated debt,* which reduces most of the effects of the difference between promised and expected yields.

Although the promised yield to maturity is not equivalent to the opportunity cost of capital for debt with high default risk, it can serve as a useful proxy for the market's estimate of default risk. Exhibit 6.1 shows the relationship between promised yields to maturity and maturity periods for portfolios of bonds varying in risk from default-free U.S. government obligations to B-rated corporate debentures. The table was plotted in the summer of 1988. Exhibit 6.2 graphs the relationship between the promised yield to maturity and the bond rating for bonds with ten years to maturity.

Exhibit 6.1 **PROMISED YIELDS VS. BOND RATINGS, SUMMER 1988,** PERCENT

Term	Default-free	AAA	AA	A	BBB	BB	B
1 month	6.27%	6.82%	7.06%	7.52%	7.95%	8.44%	10.38%
3 months	6.83	7.38	7.62	8.08	8.51	9.00	10.94
6 months	7.28	7.83	8.07	8.53	8.96	9.45	11.39
1 year	7.46	8.01	8.25	8.71	9.14	9.63	11.57
2 years	7.99	8.54	8.78	9.24	9.67	10.16	12.10
5 years	8.42	8.97	9.21	9.67	10.10	10.59	12.53
10 years	8.80	9.35	9.59	10.05	10.48	10.97	12.91
15 years	9.07	9.62	9.86	10.32	10.75	11.24	13.18
20 years	9.16	9.71	9.95	10.41	10.84	11.33	13.27
25 years	9.03	9.58	9.82	10.28	10.71	11.20	13.14
30 years	8.85	9.40	9.64	10.10	10.53	11.02	12.96

Source: Alcar, APT!

Exhibit 6.2 **PROMISED YIELDS VS. BOND RATINGS, SUMMER 1988,**
TEN-YEAR BONDS, PERCENT

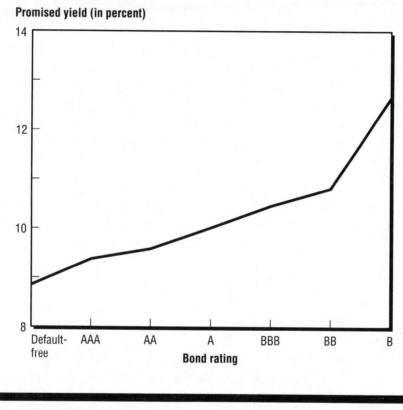

Source: Alcar, APT!

Subsidized Debt

The coupon rate on industrial revenue bonds is below the market
rate for taxable bonds of equivalent risk because they are tax-free
to investors. They should enter into the WACC at their current
market yield to maturity, where known. If the bonds are not
traded, their yield can be estimated by reference to similarly rated
tax-free issues that are actively traded (or from similar new issues
of tax-exempt debt).

Foreign-Currency-Denominated Debt

When an obligation is denominated in a foreign currency, the local currency nominal rate of return is usually an inappropriate measure of the actual cost of capital to the issuer in its home currency. This is due to the foreign exchange exposure inherent in the financing.

When a company issues foreign-currency-denominated debt, its effective cost equals the after-tax cost of repaying the principal and interest *in terms of the company's own currency*. Usually the all-in cost of borrowing in foreign currency will be close to the cost of borrowing in domestic markets due to the interest-rate parity relationship enforced by the active arbitrage engaged in by issuers, investors, and intermediaries in the cash, forward exchange, and currency swap markets.

The interest-rate parity relationship (leaving minor transaction costs and temporary, small arbitrage opportunities aside) generally guarantees the following relationship (further explained in Chapter 10):

$$1 + k_b = (X_o/X_f)\ (1 + r_o)$$

where

k_b = the domestic pretax cost of N-year debt

X_o = the spot foreign exchange rate (units of foreign currency per dollar)

X_f = the N-year forward foreign exchange rate (units of foreign currency per dollar)

r_o = the foreign interest rate on an N-year bond

To illustrate, suppose that your domestic borrowing rate is 7.25 percent and that the rate on a one-year loan denominated in Swiss francs is 4 percent. How would these rates compare? If the spot exchange rate is 1.543 francs per dollar, and the one-year forward rate is 1.4977 francs per dollar, then the equivalent *domestic* one-year borrowing rate is 7.15 percent for the Swiss franc loan.

$$1 + k_b = [1.543/1.4977] (1 + 0.04)$$
$$= 1.0715 \text{ or } k_b = 7.15\%$$

Usually, the equivalent domestic borrowing rate on foreign-currency-denominated debt will be very close to the domestic borrowing rate. Arbitrage virtually guarantees this result.

Although we can use forward rate contracts to estimate equivalent domestic rates for relatively short-term debt (less than eighteen months), no easily referenced forward markets exist farther out. For longer-term borrowing, we recommend that you assume the domestic equivalent rate is roughly equal to the actual domestic rate.

Leases

Leases, both capital and operating, are substitutes for other types of debt. Therefore, it is reasonable in most cases to assume that their opportunity cost is the same as for the company's other long-term debt.

Straight Preferred Stock

The cost of preferred stock that is perpetual, noncallable, and nonconvertible can be calculated as follows:

$$k_p = \text{div}/P$$

where

k_p = the cost of preferred stock
div = the promised dividend on the preferred stock
P = the market price of the preferred stock

If the current market price is not available, use yields on similar-quality issues as an estimate. For a fixed-life or callable preferred stock issue, estimate the opportunity cost by using the same approach as for a comparable debt instrument. In other words, estimate the yield that equates the expected stream of payments with the market value. For convertible preferred issues, option-pricing approaches are necessary.

STEP 3: ESTIMATE THE COST OF EQUITY FINANCING

To estimate the opportunity cost of equity capital, we currently
recommend using the capital asset pricing model (CAPM) or the
arbitrage pricing model (APM). Both approaches have problems
associated with their application; for example, they are subject to
measurement problems. But they are theoretically correct; they
are risk-adjusted and account for expected inflation. In contrast,
many other approaches to computing the cost of equity are conceptually flawed. For example, the dividend yield model, the
earnings-to-price ratio model, and the dividend yield model with
a growth term (sometimes called the Gordon growth model) give
incorrect results.

The Capital Asset Pricing Model

The CAPM is discussed at length in all modern finance texts (for
example, see Brealey and Myers 1984 or Weston and Copeland
1987). These detailed discussions will not be reproduced here. (In
this section, we assume that you are generally familiar with the
principles that underlie the approach.) In essence, the CAPM
postulates that the opportunity cost of equity is equal to the
return on risk-free securities plus the company's systematic risk
(beta) multiplied by the market price of risk (market risk premium). The equation for the cost of equity (k_s) is as follows:

$$k_s = r_f + [E(r_m) - r_f] \text{ (beta)}$$

where

r_f	= the risk-free rate of return
$E(r_m)$	= the expected rate of return on the overall market portfolio
$E(r_m) - r_f$	= the market risk premium
beta	= the systematic risk of the equity

The CAPM is illustrated in Exhibit 6.3. The cost of equity, k_s,
increases linearly as a function of the measured undiversifiable

risk, beta. The beta for the entire market portfolio is 1.0. This means that the average company's equity beta will also be about 1.0. In our experience it is very unusual to observe a beta greater than 2.0 or less than 0.1. The market risk premium (the price of risk), which varies from country to country, is measured as the slope of the CAPM line in Exhibit 6.3—that is, the slope is $E(r_m) - r_f$.

To implement the CAPM approach, we need to estimate the three factors that determine the CAPM line: the risk-free rate, the market risk premium, and the systematic risk (beta). The balance of this section describes a recommended approach for estimating each.

Exhibit 6.3 **THE CAPITAL ASSET PRICING MODEL**

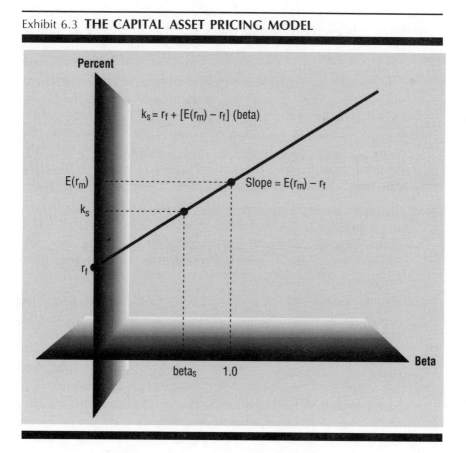

Determining the risk-free rate   Hypothetically, the risk-free rate is the return on a security or portfolio of securities that has no default risk whatsoever, and is completely uncorrelated with returns on anything else in the economy. Theoretically, the best estimate of the risk-free rate would be the return on a zero-beta portfolio. Due to the cost and complexity of constructing zero-beta portfolios, they are not available for use in estimating the risk-free rate.

We have three reasonable alternatives that use government securities: (1) the rate for Treasury bills, (2) the rate for ten-year Treasury bonds, and (3) the rate for thirty-year Treasury bonds. We recommend using a ten-year Treasury-bond rate, for several reasons.

- First, it is a long-term rate that usually comes close to matching the duration of the cash flow of the company being valued. Since the current Treasury-bill rate is a short-term rate, it does not match duration properly. If we were to use short-term rates, the appropriate ones to use would be the short-term rates that are expected to apply in each future period, not today's short-term interest rate. In essence, the ten-year rate is a geometric weighted average estimate of the *expected* short-term Treasury-bill rates over the evaluation horizon.

- Second, the ten-year rate approximates the duration of the stock market index portfolio—for example, the S&P 500—and its use is therefore consistent with the betas and market risk premiums estimated relative to these market portfolios.

- Finally, the ten-year rate is less susceptible to two problems involved in using a longer-term rate, such as the thirty-year Treasury-bond rate. It is less sensitive to unexpected changes in inflation, and therefore has a smaller beta than the thirty-year rate; and the liquidity premium built into ten-year rates *may* be slightly lower than that which is in thirty-year bonds. These are technical details, with a minor impact in normal circumstances. But they do argue in the direction of using a ten-year bond rate.

Determining the market risk premium   The market risk premium (the price of risk) is the difference between the expected rate of return on the market portfolio and the risk-free rate, $E(r_m) - r_f$. We recommend using a 5 to 6 percent market risk premium for U.S. companies. This is based on the long-run geometric average risk premium for the return on the S&P 500 versus the return on long-term government bonds from 1926 to 1988 (Ibbotson Associates 1989). Since this is a contentious area that can have a significant impact on valuations, we elaborate our reasoning in detail here.

- We use a very long time frame to measure the premium rather than a short time frame to eliminate the effects of short-term anomalies in the measurement. The 1926–1988 time frame reflects wars, depressions, and booms. Shorter time periods do not reflect as diverse a set of economic circumstances.

- We use a geometric average of rates of return because arithmetic averages are biased by the measurement period. An arithmetic average estimates the rates of return by taking a simple average of the single period rates of return. Suppose you buy a share of a non-dividend-paying stock for $50. After one year the stock is worth $100. After two years the stock falls to $50 once again. The first period return is 100 percent; the second period return is –50 percent. The arithmetic average return is 25 percent (100 percent – 50 percent/2). The geometric average is zero. (The geometric average is the compound rate of return that equates the beginning and ending value.) We believe that the geometric average represents a better estimate of investors' expected returns over long periods of time.

- Finally, we calculate the premium over *long-term* government bond returns to be consistent with the risk-free rate we use to calculate the cost of equity.

Some analysts recommend using the arithmetic average rate of return. Depending on the time frame chosen and the type of average, the market risk premium can vary significantly, as shown in the table below.

	1926–88	1962–88
Risk premium based on:		
Arithmetic average returns	7.6%	4.1%
Geometric average returns	5.4	2.7

Source: Ibbotson Associates (1989).

Clearly, your valuation can change substantially if you switch from 7.6 to 2.7 percent. Three issues must be resolved. Should one use a more recent, but shorter, time frame? Should one choose the arithmetic or the geometric average? Should the forecasted risk premium be based on historical estimates or analysts' forecasts? Since the market risk premium is a random walk, better estimates are provided by the longer time frame. Sure, things have changed, but they have not changed in a predictable fashion. Thus, the risk premium is best described as a random walk, and the longer time frame (which encompasses a stock market crash, expansions, recessions, two wars, and stagflation) is the best estimate of the future.

To contrast the geometric and average rates of return, we can go back to the earlier example where we observed two periods of return, the first with a rate of 100 percent and the second with –50 percent. What can we infer from these data? If we are willing to make the strong assumption that each return is an independent observation from a stationary underlying probability distribution, then we can infer that four equally likely return paths actually exist: 100 percent followed by 100 percent, 100 percent followed by –50 percent, –50 percent followed by 100 percent, and –50 percent followed by –50 percent. These possibilities are illustrated in Exhibit 6.4. The shaded area represents what we have actually observed, and the remainder of the binomial tree is what we have inferred by assuming independence.

The difference between the arithmetic and geometric averages is that the former infers expected returns by assuming independence, and the latter treats the observed historical path as the single best estimate of the future. If you believe that it is proper to apply equal weighting to all branches in the binomial tree, then your expected wealth is as follows:

$$\frac{1}{4} (\$200) + \frac{1}{2} (\$50) + \frac{1}{4} (\$12.50) = \$78.125$$

Exhibit 6.4 **RATE OF RETURN DATA FOR FOUR LIKELY PATHS**

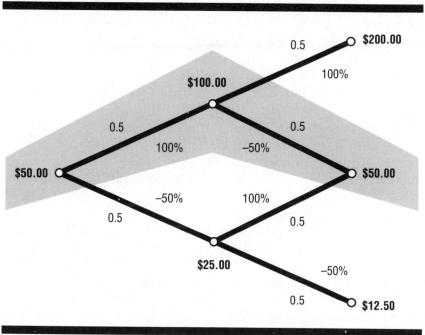

Exactly the same value can be obtained by computing the arithmetic average return:

$$\frac{1}{4}\,(100\%) + \frac{1}{2}\,(25\%) + \frac{1}{4}\,(-50\%) = 25\%$$

and applying it to the starting wealth as follows:

$$\$50\,(1.25)\,(1.25) = \$78.125$$

If you believe, as we do, that the best estimate of future wealth is the single geometric average return—that is, 0 percent—then the expected wealth after two periods is $50.

Note that the arithmetic return is always higher than the geometric return and that the difference between them becomes greater as a function of the variance of returns. Also, for a given time interval, different arithmetic average returns can be obtained by breaking the interval into different subintervals for sampling purposes. The geometric average, being a single estimate for the entire time interval, is invariant. Finally, empirical research by Fama and French (1988), Lo and MacKinlay (1988), and Poterba and Summers (1988) indicates that a significant long-term negative autocorrelation exists in stock returns. Hence, historical observations are not independent draws from a stationary distribution.

A recent example of the problematic nature of choosing a short time interval to estimate arithmetic average returns occurred during the summer of 1987. Many analysts were using the relatively low 2.5 to 3.5 percent risk premium taken from the 1962–85 time period. This low estimate helped to justify the extraordinarily high prices observed in the stock market at that time. After all, the argument went, it does not make sense to use long-term rates, because extraordinary events like a stock market crash cannot happen again. Our opinion is that the best *forecast* of the risk premium is its long-run geometric average.

Although we recommend using the long-term historical geometric average risk premium, a frequently mentioned alternative is based on analysts' forecasts. The expected rate of return on the market portfolio, $E(r_m)$, is estimated by adding the analysts' consensus estimate of growth in the dividends of the S&P 500 index, g, to the dividend yield for the index, Div/S:

$$E(r_m) = \frac{Div}{S} + g$$

The risk-free rate is then subtracted from the expected return on the market to obtain the forecast of the market risk premium. We have little faith in this method, for two reasons. First, analysts have shown limited skill in forecasting price changes (growth) for the S&P 500. And second, the formula that provides the basis for this approach implicitly assumes perpetual growth at a constant rate, g. This is a particularly stringent assumption.

Estimating the systematic risk (beta)   The approach to use in developing the estimate of beta depends on whether the company's equity is traded or not.

If the company is publicly traded, you are indeed fortunate and can use published estimates. We recommend that you use betas published by Wilshire Associates or BARRA (formerly Rosenberg Associates). BARRA betas are updated quarterly for approximately seven thousand companies listed on the New York Stock Exchange, the American Stock Exchange, and NASDAQ; these estimates of systematic risk are based on the financial ratios of each company. They change as the financial ratios do, and more accurately reflect the market's most recent estimate of equity risk.

To find that estimates of betas from different services vary is not completely unusual. We have three rules of thumb: (1) if one of the services produces higher-quality betas, throw out the others; (2) if two high-quality services provide betas that differ by no more than 0.2, take the average and use it; and (3) if the betas are farther apart than 0.2, construct an equally weighted industry average beta. Because measurement errors tend to cancel out, industry averages are more stable than company betas. When constructing the industry average, be sure to unlever the company betas and then apply the leverage of the company you are valuing, using the methodology described in Chapter 9 of this book.

If you can only find one estimate of beta, but it does not seem to make sense (for example, it is negative, greater than 2, or differs radically from betas for other similarly leveraged companies in the same industry), then use the approaches suggested in Chapter 9 for estimating betas for untraded companies.

The problem of estimating betas for business units within a company is discussed in Chapter 9, and betas for foreign companies are discussed in Chapter 10.

The Arbitrage Pricing Model

The APM can be thought of as a multifactor analogue to the CAPM. The CAPM explains security returns as a function of one factor, which is called the market index, and is usually measured as the rate of return on a well-diversified portfolio like an equally weighted New York Stock Exchange index. The APM cost of equity is defined as follows:

$$k_s = r_f + [E(F_1) - r_f] \, beta_1 + [E(F_2) - r_f] \, beta_2 + \ldots +$$

$$[E(F_k) - r_f] \, beta_k$$

where

$E(F_k)$ = the expected rate of return on a portfolio that mimics the kth factor and is independent of all others

$beta_k$ = the sensitivity of the stock return to the kth factor

Instead of one measure of systematic risk, the APM includes many. Each beta measures the sensitivity of a company's stock return to a separate underlying factor in the economy. Empirical work has suggested that five important fundamental factors are changes in

- the industrial production index, a measure of how well the economy is doing in terms of actual physical output;
- the short-term real rate, measured by the difference between the yield on T-bills and the Consumer Price Index;
- short-term inflation, measured by unexpected changes in the Consumer Price Index;
- long-term inflation, measured as the difference between the yield to maturity on long- and short-term U.S. government bonds; and
- default risk, measured by the difference between the yield to maturity on Aaa- and Baa-rated long-term corporate bonds.

Empirical evidence also confirms that the APM explains expected returns better than the single-factor CAPM (for example, see Chen 1983; Chen, Ross, and Roll 1986; or Berry, Burmeister, and McElroy 1988). In addition, the APM can add insight into the type of risk that is relevant. This is illustrated in Exhibit 6.5. The axes are two of the fundamental factors, the industrial production index and short-term inflation. The diagonal dotted lines represent constant returns with different combinations of risk.

Exhibit 6.5 **THE ARBITRAGE PRICING MODEL**

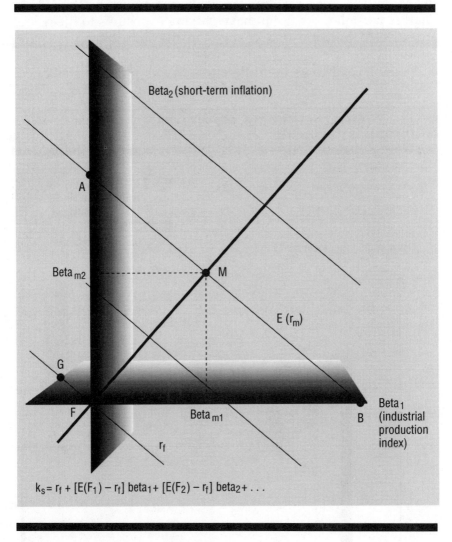

$$k_s = r_f + [E(F_1) - r_f]\, beta_1 + [E(F_2) - r_f]\, beta_2 + \ldots$$

Any portfolio at the origin (point F) has no exposure to either factor, and therefore earns the riskless rate, r_f.

For a portfolio at point G, exposure to the systematic risk of unexpected inflation has increased but is offset by decreased risk relative to the industrial production index. The net result is that point G earns the riskless rate, just like point F, but is exposed to a different bundle of risks. A similar story can be told about points A, M, and B. All earn the same expected return as the CAPM market portfolio, $E(r_m)$, but have varying exposures to the risk of unexpected inflation and changes in the industrial production index.

Exhibit 6.6 shows the differences in risk premiums as calcu-

Exhibit 6.6 **DIFFERENCES IN RISK PREMIUMS BETWEEN APM AND CAPM, BY INDUSTRY**

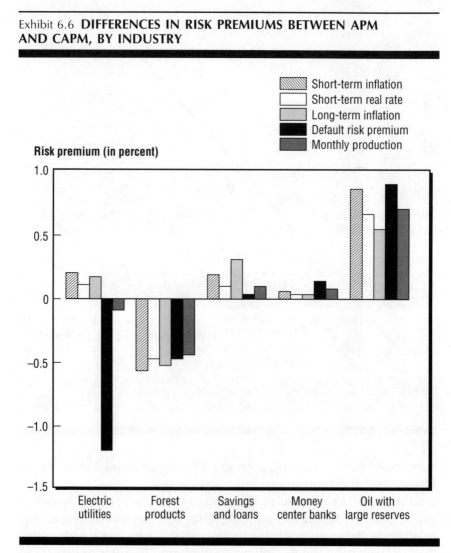

Source: Alcar's APT!, McKinsey analysis.

lated by the APM and the CAPM for five industries. Oil, savings and loans, and money center banks are riskier in every dimension. Forest products are less risky, and electric utilities have much less default risk. A larger risk premium means that the industry is more sensitive to a given type of risk than would be predicted by the CAPM. For example, savings and loans are more sensitive to unexpected changes in long-term inflation, and the market charges a risk premium—that is, it requires a higher cost of equity.

Exhibit 6.7, produced using Alcar's APT! program, shows the net effect of using the CAPM versus the APM to estimate the cost of equity for nine industries. The importance of these differences for valuation of an all-equity perpetual stream of cash flows is reflected in the last column. For example, the 4.7 percent higher APM cost-of-equity estimate in the oil industry means that equity cash flows discounted using the CAPM would be overvalued by 25 percent. Cost-of-equity estimates using the APM are significantly lower for forest products and electric utilities and significantly higher for money center banks, large S&Ls, and for oil companies with more than 50 percent of their assets in oil reserves.

Exhibit 6.7 **COMPARISON OF CAPM AND APM COST-OF-EQUITY ESTIMATES**

| Industry | Number of companies | Cost-of-equity estimate | | | Percentage change in value |
		CAPM	APM	Difference	
Brokerage	10	17.1%	17.4%	−.3%	−1.7%
Electric utilities	39	12.7	11.8	.9	7.6
Food and beverage	11	14.4	14.3	.1	0.7
Forest products	7	16.8	15.0	1.8*	12.0
Large savings and loans	18	15.8	19.6	−3.8*	−17.7
Mining	15	14.7	14.2	.5	3.5
Money center banks	12	15.9	16.9	−1.0*	−5.9
Oil with large reserves	12	14.4	19.1	−4.7*	−24.6
Property and casualty insurance	13	14.6	13.7	.9	6.6

*Statistically significant at the 5% confidence level. Source: Alcar's APT!, McKinsey analysis.

PRESTON CORPORATION

ESTIMATING THE COST OF CAPITAL

We estimated Preston's WACC to be 9.9 percent on July 1, 1988, calculated as follows:

	Target weight	Pretax cost	After-tax cost	Contribution to WACC
Short-term debt	7.4%	11.0%	6.7%	0.5%
Industrial revenue bonds	6.4	7.7	4.7	0.3
Convertible debt	7.8	11.0	8.3	0.7
Other long-term debt	33.8	11.0	6.7	2.3
Capital leases	1.0	11.0	6.7	0.1
Operating leases	3.5	11.0	6.7	0.2
Common equity	38.2	14.4	14.4	5.5
$5.58 options	0.5	24.6	24.6	0.1
$10.26 options	1.4	17.0	17.0	0.2
WACC				9.9%

We assumed that Preston would maintain its capital structure at current levels, so the target weights are based on the market values of its capital on July 1, 1988, summarized as follows:

	Book value ($millions)	Estimated market value ($millions)	Percentage of total market value
Short-term debt	$ 17.6	$ 17.6	7.4%
Industrial revenue bonds	15.2	15.2	6.4
Convertible debt	27.7	18.6	7.8
Other long-term debt	80.3	80.3	33.8
Capital leases	2.3	2.3	1.0
Operating leases	—	8.4	3.5
Total debt	$143.1	$142.4	59.9%

	Book value ($millions)	Estimated market value ($millions)	Percentage of total market value
Common equity*	129.7	90.7	38.2
$5.58 options	—	1.2	0.5
$10.26 options	—	3.3	1.4
Total capitalization	$272.8	$237.6	100.0%

*Includes deferred income taxes of $20.3 million in the book value.

The following sections describe how we estimated the cost of each capital source and its market value.

SHORT-TERM DEBT

Short-term debt matures within one year, so in most cases its book value approximates its market value. The cost of Preston's short-term debt was assumed to equal the cost of its long-term debt, 11 percent (this calculation is described later), since the short-term debt will probably be continuously rolled over. Applying Preston's marginal tax rate of 39 percent resulted in an after-tax cost of 6.7 percent.

INDUSTRIAL REVENUE BONDS

Lacking any details, we assumed that Preston's industrial revenue bonds had a pretax cost roughly 30 percent less than its other long-term debt. This resulted in a pretax cost of 7.7 percent and an after-tax cost of 4.7 percent. We also assumed that the book value of these bonds approximated their market value.

CONVERTIBLE DEBT

At the time of our estimate, Preston had $27.8 million of subordinated convertible debentures outstanding, with a coupon rate of 7 percent. They were convertible into Preston's common stock at $26 per share. Because the current share price was $15.75, these bonds were so far out of the money that we believed they behaved as straight debt and had the same pretax cost as Preston's other long-term debt (11 percent). Because of their conversion feature, convertible bonds have lower coupon rates than straight debt. As a result of these lower interest payments, Preston's convertible debt had a lower interest tax shield and thus a higher after-tax cost than its other debt. We calculated the market value of the convertible bonds, approximately $18.5 million, by discounting their coupon payments and principal repayment at Preston's pretax cost of long-term debt, 11 percent.

The after-tax cost of Preston's convertible debt was estimated as follows:

$$\text{After-tax cost of convertible debt} = \text{Pretax cost}\left(1 - \frac{\text{Coupon rate}}{\text{Opportunity cost}} \times \text{Tax rate}\right)$$

$$= 11\%\left(1 - \frac{7\%}{11\%} \times 39\%\right)$$

$$= 8.3\%$$

OTHER LONG-TERM DEBT

Most of Preston's long-term debt was not publicly traded, so market quotes were not available. Some of Preston's debt was, however, rated by Moody's at Ba. We assumed that Preston's cost of long-term debt was equal to the cost for other similarly rated companies, or 11 percent. In addition, since much of Preston's long-term debt had floating rates, we assumed that its book value approximated its market value.

CAPITAL LEASES

We estimated the cost of Preston's capital leases to equal the cost of long-term debt, 11 percent. We also assumed that their market value was equal to their book value, $2.3 million.

OPERATING LEASES

We estimated the cost of Preston's operating leases to equal the cost of long-term debt, 11 percent. Our estimate of the principal amount of the operating leases, $8.4 million, was derived by assuming that the ratio of the principal amount to annual payments for the operating leases was the same as that for the capital leases.

$$\text{Operating lease value} = \frac{\text{Present value of future minimum capital lease payments}}{\text{Total minimum capital lease payments}} \times \text{Total minimum operating lease payment}$$

$$= \frac{2.3}{2.7} \times \$9.7 \text{ million} = \$8.4 \text{ million}$$

COMMON EQUITY

Using the CAPM, we estimated Preston's cost of equity to be 14.4 percent, as follows:

$$k_s = r_f + [E(r_m) - r_f] \text{ (beta)}$$
$$k_s = 8.8\% + (6.0\% \times 0.925) = 14.4\%$$

The following assumptions were used:

- A risk-free rate of 8.8 percent, the yield to maturity of ten-year Treasury bonds
- A market risk premium of 6 percent
- A beta of 0.925 from BARRA's equity beta book

On July 1, 1988, the market value of Preston's equity was $90.7 million, based on a share price of $15.75 and a total of 5.8 million shares outstanding.

OPTIONS

Roughly 2 percent of Preston's current capital structure was executive stock options. Although option pricing is beyond the scope of this chapter, we used the Black-Scholes European call option formula (see Copeland and Weston 1988, 268–76, for details) as a method of approximating the market values of the two classes of stock options outstanding. Our calculations indicated that the $5.58 options (that could not be exercised until the stock price reached $21.25) had an opportunity cost of approximately 24.6 percent and a market value of $1.2 million; and the $10.26 options had an approximate opportunity cost of 17 percent and a market value of $3.3 million. The before-tax and after-tax cost was the same.

7

Estimating
Continuing Value

Chapter 4 introduced the idea of estimating continuing value as a
device for simplifying company valuations. This chapter describes several approaches to estimating continuing value and
how they can be applied.

As we stated earlier, a company's expected cash flow can be
separated into two time periods and the company's value defined
as follows:

$$\text{Value} = \begin{array}{c}\text{Present value of cash} \\ \text{flow } during \text{ explicit} \\ \text{forecast period}\end{array} + \begin{array}{c}\text{Present value of cash} \\ \text{flow } after \text{ explicit fore-} \\ \text{cast period}\end{array}$$

The second term is the *continuing value*. It is the value of the
company's expected cash flow beyond the explicit forecast period. Using simplifying assumptions about the company's performance during this period—for example, assuming a constant rate of
growth—permits us to estimate continuing value with one of
several formulas. Using a continuing-value formula eliminates
the need to forecast in detail the company's cash flow over an
extended period.

A high-quality estimate of continuing value is essential to any valuation, because continuing value often accounts for a large percentage of the total value of the company. Exhibit 7.1 shows continuing value as a percentage of total value for companies in four industries. In these examples, continuing value accounts for anywhere from 56 percent to 125 percent of total value. While these continuing values are large, this does not mean that most of a company's value will be realized in the continuing-value period. It often just means that the cash inflow in the early years is being more than offset by outflow for capital spending and working

Exhibit 7.1 **CONTINUING VALUE AS A PERCENTAGE OF TOTAL VALUE, EIGHT-YEAR FORECAST PERIOD**

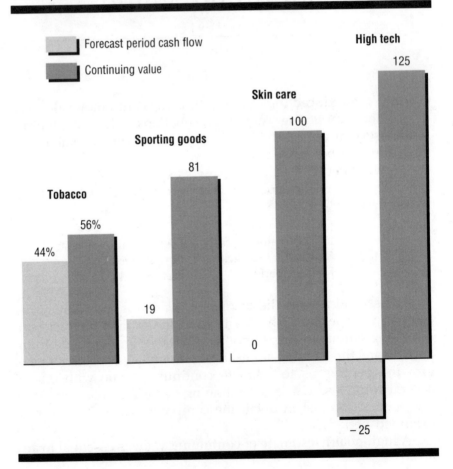

capital investment—investments that should generate higher cash flow in later years. The proper interpretation of continuing value will be discussed in more detail later in this chapter.

The continuing-value approaches outlined in the following pages are all consistent with the overall discounted cash flow framework. We often see continuing value treated as though it is somehow different, as if the company were to be arbitrarily sold or liquidated at the end of the forecast period. While this may be appropriate in some special cases—for example, limited-life joint ventures—such an interpretation often leads to a valuation that is not consistent with the expected economic performance of the company. The approaches that we recommend not only provide consistency, but also provide insight into the underlying economic forces driving the value of the company.

Estimating continuing value involves four steps:

1. Select an appropriate technique.
2. Decide on a forecast horizon.
3. Estimate the valuation parameters and calculate the continuing value.
4. Discount the continuing value to the present.

STEP 1: SELECT AN APPROPRIATE TECHNIQUE

We recommend using one of three discounted cash flow techniques for estimating continuing value. Since all three are based on discounted cash flow, if we use the same underlying assumptions, they all provide the same continuing-value estimate.

The Three Recommended Techniques

The recommended techniques are the long explicit forecast, the growing free cash flow perpetuity formula, and the value-driver formula.

Long explicit forecast Using this technique, we carry out the explicit forecast for a very long period of time (seventy-five or more years) and ignore the continuing value since it would be

insignificantly small. This technique uses the discounted cash
flow framework in its most basic form and is the most intuitive
technique, since it represents what the company is actually expected to experience.

Growing free cash flow perpetuity formula   The growing free cash
flow perpetuity technique uses the following formula:

$$\text{Continuing value}_T = \frac{FCF_{T+1}}{WACC - g}$$

where

FCF_{T+1} = the normalized level of free cash flow in the first
year after the explicit forecast period

$WACC$ = the weighted average cost of capital

g = the expected growth rate in free cash flow in perpetuity

This technique is identical to the first whenever the company's free cash flow is forecast to grow at a constant rate each
year. The formula is simply the algebraic simplification of a growing perpetuity. (See Copeland and Weston 1988, Appendix A, for
the derivation of the formula. This formula is only valid if g is less
than WACC.)

Caution! This formula is easily misused. It is particularly important to correctly estimate the normalized level of free cash flow
that is consistent with the growth rate you are forecasting. Later
in this chapter we give an example that illustrates what can go
wrong when using this formula.

Value-driver formula   The third technique uses the growing free
cash flow perpetuity formula, but expressed in terms of value
drivers, as follows:

$$\text{Continuing value}_T = \frac{NOPLAT_{T+1}\,(1 - g/r)}{WACC - g}$$

where

NOPLAT_{T+1} = the normalized level of net operating profits less adjusted taxes in the first year after the explicit forecast period

g = the expected growth rate in NOPLAT in perpetuity

r = the expected rate of return on net new investment

This value-driver formula produces the same result as the growing cash flow perpetuity formula because the denominators are identical and the numerator is a way of expressing free cash flow in terms of the key value drivers. The expression g/r represents the proportion of NOPLAT investment in additional capital. So the overall expression represents NOPLAT less investment, or free cash flow. Appendix A proves the equivalence of the two formulas.

A simple example demonstrates that all three techniques produce the same continuing-value estimate when the same underlying assumptions are used. We begin with the following cash flow projections:

	Year 1	2	3	4	5
NOPLAT	100	106	112	120	126
Net investment	50	53	56	60	63
Free cash flow	50	53	56	60	63

In this example, the growth rate in NOPLAT and free cash flow each period is 6 percent. The rate of return on net new investment is 12 percent, calculated as the increase in NOPLAT from one year to the next divided by the net investment in the prior year. The WACC is assumed to be 11 percent. First, use a long forecast, say 150 years:

$$\text{Continuing value} = \frac{50}{1.11} + \frac{53}{(1.11)^2} + \frac{56}{(1.11)^3} + \cdots + \frac{50(1.06)^{149}}{(1.11)^{150}}$$

$$\text{Continuing value} = 999$$

Next, use the growing free cash flow perpetuity formula:

$$\text{Continuing value} = \frac{50}{11\% - 6\%}$$

$$\text{Continuing value} = 1{,}000$$

Finally, use the value-driver formula:

$$\text{Continuing value} = \frac{100\,(1 - 6\%/12\%)}{11\% - 6\%}$$

$$\text{Continuing value} = 1{,}000$$

All three approaches yield the same result (though the long fore-cast approach is slightly off because it ignores the cash flow beyond 150 years).

Which of the approaches should you use? Use the technique that is easiest to apply under your particular circumstances. For example, if it is relatively easier to forecast cash flow than returns on incremental capital, use the free cash flow perpetuity formula. If it is easier to evaluate and forecast returns on capital, use the value-driver formula.

Comparison with Other Continuing-Value Approaches

A number of other continuing-value approaches are used in prac-tice, often with misleading results. Some of these are acceptable if used carefully. However, we prefer the recommended ap-proaches because they explicitly rely on the underlying economic assumptions embodied in the company analysis. The other approaches tend to hide the underlying economic assumptions. Exhibit 7.2 illustrates, for a sporting goods company, the wide dispersion of continuing-value estimates arrived at by different techniques.

Exhibit 7.2 **CONTINUING-VALUE ESTIMATES FOR A SPORTING GOODS COMPANY, ARRIVED AT BY DIFFERENT TECHNIQUES**

Technique	Assumptions	Continuing value, $ Millions
Book value	Per accounting records	$268
Liquidation value	80% of working capital	186
	70% of net fixed assets	
Price-to-earnings ratio	Industry average of 15X	624
Market-to-book ratio	Industry average of 1.4X	375
Replacement cost	Book value adjusted for inflation	275
Perpetuity based on final year's cash flow	Normalized FCF growing at inflation rate	428

We classify the most common techniques into two categories: (1) DCF approaches, and (2) non-cash-flow approaches.

Other DCF approaches   The recommended DCF formulas can be modified to derive additional continuing-value formulas with more restrictive (and sometimes unreasonable) assumptions.

The first variation is the convergence formula. For some companies in competitive industries, the return on net new investment can be expected to eventually converge to the cost of capital as all the excess profits are competed away. This assumption allows a simpler version of the value-driver formula, as follows:

$$CV = \frac{NOPLAT}{WACC}$$

The derivation begins with the value-driver formula:

$$CV = \frac{NOPLAT(1 - g/r)}{WACC - g}$$

Assume that r = WACC. In other words, the return on incremental invested capital equals the cost of capital.

$$CV = \frac{NOPLAT(1 - g/WACC)}{WACC - g}$$

$$CV = \frac{NOPLAT \dfrac{[WACC - g]}{[WACC]}}{WACC - g}$$

Cancelling the term WACC – g leaves a simple formula:

$$CV = \frac{NOPLAT}{WACC}$$

The growth term has disappeared from the equation. This does not mean that growth will be zero. It means that growth will add nothing to value, because the return associated with growth just equals the cost of capital.

This formula is sometimes interpreted as implying zero growth (not even with inflation), even though this is clearly not the case. Because of the confusion, it may be sensible to avoid using this formula.

The misinterpretation of the convergence formula has led to another variant: the aggressive formula. This formula assumes that earnings in the continuing-value period will grow at some rate, most often the inflation rate. The conclusion is then drawn that earnings should be discounted at the real WACC rather than the nominal WACC. The resulting formula is as follows:

$$CV = \frac{NOPLAT}{WACC - g}$$

Here, g is the inflation rate. This formula can substantially over-state continuing value because it assumes that NOPLAT can grow without any incremental capital investment. This is very unlikely (or impossible), because any growth will probably require additional working capital, and even maintenance fixed capital investment is likely to exceed depreciation due to inflation.

To show how this formula relates to the value-driver formula, let us assume that the return on incremental capital investment (r) approaches infinity.

$$CV = \frac{NOPLAT \ (1 - g/r)}{WACC - g}$$

$r \to \infty$ therefore $g/r \to 0$

$$CV = \frac{NOPLAT \ (1 - 0)}{WACC - g}$$

$$CV = \frac{NOPLAT}{WACC - g}$$

Exhibit 7.3 compares the two new DCF formulas. This exhibit shows how the return on total invested capital (both existing and new investment) behaves under the two assumptions. In the aggressive case, NOPLAT grows without any new investment so the return on total capital eventually approaches infinity. In the convergence case, the return on total capital moves toward the weighted average cost of capital (WACC) as new capital becomes a larger portion of the total capital base. For most cases, the recommended formulas result in a value between these two extremes.

Non-cash-flow approaches   In addition to the DCF techniques, non-cash-flow approaches to continuing value are sometimes used. Five commonly used approaches are liquidation value, replacement cost, price-to-earnings ratio, market-to-book ratio, and book value.

The liquidation-value approach sets the continuing value equal to an estimate of the proceeds from the sale of the assets of the business after the explicit forecast period. Liquidation value is often far different from the value of the company as a going concern. In a growing, profitable industry, a company's liquidation value is probably far below the going-concern value. In a dying industry, liquidation value may exceed going-concern value. Do not use this approach unless liquidation is likely at the end of the forecast period.

The replacement-cost approach sets the continuing value equal to the expected cost to replace the company's assets. This approach has a number of drawbacks. Most important are the following:

Exhibit 7.3 **RATES OF RETURN IMPLIED BY ALTERNATIVE CONTINUING-VALUE FORMULAS**

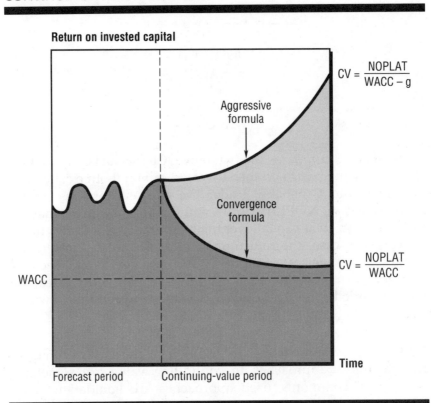

- Only tangible assets are replaceable. The company's "organizational capital" can be valued only on the basis of the cash flow the company generates. The replacement cost of the company's tangible assets may greatly understate the value of the company.
- Not all the company's assets will ever be replaced. Consider a machine used only by this particular industry. The replacement cost of the asset may be so high that it is not economic to replace. Yet, as long as it generates a positive cash flow, the asset is valuable to the ongoing business of the company. Here, the replacement cost may exceed the value of the business as an ongoing entity.

The price-to-earnings (P/E) ratio approach assumes that the company will be worth some multiple of its future earnings in the continuing period. Of course, this will be true; the difficulty arises in trying to estimate an appropriate P/E ratio.

Suppose the current industry average P/E ratio is chosen. Today's P/E ratio reflects the economic prospects of the industry during the explicit forecast period as well as the continuing-value period. However, prospects at the end of the explicit forecast period are likely to be very different from today's. Therefore, we need a different P/E ratio that reflects the company's prospects at the end of the forecast period. What factors will determine that ratio? As we discussed in Chapter 3, the company's expected growth, the rate of return on new capital, and the cost of capital are the primary determinants of its P/E ratio. How do these translate into a P/E ratio? Not very easily. Yet they are the same factors that are in one of our DCF formulas. We suggest that using the DCF approach is easier than using the P/E approach. (We should note here that one trap analysts fall into in acquisitions situations is the circular reasoning that the P/E ratio for the continuing value will equal the P/E ratio paid for the acquisition. In other words, if I pay eighteen times earnings, I should be able to sell the business for eighteen times earnings. However, in most cases, the reason a company is willing to pay a high P/E for an acquisition is that it believes it can take actions to greatly improve earnings. So the effective P/E it is paying on the improved level of earnings will be much less than eighteen. Once the improvements are in place and earnings are higher, buyers will not be willing to pay the same P/E unless they can make additional improvements.)

The market-to-book ratio approach assumes that the company will be worth some multiple of its book value, often the same as its current multiple or the multiples of comparable companies. This approach is conceptually similar to the P/E approach and therefore faces the same problems. In addition to the complexity of deriving an appropriate multiple, the book value itself is distorted by inflation and the arbitrariness of some accounting assumptions. Once again, the DCF approaches are easier to use.

The book-value approach assumes that the continuing value equals the book value of the company. Often, the implicit assumption of this approach is that the company will earn a return on capital (measured in terms of book values) exactly equal to its cost of capital. Therefore, the book value should represent the discounted expected future cash flow. Unfortunately, book values are affected by inflation and the choice of accounting rules. Therefore, they do not provide a reliable base for these assumptions.

STEP 2: SELECT THE FORECAST HORIZON

After selecting a continuing-value method, the next step is to decide how long to make the explicit forecast period. If a very long forecast period is used (seventy-five or more years), then continuing value is irrelevant; this step and the next can be skipped.

While the length of the explicit forecast period you choose is important, it does not affect the value of the company but only the distribution of value between the explicit forecast period and the years that follow. Exhibits 7.4 and 7.5 illustrate this fact. In this example, no matter what the length of the forecast period is, the company value is $893. With a forecast horizon of five years, the continuing value accounts for 79 percent of total value, while with a ten-year horizon, the continuing value accounts for only 60 percent of total value.

The choice of forecast horizon can have an indirect impact on value if it is associated with changes in the economic assumptions underlying the continuing-value estimate. Analysts often unknowingly change their performance forecasts when they change their forecast horizon. For example, many forecasters assume that the rate of return on new invested capital equals the cost of capital in the continuing-value period, but that the company will earn returns exceeding the cost of capital during the explicit forecast period. When they extend the explicit forecast period, they also extend the time period during which returns on new capital are expected to exceed the cost of capital. Therefore, extending the forecast period leads to an increase in value, attributable to the increase in the rate-of-return assumptions.

The explicit forecast period should be long enough so that the business will have reached a steady state of operations by the end

---

Exhibit 7.4 **COMPARISON OF TOTAL VALUE ESTIMATES BASED ON DIFFERENT FORECAST HORIZONS**

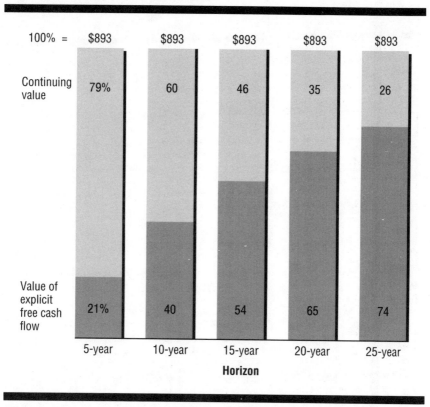

of the period. This is because any continuing-value approach relies on the following key assumptions:

- The company earns constant margins, maintains a constant capital turnover, and, therefore, earns a constant return on invested capital.
- The company grows at a constant rate and invests the same proportion of its gross cash flow in its business each year.
- The company earns a constant return on all new investments.

For example, suppose that you expect the company's margins to decline over time as its customers become more powerful.

Exhibit 7.5 **COMPARISON OF TOTAL VALUE CALCULATIONS FOR FIVE-YEAR AND TEN-YEAR HORIZONS,**
$ MILLIONS

Overall Assumptions					Yrs 1–5	Yrs 6+	
Return on new investment (r)					16%	12%	
Growth rate (g)					9	6	
WACC					12	12	
							Continuing
							base

5-year horizon	1	2	3	4	5		
NOPLAT	$100.0	109.0	118.8	129.5	141.2		$149.6
Depreciation	20.0	21.8	23.8	25.9	28.2		
Gross cash flow	$120.0	130.8	142.6	155.4	169.4		
Gross investment	76.3	83.1	90.6	98.7	107.6		
FCF	$ 43.8	47.7	52.0	56.7	61.8		
Discount factor	0.893	0.797	0.712	0.636	0.567		
Present value of cash flow	39.1	38.0	37.0	36.0	35.0		

$$\text{Continuing value} = \frac{\text{NOPLAT}(1 - g/r)}{\text{WACC} - g} \quad [1/(1 + \text{WACC})]^5 = \frac{\$149.6(1 - 6\%/12\%)}{12\% - 6\%} \; (.5674) = \$707.5$$

Present value of FCF 1–5	$185.1
Continuing value	707.5
Total value	$892.6

Exhibit 7.5 Continued

10-year horizon	1	2	3	4	5	6	7	8	9	10	Continuing base
NOPLAT	$100.0	109.0	118.8	129.5	141.2	149.6	158.6	168.1	178.2	188.9	200.2
Depreciation	20.0	21.8	23.8	25.9	28.2	29.9	31.7	33.6	35.6	37.8	
Gross cash flow	$120.0	130.8	142.6	155.4	169.4	179.6	190.3	201.7	213.9	226.7	
Gross investment	76.3	83.1	90.6	98.7	107.6	104.7	111.0	117.7	124.7	132.2	
FCF	$ 43.8	47.7	52.0	56.7	61.8	74.8	79.3	84.1	89.1	94.5	
Discount factor	0.893	0.797	0.712	0.636	0.567	0.507	0.452	0.404	0.361	0.322	
Present value of cash flow	39.1	38.0	37.0	36.0	35.0	37.9	35.9	34.0	32.1	30.4	

$$\text{Continuing value at year 0} = \frac{\text{NOPLAT}(1 - g/r)}{\text{WACC} - g} \quad [1/(1 + \text{WACC})]^{10} = \frac{\$200.2(1 - 6\%/12\%)}{12\% - 6\%} \quad (.3220) = \$537.2$$

Present value of FCF 1–10	$355.4
Continuing value	537.2
Total value	$892.6

Margins are currently 12 percent and you forecast that they will fall to 9 percent over the next seven years. The explicit forecast period in this case must be at least seven years, because continuing-value approaches cannot account for the declining margin (at least not without much computational complexity). The business must be operating at an equilibrium level for the continuing-value approaches to be useful.

Exhibit 7.6 illustrates for Innovation, Inc., how a company's cash flow patterns can also affect the choice of the forecast period. The company is making value-creating investments in the early years of the forecast, but free cash flow is negative due to these large up-front investments. After the early years, free cash flow increases significantly as the projects begin to pay off and additional investment declines. Finally, free cash flow levels off and begins to grow at a steady rate. In this example, the forecast

Exhibit 7.6 **INNOVATION, INC., FREE CASH FLOW FORECAST AND VALUATION**

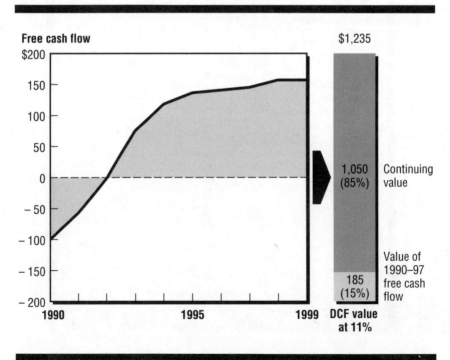

should be extended until the free cash flow growth becomes constant.

The cash flow pattern for Innovation, Inc., raises the important issue of interpretation of continuing-value estimates. It appears from Exhibit 7.6 that 85 percent of Innovation's value comes from the continuing value. Exhibit 7.7 suggests an alternative interpretation of where value is coming from. Innovation has a base business that earns a steady 12-percent return on capital and is growing at 4 percent per year. It also has developed a new product line that will require several years of negative cash flow due to the construction of a new plant. Exhibit 7.7 shows that the base business has a value of $877 or 71 percent of Innovation's total value. So 71 percent of the company's value comes from operations that are currently generating strong cash flow. But the company has decided to reinvest this cash flow in a profitable new product line. This does not mean that 85 percent of the value is more than eight years out. It just means that the cash flow

Exhibit 7.7 **INNOVATION, INC., VALUATION BY COMPONENTS**

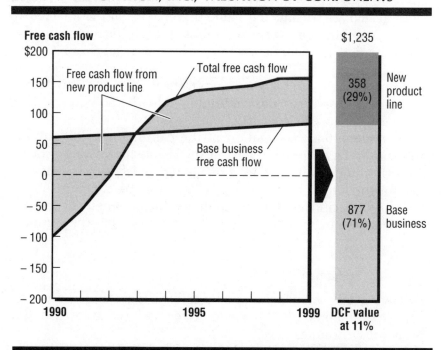

pattern mechanically results in the appearance that most of the value is a long way off.

When in doubt, choose a longer rather than a shorter forecast period. We rarely use a forecast period shorter than seven years. Furthermore, the forecast period should not be determined by the company's internal planning period. Just because the company forecasts out only three years does not justify a three-year forecast period for purposes of valuation. A rough forecast beyond three years is better than no forecast.

STEP 3: ESTIMATE THE PARAMETERS

The parameters that must be defined in order to estimate continuing value are net operating profits less adjusted taxes (NOPLAT), free cash flow (FCF), rate of return on new investment (r), rate of growth (g), and weighted average cost of capital (WACC). Careful estimation of these parameters is critical, because continuing value is highly sensitive to the value of these parameters, particularly the growth assumption. Exhibit 7.8 shows how continuing value (calculated using the value-driver formula) is affected by various combinations of growth rate and rate of return on new investment. The example assumes a $100 base level of NOPLAT and a 10-percent WACC. Notice that at a 14-percent expected rate of return on new capital, changing the growth rate from 6 percent to 8 percent increases the continuing value by 50 percent, from about $1,400 to about $2,100.

Fundamentally, estimation of the continuing-value parameters should be an integral part of the whole forecasting process. The continuing-value parameters should reflect a coherent forecast for the long-term economic situation of the company and its industry. Specifically, the continuing-value parameters should be based on the expected steady state condition that the company will migrate toward.

General Guidelines

Following are some general suggestions regarding continuing-value parameters for the value-driver and the free cash flow perpetuity formulas.

Exhibit 7.8 **IMPACT OF CONTINUING-VALUE ASSUMPTIONS (WACC = 10%; NOPLAT = $100)**

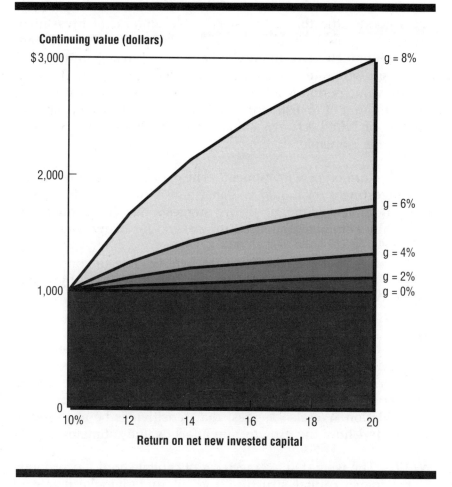

NOPLAT The base level of net operating profits less adjusted taxes should reflect a normalized level of earnings for the company at the midpoint of its business cycle. For example, revenues should generally reflect the continuation of the trends in the last forecast year adjusted to the midpoint of the business cycle. Operating costs should be based on sustainable margin levels, and taxes should be based on long-term expected rates.

Free cash flow First, estimate the base level of NOPLAT as just described. Although NOPLAT is usually based on the last forecast year's results, the prior year's level of investment is probably not a good indicator of the sustainable amount of investment needed for growth in the continuing-value period. Carefully analyze how much investment will be required to sustain the forecasted growth rate. Often the forecasted growth in the continuing-value period is lower than in the explicit forecast period, so the amount of investment should be a proportionately smaller amount of NOPLAT. An exhibit later in this chapter demonstrates this principle.

Rate of return on new investment The expected rate of return on new investment (r) should be consistent with expected competitive conditions. Economic theory suggests that competition will eventually eliminate abnormal returns, so for many companies, set r = WACC.

If you expect that the company will be able to continue its growth and to maintain its competitive advantage, then you might consider setting r equal to the return the company is forecasted to earn during the explicit forecast period.

Growth rate The expected growth rate (g) must be realistic. Few companies can be expected to grow faster than the economy for long periods of time. The best estimate is probably the expected long-term rate of consumption growth for the industry's products plus inflation. We also suggest that sensitivities be analyzed to understand how the growth rate affects value estimates.

WACC The weighted average cost of capital should incorporate a sustainable capital structure and an underlying estimate of business risk consistent with expected industry conditions.

Exhibit 7.9 shows the likely relative positions of various industries along different continuing-value parameters for the foreseeable future.

Potential Pitfalls

Some of the common mistakes made in estimating continuing values include naive base-year extrapolation, naive overconservatism, and purposeful overconservatism.

Exhibit 7.9 **LIKELY RELATIVE POSITIONS OF SELECTED INDUSTRIES ALONG CONTINUING-VALUE PARAMETERS**

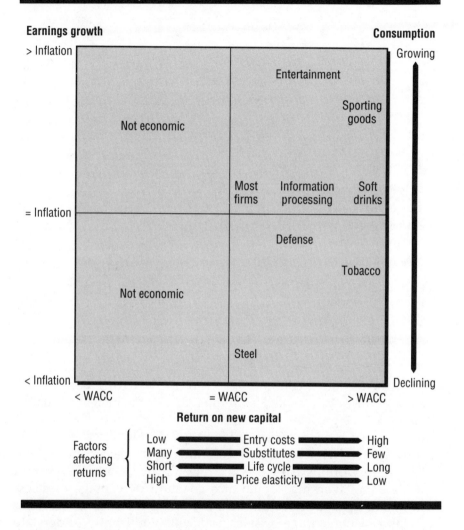

Naive base-year extrapolation   Exhibit 7.10 illustrates a common error in forecasting the base level of free cash flow. From year 9 to year 10 (the last forecast year), the company's earnings and cash flow grew by 10 percent. The forecast suggests that growth in the continuing-value period will be 5 percent per year. A naive, and incorrect, forecast for year 11 (the continuing-value base year) simply increases every cash flow from year 10 by 5 percent, as

Exhibit 7.10 **RIGHT AND WRONG WAYS TO FORECAST THE BASE FREE CASH FLOW**

	Year 9	Year 10	Year 11 (5% growth) Incorrect	Year 11 (5% growth) Correct
Sales	$1,000	$1,100	$1,155	$1,155
− Operating expenses	(850)	(935)	(982)	(982)
= EBIT	150	165	173	173
− Cash taxes	(60)	(66)	(69)	(69)
= NOPLAT	90	99	104	104
+ Depreciation	27	30	32	32
= Gross cash flow	$ 117	$ 129	$ 136	$ 136
Capital expenditures	30	33	35	35
+ **Increase in working capital**	27	30	32	17
= Gross investment	$ 57	$ 63	$ 67	$ 52
Free cash flow	**$ 60**	**$ 66**	**$ 69**	**$ 84**
Memo: Year-end working capital	$ 300	$ 330	$ 362	$ 347
Working capital/sales	30%	30%	31%	30%
Increase in working capital/sales	2.7%	2.7%	2.7%	1.5%

shown in the third column. This forecast is wrong because the increase in working capital is far too large for the increase in sales. Since sales are growing more slowly, the proportion of gross cash flow devoted to increasing working capital should decline significantly, as shown in the last column. In the last column, the increase in working capital is the amount necessary to maintain the year-end working capital at a constant percentage of sales. The naive approach results in a continual increase in working capital as a percentage of sales and will significantly understate the value of the company. Note that in the third column, free cash flow is 18 percent lower than it should be.

Naive overconservatism Many analysts always assume that the incremental return on capital in the continuing-value period will equal the cost of capital. This also relieves them of having to forecast a growth rate, since growth in this case neither adds nor destroys value. For some businesses, this is obviously wrong. For example, both Coca-Cola's and Pepsi's soft drink businesses earn very high returns on invested capital, and their returns are unlikely to fall substantially as they continue to grow. Assuming that r = WACC for these businesses would substantially understate their values. This applies equally to just about any business that sells something proprietary that is unlikely ever to be duplicated.

Purposeful overconservatism   Analysts sometimes are overly conservative because of the uncertainty and size of the continuing value. If continuing value is estimated properly, the uncertainty cuts both ways: the results are just as likely to be higher than the estimate as lower. So conservatism overcompensates for the uncertainty. This is not to say, however, that you should not be concerned about the uncertainty. That is why careful development of scenarios is a critical element of any valuation.

STEP 4: DISCOUNT THE CONTINUING VALUE TO THE PRESENT

The continuing value that you have estimated is the value at the end of the explicit forecast period. This estimate must be discounted back to the present at the WACC before it can be added to the present value of the explicit free cash flow.

PRESTON CORPORATION

ESTIMATING CONTINUING VALUE

We will use the value-driver approach to estimate Preston's continuing value, and will estimate the parameters as follows:

- The NOPLAT at the beginning of the continuing-value period (one year after the last forecast year) is simply 1997's NOPLAT increased by a rate of growth reflecting our forecast for 1998. In Chapter 5, we forecast Preston's 1998 NOPLAT to be $63.8 million.

- Preston's WACC is forecasted to remain at 9.9 percent. We do not foresee any significant change in Preston's capital structure or business risk.

- Preston's return on net new invested capital beyond 1997 is forecasted to equal its WACC, 9.9 percent. The trucking industry is highly competitive, so it is reasonable to expect that industry returns on new capital will be driven toward the cost of capital in the long run. Preston does not possess any proprietary skill or assets that are likely to enable it to earn better returns than the industry as a whole.

- We expect that Preston's NOPLAT will grow at slightly above the rate of inflation. This forecast is based on the assumption that the nominal growth in its level of business is tied to nominal industrial production growth. Therefore, we forecast a nominal growth rate of 9.0% (3.0% real growth plus 6.0% inflation).

Using these parameters in the recommended continuing-value formula results in an estimated continuing value of $644 million in 1997.

$$CV = \frac{NOPLAT(1 - g/r)}{WACC - g}$$

$$CV = \frac{\$63.8\ (1 - 9.0\%/9.9\%)}{9.9\% - 9.0\%}$$

$$CV = \$644$$

8

Calculating and Interpreting Results

The final phase of the valuation process involves calculating and testing the company's value, then interpreting the results in terms of the decision context involved.

STEP 1: CALCULATE AND TEST RESULTS

Once the preceding valuation steps have been completed for each scenario being examined, calculating the company's equity value is a relatively straightforward process. It involves the following tasks:

1. Discounting the forecasted free cash flow and continuing value at the company's weighted average cost of capital to determine the total value of the company's operations.

2. Adding the value of any nonoperating assets whose cash flows were *excluded* from free cash flow to estimate the value of the total entity. Such items might include excess marketable securities, the overfunding in a pension plan (after tax), and investments in unrelated subsidiaries. The value of these assets should be estimated on the basis of

their respective expected cash flows and appropriate discount rates, or by reference to their market values. For example, because excess marketable securities are zero-net-present-value investments, the present value of all future cash flow related to marketable securities equals their current market value (which for most money market instruments also equals their book value).

3. Subtracting the market value of all debt, hybrid securities, minority interest, or other claims superior to the residual equity. The estimation of market values of these financings was explained in Chapter 6.

Exhibit 8.1 illustrates what this typical calculation of equity value might look like.

After estimating the equity value for each scenario, you should perform several checks to test the logic of the results, minimize the possibility of errors, and ensure that you have a

Exhibit 8.1 **SAMPLE VALUATION SUMMARY**

Discounted free cash flow	$5,000
+ Overfunded pension fund	50
+ Excess marketable securities	300
+ Other nonoperating assets	0
= **Company value**	**$5,350**
Short-term interest-bearing debt	$ 200
+ Operating leases	100
+ Long-term interest-bearing debt	1,200
+ Capital leases	300
+ Preferred stock	500
+ Warrants	0
= **Value of liabilities**	**$2,300**
Company value	$5,350
− Value of liabilities	$2,300
= **Equity value**	**$3,050**

good understanding of the forces driving the valuation. These checks involve asking such questions about the results as the following:

- Is the resulting value consistent with the value drivers implied by the forecast? For example, a company that has been projected to earn rates of return on invested capital far above its WACC should have a value far above such benchmarks as its book value. If the resulting value is low, a computational error has probably been made.

- How does the resulting value compare to the company's market value? If your estimate of value is far from the market value, try to identify the causes of the difference as concretely as possible. Do you expect higher revenue growth? Higher margins? Lower capital spending? If the market value is higher than your estimate, is the difference attributable to a pending takeover?

- Do any of the results require special explanation? Are there obvious issues, such as significant deviations from historical trends, that should be explained? Are the results as expected? If not, can you explain why not? What factors caused the results to be different from expected?

- Are the financial aspects of the forecast (amounts of debt and marketable securities) achievable and desirable? If debt or excess marketable securities are excessive relative to the company's targets, how should the company resolve the imbalance? Should it raise equity if too much debt is projected? Should the company be willing to raise equity at its current market price?

As you begin to synthesize the results of your valuations, we suggest that you lay out the value of each scenario against its value drivers and any critical operating assumptions (like gross margins or capital spending), including nonquantified assumptions like new product development and the expected competitive response. This should help provide an overall perspective on each scenario and the relationships among them.

STEP 2: INTERPRET THE RESULTS WITHIN
THE DECISION CONTEXT

The purpose of valuing a company is always to help guide some management decision, be it acquisition, divestiture, or adoption of internal strategic initiatives. The results must be analyzed from the perspective of the decision at hand. And since uncertainty and risk are involved in most business decisions, *you should always think of value in terms of scenarios and ranges of value that reflect this uncertainty. Do not express values as single-point estimates; this can be dangerously misleading and often wrong.*

The decision based on any one scenario will generally be obvious, given its estimated impact on shareholder value. But interpreting multiple scenarios, developing the range of confidence you should have in your results, and determining how they should be presented (all relative to the decision at hand) are considerably more complex. At a minimum, we would suggest that you do the following:

1. Clearly identify the primary value drivers in each scenario tested and differences in value among scenarios, as well as the key assumptions underlying those drivers.

2. Understand how much the key variables underlying the results of each scenario could change without altering the decision. This provides a sense of the margin for error in the decision. Obviously, a large margin gives greater comfort in the decision. But too large an error margin is suspicious. Reconsider your assumptions by asking the following questions:
   - If the decision is clearly affirmative (to go ahead with the contemplated action), what would have to go wrong to invalidate the decision? How likely is that to occur?
   - If the decision is negative, what are the upside possibilities that are being passed up?

3. Assess the likelihood of change in the key assumptions underlying each scenario (assigning each a probability of occurrence). For example, consider the following:
   - The impact and likelihood of change in the broad en-

vironmental assumptions underlying the scenario. How critical are they to the results? Some industries are more dependent on basic environmental conditions than others. Home building, for example, is highly correlated with the overall health of the economy. Branded food processing, on the other hand, is less affected by broad economic trends.

- Assumptions about the competitive structure of the industry. A scenario that assumes substantial market share increases is probably less likely in a highly competitive and concentrated market than in an industry with fragmented and inefficient competition.

- Assumptions about the company's internal capabilities to achieve the results predicted in the scenario. For example, can the company develop the products on time and manufacture them within the expected range of costs?

4. Develop alternative scenarios suggested by the preceding analyses. The process of examining initial results may well uncover unanticipated questions that are best resolved through evaluating additional scenarios. This implies that the valuation process is inherently circular. Doing the valuation itself often provides insights that lead to additional scenarios and analyses.

A FEW LAST THOUGHTS

Valuation depends mainly on understanding the business, its industry, and the general economic environment, and then doing a careful job of forecasting. Careful thought and hard work leads to foresight. Correct methodology is only a small, but necessary, part of the valuation process. Over the years we have seen many pitfalls that can easily be avoided. What follows are a few words of wisdom about common problems.

Avoid Shortcuts

Always forecast the full set of financial statements: income statement, balance sheet, and cash flow. Too often, analysts forecast only the income statement and a partial balance sheet—for example, changes in working capital and new investment. This approach does not allow them to cross-check the validity of their assumptions by studying financial ratio changes during the forecast period. An even worse mistake is to forecast only the income statement, and then discount projected net income at the cost of equity. Remember, cash flow to equity holders is not net income, but rather dividends.

Avoid Hockey Sticks

The obvious example of a hockey stick is the forecast that predicts a remarkable turnaround for an underperforming company in a declining industry. A good preventive for analyst forecasts that are wildly optimistic is to require specification of the exact actions necessary to cause the turnaround and why current management is likely to implement them. A more subtle, but no less relevant, pitfall can trip up those who forecast in cyclical industries. Continuing-value estimates are particularly sensitive to the phase of the cycle on which the estimates are based. As illustrated in Exhibit 8.2, problems can occur if the end of the forecast period falls anywhere other than on an average year. In Exhibit 8.2, the end of the forecast period falls near the peak of the earnings cycle. Consequently, the company will be overvalued because the peak earnings are used in the continuing-value assumption. The solution to this problem is to forecast far enough out to capture a complete cycle, and to use an average year as the NOPLAT input to the continuing-value formula.

Use Longer Forecast Horizons

Longer forecast horizons are better than shorter horizons, for two reasons. First, a long forecast horizon forces you to be explicit about your forecast assumptions over a longer period of time. Second, analysts feel a strong tendency to use the perpetuity continuing-value model, and it may be entirely inappropriate for the case at hand. For example, the perpetuity model assumes that the return on new investment equals the weighted average cost of capital. For companies like PepsiCo that have returns well above their WACC and established brand names, it is completely unrea-

Exhibit 8.2 **A FORECAST PERIOD THAT WILL RESULT IN A POOR VALUATION OF A CYCLICAL BUSINESS**

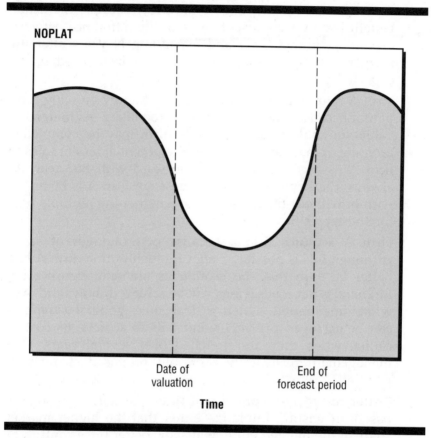

NOPLAT

Date of valuation

End of forecast period

Time

sonable to assume that their return falls to WACC all at once after, let's say, a ten-year forecast horizon. Either the forecast horizon should be much longer or the perpetuity model should not be used. If you use the perpetuity model in your valuation, test its validity by doubling your forecast period to see how sensitive your valuation is to the perpetuity assumption.

Be Realistic About Synergies

Too often, mergers are based on fictional synergies. Although the list is endless, here are a few examples:

- Firm A, needing to expand, purchases firm B because it has excess capacity. The valuation analysis adds the full excess capacity as a benefit. This is an error, because the actual benefit is only the present value of the difference between expanding immediately and expanding N years after the merger, when the excess capacity has been used up by expected growth.

- Firm A refuses to acquire a small but rapidly growing competitor because "the P/E multiple is too high." Although the valuation analysis of the smaller firm may be completely accurate, it may fail to consider the potential loss in sales to firm A as a cost of not going forward with the deal. As always, the key issue is whether or not firm A is better off with or without the merger—not whether the multiple paid for the target firm is too high.

- Firm A acquires firm B because of economies of scale. Although this is possibly a relevant justification, firm A had better be sure that the economies are real, figuring beforehand what cost savings will be achieved, how, and over what time period. Often a deal looks good if synergies can be achieved overnight, but fails to achieve its cost of capital when they are stretched over several years. Can management realistically carry out proposed changes as planned?

- "After the merger, prices will firm." Usually, this idea is based on wishful thinking—either that the higher market share of the merged entity will allow better price control, or that shutting down high-cost production facilities will result in firmer prices. In both cases, the analysis usually ignores close substitutes for the product and/or international competition.

- Cost cuts resulting from a merger rarely take place all at once. They take time. And severance pay, pension payments, and plant shut-down costs all can diminish projected savings from cost cuts.

- An almost irresistible temptation is to double count undervalued assets on the balance sheet. For example, Cannon Mills owned hundreds of houses in the town of

Cannonapolis and they were carried on the books at 1920 prices. Assuming that rents were properly forecasted in the company's cash flows, the value of the houses is already included in its present value. Adding in the current market value of the houses would be double counting.

Look Out for Off-Balance-Sheet Items

If off-balance-sheet items are found in publicly available information, they are probably already reflected in the market price of a company. For example, LIFO inventory reserves or overfunded pension plans are probably already reflected in the market price. The way you put them in your valuation depends on your cash flow forecast. For example, if your forecast assumes continued above-normal rates of pension contributions, you need to add the present value of pension overfunding to your valuation. The biggest problem with off-balance-sheet items, however, occurs when they are not publicly available. For example, how would you change the valuation of a company if you knew that its founder and key executive was having health problems?

PRESTON CORPORATION

CALCULATING AND INTERPRETING THE RESULTS

We will now complete and analyze the Preston valuation using the explicit DCF approach. The first part of this section puts together the results of the data presented and the steps described in the prior three chapters of the book. The second part analyzes those results and evaluates two scenarios for Preston Corporation.

RESULTS OF THE PRESTON VALUATION

To recap, the valuation approach involves discounting our forecasted free cash flow (FCF) and continuing value at the weighted average cost of capital (WACC), and adding the market value of nonoperating assets excluded from the FCF to determine the value of the entity as a whole. The market value of debt and other nonequity financing must then be deducted to determine the residual equity value of the company.

In addition to its discounted free cash flow and debt, three other items are included in the valuation of Preston's equity:

1. Preston owned $3.2 million of excess marketable securities at the end of 1987.
2. Preston had an after-tax unfunded pension liability of about $12.2 million.
3. Outstanding executive stock options were worth about $4.5 million.

Exhibit 8.3 summarizes the results of the valuation. The first part displays the free cash flow for each year during the ten-year forecast period, the appropriate discount factor (based on 9.9 percent WACC), and the present value of each free cash flow. To these we add the present value of the continuing value. Note that the discount factors assume that the cash flow is received or paid out midway through the year rather than at the end of the year. With the addition of the present value of excess marketable securities, we value the company at $245.5 million. Subtracting the market value of Preston's debt and other nonequity financing, the resulting equity value totals $86.4 million, or $15 per share.

At the time of the valuation, Preston's shares were trading at about $15.75 per share—close to our estimated value. This suggests that the market expected Preston to perform in much the same way as our forecast did. Analysts generally believed Preston's equity to be slightly overpriced. This conclusion was based on their skepticism regarding rate increases recently enacted by the industry. They believed that the historical tendency for these increases to be discounted by carriers eager to capture market share would continue. However, it appears that the rate increases are largely holding.

CHECKING THE RESULTS

We examined the Preston valuation in light of its assumptions and value drivers and found them reasonably consistent; however, our forecast does contain substantial deviations from Preston's historical performance because of expected changes in the competitive nature of the industry. A

Exhibit 8.3 **PRESTON CORPORATION'S ESTIMATED VALUE USING THE DCF APPROACH,** $ MILLIONS

Year	Free Cash Flow	Discount Factor	Present value of FCF
1988	($3.9)	0.9539	($3.7)
1989	(2.9)	0.8680	(2.5)
1990	0.9	0.7898	0.7
1991	0.7	0.7186	0.5
1992	1.1	0.6539	0.7
1993	(6.1)	0.5950	(3.7)
1994	(7.1)	0.5414	(3.8)
1995	(7.4)	0.4926	(3.6)
1996	(6.6)	0.4482	(3.0)
1997	(4.8)	0.4079	(1.9)
Continuing value	644.0	0.4079	262.7
Operating value			$242.3
Excess marketable securities			3.2
Entity value			245.5
Debt and leases			(142.4)
Unfunded pension			(12.2)
Value of stock options			(4.5)
Equity value			$86.4
Value per share			$15.00

noteworthy aspect of the forecast is that despite the need for Preston to reinvest nearly all of its NOPLAT in order to grow at its expected rate, we also forecast the dividend payout to remain at its historical level. Our forecast therefore projects that Preston will take on greater amounts of debt to meet its investment and dividend requirements.

The following table displays the results of a simple sensitivity analysis of the Preston valuation. The columns show the percentage changes in the total entity and equity values caused by altering key input parameters—for example, by raising Preston's operating margin and capital turnover ratios to industry-average levels.

| | Change in value ||
	Entity	Equity
Operating margin at industry average	+54.3%	+154.3%
Capital turnover at industry average	+22.9	+ 65.2
Operating margin and capital turnover at industry average	+69.5	+197.5
Revenue growth of 1.75% more per year without improved margin	+13.7	+ 39.0

From this analysis, it is evident that Preston is very sensitive to changes in its operating margin. For example, if its operating margin rises to equal the industry average, its stock price will more than double. This indicates to us that the next step is to look for means to improve its operating margin as keys to providing value-creating opportunities for Preston. The company has much to gain from improved performance.

As we have noted, after years of very costly and intense rate competition in the industry, rates appear finally to have begun to climb again. Our valuation contains the assumption of continued moderate rate growth in the industry that will eventually approach the rate of inflation. However, this forecast is by no means certain. It is therefore necessary to analyze the effects of different scenarios on Preston.

One possible scenario is that in the near future at least one large carrier or several smaller carriers will attempt to gain market share by discounting away the recent rate increases enacted by the industry. Such rate discounting has plagued industry profitability since deregulation. The history of the industry suggests that the result of such discounting would be the provocation of renewed rate wars over market share. This scenario assumes that this competition will continue until early 1990, at which time the long-overdue rate growth finally commences.

The effect of such a scenario on Preston would be devastating. Preston is a relatively small carrier that has suffered greatly since the deregulation of the industry. Preston would be earning very close to its cost of capital even if recent rate increases persist. A prolonging of the severe rate competition in the industry could be fatal to Preston. If rates were not to begin their slow rise until 1990, Preston's already small operating margins would be erased by rising costs. As a result, Preston's invested capital would be earning less than its cost of capital—that is, the company would be destroying shareholder value. Our forecast indicates that Preston's equity would be worth −$127 million under this scenario. Preston would probably be bankrupt.

However, an alternative positive scenario is also possible. If the industry is successful in maintaining the recently enacted rate increases, its members could successfully attempt to recover even more of the lost profitability of recent years. Under this scenario, the industry will adopt additional rate increases of 1.75 percent each year until 1992 (after which rates will rise at the rate of inflation). Although such a scenario would require near-uniform rate discipline in the industry, it would have a strong positive effect on Preston's and the rest of the industry's revenues and operating margins. Our analysis indicates that under this scenario, Preston's equity value would rise to $96 per share.

We do not believe that larger additional rate increases are likely. High profitability in the industry attracted numerous new entrants upon deregulation, leading to the financial troubles encountered by the industry through the 1980s. The industry is unlikely to allow rates to once again rise to the point where new firms find it profitable to enter.

Part III

Applying Valuation

9

Multibusiness
Valuation

Many valuations involve multibusiness companies whose futures depend on successful management of the portfolio of business units under their control. Multibusiness valuation is useful for several purposes, not the least of which is simply *understanding the business*. Strategic decisions for most multibusiness companies take place at the business-unit level. Thorough understanding of the company requires careful analysis of the threats and opportunities faced by each business unit. Hence, a company valuation built from separate valuations of business units provides much deeper insight than a company valuation that looks at the organization as a whole. The separate valuation of business units is at the heart of value-based planning at such companies as Pepsico, Contel, Westinghouse, Hillenbrand, Heinz, Marriott, and Union Carbide. More arcane planning targets, such as return on equity or return on assets, fail to link directly to value and are easier for division managers to manipulate.

Multibusiness valuation is also useful for determining break-up value and for assessing acquisition candidates. It can help to create a clearer picture of headquarters costs and benefits since headquarters can be valued as if it were a stand-alone business.

The central question is usually whether benefits of headquarters are commensurate with costs or if some of the extra layers of overhead can be trimmed.

Perhaps the most important use of multibusiness valuation is assessing opportunities for *restructuring* a company by taking advantage of all conceivable value enhancements, either internal or external. For example, an outside-in form of multibusiness valuation that might be called a "raider analysis" can be used to demonstrate how a raider, using publicly available information, could reshape the company.

The focus of this chapter is using multibusiness valuation to assess restructuring opportunities. We begin by reviewing the pentagon model introduced in Chapter 2.

THE RESTRUCTURING PENTAGON

Exhibit 9.1 provides a pentagon framework for thinking about value creation in a multibusiness company using internally available information. Recall that this is the pentagon used by Ralph Demsky in our example in Chapter 2.

First, the *"as is" discounted cash flow* valuation is compared with the *current market value* of the company. Any difference between these values is a *perceptions gap.* If the market-determined shareholder value is less than the "as is" value, then management needs to do a better job of communicating with the market so that the market value increases. A share repurchase program is also a possibility. In the opposite case, a negative perceptions gap may mean the company is a potential takeover target and needs to close the gap by managing assets better.

One way to close a negative perceptions gap is to undertake *internal improvements* (for example, increasing operating margins and sales growth, and decreasing working-capital requirements). By taking advantage of strategic and operating opportunities, the company can realize its potential value as a portfolio of assets. These are the myriad fine-tuning opportunities that arise from understanding the relationship between operating parameters of each business unit and value creation. These key value drivers were a main focus of Chapter 5.

Exhibit 9.1 **PENTAGON FRAMEWORK FOR ASSESSING RESTRUCTURING OPPORTUNITIES**

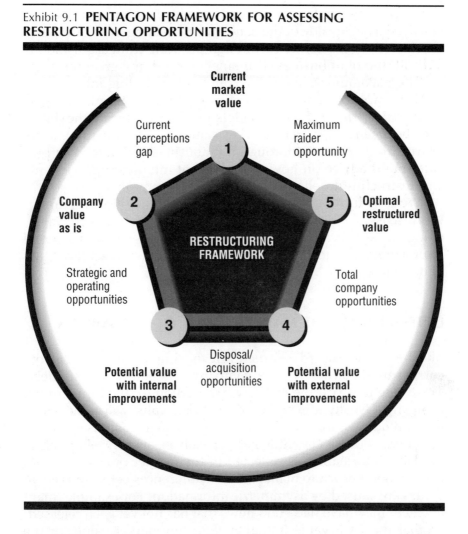

The next step, and the one that is emphasized here, is determining the value-enhancement potential that arises from *external opportunities*—shrinking the company via sell-offs, expanding it through acquisitions, or both. Unrelated businesses are particularly good candidates for sell-offs. For example, an electric utility that owns a drugstore chain may discover that it knows nothing about retail sales and that it is better off selling the chain to another owner. Divestiture can enhance value to the seller, which can then redeploy the cash received to improve its core business. The flip side of the coin, and something to be cautiously considered, is acquisition. Although profiting from acquisition is difficult, the right business combination can bring great rewards.

The maximum value of the company, including internal and external improvements and benefits from financial engineering, is its *optimal restructured value*. Raiders profit by capturing the difference between the current market value of the company and its restructured value. A thorough multibusiness valuation can provide sound advice on how to implement internal improvements and restructure to eliminate potential raider profits.

We now turn our attention to the economics of restructuring. We discuss, in turn, looking at the market-determined value, doing an "as is" valuation, then considering internal and external improvements, and finally putting it all together to achieve maximum value.

DETERMINING THE MARKET VALUE OF A COMPANY

The first step toward restructuring is simple. Just look at the current market value of the company—its equity and its debt. This value tells you the market's expectation for the future of the company. Usually, the market-determined value will agree with a discounted cash flow valuation of the company as it is currently operated, because very little gap typically exists between publicly available information as reflected in the market price and inside information known to management. Differences between the two values are caused by asymmetric information. For example, management may have had good news that has not yet been released, so that the DCF value is higher than the market value, or the market is anticipating a takeover and the premium to be received if an offer is made.

The perceptions gap can also be used as a reality test for management. Sometimes management's perception of the future of the company is unrealistic. For example, executives in the steel industry have been known to follow a policy of investing heavily in capital that returned more than the cost of debt but less than the weighted average cost of capital. Since earnings grew, they thought they were doing well, but the market had a different opinion and share prices fell. The market requires that the return on invested capital exceed the cost of capital in order for value to be created.

VALUING THE MULTIBUSINESS COMPANY "AS IS"

Valuing a multibusiness company "as is" is fundamentally the same as valuing a single-business company. The discounted cash flow process that was detailed in Chapter 4 comprises the basic knowledge needed in order to do a multibusiness valuation. What makes multibusiness valuation more complex is that each business unit has its own capital structure and cost of capital, business units often share cash flows, and headquarters costs and benefits are hard to estimate.

Exhibit 9.2 shows the steps in valuing a multibusiness company "as is." The outcome is separate valuations of each business unit and of corporate headquarters. These values provide the basis for the restructuring pentagon. The business units can be thought of as building blocks that can be fine-tuned via operating improvements, sold to owners who are willing to pay a premium to put them to a better alternative use or to manage them better, or combined with business units of another company in an acquisition.

Each step in the process of multibusiness valuation is described in detail in the following pages.

Step 1: Define Business Units

Business units are defined as separable entities that have no significant synergies with any other part of the company. In principle, they could be split off as stand-alone businesses or sold to another company. Corporate headquarters costs that can be attributed to business units should be treated as business-unit costs. The remaining headquarters costs should be kept with headquarters as a cost center.

A good rule of thumb is to define business units at the smallest practical level of aggregation. For example, a company may have a consumer products division, but consumer products can

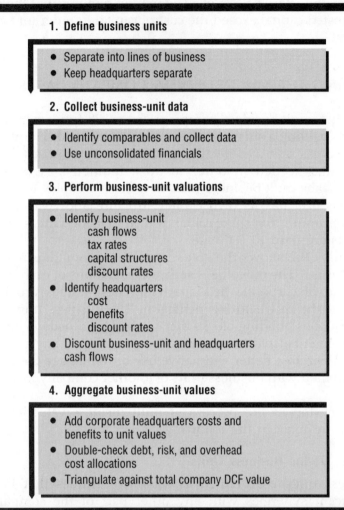

Exhibit 9.2 **STEPS IN A MULTIBUSINESS COMPANY VALUATION**

1. Define business units

- Separate into lines of business
- Keep headquarters separate

2. Collect business-unit data

- Identify comparables and collect data
- Use unconsolidated financials

3. Perform business-unit valuations

- Identify business-unit
    cash flows
    tax rates
    capital structures
    discount rates
- Identify headquarters
    cost
    benefits
    discount rates
- Discount business-unit and headquarters cash flows

4. Aggregate business-unit values

- Add corporate headquarters costs and benefits to unit values
- Double-check debt, risk, and overhead cost allocations
- Triangulate against total company DCF value

be broken down into soap, toiletries, and detergents. These are logically separable business units as long as they do not have interdependent means of production, distribution, or marketing.

Identifying business units and allocating cash flows among them is not always easy. Exhibit 9.3 illustrates a hypothetical company that markets three products: plastics, fuels, and bicycles. Plastics and fuels are joint products from a single chem-

Exhibit 9.3 **DEFINITION OF BUSINESS UNITS FOR A HYPOTHETICAL COMPANY**

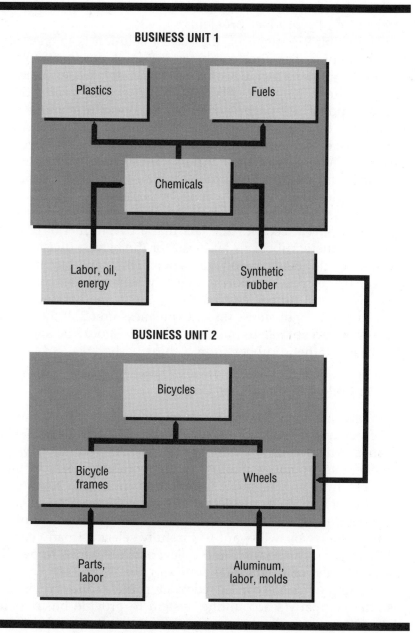

ical plant. This same plant produces synthetic rubber as a by-product that is used for the manufacture of bicycle tires. How shall business units be defined? How shall we handle the joint product and by-product problems?

As Exhibit 9.3 suggests, the easiest solution is to create two business units. The first combines the joint products—plastics and fuels—under a single roof. This is advisable because they are produced in a single facility and because their production is interdependent. Management of the business unit must maximize value by choosing the best output mix of plastics and fuels given market demand, production constraints for the two products, and the cost of their inputs. The general principle is to combine joint products (interdependent or contingent products) into a single business unit whenever possible.

Business unit 2 produces bicycles. It is clearly independent of business unit 1 except for the fact that a by-product of business unit 1, synthetic rubber, is an input for the bicycle division. This product could be acquired elsewhere from another supplier. Hence, the bicycle division is logically separable as a business unit. Synthetic rubber can be "sold," at a market-determined transfer price, by business unit 1 to business unit 2. If the transfer price is not acceptable to business unit 2, it should be allowed to purchase synthetic rubber from a third party.

Step 2: Collect Business-Unit Data

If you are analyzing a company from the outside (for example, in a merger and acquisition review), you will not have detailed business-unit accounting data to use. At best, you will have data on revenues, operating margins, and identifiable assets by line of business from the segment information in annual reports. For example, if you do not have data on capital employed, it can be estimated using asset turnover ratios of comparable companies. In any event, you will want to carefully select as many comparable companies as possible and collect data on them. (Appendix B contains a list of useful data sources.)

If your analysis is conducted from inside a company, you can use the company's accounting system to provide business-unit data. Often you will need to request that the company's information be reclassified to conform to the business-unit definitions relevant to your study. Once the internally generated data is ready, you will need to compare it with publicly available data on comparable businesses.

Step 3: Perform Business-Unit Valuations

As the how-to-do-it section, this is the longest and most detailed. The following general principles apply:

- Each business unit has its own operating cash flow. Transfer-pricing problems, if any, between business units will need to be resolved. The cost of corporate services (for example, accounting services) that the business unit would use were it self-sufficient should be allocated to it.
- Corporate headquarters is kept as a separate business unit with identifiable costs and benefits. The tradeoff between these costs and benefits determines the optimal size of headquarters.
- The effective tax rate for each business unit, when viewed as a separate entity, is different from when the unit is viewed as part of the multibusiness corporation.
- Each business unit has a unique capital structure that can be determined from its cash flow, from the assets that are attributed to it, and from studying comparable companies. A unique WACC corresponds to the business risk and financial structure of each business unit.
- Headquarters should be valued by discounting its cash flow at the relevant risk-adjusted cost of capital.

Keeping these principles in mind, we turn to a detailed discussion of the issues involved in valuing business units. From this point forward, we assume that the valuation is from an insider's point of view; that is, all internal data is readily accessible.

Identify business-unit cash flows   The guiding principle is to estimate business-unit cash flows assuming that each unit is standalone, separate from the remainder of the company. This approach will help later in determining whether the business unit should remain under the corporate umbrella or be split off. Additionally, it will provide a good perspective for analyzing the costs and benefits of corporate headquarters. To identify business-unit cash flows, we need to deal with two typical problems: transfer pricing and corporate overhead.

Transfer pricing is the problem that arises when the output of one business unit is the input of another. A high price will increase profits of the supplier at the expense of the user, and vice versa. The recommended solution is to establish a transfer price as close as possible to the market price of close substitutes. Unfortunately, this can be a difficult task if substitutes are hard to find. The main idea, however, is to approximate market prices so that profit is appropriately allocated to the supplier or to the user of the good or service.

Taxation often complicates transfer pricing. One of the benefits of the corporate umbrella (that is, of headquarters) is that it can establish a transfer-pricing system that keeps profits in the jurisdiction that has the lowest tax burden. As a result, one set of (artificial) transfer prices may be used for tax purposes and another set of (market-determined) prices for determining business unit-cash flows. This topic is covered in greater depth in Chapter 10, as multinational business valuation is an area where transfer pricing is often crucial.

Allocating corporate overhead is a problem closely related to transfer pricing. The central issue is whether business units would use corporate services if they were spun off to become separate entities. Many services *would* be used; for example, accounting, legal, computer, and internal consulting services. Whenever possible, the cost of these services should be allocated to business units on a usage basis or, failing that, on the basis of a reasonable proxy for usage, such as operating income, revenues, capital employed, or numbers of employees.

In theory, market prices should be used for allocation purposes. For example, one hour of a headquarters accountant's time should be billed to a division based on the market price of accountants' time in general—that is, at the opportunity cost to the division. Any difference between the market price and the actual salary paid to the accountant by headquarters is a benefit of, or cost to, headquarters. Clearly, record keeping for this kind of system can get out of hand with too much detail and few companies will implement it. However, the general principle remains—headquarters costs that would not be borne by business units were they separate—for example, the headquarters jet—should not be allocated.

Determine the cash flow costs and benefits of corporate headquarters Attributable to headquarters are the costs and benefits that arise from combining business units under a single corporate umbrella rather than running them as separate entities. Determining these costs and benefits is a difficult exercise that requires a great deal of judgment, but it is an important aspect of the corporate restructuring question. At one extreme, headquarters is merely an extra level of fat, and great value can be obtained by breaking up the business units, selling them, and demolishing corporate headquarters. At the opposite extreme, headquarters can be too lean for its optimal role in risk management, tax planning, and strategic planning.

Headquarters costs are all costs that should not be allocated to business units. They include the *nonallocatable portions of*

- headquarters executive salaries, wages, bonuses, and benefits;
- directors' insurance and fees;
- office space (buildings and land) and equipment;
- headquarters support staff (accounting, legal, planning, personnel, and administrative);
- corporate-level advertising;
- corporate-level research and development;
- corporate-level charitable contributions;
- transportation and communications; and
- corporate-level consulting.

The portion of each cost item to be retained at headquarters is somewhat subjective. For example, consider the remuneration of headquarters executives. If the remuneration of business-unit presidents is lower than it otherwise might be were they at stand-alone companies, then it may be reasonable to allocate a portion of headquarters executive costs to the business units. As always, the relevant consideration is: What would business-unit costs be were the companies separate?

To illustrate headquarters costs from an outsider's point of view, we took a look at the twenty-five largest companies in the Fortune 500 industrial list using fiscal 1986 publicly available data. Exhibit 9.4 shows the results.

To compute corporate headquarters expenses, we used the business segment exhibit in the annual report and looked up the corporate expense number located there. No guarantee exists that this number is defined in the same way from company to company, because of differences in the way headquarters expenses are (or are not) allocated to business units. We used the corporate expense number as reported if taxes and financing costs were not included. When they were, and when we knew the tax and financing figures, we made adjustments to estimate the pretax, prefinancing corporate expense. Occasionally, the pretax corporate expense number had to be estimated, when tax and financing expenses were unknown, by assuming interest income of 7 percent on marketable securities, a 10-percent interest expense rate on debt, and a 46-percent corporate income tax rate. After-tax corporate expenses were capitalized by dividing them by the company's real unlevered cost of equity, because we assumed no inflationary growth.

Headquarters costs averaged 1.9 percent of the 1986 year-end market value of their equity (or if you like, 1.3 percent of the market value of their assets). By comparison, management of mutual funds usually receives an average of about .5 percent of assets under management.

To compare the present value of headquarters costs with the market value of equity, we capitalized the after-tax cost stream by assuming it would grow at a real rate of 2.5 percent per year and that it had the same risk as the business as a whole. (We used the unlevered beta in the capital asset pricing model, and discounted at the real unlevered cost of equity.) The results shown in column 3 of Exhibit 9.4 are amazing. For example, if Texaco had cut its headquarters costs to 0.9 percent of its revenues (the average for twenty-one companies excluding Texaco), it would

Exhibit 9.4 **1986 HEADQUARTERS COST FOR 22 OF THE 25 LARGEST INDUSTRIALS***

Company	HQ cost $ Millions	HQ cost as percentage of market equity	Capitalized HQ cost as percentage of total equity value	HQ cost as a percentage of sales
Texaco	$ 736	8.5%	185%	2.3%
General Motors	1,015	4.8	58	1.0
Allied Signal	249	3.6	34	2.1
Mobil	456	2.8	35	1.0
Chrysler	121	2.3	15	0.5
Atlantic Richfield	213	2.0	31	1.5
Procter & Gamble	257	2.0	15	1.7
Chevron	306	2.0	23	1.3
Occidental Petroleum	82	1.8	155	0.5
Tennaco	92	1.6	130	0.6
DuPont	304	1.5	11	1.1
Shell Oil	334	1.3	16	2.0
Boeing	100	1.3	6	0.6
RJR Nabisco	139	1.1	11	0.8
General Electric	389	1.0	5	1.1
USX	54	1.0	22	0.4
Rockwell International	58	0.9	4	0.5
Exxon	406	0.8	8	0.6
Philip Morris	126	0.7	6	0.6
Amoco Corporation	113	0.7	7	0.6
United Technology	25	0.4	3	0.2
McDonnell Douglas	11	0.4	3	0.1
Average		1.9%	36%	1.0%

*The corporate expense line in the business segment section of the annual report may be defined inconsistently across companies; therefore, our average results for the entire group have greater validity than those for individual companies.

have saved $448 million per year, pretax. Its 1986 pretax operating profit, which was $1,882 million, would have increased 24 percent. If these savings were viewed as permanent, the value created for shareholders would have been astronomical. (Since 1986, Texaco has made a concerted effort to cut corporate center costs.

In 1987 its reported corporate expenses dropped to $378 million, a decline of 49 percent.)

Companies with above-average headquarters costs need to take a careful look to identify ways of trimming excess fat or to be sure that headquarters benefits exceed costs. When headquarters costs exceed benefits by a wide margin, the company, regardless of its size, is likely to become a candidate for takeover.

Headquarters benefits are usually more difficult to identify than costs. We have divided them into two broad categories: those that are quantifiable, and others that, while important, are extremely difficult to measure.

Benefits that can be quantified are tax advantages and greater debt capacity. Tax advantages attributable to headquarters arise primarily from the lack of an adequate secondary market for tax shields. A group of business units with highly variable year-to-year taxable earnings can share tax shields by operating under a corporate umbrella. The losses of unit A can be used immediately to shelter the gains of unit B, so the business unit does not have to wait for tax carry-forwards or carry-backs. Conglomerates constructed from business units with low taxable-income variability are likely to benefit less from a corporate tax umbrella than conglomerates built from diverse business units with highly variable income.

Headquarters also provides the benefit of the present value of tax shelters that arise from corporate-level tax planning. In addition to the ability to use tax losses immediately, corporate headquarters is often able to undertake international tax planning (for example, transfer pricing) that might not be available were the business units operating separately.

Finally, greater debt capacity is created because business-unit cash flows are not perfectly correlated. Once the capital structure for each business unit has been developed and business-unit debt has been totaled, a portion attributable to headquarters might yet remain. (See the discussion of determining business-unit capital structure and cost of capital, later in this step, for more on how to allocate debt to business units.) The present value of the tax shield arising from this debt is a benefit of headquarters. Of course, if the company owes no corporate-level taxes, this benefit evaporates.

Benefits that are not easily measured include prospective synergies and information advantages.

Operating synergies are an obvious benefit of combining business units. If, for example, the company makes an acquisition that allows the existing sales force to assume the duties of the target's sales force, the present value of the realized savings is a benefit due, at least initially, to headquarters, because it resulted from the decision to acquire and combine two businesses. The "vision" of headquarters is not part of continuing operations and although very valuable is impossible to forecast as part of cash flows.

Information and communications advantages complete the list of headquaters benefits. Although difficult to quantify, they can be important. Nobel laureate Kenneth Arrow contends that informational advantages of vertical integration can be valuable because they reduce uncertainty. For example, a manufacturer may decide that it is optimal to own production facilities to eliminate variability in supplies that might disrupt production.

Determine business-unit tax rates The relevant tax rate for valuing a business unit depends on the taxes it would be paying were it not under a corporate umbrella. As mentioned earlier, when a business unit is separated from the parent, it loses its ability to shelter taxable income with losses elsewhere in the parent and must resort to tax carry-forward and tax carry-back provisions of the tax code. This consideration is also relevant when deciding whether to spin off a unit or to sell it to another company. A simple spin-off may increase the unit's tax rate, whereas sale to another company that can shelter the unit's earnings may be more advisable. Effective tax rates may change for less-obvious reasons as well. For example, tax advantages of transfer pricing or multinational taxation may be different if a business unit is separated from the parent.

To determine the business unit's tax rate, first determine its taxable income as a stand-alone entity over the foreseeable future. Then use the tax code to determine its adjusted tax rate, as described in Chapter 5.

Since we are treating corporate headquarters as a separate business unit for valuation purposes, its effect on taxes must also be estimated. In most cases, headquarters (the corporate umbrella) is a means for generating tax shelters; hence, its implied tax rate is negative. The present value of headquarters tax shelters is a benefit to the company. (The appropriate discount rate is discussed in the following paragraphs.)

Determine business-unit capital structure and cost of capital   The *capital structure* of each business unit should be consistent with that of comparable companies in its industry and with the overall philosophy of its parent. For example, if the parent is aggressive and chooses a Baa bond rating, then business units will normally have capital structures that bring them to a Baa rating within their industry. (Of course, exceptions to every rule exist. If one business unit—a finance company, for example—requires a higher bond rating to do business, then its debt capacity is lower. It might carry an Aa bond rating while other business units carry a Baa rating or lower.)

The debt capacity of business units may vary considerably. An insurance subsidiary, for example, may be able to carry an 80 percent debt-to-capital ratio, while a manufacturing subsidiary might only have a 25 percent debt-to-capital ratio. The basis for determining business-unit capital structure will usually depend on cash flow or capital employed at the business unit. Internal accounting systems can help to estimate the replacement cost of capital employed, when necessary. Debt-to-capital ratios or interest-coverage ratios for comparables then provide a basis for estimating industry norms.

The difference between the sum of all business-unit debt and total companywide debt should be attributed to corporate headquarters. A portion of it may represent tied financing—for example, a real estate mortgage on the wholly owned corporate headquarters building. Any remaining debt results from the fact that the debt capacity of a portfolio of business-unit cash flows that are not perfectly correlated has less variance than the sum of the separate cash flows. Consequently, the combination of separate business units under a corporate umbrella provides greater debt capacity. The present value of the interest tax shield is a benefit of headquarters.

Having determined the target capital structure and tax rate of each business unit, you still need to estimate the cost of equity in order to establish its weighted average cost of capital. In the case of a division of a company or a nonpublic company, no betas are published. To estimate them you have to rely on wit and guile. We recommend using one of four approaches: (1) management comparisons, (2) comparison companies, (3) a multiple regression approach, or (4) earnings before interest and taxes (EBIT) regressed against a market index.

1. *Management comparisons.* A crude but often effective way of estimating betas is to elicit the help of management. Have three to five managers sit down and position the division or project being analyzed relative to the list of industries shown in Exhibit 9.5. You do not need to show managers the actual betas, or even to explain the concept. Just have a few of them circle the industry with risk closest to their division. If they closely agree (and they usually do), you will have a reasonable estimate of the levered beta of the division.

2. *Comparison companies.* A second approach is to ask management to identify the publicly traded competitors most similar to the division. Having this list is useful, because you

Exhibit 9.5 **INDUSTRY BETAS**

Levered Beta	Industry	Levered Beta	Industry
1.55	Brokerage	1.14	Real estate
1.41	Restaurants	1.09	Chemicals
1.36	Hotels	1.04	Food and kindred products
1.32	Building and construction	1.01	Banks
1.26	Electric machinery	0.98	Paper and allied products
1.25	Scientific instruments	0.96	Food stores
1.24	Airline	0.88	Metal mining
1.18	Machinery (excluding electric)	0.86	Petroleum refining
		0.73	Electric and gas utilities
1.16	Motion pictures	0.71	Railroads
1.16	Retail stores		
1.14	Textile mill products		

Source: Wilshire Associates, Inc. (1981). *Capital Market Equilibrium Statistics,* Santa Monica, California

can then look up the betas for these companies, which are presumed to have similar risk. But there is a catch. Beta is a measure of the systematic risk of the levered equity of the comparison companies, and these companies will usually employ leverage different from that used by the division you are attempting to value. To get around this problem, you have to "unlever" the betas of the comparison companies to obtain their business risk, then relever using the target capital structure of the division you are analyzing.

The unlevered beta measures the business risk of a company by removing the effect of financial leverage. The observed equity beta computed from market return data presents a picture of the risk of equity given the company's existing leverage. To unlever the beta, you need data on the company's levered beta, its target capital structure, and its marginal tax rate.

For example, suppose that the levered beta of Comparison Corporation is 1.2 and that it has a debt-to-equity ratio of 1.3. The division you are valuing has a target debt-to-equity ratio of 0.8. To estimate the unlevered equity beta of the division, the following formula will prove useful. (We should note that levering and relevering betas is a conceptually tricky business, especially for extreme situations. For example, the following formula assumes that debt is risk free. In addition, the corporate marginal tax rate may change as a function of leverage, and the formula assumes that it does not.)

$$beta_L = [1 + (1 - T_c)B/S] \, (beta_u)$$

where

$beta_L$ = the levered equity beta

T_c = the corporate marginal tax rate

B/S = the debt-to-equity ratio for the division, estimated in terms of market value

$beta_u$ = the unlevered equity beta (a measure of the business risk of the division)

To use this formula, you also need to know the marginal tax rate of both Comparison Corporation and of the division you are studying. Suppose the tax rate of Comparison Corporation is 25 percent and that your tax rate will be 34 percent. The unlevered beta (the operating risk) of Comparison Corporation is as follows:

$$\text{beta}_u = \text{beta}_L/[1 + (1 - T_c)B/S]$$
$$= 1.2/[1 + (1 - 0.25)1.3] = 0.61$$

Relying on the assumption that Comparison Corporation has the same business risk as your division, you can now estimate the levered beta of your division as follows:

$$\text{beta}_L = [1 + (1 - 0.34)0.61] = 0.93$$

Knowledge of the levered beta allows you to estimate the cost of equity for your division using the capital asset pricing model, as discussed in Chapter 6.

3. *Multiple regression approach.* One of the most difficult problems with estimating the cost of equity for business units is that good comparables can rarely be found because most companies have multiple lines of business and different percentages of their assets in each. A way around this problem is to recognize that the business risk (that is, the unlevered beta) of a multidivision company is a weighted average of the risks of each line of business, as illustrated in Exhibit 9.6. Note also that business risk, on the assets side of the balance sheet, equals the weighted average of all risks on the liabilities side. This is a demonstration of the principle of the conservation of risk.

   In the United States, at least, it is possible to use line-of-business data to estimate the percentages of assets that companies have tied up in their separate lines of business. If you have data on two companies, each with two lines of business, and know the company unlevered betas as well as the asset weights, then you can construct two equations with two unknowns:

Exhibit 9.6 **COMPANY RISK AS A WEIGHTED AVERAGE OF ITS BUSINESS-UNIT RISKS**

ASSETS

Business unit	Market value weight	Unlevered beta	Contribution to asset risk
A	W_A	β_A	$W_A\beta_A$
B	W_B	β_B	$W_B\beta_B$
•	•	•	•
•	•	•	•
•	•	•	•
Z	W_Z	β_Z	$W_Z\beta_Z$
		Asset risk* =	$\Sigma W_i\beta_i$

LIABILITIES

Source of capital	Market value weight	Beta	Contribution to liability risk
Debt	W_D	β_D	$W_D\beta_D$
Preferred	W_P	β_P	$W_P\beta_P$
Common	W_C	β_C	$W_C\beta_C$
		Liability risk* =	$\Sigma W_i\beta_i$

* Asset risk = liability risk

$$\text{beta}_{u1} = W_{A1} \text{ beta}_{UA} + W_{B1} \text{ beta}_{UB}$$
$$\text{beta}_{u2} = W_{A2} \text{ beta}_{UA} + W_{B2} \text{ beta}_{UB}$$

It is then easy to solve for the unlevered line-of-business betas, beta_{UA} and beta_{UB}.

If there are more companies than lines of business, the unlevered business-unit betas can be estimated by running a linear regression of the unlevered company betas against the weights for the lines of business, being careful to suppress the constant term. The coefficients from the regression are unbiased estimates of the business-unit betas.

Exhibit 9.7 **FOREST PRODUCTS COMPANY DATA**

Company	Levered beta	Unlevered beta	Market debt/ equity	Asset weights Forest	Asset weights Paper
Champion Int'l	1.23	0.86	70.4%	0.15	0.85
Chesapeake Corp.	0.88	0.59	82.5	0.06	0.94
Great Northern Nek.	1.21	1.10	16.9	0.04	0.96
Louisiana-Pacific	1.32	0.98	57.9	0.79	0.21
Pope and Talbot	1.18	1.06	18.9	0.51	0.49
Longview Fibre	1.16	1.01	24.6	0.26	0.74
Temple Inland	1.16	0.99	28.4	0.19	0.81

Exhibit 9.7 illustrates data for forest products companies. Our regression results based on these data indicated the following:

Unlevered beta for forest products = 1.08
Unlevered beta for paper products = 0.88

The unlevered beta represents an estimate of the operating risk of the business unit. Next, the actual tax rate and leverage of the business unit, along with the estimated unlevered beta, can be used to compute an estimate of its levered beta. Given the levered beta of a business unit, the capital asset pricing model, as discussed in Chapter 6, can be used to compute the cost of equity, k_s.

4. *Covariance of earnings before interest and taxes.* The least practical of the four recommended methods for estimating the beta of a division is to collect a history of annual or quarterly earnings before interest and taxes (EBIT) for the entity being valued, and regress EBIT against the rate of return on a market index collected for similar intervals.

$$EBIT_t = a + b \text{ (market return}_t)$$

The slope (b) of this regression is an estimate of the unlevered beta of the stock; however, it needs to be scaled because it will be expressed in dollars, not a percentage.

Therefore, it needs to be divided by an estimate of the market value of the assets in the division. This would be a good measure of beta, except for two additional problems. First, when valuing a division, historic data on EBIT is often either nonexistent or has too few observations to be useful. Second, measurement errors in the data can lead to badly biased estimates of beta. Use this method only as a last resort.

A final note about betas. When changes in risk are expected across time, you have to be prepared to estimate a changing equity beta. Sometimes a company's strategic plan implies that risk is expected to change. Usually this is the risk of the company's portfolio of assets, but it could also pertain to the portfolio of liabilities. For example, a young company, recently gone public, is risky now (high beta), but is expected to have declining risk across time. Although we cannot suggest foolproof steps for estimating the changing risk, it will change. This implies that the weighted average cost of capital may also change (decline) as the company matures. Consequently, it becomes necessary to discount year-N cash flows at a risk-adjusted rate approximate for the risk in year N, not other years when the risk might be higher or lower.

The last step is to compute the weighted average cost of capital for each business unit, to be used as a discount rate for the business-unit after-tax cash flows.

$$\text{WACC} = k_b (1 - T) \frac{B}{B + S} + k_s \frac{S}{B + S}$$

The cost of debt, k_b, is the same as the long-term rate, given the bond rating of the business unit. The tax rate is the business-unit effective tax rate. The percentage of debt in the capital structure, $B/(B + S)$, is based on target market value capital structures for comparables and adjusted for the policy (conservative or aggressive) of headquarters. The cost of equity, k_s, uses the re-levered beta of comparables, and the percentage of equity is 1 minus the percentage of debt.

Determine discount rates for headquarters You can determine the discount rates for headquarters by breaking down headquarters cash flows into three categories, each to be discounted at a rate appropriate for its risk: tax shields provided by debt, noninterest tax shields, and headquarters costs.

Tax shields provided by debt have the same risk as corporate debt and should be discounted at the pretax cost of debt, k_b. The present value of these tax shields (assuming they will be available perpetually) is the marginal tax rate, T_c, times the market value of debt, B.

Noninterest tax shields (due to transfer pricing or the fact that losses of one division can shelter gains at another) depend on the probability of realizing them. Thus, cash flows must be defined as *expected* cash flows from noninterest tax shields. The appropriate discount rate for transfer-pricing tax shields depends on the business risk of the company. Financial leverage is irrelevant because transfer-pricing schemes are expenses before interest. For these reasons, expected transfer-pricing tax shields should be discounted at the unlevered cost of equity for the company as a whole. Tax shields based on the fact that losses in one business unit can shelter gains in another should be discounted at the levered cost of equity, because they can be realized only on income after interest expenses.

Headquarters costs (for example, executive and staff compensation, or legal expenses) should be discounted at a rate somewhere between the risk-free rate and the unlevered cost of equity, depending on their covariance with general business conditions (with the market portfolio). Choice of the actual rate is difficult and subjective. Companies whose headquarters costs do not fluctuate with the economy should discount them at the risk-free rate. For most companies, however, headquarters costs tend to rise in good business conditions (as executives and staff receive higher compensation) and fall during recessions. If the changes correlate well with operating profits, then the discount rate could be as high as the unlevered cost of equity. Note that changes in headquarters costs that are not correlated with business conditions (for example, one-time, "fat-trimming" efforts) do not affect the discount rate.

Step 4: Aggregate Business-Unit Values

The final step in multibusiness valuation is to aggregate head-quarters costs and benefits with business-unit values. In addition to simply adding these up, you should also double-check your valuation by adding up the separate debt components to be sure that they equal total corporate debt. Also, you should add business-unit and headquarters cash flows to see that they come close to corporate cash flows during the historical period. (It is difficult, if not impossible, to ensure that, during the forecast period, the sum of individual business-unit cash flows equals the corporate-level forecast in a year-by year comparison, because the average of business-unit growth rates is unlikely to equal the corporate growth rate.) This is a good way of checking your assumptions for consistency.

Exhibit 9.8 shows how the values of two hypothetical divisions can be added. From these, one subtracts headquarters costs and adds headquarters benefits and the value of excess marketable securities. The result is the aggregated value of the company. When the market value of corporate debt has been subtracted, the result should be the value of equity for the company as it currently is. If your results triangulate fairly well with the present value of the discounted cash flow of the company as a whole, you have a good valuation. If not, you need to locate and deal with the discrepancy.

An important by-product of your analysis is a careful look at the costs and benefits of headquarters. If costs exceed benefits by a wide margin, then headquarters may contain too much fat and cost reduction may be in order; in extreme cases, benefits may be negligible and shareholders may be better off if the company is broken up.

A few special situations need to be discussed along with the process of aggregation. For example, how should unconsolidated subsidiaries be handled? How can double counting be avoided? And what should be done with excess debt and marketable securities?

Unconsolidated subsidiaries are often an important part of a company. They are clearly separable business units, but how should we think about the cash flows they provide to the parent?

Exhibit 9.8 **"AS IS" MULTIBUSINESS VALUATION**

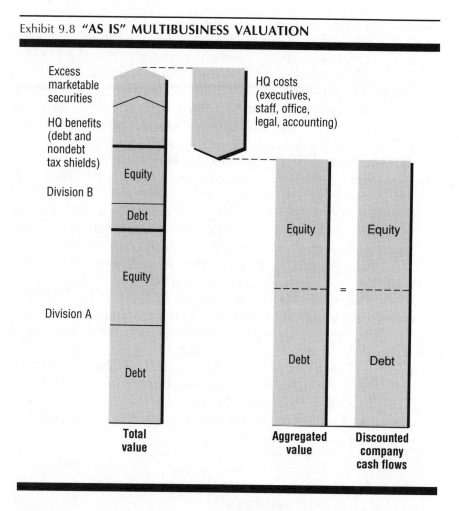

Assuming they are not foreign subsidiaries, the best approach is to value them separately, then multiply their equity value by the fraction that the parent owns, and add the result to your estimate of the parent's equity value. An alternative approach is to discount expected dividends paid from the subsidiary to the parent at a cost of equity appropriate for the riskiness of the dividend stream. This method is difficult to use because dividends are discretionary and, therefore, difficult to forecast.

Double counting can occur when an undervalued asset is carried on the books of a business unit. For example, Weyerhaeuser owns thousands of acres of timberland that is carried on the books at low value. An almost irresistible temptation exists to estimate the market value of the forest and add it to the present value of cash flow. To do so, however, would be double counting, because expected cash flow already assumes that harvested trees will be used to produce lumber. They are, in every sense, an inventory. As with inventory, their value is not added, because it is already included in future cash flow as an input to production.

Another common example of double counting is corporate headquarters or other real estate carried at low book value. The rental opportunity cost of the buildings is already reflected in a cash flow that is higher than it might otherwise be if the company were to sell its headquarters, then lease the office space. You cannot have it both ways. Either discount the cash flow as it is, or subtract the expected rental cost from the cash flow and add the market value of the headquarters building.

Excess marketable securities build up in the projected balance sheet of a business unit if it is doing well or, alternately, if extra debt is borrowed. This effect is a normal part of the forecasting process and, as discussed in Chapter 5, it has no effect on the present value of a business unit. Excess cash held by the company at the start of the valuation period is a different matter. It should not be allocated to business units. Its value should simply be kept separate and added to the other values during the aggregation stage, as shown in Exhibit 9.8.

ESTIMATING POTENTIAL VALUE WITH INTERNAL IMPROVEMENTS

After completing the valuation of the company by aggregating the separate values of all business units, the next step in restructuring is to define and implement, wherever possible, internal operating improvements. Even business units that will be sold should be fixed up as long as the cost of improvements is less than the extra sales premium that the improvements will bring. It is a little like fixing up your car or your house in an effort to attain the best possible profit from the sale.

Chapter 5 provided details on the key value drivers that affect the discounted cash flow value of companies. Exactly the same principles apply to business units. Consequently, we will not reiterate them here. Every business unit should be fine-tuned as much as possible. Furthermore, corporate headquarters costs should be carefully studied and cut back when burdensome. It is helpful to determine the present value of headquarters costs as a percentage of the value of total assets, and then compare across companies within the same industry.

ESTIMATING POTENTIAL VALUE WITH EXTERNAL IMPROVEMENTS

Once every business unit has been fine-tuned by implementing all possible internal improvements, you are ready to consider external possibilities. Some business units, even though fine-tuned, can be more valuable in alternative uses, and should be sold. In other instances they cannot be made profitable (by anyone) and should be shut down. The flip side of the coin is acquisition. Business-unit combinations that provide real synergies can do much to enhance value.

Analyze Value Creation from Breakups

Breakup is a generic term referring to several different methods of restructuring a company via the disposition of assets. This can imply the sale of individual assets, for example real estate, or the sale of entire business units.

The most common method is *divestiture* or *sell-off,* where a business unit is sold for cash to another company. The motivation is usually straightforward: the assets can be better managed by another company. Consequently, the buyer is willing to pay a higher price than the current value of the business unit to its parent. Two thousand divisions and subsidiaries were divested from parent companies in the United States in 1984 and 1985 alone. Academic studies generally indicate increases in share price for divesting companies and for companies acquiring related businesses, but not for companies that acquire unrelated businesses. (For effects on selling companies, see Jain 1985. For effects on acquiring companies, see Sicherman and Pettway 1987.)

Spin-offs involve dividending shares of a business unit to existing shareholders of the parent company in a nontaxable event. The "Dividend News" section of the *Wall Street Journal* listed 160 spin-offs between 1962 and 1981. Several reasons for spin-offs have been given. They include avoiding regulatory constraints, renegotiation of labor contracts, tax avoidance (particularly when creating oil royalty or real estate trusts), and capitalizing on situations where the value of the parts is greater than the value of the whole—the anergy effect. Academic studies indicate an average 5.02 percent positive abnormal return to shareholders of completed spin-offs. (See Copeland, Lemgruber, and Mayers 1987; and Schipper and Smith 1983.)

Leveraged buyouts (LBOs) involve the sale of a business unit to its managers, who finance the purchase with high financial leverage. Often the parent retains partial equity ownership and/or lends to the LBO. Since the company formed from an LBO is usually privately held, we have little systematic evidence on how LBO owners fare. On the other hand, ample evidence exists that the sellers benefit. (See DeAngelo, DeAngelo, and Rice 1984.)

Equity carve-outs are the least-common means for selling assets. Between 1963 and 1983, approximately seventy-six carve-outs were announced by publicly held companies. In a carve-out, new shares are issued to the public that represent ownership in the business unit to be carved out. Depending on who issues the shares either the parent or the subsidiary keeps the cash. The average effect on shareholders' wealth upon announcement of the carve-out is an increase of 1.8 percent. (See Schipper and Smith 1986.)

As illustrated in Exhibit 9.9, the analysis of asset disposition starts from a base-case market valuation of the company "as is." To this value is added the gain from disposition of the business unit—the difference between the market value of the business unit as a stand-alone entity as operated by its current parent and the market price when disposed of. From this value we must subtract tax liabilities created by sale of the business unit, expected losses of benefits provided by the current corporate umbrella (for example, tax shelters), and anticipated decreases in

Exhibit 9.9 **VALUING THE EFFECTS OF ASSET DISPOSITION (SELL-OFF)**, $ MILLIONS

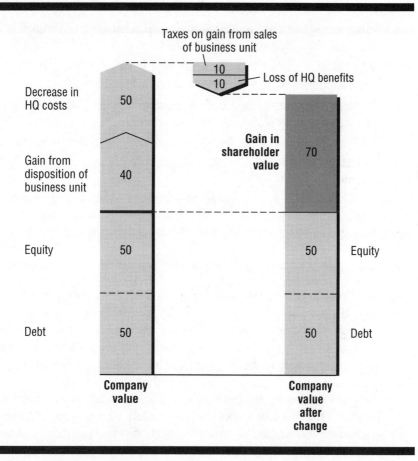

unallocated headquarters costs. For instance, as business units are disposed of, cuts should be made at headquarters (fewer administrators, less office space, and so on).

The value created from disposing of a business unit must come from cash flow benefits. It is important to search for benefits that are not related to headquarters per se. Here are a few relevant questions to ask:

• Are projected business-unit labor contract costs higher, lower, or unchanged following the disposition?

- Do any regulatory constraints change? If so, how will they affect cash flow?
- How do taxes change?
- How does the cost of accessing capital markets change? Will the cost of capital be affected?
- Would any operating changes result in higher cash flow if the business unit were owned by another company?
- Is the disposition a taxable transaction? If so, can it be structured differently to reduce taxes?
- Will disposition of the business unit result in better management incentives to create value? Why?

In each case, it is essential to consider whether breakup is really necessary. Could the company achieve the same benefits by continuing to own the business and by improving it?

Analyze Asset Acquisition

On the flip side of the restructuring coin is the search for acquisitions. Finding an acquisition candidate is only the beginning. You must also pick a strategy for enhancing the value of the company once it has been acquired, for figuring out an acquisition price that is high enough to deter competitive bids yet low enough to allow a profit, and for choosing the right approach to implement the acquisition. Since mergers and acquisitions are the main topic of Chapter 11, we only survey some broad issues here. Acquisitions are risky business. Academic studies largely agree that bidding firms, on average, do not benefit from acquisitions.

Exhibit 9.10 illustrates the economics of an acquisition. The acquiring company must identify real (not imaginary) synergies and/or operating improvements whose present value exceeds the takeover premium necessary to gain control. Additional value can be created by selling some of the acquired assets for an economic gain—that is, the difference between the "as is" economic value of the assets and their sale price less taxes.

One of the most common errors in acquisition analysis is that synergies are not properly evaluated and often amount to no more than wishful thinking. To identify and value synergies is

Exhibit 9.10 **VALUE CHANGES IN AN ACQUISITION,** $ MILLIONS

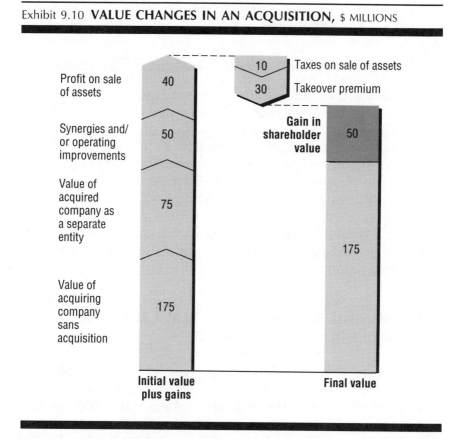

no simple task. Often economies of scale are cited as a way of cutting costs or achieving higher market share. But you should pin down exactly how the gains can be attained. For example, will quantity discounts be gained in ordering materials, will working capital be reduced, or will plant and equipment be utilized more efficiently? When two business units are combined, often savings are realized from sales force reductions. In another case, in a shrinking industry, an acquisition allowed a company to shut down one of its competitors and thereby retard further price reductions and cut transportation costs. Another possibility is that, to the extent the cash flows of the two companies are not highly correlated, their combination may reduce costs associated with cash flow variability. For example, it may be possible to carry more debt, to realize tax shelters immediately instead of having to carry them forward or back, or to avoid costly layoffs and retraining.

The proper economic perspective for acquisitions is to value the acquiring company without the acquisition and then with it. If the value does not increase after deducting the takeover premium and taxes, the merger should not be pursued. Too often a myopic perspective results in valuing the cash flow of the takeover candidate alone without placing equal weight on how the cash flow of the acquiring firm might change. For example, a well-established, mature company may wish to acquire a portfolio of small, new technology companies (even though many will fail) because if one of them succeeded on its own, the cash flow of the mature company would be significantly and adversely affected. This strategy is particularly relevant in industries where changing technology is important.

DETERMINING THE OPTIMAL RESTRUCTURED VALUE OF A MULTIBUSINESS COMPANY

The final stage of the restructuring pentagon is to determine the optimal value of the company—the sum of all internal and external improvements. The difference between this and the market-determined value of the company represents value that can be attained by a raider, or by current management if it has the will and foresight to implement changes in a timely manner. As we illustrated in Chapter 2, the best defense against takeovers is to be sure that the value gap between existing and restructured values is so small that no raider could possibly exploit the difference.

SUMMARY

Large multibusiness companies can benefit tremendously from a self-evaluation that values each business unit as well as the corporate center. Business units that would be more valuable if operated by someone else should be divested; other units that are earning less than their cost of capital and cannot be sold, should be liquidated. Viable core businesses should be improved and growth should be enhanced either through internal investment or via merger and acquisition. In a competitive environment, management must continually obtain the maximum return from its portfolio of businesses; otherwise, someone else might seize the opportunity via a takeover. Restructure your business before someone does it for you.

10

Multinational Business Valuation

Valuing foreign subsidiaries of multinational companies follows the same basic approach and employs the same principles as valuing business units of domestic companies. However, several new wrinkles need to be considered:

- Foreign currency translation
- Differences in foreign tax and accounting regulations
- The interrelationship between transfer pricing and foreign taxes
- The lack of good data (Appendix B includes a list of currently available public sources for non-U.S. company data)
- The need to evaluate political risk
- The effect of foreign exchange (FX) hedging on value
- Determining the appropriate cost of capital

We shall discuss these issues in the context of reviewing the steps in the process of valuing a foreign subsidiary.

A PREVIEW OF THE PROCESS

Exhibit 10.1 illustrates the cash flow pattern for a hypothetical parent company domiciled in the United States with a wholly-owned subsidiary domiciled in England that receives revenues from France (as well as from England), pays for raw materials supplied from Denmark (in addition to labor and raw material costs in England), and borrows in Switzerland (as well as in England). The English subsidiary receives capital and materials from its U.S. parent and returns cash flow in the form of dividends and license fees. Taxes are paid by the parent in the United States and by the subsidiary in England. This example is sufficiently rich to illustrate most of the complexities of valuing a foreign subsidiary, and we will follow it throughout this chapter. We will assume that this valuation is from inside the parent

Exhibit 10.1 **CASH FLOW FOR A U.S. COMPANY'S FOREIGN SUBSIDIARY**

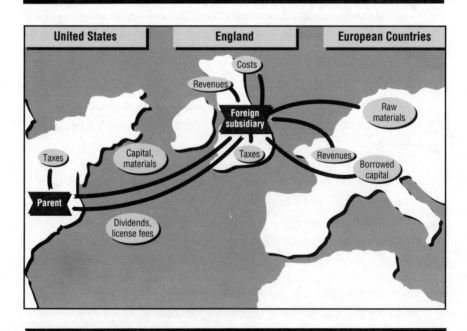

company—that is, that we have full access to internal financial and planning data for the multinational parent.

Exhibit 10.2 shows the steps in valuing a foreign subsidiary. These steps constitute the major portion of this chapter. The starting point is to forecast free cash flow in each foreign currency. For our example company, we will forecast English revenues

Exhibit 10.2 **STEPS IN VALUING A FOREIGN SUBSIDIARY**

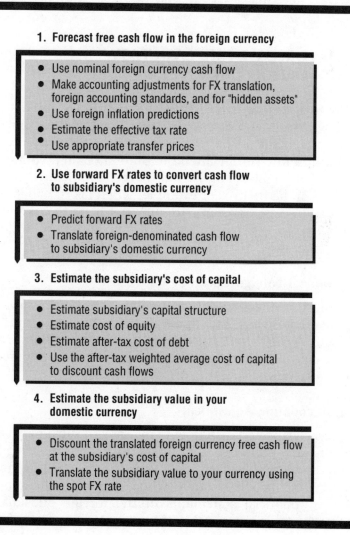

1. Forecast free cash flow in the foreign currency

- Use nominal foreign currency cash flow
- Make accounting adjustments for FX translation, foreign accounting standards, and for "hidden assets"
- Use foreign inflation predictions
- Estimate the effective tax rate
- Use appropriate transfer prices

2. Use forward FX rates to convert cash flow to subsidiary's domestic currency

- Predict forward FX rates
- Translate foreign-denominated cash flow to subsidiary's domestic currency

3. Estimate the subsidiary's cost of capital

- Estimate subsidiary's capital structure
- Estimate cost of equity
- Estimate after-tax cost of debt
- Use the after-tax weighted average cost of capital to discount cash flows

4. Estimate the subsidiary value in your domestic currency

- Discount the translated foreign currency free cash flow at the subsidiary's cost of capital
- Translate the subsidiary value to your currency using the spot FX rate

in pounds sterling and French revenues in francs. Next, we will convert nonsterling cash flow into pounds sterling by using forward FX rates. Once we have converted all expected cash flow to pounds, we will discount it at the English cost of capital. We will then convert the resulting sterling value to dollars, the home currency, by using the spot FX rate.

The last part of this chapter focuses on two valuation issues that relate to most situations but that are not discussed as steps: evaluation of political risk, and the effect of FX hedging on value.

STEP 1: FORECAST FREE CASH FLOW IN THE FOREIGN CURRENCY

In this first step, our objective is to accurately forecast foreign currency cash flow, not to translate it into the domestic currency of our foreign subsidiary. Regardless of the currency involved, it is important to carefully attend to differences in accounting standards, inflation rates, and tax rates. Transfer pricing is also important and can be tricky. For example, when tax considerations are relevant, the best transfer price may not be the market price but rather the price that minimizes the multicountry tax burden of the parent company.

Use Nominal Foreign Currency Cash Flow

Since most business executives think in terms of future cash flow forecasts that include inflationary expectations, and since market discount rates also reflect expected inflation, we recommend that foreign currency cash flow forecasts be stated in nominal rather than real terms.

Make Accounting Adjustments

To forecast expected cash flow to the foreign subsidiary in foreign currency units, certain accounting adjustments must be made. As long as foreign subsidiary cash flow is forecasted in the foreign currency, no problems arise when doing a valuation. Often, however, financial statements of the foreign subsidiary have already been converted by the parent company using U.S.

accounting standards, and it may be necessary to adjust them back to the foreign currency to avoid distorting cash flow forecasts. The following paragraphs discuss three issues: (1) how to deal with foreign exchange translation; (2) the need to understand foreign accounting standards; and (3) the need to search for "hidden assets" that can lead to understating the value.

Dealing with foreign exchange translation   When historical financials based on U.S. accounting standards are supplied by the parent, they should be restated in their original foreign currency units before an attempt is made to forecast foreign currency cash flow. This will help to avoid occasional distortions created by U.S. accounting conventions. It is especially important to focus on cash flow in high-inflation economies, because cash accounting accurately reflects the timing of cash flow while accrual accounting does not. If you cannot obtain subsidiary historical financials stated in the foreign currency from the parent, you should reverse-engineer the U.S. financial statements.

To reverse-engineer the U.S. statements, you must understand the accounting principles involved. In 1981, the U.S. Financial Accounting Standards Board issued FASB No. 52 on Foreign Currency Translation. For "normal inflation" economies (where prices *less* than double in a three-year period), translation gains and losses on the balance sheet are carried directly to the equity account under the *current method* of accounting and do not affect net income. The current exchange rate is applied to all balance sheet items except equity, and the average exchange rate for the period is used for translating the income statement. For "high inflation" economies (where prices *more* than double in three years), the *temporal method* is used (FASB No. 8). Historical exchange rates are applied to assets carried at historical costs, and current rates to monetary current assets.

Both methods are illustrated in the example set out in Exhibit 10.3. The foreign subsidiary is assumed to have acquired fixed assets at the beginning of the year when the foreign currency was at $0.95 per unit. By year's end the exchange rate was $0.85, and the average during the year was $0.90. The subsidiary used last-in-first-out (LIFO) inventory accounting with an applicable historical exchange rate of $0.91.

Exhibit 10.3 **EXAMPLE OF TRANSLATING FOREIGN SUBSIDIARY FINANCIAL STATEMENTS**

Balance sheet	Foreign currency	Temporal method Rates used	Temporal method U.S. dollars	Current method Rates used	Current method U.S. dollars
Cash and receivables, net	100	.85	$ 85	.85	$ 85
Inventory	300	.91	273	.85	255
Fixed assets, net	600	.95	570	.85	510
	1,000		$928		$850
Current liabilities	180	.85	153	.85	153
Long-term debt	700	.85	595	.85	595
Equity					
Common stock	100	.95	95	.95	95
Retained earnings	20		85		18
Equity adjustment from foreign currency translation	–		–		(11)
	1,000		$928		$850
Income statement					
Revenue	130	.90	$117	.90	$117
Cost of goods sold	(60)	.93*	(56)	.90	(54)
Depreciation	(20)	.95*	(19)	.90	(18)
Other expenses, net	(10)	.90	(9)	.90	(9)
Foreign exchange gain/(loss)	–		70		–
Income before taxes	40		103		36
Income taxes	(20)	.90	(18)	.90	(18)
Net income	20		$ 85		$ 18

Source: Peat, Marwick, Mitchell and Company (1981), p. 52.
*Historical rates for cost of goods sold and depreciation of fixed assets.

The temporal method begins by estimating the dollar equivalent for all assets and liabilities and computing retained earnings, $85, as a residual. Since no dividends are paid, retained earnings (or the change in retained earnings) must equal net income. Once all income statement items have been determined, the foreign exchange gain of $70 is computed as a plug figure. Note that since no cash flow (past, present, or future) is associated with the foreign exchange gain, it is irrelevant for valuation.

The current method, under FASB 52, starts with the income statement, converting all items at the average exchange rate during the year. Net income is transferred as retained earnings to the balance sheet; all assets and liabilities are translated at the current spot exchange rate; common stock is translated at the historical rate; and the equity adjustment from foreign currency translation is a plug figure.

Understanding foreign accounting standards This book cannot cover every accounting system in the world and the many changes that occur every year. The best that we can do is to describe a few key problems and hope that these examples will help you discover the rest. As always, the objective is to identify all cash flow to the subsidiary as a first step.

Conventions for restating balance sheets often cause problems. Many countries allow assets to be restated periodically as market or replacement value. This can make measuring the gross investment component of cash flow difficult. For the purpose of calculating free cash flow, gross investment must be a cash outlay equal to cash changes in working capital, capital expenditures, cash investment in goodwill, and cash increases in net other assets. These figures can always be determined on U.S. accounting statements because balance sheet figures are stated as book values. Any changes, therefore, are cash flow. This relationship breaks down if assets are periodically restated to market value. The solution is usually to reverse market value figures by figuring out the changes in equity that are not attributable to retained earnings.

Consolidation standards are another frequently encountered problem. For example, part of the reason that the price-to-earnings ratios of Japanese companies are high (often in the hundreds) relative to U.S. standards is that Japanese parent firms do not consolidate the earnings of their minority ownership in a large number of subsidiaries (and dividends paid by subsidiaries are extremely low). The numerator of the price-to-earnings ratio, the market value of the parent, reflects ownership of subsidiaries, but the denominator, earnings, does not—hence the high ratio. Whenever the appropriate information is attainable, all cash flow attributable to a business unit from ownership of subsidiary assets and liabilities should be consolidated for the purpose of valuing the business unit.

Searching for "hidden assets"   In some countries, the difference between the market and book values of assets can be substantial. For instance, Japanese companies customarily own minority interests in the common stock of their business partners (customers and suppliers). These securities are rarely traded and remain on the books at their historical purchase price, often a small fraction of the current worth. Their current market value should be captured in your valuation.

Real estate is another example of a hidden asset whose book value is often far below the market value you should attribute to it in your valuation. Be careful, however, because market value of real estate reflects its rental value. Only the value of underutilized land should be included. If the company is using land that it owns and if it sells the land, then it has to pay tax on the sale and it must pay rent on the property where it relocates. These costs should also be reflected in your valuation.

Use Foreign Inflation Predictions

In addition to understanding the accounting conventions of the countries in question, you should take their economic climates into account by using foreign inflation predictions to forecast nominal cash flow. Even if you are estimating cash flow for an English subsidiary, growth rates for revenues denominated in pesetas should be consistent with forecasted Spanish inflation rates, not English inflation rates. In Chapter 5, Exhibit 5.10 shows how to calculate expected inflation given the term structure of interest rates and an estimate of the real rate of return.

Estimate the Effective Tax Rate

The taxation of multinational corporations is complex. Furthermore, tax codes are constantly changing. Any valuation requires understanding of at least two perspectives: the domestic code applicable to the parent and the code of the foreign country where the subsidiary is located. And, in most cases, it also requires understanding of tax codes (and their enforcement) in every country where the parent company and its subsidiaries do business. If taxes are material to your valuation, consult a qualified tax expert.

One technical issue relevant to valuing subsidiaries of multinational companies is the treatment of foreign tax credits. Exhibit 10.4 provides examples of current U.S. tax treatment of foreign tax credits. In these examples, the local tax rates are 34 percent on U.S. income, 20 percent on income in country E, and 60 percent on country M income. U.S. taxes are computed as 34 percent of consolidated pretax income less foreign tax credits that may not exceed 34 percent of foreign income. Therefore, whenever foreign tax credits reach the maximum allowable under U.S. law, as in the first example in Exhibit 10.4, consolidated taxes paid equal the total of local taxes, and no corporate tax penalty is levied. However, when tax credits are below the maximum allowable, as in the second example in Exhibit 10.4, consolidated taxes exceed the total of local taxes, and a U.S. corporate tax penalty is levied. In effect, the U.S. tax code may raise the effective tax rate for subsidiaries located in lower-tax countries.

For the second example in Exhibit 10.4, the U.S. tax code has raised the average effective tax rate to the parent company on income in country E from 20 percent to $(30 + 80)/400 = 27.5$ percent. The marginal effective tax rate on country E income is 34 percent, the U.S. tax rate. Hence, the effective tax rate in a foreign country may not be its domestic statutory rate, because given the specific circumstances, it may depend on the parent company's tax rate. For the second example in Exhibit 10.4, if this situation were expected to persist for the long run, it might be advisable for the parent to sell company E to an owner from country E. The reason, of course, is that the after-tax cash flow would be higher from the perspective of a country E owner.

Use Appropriate Transfer Prices

Many tactics exist for reducing profits in high-tax jurisdictions. For example, you can charge out as many headquarters functions as possible; charge subsidiaries for research and development expenses; borrow at the subsidiary level; consolidate same-country profitable subsidiaries with unprofitable subsidiaries to

1. With excess foreign tax credits

	U.S.	Country E ops.	Country M ops.	Consoli-dated
Pretax income	$1,000	$200*	$300*	$1,500
Local tax rate	× 34%	×20%	×60%	
Local taxes	340	40	180	
U.S. tax rate				× 34%
Preliminary U.S. taxes				510
Less: foreign tax credits				−170**
Net U.S. taxes				340
Foreign taxes				+220
Consolidated income taxes				560
Less: total local taxes				−560
Corporate tax penalty				0

2. Without excess foreign tax credits

	U.S.	Country E ops.	Country M ops.	U.S., E, and M consoli-dated	U.S. and M consoli-dated
Pretax income	$1,000	$400*	$100*	$1,500	$1,100
Local tax rate	× 34%	× 20%	× 60%		
Local taxes	340	80	60		
U.S. tax rate				× 34%	× 34%
Preliminary U.S. taxes				510	374
Less: foreign tax credits				−140**	−34
Net U.S. taxes				370	340
Foreign taxes				+140	+60
Consolidated income taxes				510	400
Less: total local taxes				−480	−400
Corporate tax penalty				30	0

*Includes only income subject to U.S. tax rates.
**Foreign tax credit is the foreign taxes paid or the foreign income times U.S. tax rate ($500 × 34% = $170), whichever is lower.

take advantage of tax-loss carry-forwards; bill back employee stock options to other countries; use cost-plus accounting to reduce foreign profit; increase royalty charges to a foreign subsidiary; establish management-fee arrangements; consider leaving high-tax jurisdictions; and take advantage of transfer pricing. All of these maneuvers are subject to scrutiny by tax authorities. Nevertheless, tax planning obviously can have a major impact on the value of multinational corporations.

Transfer pricing between business units of a multinational company is one of the most important tax minimization methods and determines where profits are reported.* The interrelationship between transfer pricing and effective tax rates is complex. For instance, let us go back to Exhibit 10.4, and suppose that the profits reflected in the first example are based on market prices. The economics textbooks usually recommend that, tax considerations aside, all decision making should be based on market prices. In this example, however, tax considerations cannot be ignored. Suppose transfer pricing enables the parent company to shift $200 of pretax income from its subsidiary in country M, the high-domestic-tax country, to country E, the low-tax environment. The results are shown in the next-to-last column of the second example. Consolidated income taxes have declined from $560 to $510, but a corporate tax penalty of $30 emerges.

The $30 corporate tax penalty under the transfer-pricing scheme makes it tempting to consider selling subsidiary E to a foreign company also domiciled in country E. But from the perspective of the buyer, the subsidiary can earn only $200 of pretax profits, calculated using market prices, not the parent's artificial transfer prices. Therefore, the value of business unit E depends on one's point of view. From the parent's point of view, using artificial transfer prices, it is worth $3,200, given the assumptions in Exhibit 10.5.

---

*Actually, foreign income is separated into ten "income baskets" by the 1986 U.S. Tax Reform Act. Baskets are categorized by type of income—for example, passive interest, DISC dividends, foreign-trade income of foreign sales corporations, and foreign oil and gas extraction income. Income that generates high foreign tax credits can be combined with low-foreign-tax-credit income within but not across baskets.

Exhibit 10.5 **VALUE OF VARIOUS BUSINESS COMBINATIONS TO THE PARENT***

Business combination	Using example 1 in Exhibit 10.4, which assumes market pricing	Using example 2 in Exhibit 10.4, which assumes transfer pricing
Combined U.S. + M + E	$9,400	$9,900
Sell E, keep U.S. and M	9,400	8,600
Sell M, keep U.S. and E	9,120	9,640
All three separate	9,400	8,600

*Values are estimated by assuming the businesses have no debt, that cash flows are perpetuities, and that the cost of capital is 10 percent.

$$(\$400 - \$80) \div 10\% = \$3,200$$

But from the point of view of an owner domiciled in country E and using market prices, it is worth only

$$(\$200 - \$40) \div 10\% = \$1,600.$$

After considering the interaction of transfer pricing and the U.S. tax code for multinationals, the optimum decision for the U.S. parent is to employ transfer pricing to minimize taxes and to retain both of its foreign subsidiaries. As shown in Exhibit 10.5, the value of this combination is the pretax profit, $1,500, less consolidated taxes of $510, capitalized at 10 percent, for a total of $9,900. If subsidiary E were sold for $1,600 (after taxes), the total value (including the value of the U.S. operation and the subsidiary in M) would be only $8,600.

The answer would change if the situation in example 2 of Exhibit 10.4 were to reflect market prices. Then, it would be best to sell subsidiary E. The resulting value (not shown in Exhibit 10.5) would be $3,200 from selling subsidiary E plus $7,000 for the remaining U.S. plus M operation. The alternative of keeping all three operations would be worth only $9,900.

Some companies build simulation models to deal with the complexities of tax minimization and ownership. An "as is" valuation of a foreign subsidiary should assume the actual pricing mechanism employed by the parent, whether it is an artificial transfer-pricing or a market-pricing mechanism. An assessment of restructured values, however, should look at all alternatives and all points of view to discover how the greatest value can be created by changing pricing mechanisms or changing ownership.

STEP 2: CONVERT ALL CASH FLOW TO THE SUBSIDIARY'S DOMESTIC CURRENCY

Once all cash flow has been forecasted in terms of the currency where it originates, it should be converted into the currency of the subsidiary prior to discounting. We call this the *forward-rate method* for evaluating foreign cash flow. If all of the subsidiary's cash flow is already denominated in local currency, step 2 is unnecessary and you can skip to step 3.

The forward-rate method is useful when separate components of cash flow must be valued—for example, French sales revenues received by the English subsidiary but denominated in francs. This method uses the forward foreign exchange rate to convert forecasted French franc flow to sterling cash flow on a year-by-year basis. Then it combines this with other sterling-equivalent cash flow received by the English subsidiary, and discounts it at the English weighted average cost of capital. As a practical matter, for most currencies forward exchange rates are not available farther out than eighteen months. Therefore, using this method means forecasting long-term foreign exchange rates, a task that will be explained shortly.

A mathematically equivalent alternative to the forward-rate method is the *spot-rate method*. We will employ it in step 3 to discount all of the subsidiary's cash flow that has been restated in pounds sterling at the English subsidiary's cost of capital to translate its present value to U.S. dollars at the spot exchange rate.

The spot-rate method is not generally used to convert partial cash flow such as a revenue stream denominated in French francs, because no practical way exists to estimate a risk-adjusted French discount rate for the revenue stream alone. Estimating the appropriate discount rate for total cash flow from operations (NOPLAT) is hard enough.

To implement the forward-rate method, you must (1) use interest-rate parity to forecast future spot foreign exchange rates, and (2) use the future spot FX rates to convert future predicted foreign currency cash flow into the subsidiary's domestic currency. To illustrate, we will focus on a stream of revenue received from France by the English subsidiary. The forecasted French franc costs are illustrated in Exhibit 10.6.

Use Interest-Rate Parity to Forecast Forward FX Rates

Forecasting foreign exchange rates depends on using the interest-rate parity theory, which is founded on the idea that changes in foreign exchange rates are based on the ratio of expected inflation rates between two countries. Exhibit 10.7 plots the relationship between domestic inflation and domestic interest rates for forty-seven countries over the period 1977 to 1981. Indeed, inflation does explain most of the difference in nominal interest rates within each country.

Across countries, the interest-rate parity theory is expressed as follows: the expected spot foreign exchange rate in year t, X_{ft}, is equal to the current spot FX rate, X_0, multiplied by the ratio of nominal rates of return in the two countries over the forecast interval, t. (For a derivation, see Copeland and Weston 1988, pp. 790–803.)

Exhibit 10.6 **ENGLISH SUBSIDIARY'S FORECASTED FRENCH REVENUES,** FRENCH FRANCS, MILLIONS

Year	French franc revenue	Forecasted future spot FX rate, £/franc	£ equivalent cash revenue
1	106 fr.	.0947 £/fr. next year	£10.04
2	114	.0939 £/fr. 2 yrs. ahead	10.70
3	123	.0926 £/fr. 3 yrs. ahead	11.39
4	119	.0930 £/fr. 4 yrs. ahead	11.07
5	125	.0926 £/fr. 5 yrs. ahead	11.57

Exhibit 10.7 **THE RELATIONSHIP BETWEEN INFLATION AND INTEREST RATES IN 47 COUNTRIES**

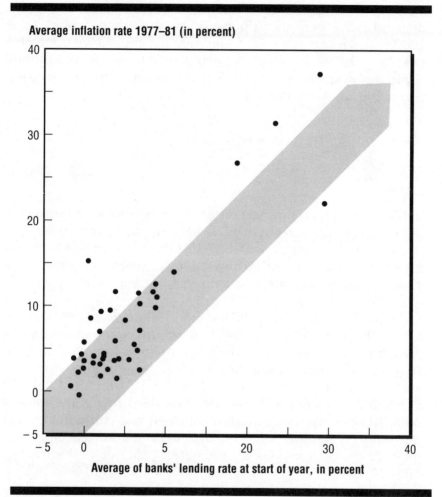

Source: Morgan Guaranty Bank World Financial Markets

$$X_{ft} = X_0 \left[\frac{1 + N_f}{1 + N_d} \right]^t$$

where

f = the foreign currency

d = the domestic currency

To illustrate the theory for a single year, suppose that our English subsidiary can borrow one-year money in Switzerland at a 4-percent nominal interest rate, N_f, while the borrowing rate in England is 7.1 percent. Suppose the spot exchange rate, X_0, is 2.673 Swiss francs per pound sterling, and the one-year forward rate, X_f, is 2.5944 Swiss francs per dollar. We can use interest-rate parity to estimate what English borrowing rate a 4-percent borrowing rate in Switzerland is equivalent to.

$$
\begin{aligned}
1 + N_d &= (1 + N_f)(X_0/X_{ft}) \\
&= (1.04)(2.673 \text{ fr./£} \div 2.594 \text{ fr./£}) \\
&= 7.15\%
\end{aligned}
$$

In this example, no practical difference exists between borrowing in England at 7.1 percent or in Switzerland at 4 percent, because the Swiss rate is equivalent to 7.15 percent in England. In our experience, the foreign borrowing rate, when converted to a domestic equivalent rate, is usually very close to the domestic rate (unless there are tax implications).

Next, let's show how to use interest-rate parity to forecast future spot FX rates and use that information to convert the French franc revenues in Exhibit 10.6 to English pounds. Exhibit 10.8 uses UK and French data to illustrate. The first two rows are the term structures of interest rates on government debt for England and France in June 1988. The third row is the ratio of nominal rates. We know from the interest-rate parity theory that the ratio of nominal rates multiplied by the current spot rate (pounds/francs) provides an estimate of the forward exchange rate.

As indicated in the fifth row, the market is forecasting that the pound will strengthen versus the franc. If the government bond market is extremely thin or even nonexistent, you will not be able to use the ratio of actual term structures (as in Exhibit 10.8) to help forecast forward exchange rates. In this situation, your best fallback position is to use interest-rate parity directly by supplying your own estimates of the expected real rates and expected inflation rates in both countries.

Exhibit 10.8 **EXAMPLE OF FORECASTING FORWARD EXCHANGE RATES***

	1-year	2-year	3-year	4-year	5-year
1. British gilts, N_d	8.71%	8.88	9.03	9.11	9.18
2. French francs, N_f	7.49%	7.86	8.06	8.30	8.43
3. $[(1 + N_f)/(1 + N_d)]^t$	.9889	.9802	.9663	.9706	.9661
4. Spot rate £/fr., X_o	.0958	.0958	.0958	.0958	.0958
5. Forecasted forward exchange rate, £/fr., X_f	.0947	.0939	.0926	.0930	.0926
6. Revenues in francs	106.00	114.00	123.00	119.00	125.00
7. Revenues in £	10.04	10.70	11.39	11.07	11.57

*N_f and N_d are, respectively, the foreign and domestic nominal interest rates; X_{ft} and X_o are, respectively, the one-year forward rate in year t and the current spot rate.
Source: Robert LeFevre, SA Supplement, Trimesterial (June 1988); *Financial Times* of London (June 1988); McKinsey analysis.

Convert Forecasted Foreign Cash Flow to the Subsidiary's Domestic Currency

The French franc revenues in line 6 of Exhibit 10.8 are converted to pound sterling revenues (line 7) by using the interest-rate parity relationship.

Once all revenues and costs of the English subsidiary have been converted to pounds sterling, the result is a complete forecast of the subsidiary income statement and balance sheet in pounds sterling. The next step is to discount this cash flow at the appropriate weighted average cost of capital.

STEP 3: ESTIMATE FOREIGN CURRENCY DISCOUNT RATE

To estimate the foreign currency discount rate, the general principle is to discount foreign cash flow at foreign risk-adjusted rates. The same assumptions about expected inflation should form the basis for both expected cash flow and the discount rate.

The fact that a subsidiary is located in a foreign country does not change the definition of the weighted average cost of capital, WACC. As before,

$$\text{WACC} = k_b (1 - T)\frac{B}{B + S} + k_s \frac{S}{B + S}$$

where

k_b = the before-tax cost of debt

T = the marginal effective tax rate

B = the market value of debt

S = the market value of equity

k_s = the opportunity cost of equity

The two most common errors in setting the WACC are (1) making ad hoc adjustments for risk; and (2) using the parent country WACC to discount foreign currency cash flow. Regarding the first point, ad hoc adjustments to the discount rate to reflect political risk, foreign investment risk, or foreign currency risk are entirely inappropriate. As we shall explain later on, political risk is best handled by adjusting expected cash flow, weighting it by the probability of various scenarios. Foreign currency or foreign investment risk is handled by the spot exchange rate, and is perfectly symmetrical. An equal chance of a gain or a loss of purchasing power exists. Regarding the second point, it should be clear that if cash flow is predicted in units of the foreign currency, then it should be discounted at the foreign country discount rate because this rate reflects the opportunity cost of capital in the foreign country, including expected inflation and the market risk premium.

Estimate the Subsidiary Target Capital Structure

The target capital structure for a subsidiary is the mix of financing, stated in market values, that it would maintain in the long run on a stand-alone basis. The actual capital structure imposed on the subsidiary by its parent may depart widely from the subsidiary's target. For tax reasons, the subsidiary may be loaded up with debt, for example. The tax effect of this type of transfer-pricing arrangement is captured when expected cash flow is estimated and should not be double counted when estimating the discount rate.

If the accounting statements of the subsidiary do not reflect its long-run target capital structure, then it may be possible to locate comparables from the same country, or even to use comparables from other countries. Be cautioned, however, that differing accounting policies regarding the treatment of the book value of assets and of equity, and regarding consolidation, can distort comparables based on book values. Another approach is to use coverage ratios. Given domestic interest rates, determine how much debt could be carried so that the ratio of pretax operating cash flow to interest and other fixed financing charges is reasonable, given industry standards.

Estimate the Cost of Equity

No evidence exists that the capital asset pricing model (CAPM) or the arbitrage pricing model (APM) are not valid within every economy. Although they have already been described earlier in the book, they are rewritten here for convenience.

The CAPM is as follows:

$$E(R_i) = R_f + [E(R_m) - R_f] \, beta_i$$

where

$$E(R_i) = \text{the market expected rate of return on the ith secur-ity}$$

$$R_f = \text{the risk-free rate}$$

$$E(R_m) = \text{the expected rate of return on the market portfolio (usually proxied by an equally weighted equity index)}$$

$$E(R_m) - R_f = \text{the market risk premium}$$

$$beta_i = \text{the undiversifiable risk of the ith security}$$

The CAPM has been used to explain the market's expected rate of return on all securities. If you have an estimate of the beta for equity, then $E(R_i) = k_s$, and the cost of equity can be estimated directly from the CAPM. The APM is as follows:

$$E(R_i) = R_f + [E(f_1) - R_f] \, beta_{i1} + \ldots + [E(f_N) - R_f] \, beta_{iN}$$

where

$E(f_1)$ = the expected return on factor 1
$E(f_N)$ = the expected return on factor N
$beta_{i1}$ = undiversifiable risk of security i relative to factor 1
$E(f_1) - R_f$ = the risk premium for factor 1

Regardless of which model is used, the major problem outside of the United States is lack of good data. Appendix B lists sources for betas for companies in most developed countries. They can be used to find comparables for business-unit betas using the methods recommended in Chapter 9. Government bond rates from the country where the subsidiary is located can be used as estimates of the risk-free rate (unless serious default risk exists). If government debt is not reasonably risk-free, then the interest rate parity theory can be used to convert U.S. government rates to foreign country equivalents.

Almost no information is readily available on market risk premiums—that is, $E(R_m)$–R_f—for non-U.S. economies. In many cases, however, it can easily be estimated from publicly available data sources. For example, an estimate for Germany was obtained by using monthly data for the difference between short-term government debt and the monthly rate of return for the Frankfurt stock index from 1970 to 1985. The average geometric difference, 3.8 percent, is an estimate of the market risk premium over this time period.* Over the same time interval, the (geometric) risk premium in the United States was 2 percent. To estimate the long-term geometric risk premium for Germany, we add the differential over the 1970 to 1985 interval—that is, 3.8 percent

---

*Our thanks to Professor Hermann Göppl at Karlsruhe Universität for providing this estimate.

minus 2 percent = 1.8 percent—to the long-term U.S. market risk premium, 6 percent, to obtain 7.8 percent. Similar logic for Japan produces a result of approximately 5.2 percent. Because of the globalization of capital markets, it is reasonable to assume that market risk premiums are approximately equal across developed nations (see Wheatley 1988 for evidence to support this point of view).

The debate about the relative costs of capital among countries continues. The overarching principle, however, is that in the absence of effective government controls to block the flow of capital, the required return on investments of equivalent risk must be the same across all national borders *after adjusting for expected inflation*. If this were not a valid principle, then enormous flows of capital would quickly bring markets into equilibrium. Understanding inflation and risk differentials is key. As we saw earlier, a 4-percent borrowing rate in Switzerland is not necessarily cheaper than a 7-percent rate in England, because Switzerland has lower expected inflation. Furthermore, a 5.2-percent risk premium in Japan is not necessarily cheaper than a 6-percent premium in the United States, because the risk of the Nikkei is less than that of the S&P 500, for two reasons: (1) the Nikkei is more a blue chip index, and (2) the Japanese bonus system of worker compensation provides a better buffer to protect shareholders in bad times. When a company is successful, Japanese workers receive very large bonuses (by U.S. standards) but when revenues are less than expected, workers may receive little or no bonus. The effect is to provide a cushion that reduces the variability of free cash flow to shareholders.

Estimate the After-Tax Cost of Debt

As with equity, the objective regarding debt is to use the foreign country opportunity cost to discount cash flow estimated in terms of the foreign currency.

The cost of nonconvertible, noncallable debt is its expected yield to maturity. If debt is callable or convertible, you can refer to Chapter 12 of this book.

The relevant tax rate is the statutory marginal tax rate in the country where the subsidiary resides. It is the tax shield that would prevail if one more unit of debt were added, or zero if no debt tax shield is available (either because other tax shields completely exhaust taxable profits or because interest on debt is not tax-deductible).

Use the After-Tax Weighted Average Cost of Capital

If the subsidiary's target capital structure is assumed to remain constant, then the WACC can also be kept constant over the relevant discount period. An exception to this rule would arise if government controls were expected to change market rates in a predictable fashion.

STEP 4: DISCOUNT FREE CASH FLOW AND TRANSLATE TO THE DOMESTIC CURRENCY

Having determined the subsidiary's weighted average cost of capital, you are ready to discount the free cash flow forecasted in step 1 and convert it to your domestic currency. Exhibit 10.9 shows expected free cash flow to our example subsidiary in England. It is discounted to the present at the subsidiary's WACC, assumed to be 11.8 percent, and then converted to dollars by multiplying the present value in pounds sterling by the spot exchange rate, .560 pounds/dollar.

One caveat is in order here: because we have discounted cash flow to the subsidiary, its present value in the domestic currency (dollars in our example) to the parent may be different if a country has restrictions that limit the expatriation of free cash flow back to the parent. Although ways around these constraints can sometimes be found—for example, barter or transfer pricing—the thing to keep in mind is that the value to the parent depends on the quantity and timing of free cash flow (or cash equivalents) that can actually be paid out.

VALUING POLITICAL RISK AND THE EFFECT OF HEDGING

Two topics remain to be discussed: how to evaluate political risk and the effect of FX hedging on value. Both topics are thorny.

Exhibit 10.9 **ENGLISH SUBSIDIARY FREE CASH FLOW, DISCOUNTED AT THE ENGLISH RATE AND CONVERTED TO DOLLARS**

	Free cash flow	Present value factor at 11.8% foreign rate	Present value
1989	£100	0.8945	£89.45
1990	115	0.8000	92.01
1991	130	0.7156	93.03
1992	142	0.6401	90.89
1993	160	0.5725	91.60
1994	180	0.5121	92.18
1995	196	0.4580	89.78
1996	225	0.4097	92.18
1997	252	0.3665	92.35
1998	280	0.3278	91.78
Continuing value	2,653	0.3278	869.61
		PV in £	£1,784.86
		÷ Spot rate £/$	÷ 0.56
		= PV in $	$3187.25

Effective evaluation of political risk, even if handled in the technically appropriate fashion (as discussed in this section) depends largely on obtaining good information. Otherwise analysis merely amounts to garbage in-garbage out. Hedging is a conceptually difficult topic mainly because it is hard to justify on theoretical grounds as beneficial to shareholders.

Evaluating Political Risk

Political risks take many forms. Exhibit 10.10 shows the results of interviews of eighty managers of multinational firms who ranked various risk categories from highest risk (1) to lowest risk (10) (Kobrin 1982). Often overlooked are the major political risks in industrialized countries (such as price controls), which can be equally as devastating as risks in less-developed countries.

The scenario approach to risk analysis used to forecast expected cash flow domestically can be applied equally well to foreign political risk. Exhibit 10.11 provides a simplified example

Exhibit 10.10 **RELATIVE IMPORTANCE OF POLITICAL RISKS,
ACCORDING TO MANAGERS OF MULTINATIONALS**

Less-developed countries		Industrialized countries	
Mean/ rank	Risk	Mean/ rank	Risk
1.8	Civil disorder	3.2	Price controls
2.4	Expropriation	3.7	Labor disruptions
3.6	War	4.4	Remittance restrictions
5.3	Remittance restrictions	5.5	Civil disorder
5.5	Labor disruptions	5.5	Fiscal changes
5.7	Partial expropriation	6.0	Expropriation
6.0	Price controls	6.9	Partial expropriation
7.3	Fiscal changes	7.2	Contract cancellation
7.6	Contract cancellation	8.4	War

Source: S. J. Kobrin (1982).

suggested by Robert Stobaugh, Jr. (1969). In this example, the economic outcomes can be regrouped into four mutually exclusive scenarios. Either the plant is not nationalized, or it is nationalized with adequate compensation, inadequate compensation, or no compensation. When these scenarios are matched with cash flow estimates, expected cash flow can be estimated year by year and discounted back to the present. The values obtained in this way can then be multiplied by the probabilities of each outcome, to obtain an expected value. Although assigning probabilities to scenarios is difficult, we recommend this approach over the alternative—arbitrarily raising the hurdle rate—because cash flow scenarios require careful thought, and as a result can provide better insights into the problem. Remember, though, that the expected (or average) outcome will never occur. It is only a probability-weighted average of all the things that might happen.

If the country where the subsidiary is domiciled imposes restrictions on the amount of capital that can be repatriated, the parent can discount only that portion of cash flow that is available for repatriation. In some cases, this may imply that the subsidiary

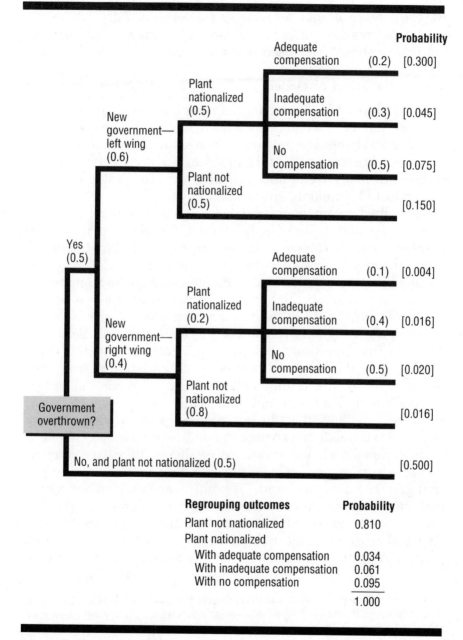

Source: R. Stobaugh, Jr. (1969).

is worth more if sold to a buyer from the country where the subsidiary resides. In other situations, it may mean that the subsidiary should be closed down entirely.

Valuing the Effect of Hedging

It is not unusual for multinational companies to take large positions in foreign exchange forward contracts to hedge against unexpected changes in floating exchange rates. Though designed to reduce currency risk, this practice is risky in itself. It has resulted in many well-publicized disasters. For example, Volkswagen lost $200 million, and Spectra Physics had an entire year's profits wiped out by inappropriate foreign exchange trading positions. Also, other ways of hedging exist. For example, if the local currency might decline in value, a company can reduce holding of local currency cash and marketable securities; delay accounts payable; invoice exports in the foreign currency and imports in the domestic currency; tighten trade credit in the foreign currency; and borrow more in the foreign currency.

Hedging programs can affect the expected cash flow of a company, its opportunity cost of capital, both, or neither. Exhibit 10.12 shows the trade-off between risk and return from two perspectives: total and undiversifiable risk. All successful hedges decrease total risk, but not necessarily undiversifiable risk.* Hedging programs that do not change expected cash flow or expected returns do not change the undiversifiable risk (the beta) of the company. They are merely diversifying; they have no effect on value because neither expected cash flow nor the discount rate changes. The company starts at point A and stays there. Other hedging programs affect expected cash flow and expected returns. Usually, expected returns decline and so do both diversifiable and undiversifiable risk (beta). The company moves from point A to point B in such a way that the decline in undiversifiable

*Total risk may be partitioned into diversifiable risk that is uncorrelated with the economy (usually company-specific events) and undiversifiable risk. Diversifiable risk has no opportunity cost because it can be eliminated at little or no cost. Therefore, diversifiable risk is unrelated to expected rates of return. Undiversifiable risk (beta) is positively related to expected return, according to the capital asset pricing model.

Exhibit 10.12 **RISK/RETURN TRADE-OFFS OF HEDGING PROGRAMS**

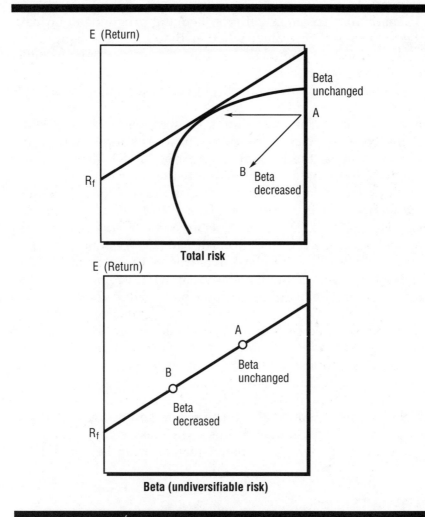

risk is offset by the decline in expected return. Although the risk-return profile of the company has been altered, no change in value necessarily results, because the risk reduction is offset by decreases in expected return. However, both the change in expected cash flow and the change in the discount rate (due to changed undiversifiable risk) should be estimated and included in your valuation if the hedging program has a material effect on the company.

Apart from secondary effects, hedging programs often have little or no effect on value, whether they are static hedges (for example, forward contracts) or dynamic hedges (for example, portfolio insurance).

Although the primary effects of hedging programs are of little concern to us, secondary effects can *sometimes* have a significant impact on value. The most significant secondary effects of hedging are costs associated with variability. Although they do not necessarily affect the opportunity cost of capital, they do affect expected free cash flow and, therefore, the value of the company. Bankruptcy costs are the most obvious example of costs associated with variability. Others are cost of business disruption (for example, loss of skilled labor), cuts in research and development, and loss of customer confidence. Altman (1984) estimates that the expected costs of bankruptcy range from 8.1 percent to 17.5 percent of the value of the company. Hedging programs that can reduce the probability of bankruptcy have their primary effect on expected cash flow. Whenever hedging programs have significant effects on expected cash flow, their impact should be captured in the valuation.

Hedging can also affect the company's effective tax rate. By smoothing cash flow, hedging makes use of carry-forward or carry-back provisions of the tax code unnecessary because tax shields are used immediately. The result is to decrease the company's effective tax rate and thus to increase value. This secondary effect of hedging is usually small and can be ignored.

SUMMARY

This chapter has focused primarily on the example of valuing the English subsidiary of a U.S. parent multinational corporation. The first step was to forecast all cash flow, wherever it occurred, in the local currency. Next, this cash flow was translated year-by-year into pounds sterling, the subsidiary's currency, by using forecasts of the future spot foreign exchange rates. Once all free cash flow was stated in sterling, it was discounted at the weighted average cost of capital for the subsidiary. The resulting sterling value of the company was then converted to dollars at the spot exchange rate.

Along the way, we covered a number of difficult issues: the need to understand foreign (and U.S.) accounting standards, the transfer-pricing problem, forecasting forward FX rates, evaluating political risk, and understanding the effect of FX hedging on value.

11

Mergers and Acquisitions

Chapter 9 discussed multibusiness valuation and restructuring. The fourth apex of the restructuring pentagon requires that one examine the potential value of a company with all possible external improvements. Obvious examples of such improvements are mergers, acquisitions, and divestitures. These are important enough to require a chapter in their own right.

THE TRENDS

Exhibits 11.1 and 11.2 demonstrate that merger and acquisition (M&A) activity has grown rapidly in nominal dollar terms in the United States, and that two "merger waves" have occurred, the first in the mid-1960s and the second, twenty years later, in the mid-1980s. Over the years, M&A activity has been highly correlated with plant and equipment expenditures, averaging between 16 and 20 percent of aggregate internal expenditures. This suggests that aside from regulatory influences, M&A activity can be viewed as an external investment alternative to internal growth. When internal growth builds up, external growth increases proportionately.

Exhibit 11.1 **FIGURES ON MERGER ACTIVITY IN THE UNITED STATES**

Year	Total dollar value paid* ($ Billions)	Total**	Number of transactions valued at $100 million or more	Number of transactions valued at $1,000 million or more	GNP deflator (1972= 100)	1972 constant dollar consideration
1968	$ 43.6	4462	46	—	82.5	52.8
1969	23.7	6107	24	—	86.8	27.3
1970	16.4	5152	10	1	91.4	17.9
1971	12.6	4608	7	—	96.0	13.1
1972	16.7	4801	15	—	100.0	16.7
1973	16.7	4040	28	—	105.7	15.8
1974	12.4	2861	15	—	115.1	10.8
1975	11.8	2297	14	1	125.8	9.4
1976	20.0	2276	39	1	132.1	15.1
1977	21.9	2224	41	—	140.1	15.6
1978	34.2	2106	80	1	150.4	22.7
1979	43.5	2128	83	3	163.4	26.6
1980	44.3	1889	94	4	178.6	24.8
1981	82.6	2395	113	12	195.5	42.2
1982	53.8	2346	116	6	207.2	26.0
1983	73.1	2533	138	11	215.3	34.0
1984	122.2	2543	200	18	223.4	54.7
1985	179.6	3001	270	36	231.4	77.6

Source: W. T. Grimm & Co. (1986); U.S. Department of Commerce.

* Based on the transactions that disclosed a purchase price.
** Total: Net merger-acquisition announcements. The W. T. Grimm & Co. Research Department records publicly announced formal transfers of ownership of at least 10% of a company's assets or equity where the purchase price is at least $500,000, and where one of the parties is a U.S. company. These transactions are recorded as they are announced, not as they are completed; canceled transactions are deducted from total announcements in the period in which the cancellation occurred, resulting in net merger-acquisition announcements for that period.

The 1990s will almost surely see a merger wave in Europe as the 1992 regulations create a single European Community. As early as December 1988, the commission of the EC proposed legislation to harmonize the widely differing rules on takeovers in its twelve member nations. This will facilitate EC mergers.

Exhibit 11.2 **A PROFILE OF MERGER ACTIVITY IN THE UNITED STATES**

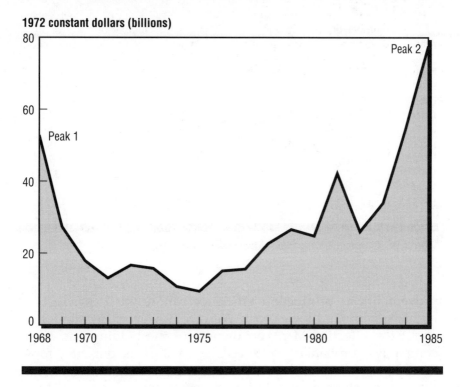

Already, companies are making acquisitions to position them-selves for an integrated EC.

Exhibit 11.3 provides data on the number of divestitures in the United States each year. Beginning in the early 1970s, corporate divestitures have represented between 40 and 50 percent of all corporate transactions. Combined M&A and divestiture activity plays a significant role in the reallocation of resources in the economy.

In this chapter, we do not attempt to provide an answer to the question of whether mergers, acquisitions, and divestitures are beneficial to the economy as a whole. A merger may be good for shareholders of both the acquiring and acquired companies but bad for the economy, because if a monopoly position is created it may be detrimental to consumers. On the other hand, real im-

Exhibit 11.3 **DIVESTITURE ACTIVITY IN THE UNITED STATES**

Year	Number of divestitures	Percentage of all transactions	Year	Number of divestitures	Percentage of all transactions
1966	264	11%	1976	1204	53%
1967	328	11	1977	1002	45
1968	557	12	1978	820	39
1969	801	13	1979	752	35
1970	1401	27	1980	666	35
1971	1920	42	1981	830	35
1972	1770	37	1982	875	37
1973	1557	39	1983	932	37
1974	1331	47	1984	900	36
1975	1236	54	1985	1237	41

Source: W. T. Grimm & Co. (1986). *Mergerstat Review, 1985.*

provements in production efficiency can result in products of higher quality and lower cost. We can, however, say something about the effect of M&A on owners of the bidding and target companies; probability of success or failure is our first topic. Second, we discuss the major reasons for failure. Finally, we discuss the steps necessary for implementing a successful M&A program.

MERGER PROGRAMS: THE PROBABILITY OF FAILURE

In the M&A arena, who wins, who loses, and why? Any company contemplating an acquisition must familiarize itself with the simple facts that external growth is extremely competitive and the probability of increasing its shareholders' wealth via such growth is low. Two broad types of research provide this warning. Academic studies have typically looked at the *ex ante* market reaction to the announcement of a merger, taking into account not only expected costs and benefits of the deal, but also the market's expectation that the deal will actually be consummated. The other approach is *ex post*, looking at the success or failure of merger programs after their completion. The bad news for potential acquirers is that neither approach provides grounds for an optimistic forecast. Therefore, M&A programs must be carefully conceived and executed.

Ex Ante Market Reactions

Exhibit 11.4 summarizes the results of dozens of academic studies. The lesson is that shareholders of acquired companies are the big winners, receiving on average a 20-percent premium in a friendly merger and a 35-percent premium in a hostile takeover. Shareholders of acquiring companies earn small returns that are not even statistically different from zero for friendly mergers.

To illustrate the usual methodology in academic studies, we have analyzed three banking mergers: Mellon/Girard, Bank of New York/Irving Trust, and Wells Fargo/Crocker. Exhibit 11.5

Exhibit 11.4 **SUMMARY OF EMPIRICAL STUDIES OF SHARE PRICE CHANGES RESULTING FROM M&A ACTIVITIES**

Type of event	Average return to shareholders (Percent)
Merger	
Acquired company	20%
Acquiring company	2–3*
Tender offer for takeover	
Acquired company	35
Acquiring company	3–5
Sell-off	
Spin-off	2–5
Divestiture	
Seller	0.5–1.0
Buyer	0.34
Equity carve-out	2

Source: Copeland and Weston 1988, 754.
* Not statistically significant.

Exhibit 11.5 **CUMULATIVE ABNORMAL RETURNS AROUND MERGER ANNOUNCEMENTS**

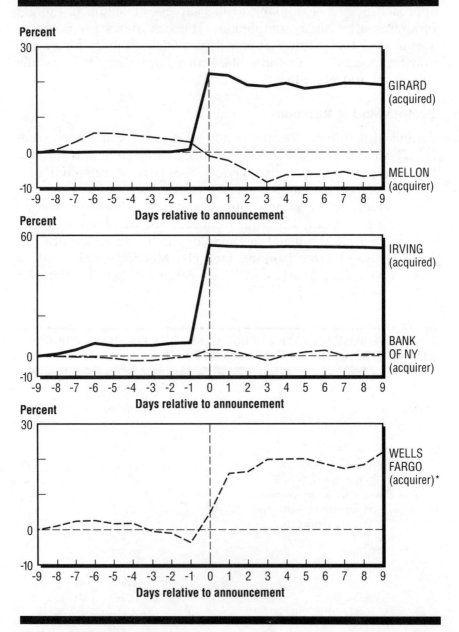

Source: McKinsey analysis
* Crocker was not publicly traded at the time it was acquired by Wells Fargo, so no CAR data are available.

shows the market reaction to the initial merger announcement in terms of the effect on common share prices for both the acquiring and the acquired company.

Shareholder returns are plotted as the cumulative abnormal returns, CARs, around the announcement date, day 0. The abnormal return each day is the error term in a regression of the security's return against that of a market index:

$$R_{jt} = \hat{a}_j + \hat{b}_j R_{mt} + e_{jt}$$

where

R_{jt} = the total return on the jth stock on day t

$\hat{a}_j, \hat{b}_j$ = the intercept and slope terms from a linear regression of R_{jt} on R_{mt} during a benchmark period (different from the period when CARs are estimated)

R_{mt} = the total return on an index representative of the entire market

This procedure provides an estimate of company-specific information on a given day, after removing the effect of general market movements. The residual, e_{jt}, is also called the abnormal return, because without a company-specific event, the difference between the actual and predicted returns will average out to zero. The CARs plotted in Exhibit 11.5 can be interpreted as the excess shareholder returns attributable to news about the merger.

The CAR patterns in Exhibit 11.5 are typical. They wander around zero prior to the unexpected announcement of the merger, and then they jump (in a few days) to a new (permanent) level that reflects the market's *ex ante* expectation of the effect of the merger on shareholders of the acquiring and acquired companies. The Mellon/Girard deal is typical, with the acquirer's shareholders losing 4.97 percent in two days and the acquired company's shareholders gaining 20.98 percent. But the Bank of New York/Irving Trust and Wells/Crocker deals are different. The acquiring shareholders earned 3.29 percent and 19.61 percent respectively in a few days, and in the Bank of New York/Irving deal, the acquired company's shareholders gained an incredible

48.16 percent. Of course, a favorable initial market reaction does not mean that the merger will ultimately succeed.

Why did Wells Fargo do so well in its acquisition of Crocker? The main reason is that unique real synergies resulting from rationalization of overlapping branch banking systems were achieved quickly during postmerger integration. Furthermore, they could not be captured by a competing bidder, so Wells Fargo shared the benefit with Crocker.

The academic evidence is primarily based on *ex ante* analysis. It reflects the market's expectation of the costs and benefits of the proposed merger and the probability that the deal will go through. On average, the market's estimate is correct. Shareholders of acquired companies receive most of the benefit, because competition among acquirers forces the target's price up to the point where little or no benefit to acquiring shareholders is left. Of course, this does not mean that acquirers never succeed. The market's initial reaction may be wrong. To learn more about why mergers succeed or fail, we must turn to *ex post* analysis.

Ex Post Analysis of Acquisitions

McKinsey & Company's Corporate Leadership Center studied 116 acquisition programs, usually involving multiple acquisitions, between 1972 and 1983. We started with companies in either the *Fortune* 200 largest U.S. industrials or the *Financial Times* top 150 U.K. industrials. We judged a program to be successful if it earned its cost of equity capital or better on funds invested in the acquisition program. In other words, income after taxes as a percentage of equity invested in the acquisition had to exceed the acquirer's opportunity cost of equity. Because it takes at least three years to determine whether an acquisition has been successful, our financial analysis looked at data available through the end of 1986. Programs usually involved multiple acquisitions. For example, General Mills made 47 acquisitions of small, high-growth, consumer-oriented companies as part of a single program.

In order to compare the market's *ex ante* reaction to our *ex post* judgment we studied the initial market reaction affecting the shareholder returns for nineteen acquisition announcements. Our *ex post* opinion is that the market was correct in ten out of the sixteen outcomes that we could judge; but only one of the five situations initially evaluated as a success by the market actually turned out that way. This does not mean the market is inefficient, only that full information on the eventual success or failure of a program is not available until well after the initial announcement.

Ex post analysis indicates that 61 percent of the programs we evaluated ended in failure, and only 23 percent in success; the results of the rest were indeterminate. Exhibit 11.6 shows the breakdown for 116 acquisition programs in the United Kingdom and the United States. Each program was categorized by the type of acquisitions it made. For the 97 programs that were either successes or failures, the greatest chance of success was only 45 percent for those programs where acquiring companies bought smaller companies in related businesses. The acquired company was judged to be small if the purchase price was less than 10 percent of the acquiring company's market value. It was classified as related if the target's markets were similar to those of the acquiring company. If the target was large and in an unrelated line of business, the success rate fell to only 14 percent. This points to the conclusion that diversification is not a good motive for mergers.

Exhibit 11.7 uses the U.S. portion of the sample to show that the probability of success is also heavily influenced by the strength of the core business of the acquirer. Companies with strong core businesses prior to the start of their acquisition programs had a much better chance than those without strong core businesses. Of the 23 percent of the U.S. programs that were successful, fully 92 percent had strong core businesses.

In sum, although the probability of success for the average buyer is only 50/50 at best, these odds can be improved by having a strong core business, buying companies in related businesses where the chance of achieving real economic synergies is highest, and buying smaller businesses so that they can easily be integrated during the postacquisition phase of the program.

Exhibit 11.6 **SUCCESS AND FAILURE RATES BY TYPE OF ACQUISITION**

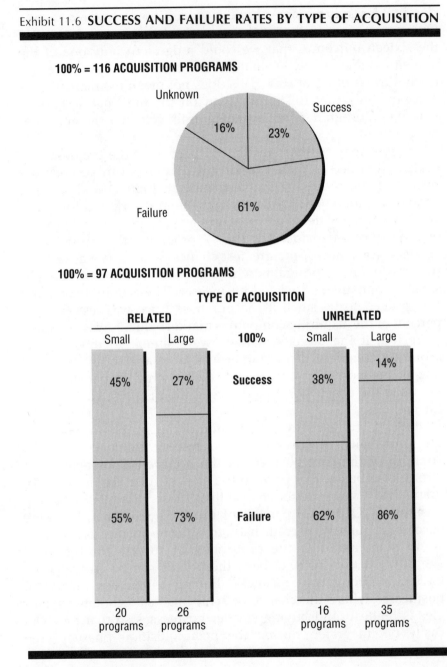

100% = 116 ACQUISITION PROGRAMS

Unknown

Success

16%   23%

Failure   61%

100% = 97 ACQUISITION PROGRAMS

TYPE OF ACQUISITION

RELATED		100%	UNRELATED	
Small	Large		Small	Large
45%	27%	**Success**	38%	14%
55%	73%	**Failure**	62%	86%
20 programs	26 programs		16 programs	35 programs

Source: McKinsey analysis.

Exhibit 11.7 **HOW CORE BUSINESSES PERFORMED PRIOR TO ACQUISITION PROGRAMS**

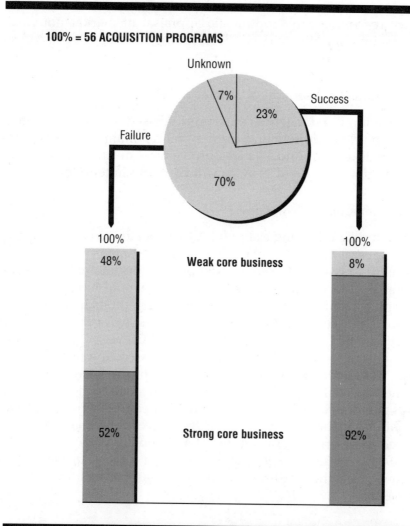

100% = 56 ACQUISITION PROGRAMS

MERGER PROGRAMS: REASONS FOR FAILURE

Why do so many acquisition programs fail? Many reasons can be given, including poor management and just plain bad luck. A pervasive reason, though, is that many acquirers pay too much.

With average takeover premiums in the 40 percent range, and with increasingly competitive markets for takeover, it is all too easy to overpay. But why do companies overpay? The four primary reasons are overoptimistic appraisal of market potential, overestimation of synergies, overbidding, and poor postacquisition integration.

Overoptimistic Appraisal of Market Potential

Acquisition is a dangerous enterprise if based on the assumption that a market will rebound from a cyclical slump or that a company will turn around. No less problematic or uncommon is the assumption that rapid growth will continue indefinitely.

Overestimation of Synergies

Consider the following example. A large health services company paid several billion for a more profitable company in a related industry segment. Given its stepped-up investment base, the target's postacquisition after-tax earnings would have had to be around $500 million for the acquirer's return on its investment to approach its cost of capital, even after divesting over $600 million worth of the newly acquired company's businesses. In 1984, the year before the transaction was consummated, the target's earnings were about $225 million. After divestiture of units that had earned $45 million the previous year, it needed to close an earnings gap of over $275 million through "operating synergies." The acquirer's inability to make improvements of this magnitude resulted in destruction of significant shareholder value. From 1984 to 1986, overall market indices increased almost 18 percent in value while the acquirer's returns to its shareholders fell 3.8 percent.

Overbidding

In the heat of a deal, the acquirer may find it all too easy to bid up the price beyond the limits of a reasonable valuation. Remember the winner's curse. If you are the winner in a bidding war, why did your competitors drop out?

Poor Postacquisition Integration

It goes almost without saying that poor implementation can ruin even the best strategy. Unfortunately, in merger and acquisition situations the execution of a sound business strategy is made especially difficult by the complex task of integrating two different organizations. Relationships with customers, employers, and suppliers can easily be disrupted during the process; and this disruption may cause damage to the value of the business. Aggressive acquirers often believe they can improve the target's performance by injecting better management talent, but end up chasing much of the talent out. Yet it is this very integration that should yield the returns to make the acquisition pay off. Failure to integrate can be as costly as integrating poorly.

Exhibit 11.8 shows a typical losing pattern for unsuccessful merger programs. This death spiral, unfortunately, is all too common. The next section of this chapter talks about the steps in a disciplined acquisition program designed to maximize the probability of success.

STEPS IN A SUCCESSFUL MERGER AND ACQUISITION PROGRAM

We can break an acquisition program into the five distinct steps shown in Exhibit 11.9. Common sense is the rule of the day every step along the way. The process begins with a preacquisition phase that involves a careful self-examination of your company and the industry it is in. And the process ends with a carefully planned postmerger integration that is executed as quickly as possible to capture the premium that was paid for the acquisition. When the odds against successful external growth are so high, it pays to develop a careful program.

Step 1: Manage the Preacquisition Phase

Getting ready for an active acquisition campaign means taking a proactive stance. The most important lesson is that secrecy must be maintained throughout the entire program. If the market gets

Exhibit 11.8 **TYPICAL LOSING PATTERN FOR MERGERS**

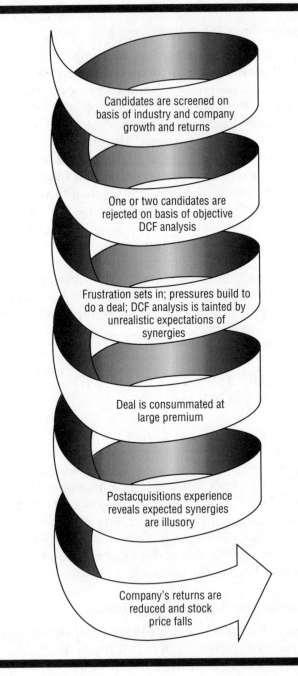

Candidates are screened on basis of industry and company growth and returns

One or two candidates are rejected on basis of objective DCF analysis

Frustration sets in; pressures build to do a deal; DCF analysis is tainted by unrealistic expectations of synergies

Deal is consummated at large premium

Postacquisitions experience reveals expected synergies are illusory

Company's returns are reduced and stock price falls

Exhibit 11.9 **STEPS IN A SUCCESSFUL MERGER AND ACQUISITION PROGRAM**

1. Manage preacquisition phase

- Instruct staff on secrecy requirements
- Evaluate your own company
- Identify value-adding approach
  - Understand industry structure, and strengthen core business
  - Capitalize on economies of scale
  - Exploit technology or skills transfer

2. Screen candidates

- Identify knockout criteria
- Decide how to use investment banks
- Prioritize opportunities
- Look at public companies, divisions of companies, and privately held companies

3. Value remaining candidates

- Know exactly how you will recoup the takeover premium
- Identify real synergies
- Decide on restructuring plan
- Decide on financial engineering opportunities

4. Negotiate

- Decide on maximum reservation price and stick to it
- Understand background and incentives of the other side
- Understand value that might be paid by a third party
- Establish negotiation strategy
- Conduct due diligence

5. Manage postmerger integration

- Move as quickly as possible
- Carefully manage the process

wind of a rumored takeover attempt, the price of the target will go up, possibly enough to kill the deal. Staff must also be trained in doing valuations from an outsider's perspective that uses a library of publicly available data. A good starting point is to value your own company by valuing its business units and doing a "raider analysis." In addition to training your staff, this exercise often provides valuable insights about how to obtain the maximum value out of your own business to keep from becoming a target yourself.

If you have valued your own company, if you understand its strengths and weaknesses, and if you understand the changing structure of your industry, then you are ready to have a brainstorming session to identify the value-adding approach that will work best for your company. Three possible approaches are as follows:

1. Strengthen or leverage your core business.
2. Capitalize on functional economies of scale.
3. Benefit from technology or skills transfer.

You can use the model of industry structure analysis illustrated in Exhibit 11.10 to think about ways of strengthening or leveraging your core business. Acquiring a foothold in a *substitute* business may be a critical defensive move to preserve the value of, for example, a strong sales/service capability. Wang's purchase of Intecom was intended, at least in part, to protect Wang's position in the front office automation business from potential substitute PBX-based systems. IBM-Rolm is a similar example. Monsanto's long-term efforts to enter the biotechnology industry have been predicated on exploiting new approaches to producing its existing product lines.

If the *customer* base is concentrating (as it is, for example, in trucking), or the company's value added to the customer's end product is diminishing (as in general aviation assembly), acquisitions to forward-integrate and/or to create a clearly differentiated product may be needed to preserve existing margins. ConAgra's forward integration from grain and poultry into higher-value-

Exhibit 11.10 **A MODEL OF INDUSTRY STRUCTURE ANALYSIS**

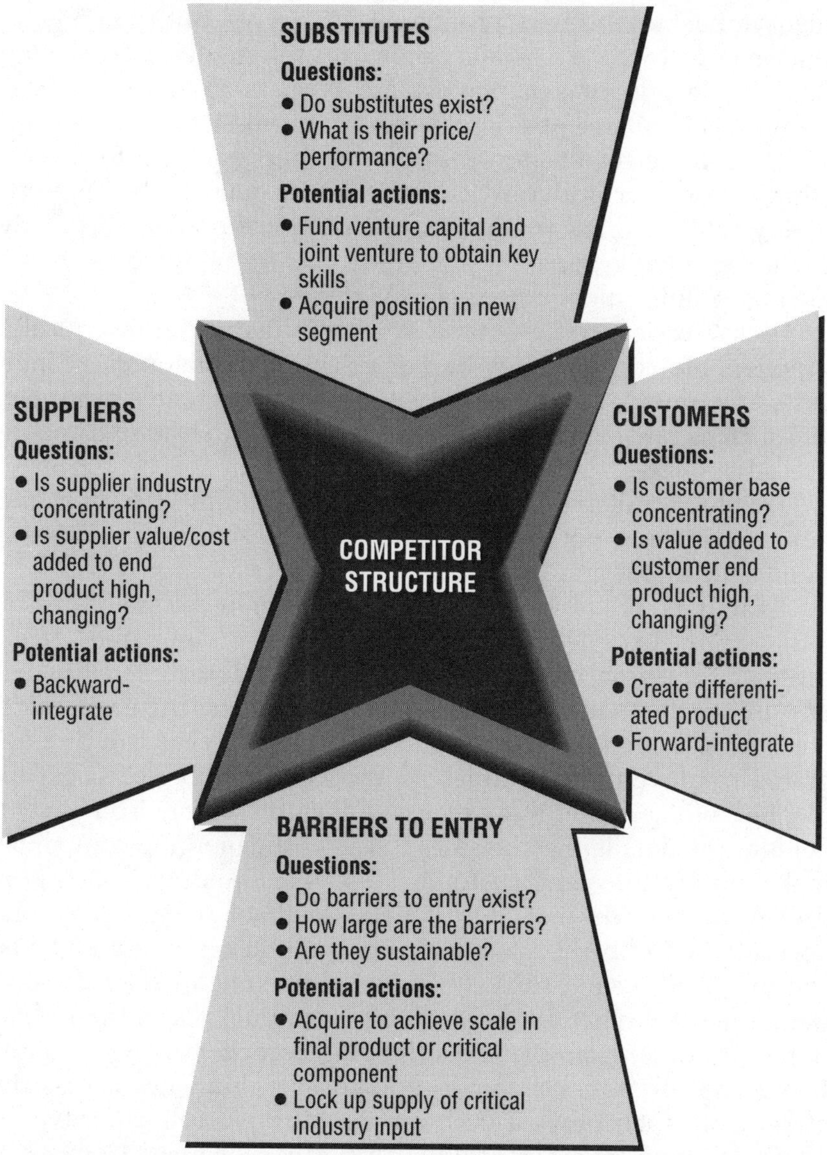

SUBSTITUTES

Questions:
- Do substitutes exist?
- What is their price/performance?

Potential actions:
- Fund venture capital and joint venture to obtain key skills
- Acquire position in new segment

SUPPLIERS

Questions:
- Is supplier industry concentrating?
- Is supplier value/cost added to end product high, changing?

Potential actions:
- Backward-integrate

COMPETITOR STRUCTURE

CUSTOMERS

Questions:
- Is customer base concentrating?
- Is value added to customer end product high, changing?

Potential actions:
- Create differentiated product
- Forward-integrate

BARRIERS TO ENTRY

Questions:
- Do barriers to entry exist?
- How large are the barriers?
- Are they sustainable?

Potential actions:
- Acquire to achieve scale in final product or critical component
- Lock up supply of critical industry input

added products has actually increased its operating margin in the face of a concentrating retail structure.

Acquisitions to preserve or create *barriers to entry* can have a major impact on industry profitability; however, antitrust regulations may restrict the feasibility of many of these deals. Achieving major scale advantages may create barriers to new entrants. Acquiring dominant positions in critical input factors can accomplish the same result—for example, (1) negotiating a long-term contract for a critical raw material; (2) acquiring the highest-quality raw materials in an area, such as gypsum deposits or fly ash for synthetic gypsum; and (3) acquiring regulated licenses such as cellular mobile or cable-TV rights.

Backward integration into a *supplier* industry can be critical if suppliers are concentrating and/or pricing like oligopolies. Similarly, ensuring continuous access to periodically scarce input factors such as raw materials or key components can lead to competitive advantages.

Finally, acquisitions to concentrate *competitor structure* and reduce cutthroat competition due to overcapacity can have a significant impact on profitability.

Exhibit 11.11 shows areas where economies of scale may be found. Our experience suggests that many companies overestimate functional economies of scale and underestimate the cost of running the matrix structure required to create the economies. For example, it is one thing to say that sales forces can be integrated to move more product via the same number of salespeople, but quite another thing to accomplish the vision. You have to get into the details. Do the sales forces of the merging companies make exactly the same customer calls? For example, it is a pipe dream to believe that two college textbook companies, one specializing in liberal arts books and the other in scientific texts, can profit from sales force savings. Salespeople in the two companies actually visit different parts of campus, with little redundancy. Another example is overlapping branch banking systems. It may not be possible to close down even branches across the street from each other if both are operating at full capacity.

Sometimes, but not often, value can be gained from skills or technology transfer via merger. But this approach, which is one we have seen often, is fraught with pitfalls. More often than

Exhibit 11.11 **ANALYSIS OF POTENTIAL ECONOMIES OF SCALE**

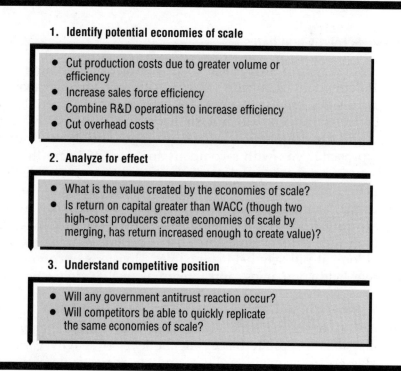

1. **Identify potential economies of scale**

- Cut production costs due to greater volume or efficiency
- Increase sales force efficiency
- Combine R&D operations to increase efficiency
- Cut overhead costs

2. **Analyze for effect**

- What is the value created by the economies of scale?
- Is return on capital greater than WACC (though two high-cost producers create economies of scale by merging, has return increased enough to create value)?

3. **Understand competitive position**

- Will any government antitrust reaction occur?
- Will competitors be able to quickly replicate the same economies of scale?

not, managerial hubris creates overly optimistic self-assessments of leverageable skills.

One successful example of skills transfer, however, was when United Technologies acquired Otis Elevator in 1981. Improvements in general management skills resulted in working capital reductions and reduced corporate overhead. Improvements in functional capabilities enabled Otis to reengineer its product line and to introduce, six years ahead of schedule, a fully electronic elevator control system that (1) consumed 40 percent less energy than the existing product; (2) reduced passenger waiting time by 33 percent; and (3) required less maintenance while reducing the cost of maintenance required.

Your approach to identifying the best value-adding approach should be to go for the low-hanging fruit first—to exploit your existing competitive advantage. Then, as refinements are needed, look for closely related opportunities.

Step 2: Screen Candidates

Successful acquirers undertake their own active screening process, independent of outside sources. Although you may explain your acquisition criteria to a broad spectrum of investment banks and business brokers, do not sit back and passively react to investment banking proposals for acquisition candidates. If someone approaches you with a company for sale, odds are that the company is being shopped around. In addition to establishing criteria for acquisition, it is also useful to develop a list of "knockout criteria," as illustrated in Exhibit 11.12. Targets that are too large, too small, or in unrelated businesses can be quickly eliminated in order to focus on a short list of serious candidates. You should look at publicly held companies, divisions of companies, privately held companies, and foreign as well as domestic companies.

At this stage in the process, you should think carefully about the role of consulting firms, law firms, and investment banks. Each has its appropriate place, but the level of activity varies at each stage of an acquisition. Legal and tax advice is necessary at all phases.

Once you have narrowed your list of candidates to a handful of realistic possibilities, you have to roll up your sleeves and get down to the detailed work of valuing each candidate and identifying an explicit strategy for earning back the merger premium that you will have to pay.

Step 3: Value Remaining Candidates

The typical takeover premium in the 1980s has been close to 40 percent above the preacquisition market value of the target company.

When doing a detailed valuation of the few remaining candidates, remember the difference between the value to you and the price you pay. Your objective should be to pay only one dollar more than the value to the next highest bidder, and an amount

Exhibit 11.12 **USE OF KNOCKOUT CRITERIA TO NARROW THE ACQUISITION CANDIDATE SAMPLE**

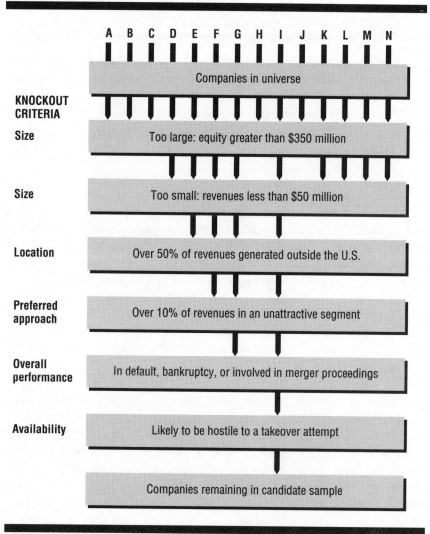

A B C D E F G H I J K L M N

Companies in universe

KNOCKOUT CRITERIA

Size
Too large: equity greater than $350 million

Size
Too small: revenues less than $50 million

Location
Over 50% of revenues generated outside the U.S.

Preferred approach
Over 10% of revenues in an unattractive segment

Overall performance
In default, bankruptcy, or involved in merger proceedings

Availability
Likely to be hostile to a takeover attempt

Companies remaining in candidate sample

that is less than the value to you. The implication is that you need to identify not only the real synergies that you can obtain but also those that may accrue to other potential acquirers.

Synergies fall into one of three broad categories, as detailed by Bill Pursche (1988).

1. *Universal.* Generally available to any logical acquirer with capable management and adequate resources. Examples are many economies of scale (such as leveraging the fixed cost of an MIS department) and some exploitable opportunities (for example, raising prices).
2. *Endemic.* Available to only a few acquirers, typically those in the same industry as the seller. These include economies of scope (broadened geographic coverage) and most exploitable opportunities (redundant sales forces).
3. *Unique.* Opportunities that can be exploited only by a specific buyer (or seller).

The value to the buyer and seller depends on the type of synergy and who has it. If the synergy is unique and held by the seller, then the buyer has little hope of capturing any value in the bidding process. But if the buyer has the unique synergy, it can pay a low price (because there is no competing buyer) and keep most of the value. Endemic synergies fall in between, with the buyer and seller sharing the value created. And universal synergies must be paid for by the buyer (because anyone can compete). The ideal bid, after a careful analysis, is one that includes most or all of the universal synergies and perhaps some of the endemic synergies.

A variety of restructuring and financial engineering approaches can result in real value added for the acquiring company. Assets that are worth more to other owners can be profitably redeployed via liquidations, divestitures, spin-offs, or leveraged buyouts. The value of core businesses can be enhanced by reducing headquarters costs, by implementing significant skills transfers, by changing the industry structure, and by capturing real synergies. Hidden asset values can be captured by exploiting overfunded pension plans, underutilized real estate, or other underutilized assets (such as timberlands, oil reserves, mineral deposits, or film libraries). Finally, alternative financing arrangements—including sale/leaseback arrangements, royalty trusts, master limited partnerships, partial equity offerings, letter stock, and contingency payment units—can also create value by better utilizing tax shelters, by reducing the capital base without cutting earnings, or by raising funds in an optimal way.

It is crucial to identify and value all restructuring and financial engineering opportunities in great detail before deciding to bid on an acquisition candidate. Before entering negotiation, you must know how much a company is worth to you, exactly what you plan to do with it, and the precise timing.

It is also important to understand the accounting and tax treatments of potential acquisitions. The two accepted accounting treatments for mergers in the United States are purchase and pooling. They are governed by Accounting Principles Board Opinions 16 and 17. Pooling of interests simply combines the financial statements of the merging companies. Purchase accounting requires that the difference between the price paid and the book value of the acquired assets be recorded as goodwill (an intangible asset) and written off as a non-tax-deductible expense over a period not to exeed forty years.

The real danger in the accounting treatment of mergers is summarized in the following quotation from an FASB discussion memorandum (August 1976): "Some have suggested that if many of the combinations (of businesses) accounted for by pooling of interests were required to be accounted for by the purchase method . . . they would not have been consummated, notwithstanding valid business reasons supporting their consummation."

Because purchase accounting requires the write-off of goodwill and therefore lower earnings, most managers prefer pooling whenever possible. However, because the write-off of goodwill does not affect taxes, it has no impact whatsoever on cash flows or on the value of the company (see the discussion of goodwill in Chapter 5).

Which treatment creates the more value? We would say that (tax considerations aside) no difference exists between pooling and purchase. The accounting treatment has no effect on value created. Empirical support for this is provided in an article by Hong, Kaplan, and Mandelker (1978). For a sample of 159 mergers, 122 used pooling and 37 used purchase. The researchers found no evidence whatsoever that shareholders of companies using the purchase treatment did worse than companies using pooling. Nevertheless, in a survey of the 122 companies that used pooling, 66 percent agreed with the aforementioned quotation that otherwise profitable acquisitions might not be consummated if the purchase treatment were required.

Six broad tests are used to determine whether the conditions for pooling of interests treatment are met. If all are met, then the combination is considered to be a merger among equals and the pooling of interests method can be employed. The six tests are as follows:

1. The acquired company's stockholders must maintain an ownership position in the surviving company.

2. The basis for accounting for the assets of the acquired entity must remain unchanged.

3. Independent interests must be combined. Each entity must have had autonomy for two years prior to the initiation of the plan to combine, and no more than 10 percent ownership of voting common stock can be held as intercorporate investments.

4. The combination must be effected in a single transaction; contingent payouts are not permitted in poolings but can be used in purchases.

5. The acquiring corporation must issue only common stock with rights identical to its outstanding voting common stock in exchange for substantially all (90 percent) of the voting common stock of the company.

6. The combined entity must not intend to dispose of a significant portion of the assets of the combining companies within two years after the merger.

In contrast, a purchase involves new owners, an appraisal of the acquired firm's physical assets, restatement of the balance sheet to reflect these new values, and the possibility of an excess or deficit of consideration given up vis-à-vis the book value of equity. The last point, of course, is the creation of goodwill.

STEPS IN A SUCCESSFUL MERGER AND ACQUISITION PROGRAM

The tax treatment of acquisitions is a constantly changing and extremely complex topic. Almost anything that we could commit to paper at this time would soon be outdated. Our recommendation, therefore, is that anyone working on a merger and acquisition should seek the counsel of a qualified tax expert.

Step 4: Negotiate

Merger fever can be a fatal disease if complicated by managerial hubris at the negotiation phase. If you have done your homework carefully, you have assessed the value to you of the acquisition candidate. If you pay even one dollar more than this reservation price, you lose. An article by Mark Mitchell and Ken Lehn (1988) of the Securities and Exchange Commission indicates that bidders who fail in an acquisition because they overbid or because they could not make the acquisition work often become targets themselves. The cost of overpaying can be severe and will be suffered immediately.

The keys to a successful negotiating strategy are as follows:

- Assess the value of the acquisition to you.
- Assess the value of the acquisition candidate to the existing owners and other potential buyers.
- Assess the financial condition of the existing owners and other potential acquirers.
- Assess the strategy and motivation of the existing owners and other potential acquirers.
- Determine whether the other parties are using or will use a negotiation intermediary, and examine the history of their approaches.
- Create a bid strategy, focusing on potential changes in value and on the initial offer, conditioned by the situation of the initial owners and of potential bidders.
- Understand the potential impact of antitakeover provisions.

Not only should you know your own reservation price, but you should also know what the target is worth to other potential buyers, including the existing management in a leveraged buyout. If all goes well, you will not need to pay any more than one dollar more than the value to the next highest bidder. If you think you will be the second highest bidder, why enter the competition in the first place?

Just prior to negotiation, many acquirers achieve a toehold in the target company by purchasing up to 5 percent of its stock on the open market, and do so without causing a noticeable run-up in the price. Once the 5 percent limit has been exceeded, the Williams Act requires full disclosure. The purpose of a toehold, of course, is to reduce the cost of the acquisition by averaging the low cost of preannouncement purchases with the high cost of shares purchased later at a premium.

Negotiation is an art. You should choose your negotiating team carefully. The best number-crunchers are usually not the best negotiators. Know the financial condition of the other side. Know the ownership structure of the target company. And develop your bidding strategies in advance. Should you start with a low bid, planning to give way later on, or should you go in with an exploding offer that is nonnegotiable and has a deadline? How much information about the target should you ask its management to supply? What will they be willing to give? What antitakeover provisions do they have in place, and how resistant will they actually be? Exactly what are the backgrounds of their board of directors? What fairness opinions will be needed and who should supply them? What tax angles can be exploited in the deal?

Knowing the answers to these and other relevant questions, preplanning, and careful choice of your negotiating team will lead to the best possible outcome.

Step 5: Manage Postmerger Integration

Now you have bought a company and paid a hefty premium to do so. Postmerger integration is a fancy phrase for figuring out how to recoup your investment.

As shown in Exhibit 11.13, most acquirers destroy rather than create value after the acquisition. For twenty recent acquisitions, we looked at the acquired company's performance relative to its industry before and after acquisition. Performance was measured as return on sales (ROS) rather than return on invested capital (ROIC) to avoid problems associated with a stepped-up asset basis. Prior to being acquired, 24 percent of the companies performed better than the industry average and another 53 percent performed better than 75 percent of their industry average. Postacquisition, these percentages dropped to 10 percent and 16 percent, respectively. Prior to being acquired, 78 percent of

Exhibit 11.13 **PRE- AND POSTACQUISITION PERFORMANCE OF 20 ACQUIRED COMPANIES RELATIVE TO INDUSTRY**

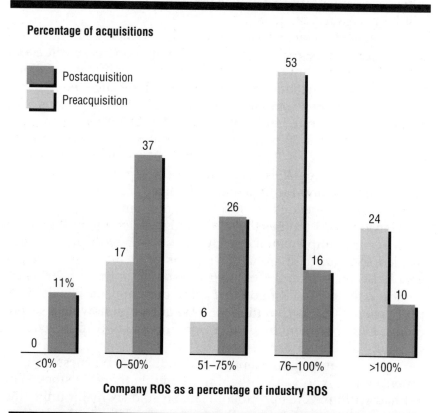

Percentage of acquisitions

Company ROS as a percentage of industry ROS

Source: McKinsey analysis.

the target companies beat the 75 percent mark, but after acquisition only 26 percent did. Clearly, postmerger integration must be carefully planned and implemented to avoid destroying value.

The appropriate management action for recouping your investment will depend on your original philosophy of value creation. In many cases, it will be possible to reduce corporate center costs by combining functions. Remember, though, to keep the best people from both organizations and fire the worst. Nothing is worse for the morale of the target company than wholesale layoffs. In other situations, it will be advisable to sell off business units that are worth more to other parent companies. And in other cases, integration of management to facilitate skills transfers will be necessary.

The speed of action is crucial. The sooner cash flow improvements can be realized the better, both to increase value and to reduce the amount of earnings dilution in the first year following acquisition. The incremental annual earnings needed to offset an acquisition premium climb precipitously as time passes. For example, as illustrated in Exhibit 11.14, if a $200-million company is purchased for a 30-percent premium at $260 million and the cost of the capital is 13 percent, then $60 million per year is needed in incremental cash flow to offset the premium if action is taken immediately. But if action is deferred three years, $87 million per year is needed to offset the premium.

Hanson Trust typifies the successful restructurer and financial engineer that implements quickly. Its success with this strategy has led to average shareholder returns of about 38 percent per year between 1975 and 1986—fifth best among the top 200 companies in the United Kingdom. Typical of its approach is the 1986 purchase of SCM Corporation for $930 million, following a seven-month tender/rebuttal battle. Hanson pursued two approaches to creating value after acquisition.

First, and most important, it sold individual business units to other owners who valued them more highly than the stock market had within SCM's portfolio. Hanson sold six major units (the paper operations, Glidden Paints, Durkee Foods, the kitchen subsidiary, a stamping machine unit, and Sylvachem) for approximately what it had paid for the entire corporation. Prospective

Exhibit 11.14 **COST TO A HYPOTHETICAL COMPANY OF DELAYING CASH FLOW IMPROVEMENTS,** $ MILLIONS

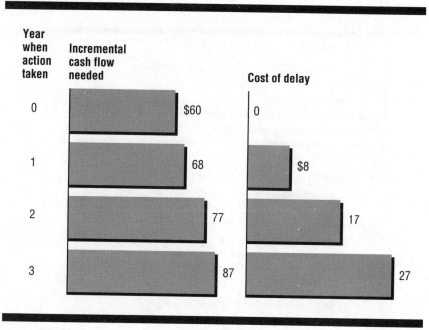

buyers for several of these businesses had been lined up prior to the deal's closing. Hanson was left with the core SCM typewriter business (well into a major profit turnaround), some paper operations, and the titanium dioxide paint business. These businesses were projected to produce over $130 million in operating income on sales of $700 to $800 million.

Second, Hanson cut corporate staff and corporate/group executive layers by 90 percent. Of the 250 executives that SCM had employed in corporate or group line and staff positions prior to acquisition by Hanson, only 25 were required to run Hanson's new U.S. operations.

As important as Hanson's approach was its timing. Within six months of the close of the acquisition, Hanson had recouped its total purchase price of $930 million on a pretax basis.

Exhibit 11.15 is a framework for postacquisition integration. Careful planning is required because of the large number of communications that need to be handled well. The extent of

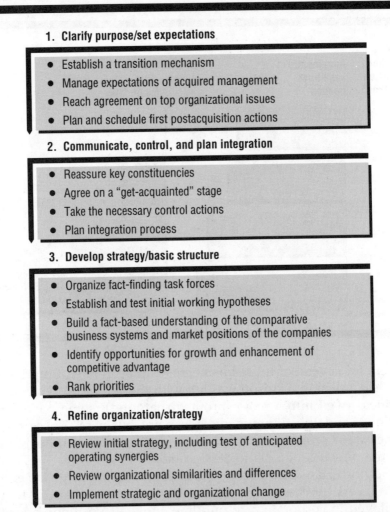

Exhibit 11.15 FRAMEWORK FOR POSTACQUISITION INTEGRATION

1. Clarify purpose/set expectations

- Establish a transition mechanism
- Manage expectations of acquired management
- Reach agreement on top organizational issues
- Plan and schedule first postacquisition actions

2. Communicate, control, and plan integration

- Reassure key constituencies
- Agree on a "get-acquainted" stage
- Take the necessary control actions
- Plan integration process

3. Develop strategy/basic structure

- Organize fact-finding task forces
- Establish and test initial working hypotheses
- Build a fact-based understanding of the comparative business systems and market positions of the companies
- Identify opportunities for growth and enhancement of competitive advantage
- Rank priorities

4. Refine organization/strategy

- Review initial strategy, including test of anticipated operating synergies
- Review organizational similarities and differences
- Implement strategic and organizational change

integration ultimately planned has to be communicated to the top management team of the acquired company to insure that their expectations are properly managed so that key players can be locked in. A communications plan for *both* organizations must be developed to allay anxieties, and organizational structures and systems must be integrated to minimize operational disruptions and departures of talented people. Ultimately, the strategy of the combined entity must be clarified.

Postmerger integration is a difficult task that becomes monumental if the two organizations are nearly the same size. Perhaps this explains why successful mergers are more likely to consist of large companies acquiring small companies in the same industry.

SUMMARY

Merger and acquisition activity (as well as divestiture) is a cyclical phenomenon correlated with the level of plant and equipment expenditures. External investment is a substitute for internal investment. It is also influenced by structural factors such as regulatory, technological, tax, and competitive changes.

An active market for corporate control dramatically reduces the chances of success for acquiring companies. Even in situations where the acquired company is in the same line of business as the acquirer and is small enough to allow easy postmerger integration, the likelihood of success is only about 50 percent.

A disciplined acquisition program is essential. You must have control of the process. Don't rely on deals brought to you by third parties. Find your own targets, starting with a self-analysis that leads to a value-adding approach. Identify knockout criteria in the screening process. Before bidding on a candidate, understand exactly how you intend to recoup a takeover premium. Identify real synergies and try to find synergies that are unique —that cannot be captured by another bidder. Decide on your maximum reservation price and stick to it as part of a carefully planned negotiation strategy. Finally, move as quickly as possible during postmerger integration and carefully manage the process.

As a closing thought, it is hard to resist the temptation to compare LBOs with mergers and acquisitions. The research on LBOs is still in a nascent stage. For example, because LBOs almost always result in privately held companies, little reliable or systematic evidence about returns to acquirers exists. Anecdotal evidence suggests that the returns have been high. Yet LBOs take place in a market for corporate control that is just as competitive as that for mergers and acquisitions. If the average return for acquirers in the mergers and acquisitions game is zero, why is it not zero for LBOs also?

12

Using Option Pricing Methods to Value Flexibility

Options give their owner the right (not the obligation) to buy or sell assets at a predetermined price (called the striking price) for a predetermined period of time (called the life of the option). Call options give the right to buy, and put options the right to sell. For valuations, it is important to remember that options can be found on both the assets and the liabilities sides of the balance sheet. Options on the assets side provide flexibility and create value when the cost of the option is lower than the benefits it provides. Options on the liabilities side affect the company's cost of capital.

Examples of options on the *assets side* of the balance sheet primarily have to do with flexibility. A company that has the option to shut down and restart operations, or to abandon them, is more flexible and therefore more valuable than the same company without these options. Asset options are important not only because they affect the values of companies that have them but also because they provide explicit criteria for deciding when operations should be opened, closed, or abandoned. For example, an option to open and close a mining operation may add 30 to 40 percent to its ordinary present value based on expected cash flow. In addition, the option provides explicit decision rules; for example, "open the mine when the price of kryptonite exceeds $100 per ounce."

In practice, we have applied option pricing to a variety of asset option situations where the value of flexibility was critical. In one case, the option value of a large mineral lease was 100 percent higher than its simple net present value. Although the mine was only marginally profitable at the time, the option to defer development until the mineral price rose made the value much higher than indicated by net present value analysis. In a large research and development effort, the option to abandon the project at critical decision nodes increased its value by 83 percent. These and other applications will be discussed in greater detail later on.

Options on the *liabilities side* of the balance sheet are easy to recognize. Convertible debt and preferred stock give their holder the right to exchange them for stock at a predetermined conversion ratio. Therefore, they contain call options. Warrants allow their owner to buy shares at a fixed price—again, a call option. Our standard approach to valuation requires that we subtract the market value of these liabilities from the entity value to estimate the value of equity. Furthermore, they have to be included in the weighted average cost of capital. This issue is far from trivial. For example, a recent random sample of one hundred companies listed on the New York Stock Exchange indicated that forty-three had convertible debt or preferred stock outstanding. Another important liabilities-side application is leasing. Most operating leases give the leaseholder the right to cancel by paying a fee (that is, an American put option) or the right to purchase for a fixed price at the end of the lease (that is, a European call). (An American option can be exercised at any time up to and including the maturity date. A European option can be exercised only on its maturity date.) These are valuable options.

The purpose of this chapter is not to turn you into a rocket scientist. Rather, we show the relation between option pricing and familiar approaches like net present value and decision-tree analysis, provide examples of asset options and show how they have been used in practice, and show how liability options can significantly affect the cost of capital.

ASSET OPTIONS

Options on assets add flexibility to managerial decision making. In the broadest sense, we can think of flexibility as one way of managing risk, but not the only method. Two strategies can be used for dealing with uncertainty: (1) anticipation, and (2) resilience. If risks can be anticipated because they are predictable, then the most effective and least costly approach is often to construct a specialized but inflexible system that works best in the anticipated environment. Alternatively, if risks cannot be anticipated, a resilient system with a great deal of flexibility becomes the best approach. Take as an example the shock to the economic system created when OPEC dramatically raised crude oil prices in the early 1970s. Heavy energy consumers had not anticipated the change and many were overspecialized because they could convert only oil. They quickly invested to create flexibility for themselves to use multiple sources of energy (for example, natural gas, hydroelectric power, and coal, as well as oil). The motivation for investment was to create a valuable asset option for themselves—the ability to switch at low cost between sources of energy. This is a typical example of the worth of asset options in a changing environment.

Asset options give various types of flexibility, such as the option to defer an investment, to expand (or contract) the scale of an investment, to abandon a project, or to start up and shut down an ongoing operation (the switching option). Asset options are important in analyzing research and development programs, new product introduction, and in valuing businesses that develop and extract natural resources.

In this section we first compare standard net present value (NPV) methodology (naively applied) with decision-tree analysis (DTA) and the option-pricing model (OPM). In so doing, we illustrate that option pricing is a generic form of decision making that encompasses NPV and DTA as special cases. Second, we provide simple examples of various types of asset options—a taxonomy of asset options. And third, we briefly illustrate how McKinsey & Company has applied option pricing by describing a few case histories.

Comparing Decision-making Approaches

Exhibit 12.1 illustrates a generic *event tree*. Good and bad outcomes (G, B) are at the event nodes, and probabilities (p_1, p_2, p_3) are along the branches. Traditional NPV techniques estimate the value of the project by estimating the expected payouts, and then estimating the appropriate risk-adjusted opportunity cost of capital based on a comparable security with equivalent risk. Everyone knows the difficulties, both of estimating the payouts and of divining the discount rate; yet NPV is a widely accepted decision technique.

Exhibit 12.2 is a generic *decision tree*. The major difference from an event tree is that the nodes allow decisions to be made after

Exhibit 12.1 **GENERIC EVENT TREE**

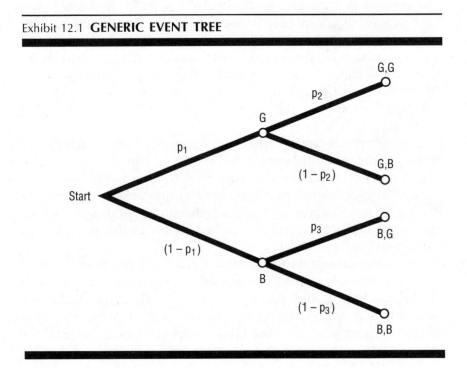

Exhibit 12.2 **GENERIC DECISION TREE**

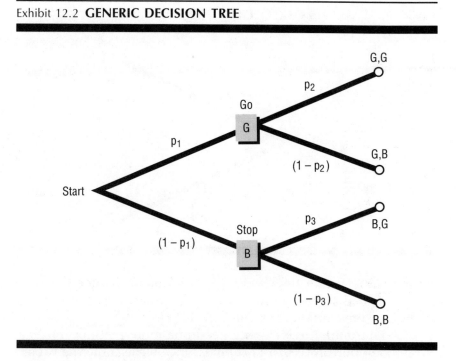

---

information has been received before proceeding. For example, if the bad (B) outcome turns up at the end of the first period, the decision maker may decide to stop the process so that the lower outcomes in the second period can never occur. Clearly, DTA is superior to the NPV technique as naively applied in Exhibit 12.1. The problem with classic DTA is that it provides no recommendation about the appropriate risk-adjusted discount rate to use. That is where the option-pricing model is useful.

The OPM allows decision nodes, like DTA, but it also searches for a comparable security with equivalent risk on which to base the discount rate. It combines the best features of NPV and DTA.

To further illustrate the differences among the three approaches, let us proceed with a numerical example, diagrammed in Exhibit 12.3. To keep things simple, suppose that two end-of-period states of nature (good and bad) are equally likely. We are asked to evaluate a project that requires an investment outlay of $104. At the end of the year, it will return a stream of cash flows

Exhibit 12.3 **PAYOUTS FOR A SIMPLE PROJECT**

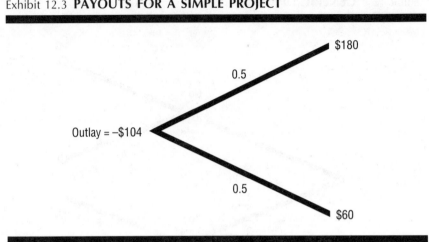

whose value at that time will be either $180 in the good state or
$60 in the bad state. The states of nature are equally likely. What
is the net present value of the project?

To determine the NPV, we need one more piece of information: the opportunity cost of capital. Since we assume the project
is not perfectly correlated with the company evaluating it, we
cannot use the company's cost of capital. Therefore, we seek
another approach. We want to find another asset whose current
value is readily observable and that has payouts that are perfectly
(or highly) correlated with our project. We need to find a good
comparable. After a long search, we come up with the security
diagrammed in Exhibit 12.4. In the good state of nature, its price
increases by a factor $u = 1.8$, and in the bad state its price falls to d
$= .6$ of its starting value. Its payouts are strictly proportional
(one-fifth of the project payouts), and the market values the
security at $20. The key is that this is a perfectly correlated *priced*
security. Without knowing its market price, we could not proceed. At this price, the market-required rate of return on the
security is

$$\$20 = \frac{.5\ (\$36)\ +\ .5\ (\$12)}{1\ +\ r} = \frac{\$24}{1\ +\ r}$$

$$r = 20\%$$

Exhibit 12.4 **DECISION TREE FOR A PERFECTLY CORRELATED SECURITY**

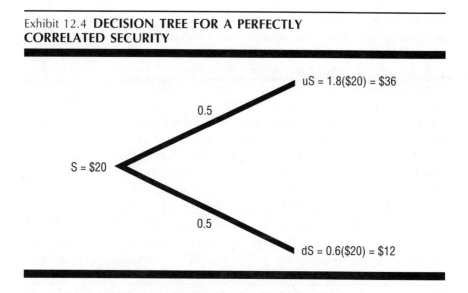

$uS = 1.8(\$20) = \$36$

0.5

$S = \$20$

0.5

$dS = 0.6(\$20) = \$12$

Now that we have estimated the required rate of return (the opportunity cost) for our risky project, we can compute its NPV.

$$\text{NPV} = \frac{\text{expected cash flows}}{1 + \text{risk-adjusted rate}} - \text{investment outlay}$$

$$= \frac{.5\ (\$180)\ +\ .5\ (\$60)}{1\ +\ .20} - \$104$$

$$= -\$4$$

Given this set of facts, our decision is obvious. We do not undertake the project, due to its negative NPV. Because NPV is a familiar methodology, we usually accept without question that the opportunity cost of capital is a reasonable approximation, even though it is based on the search for a comparable security. Keep this in mind, because our ability to understand option pricing as a practical decision-making tool depends on exactly the same leap of faith—finding a comparable security.

Next, suppose we complicate the picture by introducing a one-year license that allows management to wait one year, and then undertake the project if the good state of nature occurs or allow the license to expire if the bad state occurs. The license provides flexibility—the *option to defer*. Let us say the risk-free rate of interest is 8 percent. Now the decision tree is more complex, as shown in Exhibit 12.5. Note that the option to defer (implied by the license) dramatically alters the shape of payouts. Instead of paying $104 now to receive either $180 or $60, we can wait to see if the state of nature is favorable, then go ahead and invest, for a net of $67.68; or we can decide to abandon the project in the bad state of nature. An analogous situation is an R&D project. We invest a small sum now to find out if a product or an idea is going to turn out to be good or bad. If it is good, we invest more and proceed. If it is bad, we stop. Without the license to defer, the optimal (inflexible) NPV decision was to stop, and its payout was $0.

How shall we value the license that provides a flexibility option to defer? We will illustrate both the decision-tree and the option-pricing approaches. The problem with the decision-tree

Exhibit 12.5 **DECISION TREE WITH AN OPTION TO DEFER**

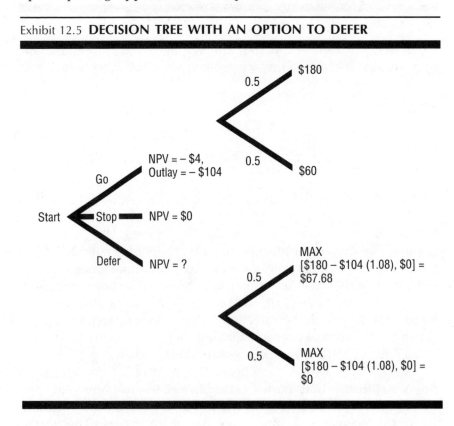

approach is that we do not know the appropriate discount rate. The 20 percent rate derived from our NPV comparable is inappropriate, because the comparable security is not even approximately correlated with the payouts from the flexibility option. But let us use it anyway, just for the heck of it. The decision-tree analysis would compute the NPV as

$$NPV = \frac{.5(\$67.68) + .5(\$0)}{1.20} = \$28.20$$

Next, we turn to the option-pricing approach. It combines the desirable features of both the NPV and DTA approaches. From the NPV approach, it borrows the idea that we must find a comparable (perfectly correlated security) to correctly evaluate risk, and from the DTA approach it uses decision nodes (not rigid event nodes) to model flexibility.

The option-pricing approach proceeds to solve the problem by creating a portfolio of observable securities whose prices (and required rates of return) are known and whose payouts exactly mimic the payouts of our decision tree. Since the market prices of the comparable securities are known, we can value the option to defer. The mimicking portfolio whose payouts are diagrammed in Exhibit 12.6 consists of m shares of the comparable stock, S, and borrowing B dollars at the risk-free rate, r_f. The payouts in the good state (\$67.68) and the bad state (\$0) exactly replicate the payouts in the decision tree, given the option to defer (Exhibit 12.5). We can solve for the value of m and the number of units of the riskless bond, B, because we have two equations and two unknowns.

$$m(uS) - (1 + r_f)B = \$67.68$$
$$m(dS) - (1 + r_f)B = \$0$$

Given that $uS = \$36$, $dS = \$12$, and $r_f = .08$, we have

$$B = \$31.33 \text{ and } m = 2.82 \text{ shares}$$

Thus, a mimicking portfolio with 2.82 shares of the comparable security and borrowing \$31.33 has exactly the same payouts as

---

Exhibit 12.6 **PAYOUTS OF A MIMICKING PORTFOLIO**

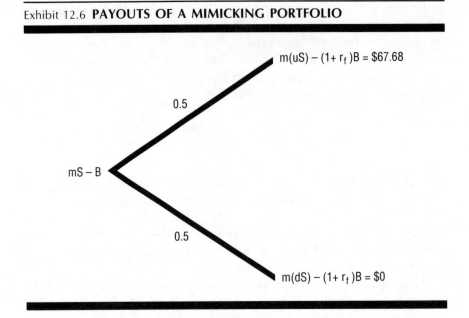

---

the flexible option to defer. Since the mimicking portfolio has the same payouts, it has the same value.

$$mS - B = 2.82\ (\$20) - \$31.33$$
$$= \$25.07$$

Going back to Exhibit 12.5, this means that if the license to defer cost less than $25.07, we would purchase it. Then, if the favorable state of nature occurred, we would proceed with the project, paying $104 (1.08) = $112.32 and receiving a cash flow stream worth $180. But if the unfavorable state turned up, we would simply decide not to go forward with the project.

If we compare the option-pricing value of the option to defer, $25.07, with the DTA value, $28.20, we see that the DTA over-valued the option because it used the 20 percent discount rate taken from the NPV analysis—but the NPV payouts did not mimic the payouts on the flexibility option. Naively applied, the DTA was comparing apples and oranges. The DTA would have given the same answer as the option-pricing approach had it used a discount rate of 35 percent:

$$\text{Value} = \frac{\text{expected cash flow}}{1 + \text{risk-adjusted rate}}$$

$$= \frac{.5(\$67.68) + .5(\$0)}{1.35}$$

$$= \$25.07$$

Alternatively, we could have used certainty-equivalent probabilities and discounted at the risk-free rate. The certainty-equivalent probabilities are

$$\text{Value} = \frac{\text{expected cash flow}}{1 + \text{risk-adjusted rate}}$$

$$\$25.07 = \frac{p(\$67.68) + (1 - p)(\$0)}{1.08}$$

$$p = .4$$

Finally, the value of the flexibility provided by the option to defer is the difference between the NPV computed using only event nodes, and the value with the option to defer. Recall that the NPV was –$4 and the value with the option to defer was $25.07; therefore, the option to defer is worth $29.07.

To summarize this section, we have shown that the option-pricing approach is superior to both the NPV technique and DTA when naively applied. It combines the use of decision nodes with the concept of using risk-adjusted comparables to correctly evaluate decisions that involve flexibility. Next, we describe the broad categories of asset options and give real-world analogues for each.

A Taxonomy of Asset Options

Ordinary NPV analysis tends to understate a project's value because it fails to capture adequately the benefits of operating flexibility and other strategic factors such as follow-on investment. To identify potential operating flexibility and strategic factors, we will classify asset options into five mutually exclusive (but not exhaustive) categories and discuss some potential implications.

Abandonment option   The option to abandon (or sell) a project—for example, the right to abandon an open pit coal mine—is formally equivalent to an American put option on the stock. Exhibit 12.7 is a decision tree with an abandonment option attached to it. If the bad outcome turns up at the end of the first period, the decision maker may decide to abandon the project and realize the expected liquidation value. Then, the expected liquidation (or resale) value of the project may be thought of as the exercise price of the put. When the present value of the asset falls below the liquidation value, the act of abandoning (or selling) the project is equivalent to exercising the put. Because the liquidation value of the project sets a lower bound on the value of the project, the option to liquidate is valuable. A project that can be

Exhibit 12.7 **DECISION TREE WITH AN ABANDONMENT OPTION**

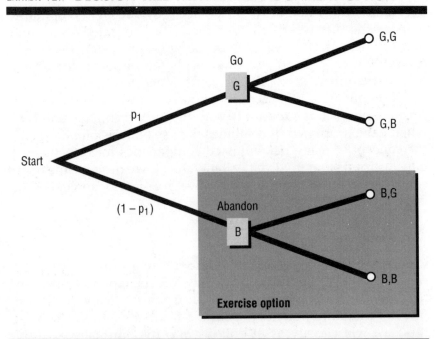

liquidated is therefore worth more than the same project without
the possibility of abandonment.

Option to defer development   The option to defer an investment
outlay to develop a property is formally equivalent to an American call option on the stock. For example, the owner of a lease on
an undeveloped oil reserve has the right to "acquire" a developed
reserve by paying a lease-on-development cost. However, the
owner can defer the development process until oil prices rise. In
other words, the managerial option implicit in holding an undeveloped reserve is in fact a deferral option. The expected development cost may be thought of as the exercise price of the call.
The net production revenue less depletion of the developed reserve is the opportunity cost incurred by deferring the investment. If this opportunity cost is too high, the decision maker may
want to exercise the option (that is, develop the reserve) before its
relinquishment date. Exhibit 12.8 illustrates this type of option.

Exhibit 12.8 **DECISION TREE WITH AN OPTION TO DEFER**

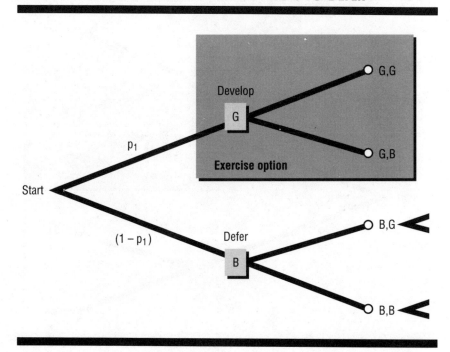

Because the deferrable investment option gives management the right, but not the obligation, to make the investment to develop the property, a project that can be deferred is worth more than the same project without the flexibility to defer development.

Option to expand The option to expand the scale of a project's operation is formally equivalent to an American call option on the stock. For example, management may choose to build production capacity in excess of the expected level of output so that it can produce at a higher rate if the product is more successful than was originally anticipated. Exhibit 12.9 illustrates this type of option. Because the expansion option gives management the right, but not the obligation, to make additional follow-on investment (for example, to increase the production rate) if project conditions turn out to be favorable, a project that can be expanded is worth more than the same project without the flexibility to expand.

Exhibit 12.9 **DECISION TREE WITH AN OPTION TO EXPAND**

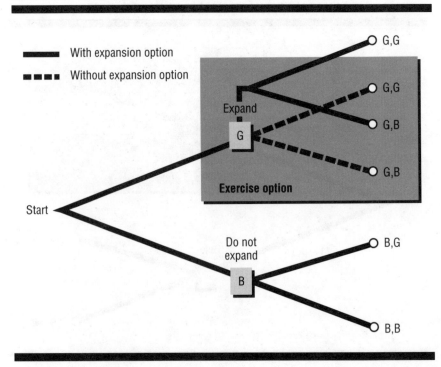

The option to expand is difficult to evaluate in practice because its decision tree is complex. For example, the option to expand can be exercised today by building excess capacity or next year by building excess capacity then, and so it goes.

Option to contract   The option to contract the scale of a project's operation is formally equivalent to an American put option on stock. Many projects can be engineered in such a way that output can be contracted in the future. For example, a project can be modularized. Foregoing planned future expenditures on the project is equivalent to the exercise price of the put. Exhibit 12.10 illustrates this type of option. Because the contraction option gives management the right to reduce the operating scale if project conditions turn out to be unfavorable, a project that can be contracted is worth more than the same project without the flexibility to contract.

Exhibit 12.10 **DECISION TREE WITH AN OPTION TO CONTRACT**

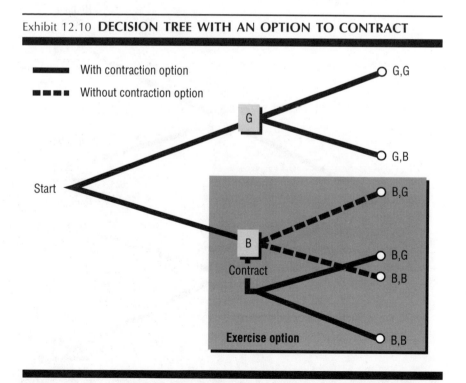

Switching options This is the most general class of asset option. The option to switch project operations is in fact a portfolio of options that consists of both call and put options. For example, restarting operations when a project is currently shut down is equivalent to an American call option. Similarly, shutting down operations when unfavorable conditions arise is equivalent to an American put option. The cost of restarting (or shutting down) operations may be thought of as the exercise price of the call (or put). A project whose operation can be dynamically turned on and off (or switched between two distinct locations, and so on) is worth more than the same project without the flexibility to switch. A flexible manufacturing system (FMS) with the ability to produce two products is a good example of this type of option. (See Exhibit 12.11.)

Exhibit 12.11 **DECISION TREE WITH SWITCHING OPTIONS**

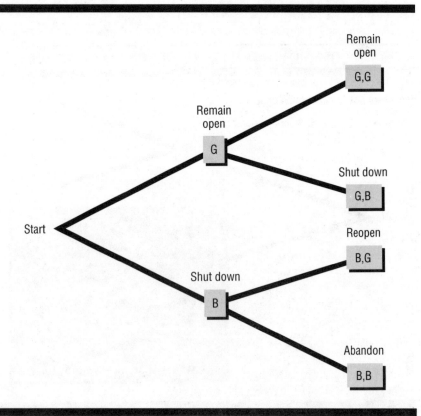

Asset Options in Practice

Drawing from our experience with clients, we now briefly describe four case histories that illustrate four types of options. Names of corporations and data are, of course, disguised to ensure confidentiality. We make explicit comparisons among different valuation approaches to show the usefulness of the option-pricing approach. Finally, we discuss some conclusions and lessons learned from each application.

Most asset option-pricing applications are limited to those situations where the option value depends on the market price of a world commodity, such as oil, coal, copper, nickel, gold, or zinc. When we have observable price data about the underlying risky asset, option pricing is feasible. Without the priced comparable security, it is guesswork at best.

Oil extraction   A major North American energy client, OILCO, planned to sell interests in an important heavy oil asset. Deferral options were important. The asset was unique in having potential expansion opportunities that could be phased in over time to significantly increase capacity with minimal geological risk. Conventional NPV approaches and assumptions considerably understated the value of OILCO's operations to an investor. The lack of industry consensus about the future behavior of oil prices led to greatly divergent NPVs. Specifically, two major operating flexibilities were present: the option of deferring a debottleneck program and the option of deferring an expansion program. These two options added significant value to OILCO's operation, an increase of 21 percent over its conventional NPV (see Exhibit 12.12).

The option premiums that the company identified placed upper bounds on the asset's market value under a given set of oil price and macroeconomic assumptions. The option-pricing approach also provided decision rules on when to time investments. Specifically, the OPM indicated that OILCO should initiate its expansion program as soon as the oil price rose above $20/bbl. Since, in practice, it might not be possible to time investments in this optimal manner, a rational investor sharing the same expectations as OILCO would in reality be prepared to pay only some portion of the option premium. However, the option

Exhibit 12.12 **AFTER-TAX VALUATION OF OILCO OPERATIONS,**
$ Millions

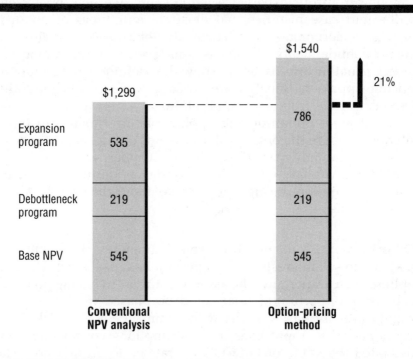

valuation provided a reasonable starting point for negotiations to sell the property.

Kryptonite mining Kryptonite is a globally traded commodity product. Kryptonite Mining Limited was the world's leading producer of kryptonite, supplying over one-third of the free world's demand. It had four production sites, each with a different layout of operating mines and a different extraction technology. The random movement of spot kryptonite prices had been extremely volatile in the past four years. Our study focused on developing a valuation method for each site as well as providing some guidance regarding the shut-down/reopen decision—a switching option. Initial estimates of Kryptonite Mining's NPV based on analysts' forecasts of kryptonite prices measured only up to 45 percent of Kryptonite Mining's current market value of equity (see Exhibit 12.13). A scenario-based NPV analysis allowing for no explicit operational flexibilities increased this estimate to 71 percent of equity value. Finally, the option-pricing valuation with shut-down/reopen and abandonment options gave us a valuation of Kryptonite Mining's equity of 116 percent of its current market value.

The shut-down, reopen, and abandonment option values as fractions of the corresponding site option-pricing values ranged between 5 and 15 percent for a spot price range of $1.75/ounce to $2.25/ounce. These option values were much higher for lower spot prices and much lower for higher spot prices.

A major benefit of the analysis was that it provided insight into the economics of when to open up and shut down each site. Given that a mine was open, it was optimal to keep it open even when the marginal revenue from a ton of output was less than the

Exhibit 12.13 **VALUATION OF KRYPTONITE MINING CORP.,**
$ Millions

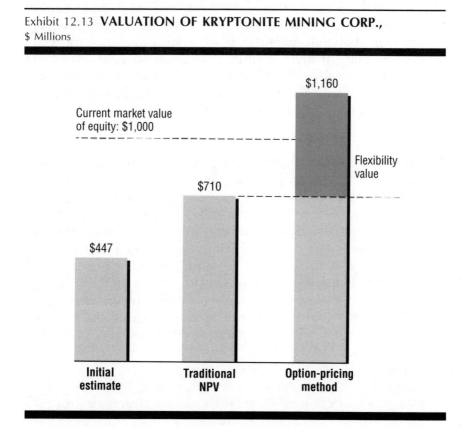

marginal cost of extraction. The intuitive explanation is that the fixed cost of closing an operation might be incurred needlessly if the commodity price rose in the near future. The opposite result applies to a closed mine. Due to the cost of reopening it, the optimal decision might be to keep it closed until the commodity price rose substantially above the marginal cost of production.

Pharmaceutical R&D   Drug & Company was a leading manufacturer of human and animal health care products. It needed to value a new drug research and development project.

Four development stages were involved: (1) initial R&D, with a 20-percent chance of success; (2) preclinical testing, with a 50-percent chance of success; (3) testing I, with a 40-percent chance of success; and (4) testing II, with a 90-percent chance of success. Exhibit 12.14 illustrates the decision tree with abandonment options. Using the traditional NPV approach—that is, neglecting the staged-abandonment option—this R&D project was valued at $18.3 million. By contrast, the OPM, taking account of the staged-abandonment option, gave a valuation of $33.5 million, 83 percent more than its traditional NPV. Exhibit 12.14 also shows the value increment from the abandonment options. This analysis ascribed put-option values to a multistage research program that could be abandoned at various phases of development.

Mineral lease   MINCO was deciding on the correct bid for a mineral lease. A very careful NPV analysis indicated a value that was 50 percent lower than the anticipated winning bid. At current prices, the project would have only marginal profitability if developed immediately. However, the NPV analysis did not account for the value of an implicit option to defer development for up to five years—that is, to wait for better prices before making capital outlays to develop the project. Given the very high production rate that was anticipated once the site was developed, analysis showed that the deferral option increased the NPV estimate by up to 100 percent, depending on the variance of mineral prices and on whether or not they were assumed to be mean-reverting.

Mean reversion played an important role in developing a realistic model, because mineral prices tend to fluctuate around a

Exhibit 12.14 **ANALYSIS OF A MULTISTAGED PHARMACEUTICAL R&D PROJECT,** $ Millions

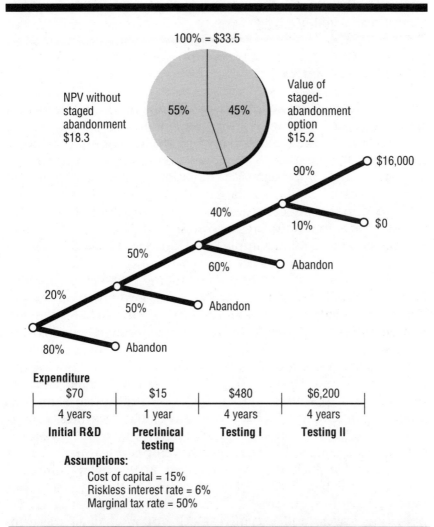

long-term average. When prices rise rapidly, they are driven down as marginal suppliers open up production and as users switch to substitutes. And when prices fall, producers shut down and users move away from alternate sources.

It is easy to see from the examples that asset options can substantially alter the value of a business. The fact that the options exist, however, does not mean that they are optimally managed. One of the important outcomes of understanding asset options is that this understanding can provide new insight into managing flexibility.

LIABILITY OPTIONS

So far we have discussed flexibility options on the assets side of the balance sheet. Now we turn to options implicit in various sources of funding. These liability options are important because they affect the company's weighted average cost of capital.

Plain vanilla approaches to valuation describe the weighted average cost of capital as the simple weighted average of the after-tax opportunity costs of debt and equity. But hybrid securities that have option features are often used as sources of capital. We looked at a random sample of one hundred companies listed on the New York Stock Exchange and found that forty-three of them had convertible securities outstanding. The yield to maturity on convertible securities is usually much lower than on straight debt with the same maturity and quality. But the yield on convertible securities is a particularly bad estimate of their actual cost of capital.

The objective of this section is to show how option pricing can be used to compute the true opportunity cost for callable, convertible debt and preferred stock, and to illustrate with a few examples that employ McKinsey's convertible securities pricing model (CSPM). Of course, a wide variety of instruments on the liabilities side of the balance sheet have option features. A non-exhaustive list includes the equity of a leveraged company, warrants, callable or convertible debt and preferred stock, variable-rate loans with caps or floors, guaranteed lines of credit, operating leases, and executive stock options. All of these instruments affect the cost of capital and, therefore, the value of equity.

The first part of our analysis will show how to value callable and convertible debt. Then we will discuss how its cost of capital is estimated. Finally, we will give a few real-world examples and discuss the complications involved.

Valuing Callable Debt

A callable bond can be repurchased by the issuing company at a fixed price for a predetermined period of time. Nearly all fixed-coupon bonds are callable. Exhibit 12.15 shows the terms for American Medical Intl. callable, convertible 9-½s due 2001 whose face value is $100. A callable bond is equivalent to a straight bond plus a call option. Since the option limits the potential capital gain of investors who hold the bond, they require a higher return on callable bonds than on equivalent noncallable bonds.

If interest rates fall low enough, it is to the company's advantage to call the bonds, pay the call premium, and then refund them at a lower rate. The variability of interest rates is crucial for pricing callable bonds. For example, assume a three-year callable bond that pays a 12-percent coupon, has a $100 face value, and that can be called for $104 from year 1 onward. The current market rate of interest is 10 percent, but it can move upward by a factor of 1.2 or down by .85 with equal probability. Exhibit 12.16 models the term structure of interest rates (the yield curve) used in our example.

Exhibit 12.15 **TERMS FOR AMERICAN MEDICAL 9-½s DUE 2001** (Data from Fall 1988)

Rating	Baa1	
Amount authorized	$125.0 million	
Amount outstanding	$124.9 million	
Issued	11/5/81	
Due	11/15/2001	
Interest dates	5/15, 11/15	
CALL TERMS	Year	Price
	1987	$104.75
	1988	103.80
	1989	102.85
	1990	101.90
	1991	100.95
	1992 on	100.00
Conversion price	$24.38/share	

Exhibit 12.16 **SIMPLIFIED TERM STRUCTURE OF INTEREST RATES**

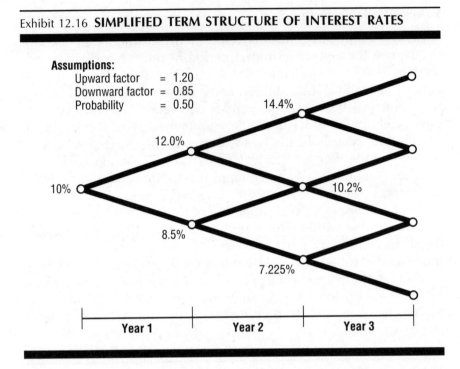

Assumptions:
Upward factor   = 1.20
Downward factor = 0.85
Probability   = 0.50

14.4%

12.0%

10%   10.2%

8.5%

7.225%

Year 1   Year 2   Year 3

Exhibits 12.17 and 12.18 show the valuation of a straight 12-percent (default-free) bond and its callable equivalent, given the assumed term structure. Note that in every state of nature where the market value of the bond exceeds its call price, it should be called. The effect is to reduce the value of the bond to investors (from $104.46 to $103.54) and therefore to increase its cost of capital to the company from 10.20 percent to 10.56 percent pretax.

Valuing Callable, Convertible Securities

Convertible bonds allow their owners to convert them into another security at a predetermined exchange ratio for a fixed interval of time. For example, the American Medical 9-½s described in Exhibit 12.15 could be converted into common stock at a price of $24.38 per share anytime during their life. The actual common stock price at the time of our data collection was $14.75. When exercising conversion rights, the bondholder gives up, as the

Exhibit 12.17 **VALUATION OF A STRAIGHT 12-PERCENT BOND**

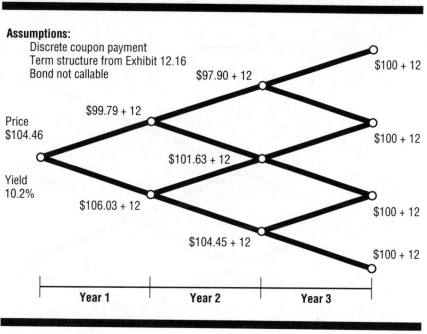

Assumptions:
Discrete coupon payment
Term structure from Exhibit 12.16
Bond not callable

exercise price, the present value of the expected bond payments. For American Medical, the bondholders would give up the bond payments in return for 4.102 shares (per $100 of face value on the bond). Thus, convertible bonds have a changing exercise price.

Exhibit 12.19 shows a numerical example of the valuation of a callable, convertible bond. The following set of assumptions details the interest rate environment, the way the value of the company varies through time, and the provisions of the callable, convertible bond.

- The constant risk-free rate is 8 percent per year.
- The company is worth $400,000 right now (no senior debt).
- There is a 60-percent probability that company value will increase by 50 percent, and a 40-percent probability that it will decrease by 50 percent.

Exhibit 12.18 **VALUATION OF A CALLABLE BOND**

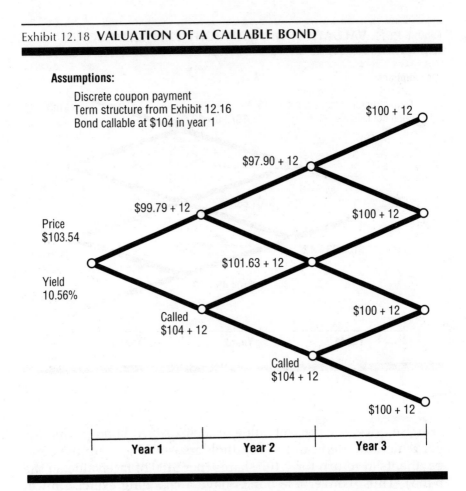

Assumptions:

Discrete coupon payment
Term structure from Exhibit 12.16
Bond callable at $104 in year 1

- Two securities are outstanding: 150 shares of stock, and 100 callable, convertible bonds that can be converted at a ratio of one-half share per bond.
- If bonds are converted, bondholders will own 50/(150 + 50) = 25 percent of the company.
- Each $1,000-face-value bond pays $100 per period coupon.
- Anytime before maturity, stockholders can call the bonds for $1,400.
- The company pays no dividends.
- The first bond coupon has just been paid.

Exhibit 12.19 **VALUATION OF A HYPOTHETICAL COMPANY AND ITS CALLABLE, CONVERTIBLE BOND,** $ Thousands

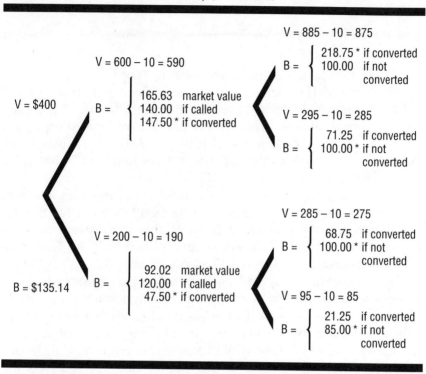

V = 885 – 10 = 875

$$B = \begin{cases} 218.75 * & \text{if converted} \\ 100.00 & \text{if not} \\ & \text{converted} \end{cases}$$

V = 600 – 10 = 590

$$B = \begin{cases} 165.63 & \text{market value} \\ 140.00 & \text{if called} \\ 147.50 * & \text{if converted} \end{cases}$$

V = \$400

V = 295 – 10 = 285

$$B = \begin{cases} 71.25 & \text{if converted} \\ 100.00 * & \text{if not} \\ & \text{converted} \end{cases}$$

V = 285 – 10 = 275

$$B = \begin{cases} 68.75 & \text{if converted} \\ 100.00 * & \text{if not} \\ & \text{converted} \end{cases}$$

V = 200 – 10 = 190

$$B = \begin{cases} 92.02 & \text{market value} \\ 120.00 & \text{if called} \\ 47.50 * & \text{if converted} \end{cases}$$

B = \$135.14

V = 95 – 10 = 85

$$B = \begin{cases} 21.25 & \text{if converted} \\ 85.00 * & \text{if not} \\ & \text{converted} \end{cases}$$

* Optimal decision.

To value the callable, convertible bonds, we start with their final payouts, determine the optimal action, and compute their value at the end of year 1 conditional on the value of the company, as illustrated in Exhibit 12.19. For example, given that the value of the company has gone up the first year, the final value of the company can be $875 thousand or $285 thousand, ex coupon. If it is $875 thousand, the bondholders receive $218.75 thousand if they convert and $100 thousand otherwise. Obviously, they will convert. If the company value is $285 thousand, they will not convert, preferring to receive the $1,000 face value per bond rather than the conversion value of $712.50. With these facts in hand, we can determine the market value of the bond at the end of year 1.

$$B = \frac{.58(\$218.75) + .42(\$100)}{1.08} + \frac{\$100}{1.08} = \$165.63$$

Note that the payouts are multiplied by their respective hedging (or certainty equivalent) probabilities

$$p = \frac{r_f - d}{u - d} = \frac{1.08 - .5}{1.5 - .5} = .58$$

and then discounted at the risk-free rate.

Since the market value of the bond is greater than the $1,400 call price, shareholders will exercise their right to call. When they do this, bondholders, who would not voluntarily convert, are forced to do so at a value of .25 ($590) = $147.50. Thus, we see that the year-1 value of the callable, convertible bond, given that the company value goes up, is $147.50.

By working backward from the final set of payouts, we find that the current market value of the bond is $135.14. Similar calculations can be performed to show that the present value of the same bond if callable but not convertible is $101.30. The value of the conversion feature is $33.84 per bond.

Whenever the entity approach for valuing a company is used, the market value of equity is estimated by first valuing the whole company—the entity—and then subtracting the market value of debt to estimate the value of equity. Having a good estimate of the market value of convertible securities is often crucial. In our example, the best estimate of the market value of equity is the value of the company, $400,000, less the market value of callable, convertible debt, $135,140. The value of equity is $264,860. Had we used the face value of the debt, $100,000, we would have overestimated the equity value by 13.3 percent.

The Cost of Capital for Callable, Convertible Securities

In 1966, Eugene Brigham surveyed the chief financial officers of twenty-two companies that had issued convertible debt. Of them, 68 percent said they had used convertible debt because they believed their stock price would rise over time and that convertibles would provide a way of selling common stock at a price above the existing market. Another 27 percent said that their company had wanted straight debt but had found conditions to be such that a straight bond issue could not be sold at a reasonable rate of interest.

The problem with these responses is that neither reason makes much sense. Convertible bonds are not "cheap debt." Because convertible bonds are riskier, their true cost of capital is greater (on a before-tax basis) than the cost of straight debt. Also, convertible bonds are not equal to deferred sale of common stock at an attractive price. The uncertain sale of shares at $28, for example, each at some unknown future date, can hardly be compared directly with a current share price of $25.

The risk of convertible debt is higher than that of straight debt and lower than that of equity, so its true opportunity cost lies between these limits. The yield to maturity on convertible debt (often lower than on the company's senior debt) has nothing to do with its opportunity cost, because convertible debt has an option embedded in it, and options are much riskier than debt.

Three broad categories of information are needed to value a callable, convertible bond and to determine its cost of capital:

1. *The interest rate environment.* Ideally, we would capture the entire term structure and its expected variability. However, our model can handle only one random variable at a time, and the variability of the company's common stock is the most important element. Consequently, the interest rate environment is captured by the yield to maturity on a Treasury bond with the same maturity as the convertible bond.

2. *Characteristics of the bond.* We need to know the amount outstanding, the face value, the number of months to maturity, the conversion price, the number of months until the first coupon date, the time between coupons, the annual coupon rate, and the call provisions (the call prices and their timing).

3. *Characteristics of the common stock.* Since the bond is convertible into common stock, we need to know the current stock price, the equity beta, the expected dividend per share, the ex dividend dates, the number of shares outstanding, the equity volatility, and the amount of senior debt outstanding.

Exhibit 12.20 shows our estimate of the value and the before-tax cost of capital for a sample of seven callable, convertible bonds. The results were provided by McKinsey's in-house convertible securities pricing model (CSPM). In every case, the before-tax cost of capital for the callable, convertible bond is higher than the coupon rate, and in all but one case (Baker Hughes) the difference is substantial.

The after-tax cost of the bond depends on the percentage of its opportunity cost that is actually tax deductible. Thus, an estimate of its after-tax cost is

$$\text{After-tax } K_{CV} = K_{CV}\left[1 - \frac{\text{coupon rate}}{Kcv} (\text{tax rate})\right]$$

Exhibit 12.20 **COST OF CAPITAL FOR SEVEN CALLABLE, CONVERTIBLE BONDS**

Company	Common Stock		Convertible Bond	
	Price	Beta	Coupon rate	Cost of capital
American Medical Int'l.	$14.88	1.15	9.50%	18.00%
Baker Hughes	16.75	1.21	9.50	10.40
Bally	17.00	1.35	6.00	26.10
Bank of Boston	25.75	1.06	7.75	19.90
General Instrument	31.00	1.40	7.25	12.40
Humana	22.25	1.11	8.50	11.60
Loral	39.38	1.04	10.75	14.60

Company	Callable, Convertible Bond			
	Exercise price	Market price	Model price	Percent difference
American Medical Int'l.	$24.38	$ 932.50	$ 798.84	−14.3%
Baker Hughes	47.13	977.50	913.86	−6.5
Bally	28.99	760.00	622.47	−18.1
Bank of Boston	23.42	1,135.00	1,103.67	−2.8
General Instrument	40.57	1,015.00	1,066.07	+5.0
Humana	37.80	935.00	902.29	−3.5
Loral	44.25	1,020.00	969.16	−5.0

Source: McKinsey analysis.

For example, if American Medical's tax rate were 39 percent, the after-tax cost of the 9-½s would be

$$\text{After-tax } K_{CV} = .180 \left[1 - \frac{.095}{.180} (.39) \right] = 14.3\%$$

SUMMARY

Option pricing is analogous with flexibility in decision making because the holder of an option can exercise the option at his or her discretion to take advantage of an opportunity. Viewed broadly, options can affect every arena of management. We have illustrated only a few applications. On the assets side of the balance sheet are options to defer, expand, contract, abandon, or switch projects on and off. Net present value analysis, rigidly applied, often undervalues assets because it fails to account for the rich set of flexibility options involved in business decisions. On the liabilities side, options can have a significant impact on the cost of capital. We analyzed callable, convertible debt and saw that the true opportunity cost is often substantially higher than the coupon rate. Convertible debt is not a free lunch. It is neither cheap debt nor cheap equity.

Valuing options is a complex task, generally beyond the capability of an analyst with a pocket calculator. Although PC-based programs are available for standard situations, it is usually advisable to seek the advice of an expert, especially when asset options (with their extreme complexity) are involved.

13

Valuing Banks

The banking and thrift industries have been going through a decade of change catalyzed by the globalization of financial markets, deregulation that has enhanced competition among financial institutions, the growing popularity of nonbank substitutes that channel individual savings into corporate investment, greater interest-rate volatility, and changes in tax laws. These powerful forces have led banks and savings and loans (S&Ls) to take greater risks in order to enhance their perceived profitability. The pitfalls have been numerous and nearly every financial institution has experienced some difficulty. Bank managers have created large lending positions in less-developed countries (LDCs) and in leveraged-buyout (LBO) situations; S&L managers have overextended mortgage credit, and engaged in risky land speculation.

The inevitable result is massive restructuring in the banking and thrift industries. In the fourth quarter of 1988, the Bank of New York successfully completed its hostile takeover of Irving Trust. Many commercial banks have adopted a "poison pill" defense against potential takeover. Recently, NCNB Corporation made an unsolicited offer for Citizens & Southern only to withdraw it a month later. Although these events do not necessarily portend a wave of hostile restructurings within the industry, they do suggest that a substantial level of internal restructuring and "friendly" acquisitions or divestitures will occur.

Valuation is an important tool for understanding restructuring. Managers who focus on value creation rather than being misled by accounting models of their businesses will have a competitive advantage. Banks that restructure themselves to maximize value for their shareholders are less subject to takeover attempts and regulatory pressure. They are also in the best position to acquire other financial institutions in order to create value through superior management skills.

THE DIFFICULTY OF VALUING BANKS

Valuing banks is conceptually difficult. For an outsider, determining the quality of the loan portfolio, measuring the amount of current accounting profits attributable to interest-rate mismatch (for example, the difference between long-term rates earned on loans and short-term rates paid on deposits), and understanding which business units are driving the bank's profit potential are all hard to do.

For an insider attempting to value a bank, the major issue is transfer pricing. As illustrated in Exhibit 13.1, most banks can be separated into three basic business units (although most have dozens of distinct businesses): a retail bank that has only twenty cents in loans for each dollar in deposits, a wholesale bank with only twenty cents in deposits for each dollar in loans, and a treasury that stands between them and carries on activities of its own such as securities trading. The excess funds generated by the retail bank can be loaned to the marketplace or to the wholesale bank. If loaned internally, the rate credited to the retail bank and paid by the wholesale bank is a crucial transfer price. If this price is set too high, the retail bank appears more profitable, and vice versa. It is critical to establish the correct transfer price in order to determine where the bank should allocate its marginal re-sources—to the retail bank or to the wholesale bank.

This short chapter does not present all the answers to bank valuation, but focuses mainly on the issue of how to value banks. First, we discuss the practical reasons why it is easier to use an equity approach than an entity approach to valuing banks.

Exhibit 13.1 **BUSINESS-UNIT STRUCTURE OF BANKS**

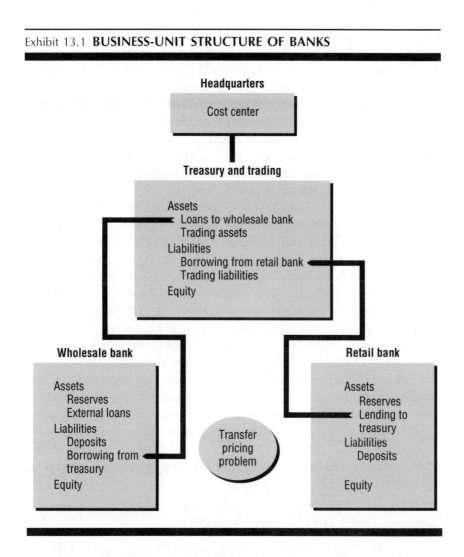

Second, we cover the issues involved in an outsider's approach, and finally we turn to the problems of an insider's approach.

THE EQUITY APPROACH TO VALUING BANKS

Throughout the book we have recommended and used the entity approach to valuing companies. (The entity approach discounts the after-tax free cash flow from operations at the weighted average cost of capital to first obtain the estimated entity value, then subtracts the market value of debt to estimate the equity value.) Banks are the exception that proves the rule. Although the equity and entity approaches are mathematically equivalent, the equity approach to valuing banks is easier to use. Therefore, we recommend that for banks you forecast free cash flow to equity holders and discount it at the cost of equity.

The entity method is more difficult to use for banks because a main source of financing is non-interest-bearing customer deposits raised through the retail bank, not borrowing in capital markets. The cost of capital for these deposits can be very difficult to estimate. Furthermore, the retail bank is legitimately a separate business in its own right, unlike the treasury function of most corporations. These facts make it difficult, if not impossible, to value the bank's equity by first valuing its assets (that is, its lending function) by discounting interest income less administrative expenses at the weighted average cost of capital; then subtracting the present value of its deposit business (interest expenses plus consumer bank administrative costs, discounted at the cost of debt). Still another problem with the entity approach for banks is that the spread between the interest received on loans and the cost of capital is so low that small errors in estimating the cost of capital can result in huge swings in the value of the entity.

The equity approach is the straightforward approach to valuing banks. To implement it you need to know (1) how to define free cash flow to shareholders; and (2) how to use the "spread" or "income" model.

Defining Free Cash Flow to Shareholders

Free cash flow to shareholders is net income plus noncash charges less cash flow needed to grow the balance sheet. The value of equity is not simply net income discounted at the cost of equity, because not all of net income can be paid to shareholders. In fact, only dividends can be paid to shareholders.

Exhibit 13.2 shows the definition of free cash flow to shareholders of a bank. The best way to think about it is to keep your eye on actual cash in and cash out. Cash flow from the income statement is reasonably straightforward except for the fact

Exhibit 13.2 **FREE CASH FLOW TO SHAREHOLDERS OF A BANK**

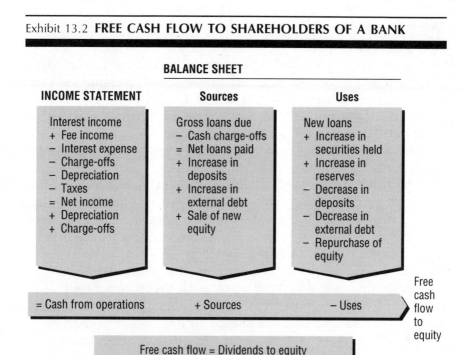

BALANCE SHEET

INCOME STATEMENT	Sources	Uses

Interest income
+ Fee income
− Interest expense
− Charge-offs
− Depreciation
− Taxes
= Net income
+ Depreciation
+ Charge-offs
	Gross loans due
	− Cash charge-offs
	= Net loans paid
	+ Increase in
	   deposits
	+ Increase in
	   external debt
	+ Sale of new
	   equity
		New loans
		+ Increase in
		   securities held
		+ Increase in
		   reserves
		− Decrease in
		   deposits
		− Decrease in
		   external debt
		− Repurchase of
		   equity

= Cash from operations   + Sources   − Uses

Free cash flow to equity

Free cash flow = Dividends to equity

that depreciation and loan charge-offs are not cash flow. Their only effect is to reduce taxes. Balance sheet cash flow starts with cash in as loans are repaid. Actual cash received is gross loans due less cash charge-offs, resulting in net loans paid. To this number we must add increases in deposits and external debt, and sale of new equity, all sources of funds. On the uses side, new loans and increases in cash reserves and in securities held represent the main cash outflows.

When cash from operations is combined with sources and uses from the balance sheet, the result is free cash flow to shareholders, which is mathematically identical to dividends. Note that the creation of loan-loss reserves is not treated as a cash flow in our definition. Charge-offs are not a cash flow either, but they do affect taxes. Actual net loans paid and their timing is one of the key factors affecting our estimate of a bank's value.

Using the Spread or Income Model

The language of banking expresses income as "spreads" earned on balances—that is, the difference between the rate paid on borrowings and the rate received on loans and investments. Consequently, as a first step it is useful to show the equivalence between the traditional computation of earnings as reported in financial statements for nonfinancial companies, which for lack of a better phrase we shall call the "income model," and the "spread model" that is common practice in banking.

The balance sheet and income statement for the hypothetical bank in Exhibit 13.3 show the traditional income model computation of net income. We assume that loans earn 12 percent, cash reserves at the Federal Reserve Bank earn nothing, deposits pay 5 percent, and the tax rate is 40 percent.

The spread model is an alternative but equivalent approach for computing net income. It starts with the assumption that an opportunity cost of money (call it the money rate, MR) is charged to the wholesale bank and credited to deposits. For the sake of argument, suppose it is 8 percent in our example. The spread model calculates net income by adding spreads times balances. It then adds a credit for the equity component of the bank's financing, since the spreads used assume that investments are 100

Exhibit 13.3 **FINANCIAL STATEMENTS FOR ABC BANK, ILLUSTRATING THE INCOME MODEL,** $ MILLIONS

Balance sheet		Income statement	
Assets		Interest income, 12% ($933) =	$111.96
Cash reserves	$ 120	− Interest expense, 5% ($1,000) =	−50.00
Loans	933	− Other expenses	−48.00
	1,053		
		Net profit before tax	13.96
Liabilities		− Taxes at 40%	−5.58
Deposits	1,000	Net income	$ 8.38
Equity	53		
	$1,053		

percent from borrowings. Likewise, income is reduced for reserves at the Fed since they do not earn interest. Exhibit 13.4 illustrates the spread model net income calculation.

The spread model gives the same answer as the income model, but should be used with care. For example, the money rate used in the equity credit is not equivalent to the cost of equity: it is merely an accounting convention necessary to provide the right answer.

VALUING BANKS FROM THE OUTSIDE

Banks remain among the most difficult companies to value, because in spite of the multitude of regulatory and reporting requirements imposed on them, it is hard to determine the quality of their loan portfolio, to figure out what percentage of their accounting profits results from interest-rate mismatch gains, and to understand which business units are creating or destroying value.

Exhibit 13.5 illustrates an outsider's valuation of a money center bank using publicly available information. The method was to forecast free cash flow to equity holders and discount it at the cost of equity, business unit by business unit. The analysis

Exhibit 13.4 **INCOME CALCULATED FOR ABC BANK USING THE SPREAD MODEL,** $ MILLIONS

Definition	Calculation		
(Spread on loans) × (Loan balance)	(12% − 8%) ($933)	=	$37.32
+ (Spread on deposits) × (Deposit balance)	+ (8% − 5%) ($1,000)	=	+30.00
+ (Equity credit) × (Equity)	+ (8%) ($53)	=	+4.24
− (Reserve debit) × (Reserves)	− (8%) ($120)	=	−9.60
− Expenses			−48.00
= Net profit before tax			13.96
− Taxes at 40%			−5.58
Net income			$ 8.38

Exhibit 13.5 **AN OUTSIDER'S ESTIMATE OF SOURCES OF VALUE FOR
A LARGE BANK,** $ MILLIONS

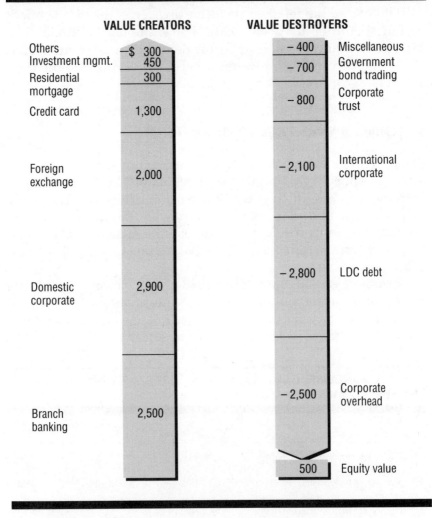

Source: McKinsey analysis.

raises numerous issues. Can the businesses that appear to be
destroying value be turned around, and if so, how long will it
take? If the losing businesses cannot be turned around, can they
be sold to someone else for whom they would have greater value?
For example, if the government bond trading and corporate trust

units were sold for only one dollar each, the equity value of the bank would quadruple. Can corporate overhead be cut? If so, by how much? For the value-creating units, one must examine ways to improve them further and to secure their competitive advantage, or to sell them if they would have higher value to someone else.

Exhibit 13.5 shows the power of valuation for coming to grips with the strategic issues facing a money center bank, and the potential for creating value. But great care should be used before taking action. Let's turn to some of the conceptual problems involved in getting the valuation right.

Understanding Mismatch Gains and Losses

Normally, the term structure of interest rates is upward sloping, as shown in Exhibit 13.6. A bank that lends three-year money and

Exhibit 13.6 **THE SLOPE IN THE TERM STRUCTURE, WHICH CREATES MISMATCH PROFITS**

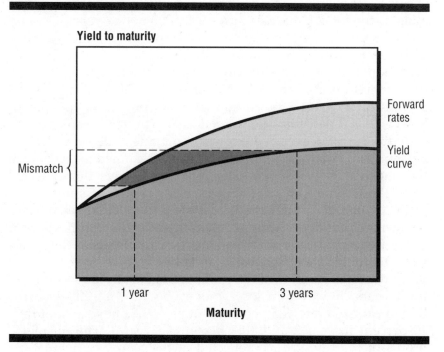

borrows one-year money will earn a mismatch profit equal to the difference between the longer- and shorter-term rates of interest. However, much of this profit is illusory because the one-year funds must be rolled over twice at future one-year spot rates that are expected to be higher than today's one-year rate. The mismatch profit observed in today's market should not, in most circumstances, be forecasted to persist over time.

To illustrate how spreads would be expected to change over time, suppose a bank lends $1 million of three-year fixed-rate money and borrows $900,000 of one-year CDs that are rolled over each year for three years. The assumed term structure is as follows:

Maturity	Yield	1-year forward rate
1 year	8.0%	8.0%
2 years	9.0	10.0
3 years	9.5	10.5

Exhibit 13.7 shows the forecasted income statements and balance sheets for three units of a bank: the wholesale bank that lends $1 million, the retail bank that raises $900,000 in one-year CDs, and the treasury. To keep the example as simple as possible, we have assumed no reserve requirements and no taxes. The wholesale bank is match-funded with three-year money that costs 9.5 percent; therefore, it earns 9.5 percent on $1 million and pays 9.5 percent on $900,000, for an annual profit of $4,750. Its spread, however, is 0 percent—not a good deal. The retail bank is forecasted to earn the expected one-year spot rate (8 percent, then 10 percent, and finally 10.5 percent), which is assumed to be equal to the one-year forward rate. The retail bank pays the expected one-year spot rate on CDs. It, too, has a 0-percent spread.

In Exhibit 13.7, both the wholesale and retail banks are perfectly match-funded; therefore, all of the mismatch profits appear in the treasury. In the first year, the treasury lends at the three-year rate (to the wholesale bank) and borrows at the one-year rate (from the retail bank) for a net profit of $14,250. In the second and third years, however, it loses money because it still earns the three-year fixed rate, 9.5 percent, but pays the one-year spot rate, 10 percent in year 2 and 10.5 percent in year 3. The mismatch profits of the treasury are reflected in the bank as a whole.

Exhibit 13.7 **FINANCIAL STATEMENTS FOR THREE UNITS OF A BANK, ILLUSTRATING HOW CURRENT ACCOUNTING PROFITS OVERSTATE LONG-TERM CASH FLOW**

Balance sheets
$ Thousands

Income statements
$ Thousands

Wholesale bank

					Year 1	Year 2	Year 3
Loans	$1,000.00	Borrowing from		Interest income	95.00	95.00	95.00
		treasury	$950.00	Interest expense	90.25	90.25	90.25
		Equity	50.00	Wholesale bank			
	$1,000.00		$1,000.00	profit	4.75	4.75	4.75

Retail bank

Lending to		CDs	$900.00	Interest income	76.00	95.00	99.75
treasury	$950.00	Equity	50.00	Interest expense	72.00	90.00	94.50
	$950.00		$950.00	Retail bank			
				profit	4.00	5.00	5.25

Treasury (mismatch)

Lending to wholesale		Borrowing from retail		Interest income	90.25	90.25	90.25
bank	$950.00	bank	$950.00	Interest expense	76.00	95.00	99.75
	$950.00		$950.00	Treasury profit	14.25	-4.75	-9.50

Total bank

Loans	$1,000.00	CDs	$900.00	Interest income	95.00	95.00	95.00
		Equity	100.00	Interest expense	72.00	90.00	94.50
	$1,000.00		$1,000.00	Total bank profit	23.00	5.00	0.50

If one were to build a valuation model that forecasted profits to be $23,000 perpetually (that is, a 23-percent return on equity), the bank would appear profitable. The reality is that the bank return on equity is 5 percent or less in the second year and .5 percent or less in the third year. Its high mismatch profits in the first year are an illusion that is discovered only when the forecast of profit over time takes into account the fact that short-term rates are forecasted to rise.

The key to handling the problem of mismatch gains or losses is to build a good forecast that takes into account:

- the way spreads are forecasted to change across time with changing interest rate environments,
- the inflow of funds from loans being paid off and the outflow of funds at new rates as new loans are made,
- the substitution between interest-bearing and non-interest-bearing deposits as interest rate environments change, and
- the portion of mismatch profits that is sustainable because forward rates tend to be higher than their corresponding realized spot rates.

It is not easy to build all of these variables into your forecast. Even if you decide not to do so, it helps to understand the illusion of mismatch profits.

Determining the Quality of Loans

Determining the quality of loans is the most difficult problem for an outsider's valuation, and very little information is available to help solve it. Take loans to LDCs as an example. Although they are sometimes sold in secondary markets for fifty cents on the dollar, this kind of markdown must be viewed with healthy cynicism. The loans that banks keep are probably worth more than those they choose to sell in the secondary market.

The market value of the loan portfolio constantly changes with changes in interest rates and with changes in the creditworthiness of debt in the bank's loan portfolio. It is usually possible to find out what percentage of the portfolio is represented by LDC and LBO debt (in some cases). These can then be marked to market (at least approximately) as market conditions change.

VALUING BANKS FROM THE INSIDE

The main objective of an insider's valuation is to value the bank's business units. Even with complete information, this is a difficult problem because of transfer pricing and shared costs. We will discuss valuation from the inside by focusing on issues concerning the retail bank, the wholesale bank, and the treasury.

The Retail Bank

Most retail banks are in the business of collecting deposits: non-interest-bearing demand deposits, interest-bearing demand deposits, money market accounts, and certificates of deposit. For each dollar in deposits there *might* be twenty cents in external consumer loans, and the remaining eighty cents is lent to the treasury at a transfer price we call the money rate. The first of several issues central to valuing the retail bank is the correct money rate to use. Next is the value of "deposit stability." Conceptual issues concerning capital structure and the cost of equity are also important.

The money rate for the retail bank The usual economic principle for transfer pricing is to use the market price. But what is the correct opportunity cost for deposits? Logically, it should be the market rate for securities that have the same duration—that is, the same sensitivity of market value to changes in interest rates. Determining the duration of demand deposits and deciding how to match-fund them are tricky topics, for two reasons. First, most banks confuse the length of time a dollar stays in a demand deposit (that is, its maturity) with the sensitivity of balance values to changes in interest rates (that is, their duration). A propensity exists to choose a money rate that eliminates fluctuations in net interest income rather than to choose a rate that stabilizes shareholder value. Second, one has to decide whether to match-fund to immunize demand deposits or to immunize the entire retail bank against changes in interest rates. In the example that follows, we have chosen to immunize the entire business unit.

Exhibit 13.8 illustrates how the choice of a money rate affects the stability of net income versus shareholder value. To keep this example simple, we have assumed that the retail bank has deposits that pay no interest but will be withdrawn in year 5. Reserves at the Federal Reserve Bank will be recovered at the same time. The initial situation assumes that the market rate is 10 percent and that loans to the treasury earn 10 percent, so that their market value equals their book value. Reserves and deposits are like zero-coupon notes, so their market value is less than book.

The bank can choose to match-fund deposits at the five-year rate, the time interval equal to their maturity, or the shorter

---

Exhibit 13.8 EXAMPLE OF HOW CHOICE OF MONEY RATE AFFECTS STABILITY OF NET INCOME VS. EQUITY VALUE

Initial situation:
Reserves and deposits are paid off in 5 years
Current interest rate is 10%

Book value balance sheet

Reserves	$240.00	Deposits	$2,000.00
Loans to		Equity	128.00
treasury	1,888.00		
	$2,128.00		$2,128.00

Market value balance sheet

Reserves	$149.02	Deposits	$1,241.84
Loans to		Equity	795.14
treasury	1,888.00		
	$2,037.02		$2,037.02

Match-fund deposits with 5-year loan:
Interest rate rises to 15%

Market value balance sheet

Reserves	$119.32	Deposits	$944.36
Loans to		Equity	696.50
treasury	1,571.54		
	$1,690.86		$1,690.86

Year	Net income
1	$188.80
2	188.80
3	188.80
4	188.80
5	188.80

Result
Net income constant
Equity value varies

Match-fund deposits with 3-year loan:
Interest rate rises to 15%

Market value balance sheet

Reserves	$119.32	Deposits	$994.36
Loans to		Equity	797.42
treasury	1,672.46		
	$1,791.78		$1,791.78

Year	Net income
1	$188.80
2	188.80
3	188.80
4	283.20
5	283.20

Result
Net income varies
Equity value constant

---

three-year rate. The five-year rate keeps net income constant for five years, but fails to immunize shareholders' wealth. Equity value declines from $795.14 to $696.50 when interest rates rise from 10 percent to 15 percent. This happens because the value of assets falls faster than the value of deposits. This problem is alleviated when deposits are match-funded with three-year money, because the interest rate credited to loans to the treasury rises from 10 percent to 15 percent in year 4. Consequently, loans to the treasury decline less in value when interest rates rise and the value of equity remains unchanged (immunized against changes in interest rates).

If you wish to centrally manage all interest-rate risk in the treasury, the correct money rate to use for match-funding deposits is the rate that immunizes the value of equity in the retail bank against changes in interest rates. To find this rate, you must take into account the sensitivity of balance levels to changes in interest rates, the ratio of fixed to variable costs in the business unit, and the duration of external loans held by the retail bank.

The value of deposit stability   In valuing retail banks, the issue often arises of whether deposit-taking units should receive a credit for deposit stability. The logic for a credit is that depositors understand and value the FDIC insurance attached to demand deposits. When banks get into trouble (for example, when their credit rating is downgraded), customers usually do not withdraw their deposits and place them in "safer" institutions. As a result, FDIC-insured deposits tend to be stable. Troubled institutions that have fewer insured deposits have to pay higher yields to obtain short-term funding. For example, the Bank of America, with its large deposit base, was able to retain its FDIC-insured deposits during troubled times; but Continental Illinois, without a large deposit base, had to pay relatively higher yields to keep itself funded during a time of crisis.

The benefit of FDIC insurance to a retail bank is directly related to the lower cost of funds that banks have to pay, compared with nonbank institutions, for similar duration liabilities. The lower the credit rating of the bank, the higher the benefit of FDIC insurance to it. The cost of FDIC insurance is deducted directly from the cash flow of the retail bank. The value of FDIC insurance is the difference between the indirect benefit and the direct cost.

FDIC insurance is a put option. (See Chapter 12 for a description of put options.) In the event of bank default, insured depositors receive the face value of their deposits rather than the fraction of the face value they might otherwise receive following bankruptcy or reorganization. The maturity date of the FDIC "put option" is the interval until completion of the next audit of the bank's assets. Since the FDIC charges a uniform fee, riskier banks receive a subsidy. The value of the subsidy depends primarily on

- the market value of the bank's assets,
- the variability of the market value of the bank's assets,
- the *total* debt of the bank, and
- the proportion of total debt represented by insured deposits.

Although the procedure is somewhat crude, it is possible to obtain cross-sectional estimates of the per-dollar value of the deposit insurance premium by using a put option pricing model. Exhibit 13.9 shows some estimates obtained by Ronn and Verma (1986) for a cross-section of banks in 1983. The highest value was 72.41 basis points per dollar of FDIC-insured deposits for the troubled First Pennsylvania Corp., while the average value was 8.08 basis points. Since normal discounted cash flow methods cannot capture the value of deposit stability, the retail bank should be credited with a value equal to its insured deposit balance times an estimate of the average annual deposit insurance premium.

Capital structure   Exhibit 13.10 shows a simplified balance sheet of a hypothetical retail banking unit.

Two broad approaches exist for deciding how much equity should be allocated to the retail banking unit. Since most retail banks have required reserves as a buffer against unanticipated account withdrawals, they would carry less equity than the regulatory requirement. We assume, therefore, that the regulators determine the percentage of equity to be carried on the balance sheet. We could compute equity either as a percentage of total assets, or as a percentage of external assets only (reserves, consumer loans, and small business loans). If we adopt the former approach, then equity is a percentage of a major intercompany account, namely loans to the treasury. This philosophy over-allocates equity, because the total equity of all business units will

Exhibit 13.9 **PER-DOLLAR VALUE OF FDIC DEPOSIT INSURANCE, 1983**

Bank	Market value of assets, $ millions	Face value of total debt, $ millions	Ratio of assets to debt	Average annual deposit ins. premium,%
First Pennsylvania	$ 3,857	$ 3,866	.998	.7241%
Crocker National Corp.	15,247	15,195	1.003	.2666
Continental Illinois	22,289	22,073	1.010	.1944
Wells Fargo	22,200	21,911	1.013	.1838
Manufacturers Hanover	34,626	34,313	1.009	.1269
BankAmerica	74,642	73,714	1.013	.1035
First Interstate	37,039	36,405	1.017	.0856
Chase Manhattan	36,184	35,674	1.014	.0577
Bankers Trust	20,996	20,266	1.036	.0568
Citicorp	66,129	63,407	1.143	.0440
Chemical, New York	32,754	31,718	1.033	.0270
Security Pacific	29,699	28,682	1.035	.0162
Mellon	19,864	19,122	1.039	.0157
NCNB	10,301	9,890	1.042	.0129
Bank of Boston	10,690	10,231	1.045	.0106
Morgan, J. P.	28,913	26,981	1.072	.0001
Average				.0808%

Source: Ronn and Verma (1986).

exceed total equity in the bank. To avoid this aggregation problem, it is better to allocate equity to external assets only. Given the numbers in Exhibit 13.10, and assuming that book equity must be 5 percent of external assets, equity in the retail bank would be $14 million and loans to the treasury would be $1.434 billion.

The cost of equity As always, the cost of equity is the rate of return investors would require for other investments of equivalent risk.

Preliminary thinking would indicate that no good market comparable exists for the retail banking unit as we have structured it because no stand-alone banks exist with 80 percent of

---

Exhibit 13.10 **BALANCE SHEET OF A RETAIL BANKING UNIT,**
$ MILLIONS

Assets		Liabilities	
Reserves	180	Demand deposits	1,000
Consumer loans	100	Money market accounts	500
Small business loans	100	Certificates of deposit	300
Loans to treasury	1,420+	Equity	?
	?		?

their assets invested in "loans to treasury" (or in government securities that return the money rate, the bank's transfer price). We have deliberately chosen the money rate to immunize the value of shareholders' equity against changes in market rates of interest. Consequently, even though in our allocation scheme the book equity of the retail banking unit is only about 1 percent of total assets, it has very little interest-rate risk. Furthermore, reserves serve as a buffer to protect against account withdrawals and loan defaults.

Further thought leads to the realization that the major risk borne by equity in the retail bank is the portion of loan default risk correlated with the economy, a risk that affects only the external assets of the retail bank. Since equity is roughly 5 percent of external assets (that is, the amount required by regulation in our hypothetical example), equity risk will be roughly the same as for comparable retail banks that have a low ratio of loans to deposits.

The Wholesale Bank

The primary business activity of the wholesale bank is making loans. For each dollar of loans, there might be only twenty cents in deposits; therefore, the wholesale bank funds itself by borrowing from the bank's treasury. Once again, the critical issue is how to determine the correct transfer price or money rate the wholesale bank must pay for the funds it uses. Once this issue has been resolved, we can turn to capital structure and the cost of equity.

The money rate for the wholesale bank The opportunity cost of funds for a loan portfolio depends on those factors that affect its

Exhibit 13.11 **EXPECTED PAYOUTS FOR A LOW-QUALITY LOAN**

Year	Cumulative default rate	Promised payments	Assumptions
1	1%	$ 200	• $1,000 lent at year 0
2	2	200	• When the loan defaults, nothing can be recovered
3	5	200	
4	10	200	
5	20	1,200	

systematic risk: (1) duration, the sensitivity of its value to changes in interest rates; and (2) the portion of its credit or default risk that cannot be diversified away. Diversifiable credit risk does not affect the opportunity cost of funds; rather, it is reflected in the computation of the expected cash flow to the loan portfolio. To illustrate, suppose we are evaluating the opportunity cost of capital for the low-quality loan in Exhibit 13.11. We lend $1,000 in return for promised payments of $200 per year plus repayment of the principal, $1,000, at the end of the fifth year. The *promised* yield to maturity is 20 percent; however, the cumulative default rate rises each year until only 80 percent of loans of this type reach maturity without defaulting. Asquith, Mullins, and Wolff (1989) indicate that actual cumulative default rates on five- to nine-year-old portfolios of original issue junk bonds were between 19 and 26 percent. We need to figure out the *expected* yield to maturity. This can be done by finding the rate that equates the expected cash flow with the amount we lent out.

$$\$1,000 = \frac{.99(\$200)}{1+y} + \frac{.98(\$200)}{(1+y)^2} + \frac{.95(\$200)}{(1+y)^3} + \frac{.9(\$200)}{(1+y)^4} + \frac{.8(\$1,200)}{(1+y)^5}$$

In our formula, the expected yield, y, turns out to be approximately 15.8 percent. Thus, the expected yield is 420 basis points lower than the promised yield.

Once the difference between the expected and promised yields has been clarified, the choice of the appropriate money rate to charge the wholesale bank for borrowing from the treasury becomes a matter of taste. If expected cash flow estimates forecast charge-offs, then the money rate should be the expected yield for loan portfolios of equivalent credit risk and duration. Alternately, if expected charge-offs are not computed (and by default, all payments are assumed to be made as promised), then the money rate should be the promised yield to maturity for loan portfolios of equivalent credit risk and duration.

A commonly used source of data for yields on loan portfolios of equivalent credit risk and duration is market prices of publicly traded debt issues. However, a certain amount of distrust is appropriate when drawing comparisons, because the covenants on publicly held debt issues are often different from bank debt covenants. Consequently, a direct comparison of yields may be inappropriate unless they are adjusted for the effect of differences in covenants.

Capital structure   As with the retail bank, the dominating consideration is that the equity for all of the pieces of the bank should aggregate to equal the total bank equity. Therefore, we recommend that book equity in the wholesale bank be determined as a percentage of its external assets (usually equal to total assets).

Cost of equity   Because each loan portfolio is match-funded with a money rate that accounts for both credit risk and interest-rate (duration) risk, and because the ratio of equity to total assets will be close to the regulatory requirement, the cost of equity for the wholesale bank will be less than for the bank as a whole. Business risk is the primary risk left in the wholesale bank after match-funding; hence, its cost of equity will be close to the unlevered cost of equity for the entire bank, which, of course, is an estimate of business risk for the entire bank.

Treasury and Headquarters

The bank treasury borrows from the retail bank and lends to the wholesale bank. It also handles the bank's trading business and is responsible for centralized risk management. And, for the sake of argument, we will assume that it is responsible for solving the shared-cost problem. To organize our discussion of these issues, we cover, in turn, the mismatch problem, centralized risk management, the cost of equity, and the shared-cost problem. We will not discuss the treasury's capital structure except to say that, as before, equity will be allocated to the treasury based on the amount of external assets it holds.

Mismatch profits and losses The philosophy that we have adopted is to match-fund the retail and wholesale banks as closely as possible for credit and interest-rate (duration) risk. The business reason for doing so is to provide business-unit managers with guidelines that lead directly to positive net present value decisions. For example, a loan officer must earn an all-in rate (fees plus interest) that exceeds a money rate that is adjusted both for credit and duration risk.

To the extent that the risk and duration of deposits is less than for loans, the treasury unit will record a mismatch profit. We have already illustrated, in Exhibit 13.7 and the accompanying discussion, that mismatch profits can be illusory. Recall that the key to handling mismatch gains or losses is to build a good cash flow forecast that takes into account (1) the way spreads are forecasted to change across time with changing interest rate environments; (2) the inflow of funds from loans being paid off and the outflow of funds at new rates as new loans are made; (3) the substitution between interest-bearing and non-interest-bearing deposits as interest-rate environments change; and (4) the portion of mismatch profits that are sustainable because forward rates tend to be higher than their corresponding realized rates.

Centralized risk management Although current mismatch profits or losses may be illusory because they will not persist across time, the fact that they fluctuate with unexpected changes in the term structure of interest rates means that mismatch creates risk for shareholders. Financial futures positions can be used to offset this mismatch risk. A bank or savings and loan that lends long term and borrows short term can hedge against the risk of an increase in interest rates by taking an offsetting short position in financial futures. This form of risk management is best implemented by the treasury unit, which has a centralized point of view.

The cost of equity The recommended transfer-pricing mechanism collects interest-rate risks in the treasury unit. If the treasury does nothing to hedge these risks, then the cost of equity will generally be higher for the treasury than for the bank as a whole. To the extent that risks are hedged, the cost of equity will be lower.

The shared-cost problem Most banks try to use cost accounting systems to push all overhead costs down to the business-unit level. It is better, we believe, to allocate only those costs that the business units would incur were they standing alone. Un-allocated headquarters costs should be kept at headquarters as a cost center. Furthermore, business units should be encouraged to compare costs of providing services via outsourcing with internal costs. This provides a means of checking to be sure that internally provided services are cost-efficient.

The shared-cost problem arises from the fact that multiple business units may use the same resource. For example, a teller may provide services for non-interest-bearing checking, money market accounts, coupon clipping, and mortgage loan payments. If all these activities are within the same business unit—for example, retail banking—no problem results for valuation at the business-unit level. However, if the costs are shared between business units—for example, retail banking and the trust department—then an effort should be made to allocate the costs on the basis of services used.

SUMMARY

At the outset we said this short chapter would not present all the answers. However, by raising issues we hope to catalyze an ongoing discussion among banking managers. We firmly believe that valuation is a useful tool in the banking industry and that for planning purposes it should supplement and even replace more arcane and myopic performance standards such as growth in net income or return on equity.

However, difficult and unresolved issues are present in valuing banks. From an outsider's point of view, banks are particularly opaque businesses because of blind pool risk in their loan portfolios and because adequate information is not available concerning their actual hedging practices. From an insider's perspective, a variety of transfer-pricing schemes are possible. We have discussed an approach that match-funds each business unit for interest rate and credit risk, thereby collecting these risks in a centralized treasury operation where they can be explicitly managed. One of the by-products of this approach is that each match-funded unit, as well as the treasury, has no good market comparables that can be used to estimate the cost of equity. Consequently, some guesswork is involved in this area and the answers are soft, requiring us to use ranges rather than point estimates. Nevertheless, the most relevant differences among banking business units are reflected in their expected free cash flow to shareholders, and these are adequately captured in the valuation process.

Proof of the Equivalence of Two Formulas for Estimating Continuing Value

This appendix proves the equivalence of the two recommended continuing-value formulas: the free cash flow perpetuity formula and the value-driver formula. The two formulas are as follows:

$$\text{Continuing value} = \frac{\text{FCF}}{\text{WACC} - g} = \frac{\text{NOPLAT} (1 - g/r)}{\text{WACC} - g}$$

Since the denominators are identical, we only need to prove that free cash flow can be expressed by the following equation:

$$\text{FCF} = \text{NOPLAT} (1 - g/r)$$

where

FCF	= free cash flow
NOPLAT	= net operating profits less adjusted taxes
g	= growth rate in NOPLAT
r	= rate of return on net new capital invested

First, let us define free cash flow as the company's operating profits less the net new capital invested.

$$FCF = NOPLAT - In$$

where

In = net increase in invested capital over and above replacement capital

As long as the return on existing capital employed remains constant, a company's NOPLAT in any period equals last period's NOPLAT plus the return it earns on last period's net investment in new capital.

$$NOPLAT_T = NOPLAT_{T-1} + (r \times In_{T-1})$$

This equation can be rearranged to show that the change in NOPLAT equals the rate of return on new investment times the amount of new investment.

$$NOPLAT_T - NOPLAT_{T-1} = (r \times In_{T-1})$$

Dividing both sides by last year's NOPLAT calculates the growth rate in NOPLAT.

$$g = \frac{NOPLAT_T - NOPLAT_{T-1}}{NOPLAT_{T-1}} = \frac{r \times In_{T-1}}{NOPLAT_{T-1}}$$

$$g = r \times \frac{In}{NOPLAT}$$

Solving for the amount of investment required to increase NOPLAT at the rate g and substituting for the first definition of free cash flow gives the free cash flow calculation in terms of the key value drivers.

$$
\begin{aligned}
\text{In} \quad &= \text{NOPLAT} \times g/r \\
\text{FCF} \quad &= \text{NOPLAT} - (\text{NOPLAT} \times g/r) \\
\text{FCF} \quad &= \text{NOPLAT}\,(1 - g/r)
\end{aligned}
$$

The ratio g/r can be called the net investment rate, as it represents the ratio of net new investment to NOPLAT that is consistent with a growth rate of g and a rate of return r.

Sources of
Valuation Data

U.S. COMPANIES

Source	Brief description
Public Companies: Printed Data	
Moody's Manuals	Historical financials, detailed descriptions of securities outstanding, bond ratings
Standard & Poor's Stock Reports	Financial information, business segment descriptions, current information on company activities
Standard & Poor's Industry Reports	Discussion of industry trends, including company-specific information
Value Line Investment Survey	Financial information on 1,700 public companies, including forecasts
SEC filings:	
• 10-K	Detailed annual financial information
• 10Q	Quarterly financial information
• Proxy statement	Details regarding security issues
• 13D	

Source	Brief description
• Insider trading	Historical data on transactions by insiders
Annual report	Audited annual report to shareholders
Wall Street Transcript	Summaries of analyst reports, CEO speeches
Dun & Bradstreet:	
• Business Rankings	Ranking by sales of both public and private companies within SIC codes
• Million Dollar Directories	Listings of both public and private companies within SIC codes
• Corporate affiliations	Listing of divisions, product lines, and subsidiaries with SIC codes
Magazine indexes:	
• F&S index	List of recent articles about a company
• Business Periodicals Index	List of recent articles about a company
• Wall Street Journal Index	List of *Wall Street Journal* cites of a company
Analysts' reports	Detailed studies often containing forecasts
Newspaper articles	Miscellaneous data
Trade journals	Miscellaneous data

Public Companies: Computer-readable Data

Datext	Compact-disc-based information on 10,000 publicly held companies, organized by groups (Technology, Industrial, Service, Consumer, Corp-Tech, and Commercial Bank); contains financials, subsidiaries, directors, stock reports, recent articles, comparable financials
Dialog:	
• Disclosure	Historical financials, officers, subsidiary list, annual report
• Moody's Corporate Profiles	Condensed financials, institutional holdings
• Media General	Weekly prices, dividends, ratios
• Investext	Analysts' reports
• Predicast	Financial abstracts
• Newspaper Index	Index of newspaper articles
• Business Wire	News summaries

Source	Brief description
Dow Jones:	
• Stock quotes	Recent stock quotes
• Current news	News wire service
• Media General	Summary data on prices, dividends, shareholdings
• Disclosures	Historical financials, ratios, ownership information, analysts' reports
• Wall Street Journal	Search for routine Wall Street Journal articles
Nexis:	
• Full text	Text of articles on a company
• Exchange	Search capability
Privately Held Companies: Printed Data	
Dun & Bradstreet Reports	Brief financial and nonfinancial profiles on private companies; includes sales, SIC, and number of employees
Standard & Poor's Corporate Register	List of officers, products, SIC
Thomas Register	CEO, SIC, sales, number of employees
Privately Held Companies: Computer-readable Data	
Dialog	See description under "Public companies"
Nexis	See description under "Public companies"
Dun & Bradstreet Credit Rating	Credit rating, special events, financials, officers
Newsnet	TRW business profiles
Industry Sources: Printed Data	
U.S. Industrial Outlook	Description of two-digit and three-digit SIC industry groups; industry sales forecasts
Standard & Poor's Industry Surveys	Industry overviews by S&P analysts
Value Line Investment Surveys	Industry analysis and forecasts of sales growth, operating margins, tax rates, capitalization
Wall Street Transcript	Panel discussions of industry outlook
Dun & Bradstreet	Key business ratios and industry norms
Moody's Industry Review	Comparative statistics for major companies within an industry classification
Predicast	Summary of industry data, employment, capital expenditures, etc.

Source	Brief description
Encyclopedia of Associations	Listing of industry associations that can be contacted for further data, lobbying efforts, etc.

Industry Sources: Computer-readable Data
Dialog:

• Predicast	Sales growth rates
• Trade & Industry Index	Abstracts of trade journal articles
• Investext	Abstracts of market/industry studies
• Arthur D. Little/on-line	A.D. Little industry reports
• Encyclopedia of Associations	Industry associations
Nexis	See description under "Public companies"
Dow Jones	See description under "Public companies"

Other Sources

U.S. Government	Specific department publications
Yellow Pages	Phone book
Statistical Abstracts	Summary of government data (for example, Federal Reserve, Commerce Department)

NON-U.S. COMPANIES

BARRA International   Produces individual company betas using a Goldman Sachs monthly rate of return database. The betas are computed using BARRA methodology that incorporates regression toward the mean and a multifactor approach. Currently available are

• The World Book, containing 2,500 companies from the *Financial Times* list
• Separate, more complete, country books:
  • United Kingdom, with 1,300 companies
  • Japan, with 1,800 companies
  • West Germany, with 250 companies
  • Australia
• More complete data for Sweden, France, and Holland is expected soon

Although BARRA produces betas, it unfortunately does not provide information on the number of shares outstanding, market risk premiums, or line-of-business breakdowns of company assets. For more information contact: BARRA International,   65 London Wall, London EC2M 5TU, England. Phone: 01-920-0131

London Business School, London, England Has a share price database and a risk measurement service. The share price database is updated annually and contains monthly rate of return data for over 4,500 U.K. companies from 1975 to present (with some as early as 1955). It also contains indexes (dividend yields, earnings yields, exchange rates, interest rates on government bonds, and the *Financial Times* A Classified Index), shares outstanding, dividends, earnings, and adjustments (for splits, script, and rights). The LBS risk measurement service produces quarterly updates of total volatility and betas that are adjusted for thin trading and for regression toward the mean. For more information contact: London Business School, Sussex Place, Regent's Park, London NW1 4SA, England. Phone: 01-262-5050

Erasmus University, Rotterdam, Holland Has an effort under the direction of Professor Roberto Wessels that will produce both capital asset pricing model (CAPM) and arbitrage pricing model (APM) betas for nine European countries (Belgium, Denmark, France, Germany, Great Britain, Holland, Italy, Sweden, and Switzerland). Risk-free rates of return, market indexes, and individual stock rates of return will also be available. For more information contact: Professor Roberto Wessels, Erasmus University, Rotterdam, Holland. Phone: 10-408-1294

Karlsruhe Universität, Karlsruhe, West Germany Has the most complete source of German data. Under the direction of Professor Herman Göppl, the Karlsruhe Kapitalmarktdatenbank has been produced. It has 7 stock market indexes, monthly rates of return for 234 German stocks, 13 foreign stocks listed in Germany, 62 call and put options, 44 warrants, and 300 government bonds. Although no commercial service for betas yet exists, the computer programs are available and the institute is willing to produce data under contract. For more information contact: Professor Herman Göppl, Institut fur Entscheidungstheorie und Unternehmensforschung, Universität Karlsruhe, Postfach 6980 D-7500 Karlsruhe 1, West Germany. Phone: 721-608-3427

Morgan Stanley Capital International, New York, New York, USA Provides stock market return indexes for nineteen countries as well as European and World indexes. They also have P/E, price-to-cash-earnings, and price-to-book ratios; limited balance sheet information; shares outstanding; earnings and dividends per share. Their sample contains roughly 1,700 of the largest companies in the world (1970 to present). For more information contact: Morgan Stanley, Inc., 1633 Broadway, New York, New York 10019. Phone: 212-765-3114

Compass Very large database with heavy product/service offering orientation but with some financial information, covering
• All significant U.K. companies
• Major European companies (Euro-Compass)

Datastream Online database service providing
• Equity data for
  • All U.K. quoted companies

- Foreign companies quoted in
  - Canada
  - France (190 companies)
  - Germany (4,000 companies)
  - Hong Kong
  - Japan
  - Netherlands
  - Switzerland
  - U.S.
- Company accounts information for
  - Quoted companies
  - 40,000 unquoted U.K. companies

Extel   Authoritative card-based five-year summary (for main market, USMA, third market, and major unquoted companies) of financial statements and
- Capital and restructuring transactions
- Acquisitions and disposals
- Dividends

Hoppenstat   German database of company financial information.

ICC   Archive service for company accounts, public documents, and brokers' reports.

Investex   Online brokers' reports, including all major U.K. brokers (and some foreign) and covering all major U.K. and most major foreign corporations.

Japan Company Handbook   Useful reference for Japanese companies in first and second section with summary financial information.

M&A Database   Based on M&A magazine data, covers all major transactions, most smaller U.K. deals, and many smaller U.S. deals.

Topic   Real-time stock exchange information.

World Scope   CD-ROM system with financial information on major global and U.S. corporations.

SUMMARY OF VALUATION DATA SOURCES

Country	Indexes		Risk-free rate	Betas		Individual security returns			
	Market portfolio	Industry		CAPM	APM	Stock	Bonds	Options	Shares outstanding
Austria	MS	X	X	X	X	X	X	X	MS
Australia	MS	X	X	B	X	X	X	X	MS
Belgium	MS	X	X	X	X	X	X	X	MS
Canada	MS	X	—	—	X	D	X	X	MS
Denmark	MS	X	X	X	X	X	X	X	MS
France	MS	X	X	X	E	D	X	X	MS
Germany	MS	X	K	B,K	E	E,K,D	X	X	MS
Hong Kong	MS	X	X	X	X	D	X	X	MS
Italy	MS	X	X	X	RR	X	X	X	MS
Japan	MS	X	RR	B	X	RR,D	X	X	MS
Mexico	MS	X	X	X	E	X	X	X	MS
Netherlands	MS	X	E	E	E	E,D	X	X	MS
Norway	MS	X	X	X	X	X	X	X	MS
Singapore	MS	X	X	X	X	X	X	X	MS
South Africa	MS	X	X	X	X	X	X	X	MS
Spain	MS	X	X	B	X	X	X	X	MS
Sweden	MS	X	X	X	X	X	X	X	MS
Switzerland	MS	X	X	X	X	D	X	X	MS
United Kingdom	LBS,MS	LBS	LBS	LBS,B	E	LBS,D	X	X	LBS,MS
United States	MS	X	CRSP	B	A	CRSP,C,D	CRSP	Berk	CRSP,MS

A   = Alcar
B   = BARRA International
Berk = University of California, Berkeley
C   = Compuserve
CRSP = Center for Research in Securities Prices, University of Chicago Graduate School of Business
D   = Datastream
E   = Erasmus University
K   = Universität Karlsruhe
LBS = London Business School Financial Services
MS   = Morgan Stanley Capital International
RR   = Roll and Ross, Inc., Culver City, California
X   = No known data source

References

Altman, E. 1984. A further empirical investigation of the bankruptcy cost question. *Journal of Finance,* September, 1067–89.

Asquith, P., D. Mullins, Jr., and E. Wolff. 1989. Original issue high-yield bonds: Aging analysis of defaults, exchanges, and calls. Working paper, Harvard University, March.

Berry, M., E. Burmeister, and M. McElroy. 1988. Sorting out risks using known APT factors. *Financial Analysts Journal,* March/April, 29–42.

Biddle, G. C., and F. W. Lindahl. 1982. Stock price reactions to LIFO adoptions: The association between excess returns and LIFO tax savings. *Journal of Accounting Research,* Autumn, 551–558.

Brealey, R., and S. Myers. 1984. *Principles of corporate finance,* 2nd edition. New York: McGraw-Hill.

Brigham, E. 1966. An analysis of convertible debentures. *Journal of Finance,* March, 35–54.

Chen, N. F. 1983. Some empirical tests of the theory of arbitrage pricing. *Journal of Finance,* December, 1393–1414.

Chen, N. F., S. Ross, and R. Roll. 1986. Economic forces and the stock market. *Journal of Business,* July, 383–403.

Copeland, T. E., and W. H. Lee. 1988. Exchange offers and stock swaps—A signaling approach: Theory and evidence. Working paper, UCLA.

Copeland, T. E., E. F. Lemgruber, and D. Mayers. 1987. Corporate spinoffs: Multiple announcement and ex-date abnormal performance. In

Modern finance and industrial economics, ed. T. E. Copeland, Ch. 7. New York: Basil Blackwell.

Copeland, T. E., and J. F. Weston. 1988. *Financial theory and corporate policy,* 3rd edition. Reading, MA: Addison-Wesley.

DeAngelo, H., L. DeAngelo, and E. Rice. 1984. Going private: The effects of a change in corporate ownership structure. *Midland Corporate Finance Journal,* Summer, 35–43.

Fama, E., and K. French. 1986. Dividend yields and expected stock returns. *Journal of Financial Economics,* October, 3–25.

Fama, E., and M. Gibbons. 1984. A comparison of inflation forecasts. *Journal of Monetary Economics,* May, 327–48.

Financial Accounting Standards Board. 1976. Statement of financial accounting standards, no. 13, *Accounting for leases.* Stamford, CT.

Grimm, W. T., & Co. 1986. *Mergerstat review 1985.* Chicago.

Hardouvelis, G. 1988. The predictive power of the term structure during recent monetary regimes. *Journal of Finance,* June, 339–56.

Hector, C. 1988. Yes, you can manage long term. *Fortune,* November 21, 63–76.

Hong, H. R., R. S. Kaplan, and G. Mandelker. 1978. Pooling vs. purchase: The effects of accounting for merger on stock prices. *Accounting Review* 53:31–47.

Ibbotson Associates, Inc. 1989. *Stocks, bonds, bills, and inflation 1989 yearbook.* Chicago, IL.

Jain, P. C. 1985. The effect of voluntary sell-off announcements on shareholder wealth. *Journal of Finance,* March, 209–24.

Kobrin, S. J. 1982. *Managing political risk assessment: Strategic response to political change.* Berkeley, CA: University of California Press.

Lo, A. and C. MacKinlay. 1988. Stock market prices do not follow random walks: Evidence from a simple specification test. *Review of Financial Studies,* Spring, 41–66.

McConnell, J. J., and C. J. Muscarella. 1985. Corporate capital expenditures decisions and the market value of the firm. *Journal of Financial Economics,* March, 399–422.

Mercer, G. 1987. A review of major corporate write-offs, 1984–86. Unpublished manuscript.

Mitchell, M. L., and K. Lehn. 1988. Do bad bidders become good targets? Working paper, Office of Economic Analysis, Securities and Exchange Commission, Washington, DC, August.

Office of the Chief Economist. 1985. *Institutional ownership, tender offers, and long-term investment.* Securities and Exchange Commission, Washington, DC.

Peat, Marwick, Mitchell and Company. 1981. Statement of financial accounting standards, no. 52, *Foreign currency translation.*

Poterba, J., and L. Summers. 1988. Mean reversion in stock prices: Evidence and implications. *Journal of Financial Economics,* October, 27–59.

Pursche, B. 1988. Building better bids: Synergies and acquisition prices. *Chief Financial Officer USA: 1988,* 63–64.

Ronn, E. and A. Verma. 1986. Pricing risk-adjusted deposit insurance: An option-based model. *Journal of Finance,* September, 871–895.

Ruback, R. S. 1982. The Conoco takeover and stockholder returns. *Sloan Management Review* 23(2): 13–32.

Schipper, K., and A. Smith. 1983. Effects of recontracting on shareholder wealth. *Journal of Financial Economics,* April, 437–67.

Schipper, K., and A. Smith. 1986. A comparison of equity carve-outs and seasoned equity offerings. *Journal of Financial Economics,* January/February, 153–86.

Sicherman, N. W., and R. H. Pettway. 1987. Acquisition of divested assets and shareholders' wealth. *Journal of Finance,* December, 1261–73.

Stobaugh, R., Jr. 1969. How to analyze foreign investment climates. *Harvard Business Review,* September/October, 108.

Sunder, S. 1973. Relationship between accounting changes and stock prices: Problems of measurement and some empirical evidence. *Empirical Research in Accounting: Selected Studies,* 18.

Weston, J. F., and T. E. Copeland. 1987. *Managerial finance,* 8th edition. New York: CBS College Publishing.

Wheatley, S. 1988. Some tests of international equity integration. *Journal of Financial Economics,* September, 177–212.

Wilshire Associates, Inc. 1981. *Capital market equilibrium statistics.* Santa Monica, CA: Author.

Woolridge, R. 1988. Competitive decline and corporate restructuring: Is a myopic stock market to blame? *Journal of Applied Corporate Finance* 1(1):26–36.

Index